A Program for Families of Children With Learning and Behavior Problems

A Program for Families of Children with Learning and Behavior Problems

MARTIN A. KOZLOFF
Boston University

A WILEY–INTERSCIENCE PUBLICATION
JOHN WILEY & SONS
New York • Chichester • Brisbane • Toronto

Library of Congress Cataloging in Publication Data

Kozloff, Martin A

A program for families of children with learning and behavior problems.

"A Wiley–Interscience publication."

Includes bibliographical references and index.

1. Learning disabilities. 2. Problem children.
3. Family psycho therapy. 4. Behavior therapy.
I. Title.

LC4704.K69 371.9'2 78–26578

ISBN 0-471-04434-2

Printed in the United States of America

10 9 8 7 6 5 4 3 2 1

For my son, Anthony

To accept one's limited freedom
to accept one's isolation
to accept this responsibility
to learn one's particular powers
and then with them to humanize the whole
that is the best for this situation

John Fowles, The Aristos

PREFACE

This book is the result of work over the past ten years with families of children with learning and behavior problems—the autistic child, the mentally retarded child, the emotionally disturbed child, the oppositional child, the child with speech and language problems. It was written for those who are either working with families of such children or who are in a position to do so—psychologists and psychiatrists, teachers, pediatricians, social workers, and parents. The book provides the reader with both detailed descriptions of procedures and a variety of instruments for conducting a comprehensive program with families.

In step-by-step fashion, it focuses on: 1) first *contacts* with families; 2) conducting *Initial Interviews*; 3) strengthening *readiness* to change; 4) *formalizing* a working relationship; 5) *assessing* the strengths and needs of the family system—via interviews, direct observation, and an Assessment and Programming Guide; 6) establishing short-term and long-term *goals*; 7) *planning* a program; 8) *conducting programs* for individual families or for groups—which includes teaching parents a wide range of skills for evaluating the family system and their children's needs, planning an educational program, managing productive patterns of interaction, conducting home teaching programs, problem-solving, and working to maintain and generalize beneficial change; and 9) conducting ongoing and summative *evaluations* of the program, revising it as necessary.

The organization and orientation of the book and the program it describes will perhaps be clarified by a recounting of past work. Between 1967 and 1970, I worked in the Autism Program at Washington University in St. Louis, Missouri—a laboratory-school for autistic and autistic-like children funded by the United States Office of Education through the Central Midwestern Regional Educational Laboratory, Inc., and directed by Dr. Robert L. Hamblin, now Professor of Sociology at the University of Arizona. There, I conducted a program for four families, which consisted of teaching parents basic principles of learning and social exchange; helping them to teach simple skills to children in the classroom via direct coaching—sometimes using a wireless communication system; working with them to develop "behavioral prescriptions" for teaching in the home; and helping them to institute their home programs through weekly home visits. A description of the operation and results of the program is found in *Reaching the Autistic Child* (Martin A. Kozloff, Research Press Co., 1973).

Although the program was generally successful, it contained a number of shortcomings. In particular, parents were taught a rather narrow range of skills—they were not taught to evaluate their children's strengths and needs, nor their own, nor to develop alternative teaching programs, nor to solve problems in a creative and sequential fashion. Second, they were not provided with comprehensive, easy-to-read materials (such as a book) on how to evaluate and educate their children, which might have helped them to become more independent of their consultant. Third, they did not work with other parents, in a group, which might have helped them to generalize their skills to different situations and problems and to maintain their enthusiasm. And, fourth, additional problems in some families, such as marital conflict, difficulties with siblings, and lack of organization in certain household routines, were not solved, which seemed to hinder parents' efforts throughout the program.

Between 1972 and 1975, I attempted to remedy some of the above shortcomings in parent programs conducted under grant number MH 12873, awarded to the Boston University Center for Applied Social Science, then directed by Dr. George Psathas, by the Experimental and Special Projects Branch of the National Institute of Mental Health. In those programs, parents were taught a wide range of skills for evaluating their children, planning a comprehensive educational program, conducting teaching programs in seven skill areas, and solving problems. In addition, programs were conducted with small groups of families, so as to generate esprit de corps, a sharing of ideas, and the nucleus of a network of backup support. And, finally, parents were provided with written materials which were, in effect, a major part of the curriculum of the program. The materials were later published in book form in *Educating Children with Learning and Behavior Problems* (Martin A. Kozloff, Wiley-Interscience, 1974).

For two years, 1975–1976, I conducted a summative or overall evaluation of the NIMH-funded programs for families. Every videotape made in the homes (almost one per week) was viewed and reviewed by from one to three scorers; audiotape recordings of all meetings were listened to again and again; logs written by parents, notes taken by family consultants on phone calls, home visits and group meetings, and data recorded by parents on home teaching programs were read and reread. At the same time, the programs were being replicated by Dr. Kenneth Kaufman and his staff at the Sagamore Children's Center, Melville, New York. The conclusions were that: 1) the book alone *(Educating Children)* resulted in substantial beneficial change in parents and children; 2) the improvement in parents' skills and children's behaviors was generally greater when parents, using the book, participated in group programs; and yet 3) progress throughout the change process, from the first contact through maintenance and follow-up, was affected by so many variables both inside and outside the family system that a perspective broader than that of social learning theory, and a set of methods for facilitating change more comprehensive than that found in traditional behavior therapy, seemed to be called for. Thus, in an effort to better understand and improve the change process, I consulted works on communication theory; family therapy; the sociology of the family, work, and deviance; women's studies; political and social philosophy; and psychodynamic psychotherapy. The seminal ideas, research findings, and change methods of major writers in these fields were of great importance in the final stage in the development of the program. They helped me to understand the complex processes taking place in families from the time a child is recognized as deviant—processes that must be reckoned with in working with families. And, they helped me and my colleagues to develop and apply methods for helping families to avoid or solve a wide variety of problems.

In sum, the perspective, methods, and instruments described in this book constitute a synthesis of the efforts by myself and my colleagues to develop more effective, efficient, and comprehensive programs for families, and of the major ideas of researchers, theorists, and clinicians in other disciplines. The program has been replicated twice under grant number MH 14761, awarded to the Boston University Department of Sociology by the Experimental and Special Projects Branch of the National Institute of Mental Health.

I am grateful to many persons for their help over the years: Dr. Ralph Simon, Dr. Sam Silverstein, and Dr. Beatrice Shriver of the Experimental and Special Projects Branch of the National Institute of Mental Health for their long-standing trust, interest, and encouragement; Dr. Robert L. Hamblin for the continuing power and elegance of his formulation of structured exchange in socialization, and for the faith, often put to the test, which he placed in his former student; Professors George Psathas, Sol Levine, Murray Melbin, James Teele, Paule Verdet, and Richard Frankel of the Boston University Department of Sociology for their friendship and judgment during the easy and the difficult times; the parents, with whom I have been privileged to work, for their energy, fortitude, and wisdom; Dr. Kenneth Kaufman, Julie Bakalor, Barbara Paradise, Barbara Price, and Robin Tyson for their friendship, abundant positive reinforcement, and not-so-uncritical acceptance of many of the ideas in this book; my colleagues on programs past and present—Barbara Cutler, Dr. Barbara Bruno-Golden, James Delphin, Maureen Murphy, Agnes Myles, Martin Sawzin, Beth Solomon, Karen Gardner, Michelle O'Steen, Gregory E. Hudson, Virginia Hudson, John Peters, Shelley Leavitt, and Joel Vatter—who helped in the planning of the programs, worked as family consultants, and stayed with me through revisions too painful to remember; Susan Arnold for managing the grant and for managing a smile at the receipt of each chapter; and my wife and son for things I will probably never understand.

MARTIN A. KOZLOFF

Boston, Massachusetts
January 1979

A FEW TIPS FOR THE READER

This book should be used along with its companion book, *Educating Children with Learning and Behavior Problems* (Kozloff, Wiley-Interscience, 1974), referred to as *Educating Children,* which will provide you and the parents with step-by-step methods for evaluating children's strengths and needs and for planning, conducting, evaluating, and revising teaching programs in seven skill areas. Additional readings on physical disabilities in children, sign language, relaxation training, and self-control are cited in later chapters.

M. A. K.

CONTENTS

TABLES

FIGURES

A Program for Families of Children With Learning and Behavior Problems

1 PARENTS AND THE EDUCATIONAL PROCESS

I. WHY WORK WITH PARENTS?

Unless you picked up this book by accident, you already know many good reasons for working with parents of children with learning and behavior problems. I repeat some of those reasons here because the Program in this book is based on them.

1. For a long time many professionals thought that the problems of children (for example, emotionally impaired, autistic) had been caused by their parents. So, instead of teaching parents how to work with or educate their children, it was thought that the parents either needed therapy along with their children or were irrelevant to the treatment process. Today, however, the idea that parents cause their children's learning and behavior problems is being seriously criticized, simply because there is so little solid evidence for the idea. Instead, more and more people think that children with severe learning and behavior problems got off the track (or never got on the track) because of biological problems for which their parents were not responsible. And they see many ways in which parents can help in their children's education or socialization.

2. Studies show that many children who need special help are not getting it, partly because few people are trained to help them (Arnstein, 1965; Mosher et al., 1970; Lindsley, 1966; Guerney, 1969). By supporting and training parents, the number of people who can educate the children would be increased.

3. Even though all states have laws that require communities to provide an education to all children regardless of their handicaps, many children are left out or receive an inadequate education, either because not enough good schools exist or because some children are considered too severely handicapped to fit into existing educational programs. So, it is necessary to provide parents with special skills so that they can either give their children a head start until good schools are available or prepare their children for entrance into schools (for example, by helping them learn such "readiness" skills as paying attention, sitting, and cooperating with simple requests).

4. Even if every child had a good school, the problem of educating children with severe learning and behavior problems would not be solved, because there is usually a big difference between what goes on in a school (or special treatment) setting and what goes on in other settings (such as the home or public places). In fact, many studies have shown that children's behaviors may be quite different from one setting to another (Johnson et al., 1976; Bernal et al., 1976). Also, it is possible that the behavioral gains made by a child in an educational or treatment setting will not generalize to, or be maintained in, home and community settings unless persons in those settings (such as parents) are given special training (Lovaas et al., 1973; Wahler, 1969).

For example, even if a mute child is taught to speak in school, unless his parents are taught how to give the child many "occasions" to talk and to reinforce proper speech, the child would most likely remain nearly mute in the home. Besides, many behaviors are easier or more "natural" to teach outside of school settings (for example, getting ready for bed, doing household chores, or buying things in a store).

5. Not only can parents help spread (generalize) and maintain their children's educational gains, but our research in a school in St. Louis suggests that parents working with their children at home can actually increase the rate at which their children learn (Hamblin et al., 1971; Kozloff, 1973).

6. Parents have a right to available information on how to help themselves and their children. After all, their tax dollars have supported the thousands of studies that have been done over the years on the learning process and on methods for educating children.

7. We can increase the number of people who are skilled at planning and evaluating services for children. As consumer-evaluators, parents could make important contributions to planning, implementing, and revising local and state services.

8. A counterproductive relationship sometimes exists between schools and parents of special-needs children. As a result of the past lack of services for children and the increasing availability of services stemming from Public Law 94-142 (the Education for All Handicapped Children Act), some parents' expectations are justifiably rising. To the extent that their expectations are not met, however, parents may put pressure on teachers and administrators for more services or for services of a different kind, sometimes resulting in conflict (e.g., blaming, protest, law suits). In an atmosphere of mutual distrust and antagonism, it is difficult for parents and schools to work together to plan and implement services, for school personnel to feel comfortable about conducting programs for families, or for the conflicting parties to change their relationship for the better. However, if schools offered programs for families from the start (e.g., from the time children were enrolled or were evaluated), the vicious cycles might be avoided, and a cooperative, problem-solving relationship established.

The Program offered in this book was designed with all of the above reasons in mind. It also remedies some of the deficiencies in past programs for families of children with learning and behavior problems.

II. WHAT KIND OF WORK HAS BEEN DONE?

Over the past fifteen years or so, many programs for parents have been conducted and most were reportedly successful in teaching parents to change their children's behavior (O'dell, 1974). The programs differed in several ways. For example, not only did the children have different problems (autistic, aggressive, oppositional, mentally retarded, emotionally disturbed) but some programs were conducted with individual families and others were conducted with groups (Kovitz, 1976; Peine, 1971; Mira, 1970; Tams and Eyberg, 1976). Some were done in connection with the school where the children were enrolled and others were done apart from any school.

The groundbreaking work was done by the following persons, as well as others too numerous to list. Patterson (1966), for example, taught parents to help a child with school phobia. Parents of children who were aggressive, oppositional, or had other problem behaviors were taught by such people as Hamblin et al. (1971), Bernal et al. (1968), Tharp and Wetzel (1969), Miller (1975), Wahler et al. (1965), Patterson and Brodsky (1966), Patterson et al. (1969), Patterson et al. (1975), Engeln et al. (1968), and Mira (1970). Russo (1964), Williams (1966), and Hawkins et al. (1966) taught parents to decrease tantrum behaviors. Allen and Harris (1966) taught parents to decrease self-injurious scratching, while Reid et al. (1967) conducted a program for parents of a selectively mute child. Parents of children called autistic, disturbed, schizophrenic, or mentally retarded, finally, have been in programs conducted by Wolf et al. (1966), Lindsley (1966), Risley and Wolf (1966), Johnson and Brown (1969), Hamblin et al. (1971), Schell and Adams (1968), Davison (1964), Walder (1968), Kozloff (1973, 1976, 1977), and Kaufman (1976).

What We Have Learned from the Early Work with Families

We have learned two things. First, all of the studies listed above showed that by teaching parents to alter their own behaviors (especially the ways they interacted with their children), it was possible for the parents to produce important changes in some of the behaviors of their children. For example, when parents systematically reinforced cooperative behavior rather than yelling at their children for misbehaving, the children began to cooperate more and misbehave less. As the early studies showed that parents, in a short time, could learn how to change their children's behaviors, many more people began to "get into the act" and run programs for parents. In fact, some journal articles gave the impression that all the parents had to do was reinforce appropriate behaviors and ignore problem behaviors and the family would change for the better. However, the second thing we learned over the years was that helping parents to change their own behaviors, change their children's behaviors, and maintain the behavior changes was not as easy to do as it was to write about!

For example, looking back on his work of about ten years with families of aggressive children, Gerald Patterson, a pioneer in the field, pointed out that simply teaching parents "the specific skills for changing child behaviors" was sufficient for only about one-third of the families he worked with. Another third of the families needed a lot more help (e.g., to solve marital conflicts and to alleviate feelings of depression) before they could effectively change their children. And the last third of the families with whom he worked seemed to "fail in spite of our best efforts" (Patterson, 1976). I found just about the same thing in my work with families of children with severe learning and behavior problems. For example, some parents never become interested in participating in a free training program, even though they are shown videotapes indicating how much they could teach their children in a short time. In addition, some parents who participate do not conduct home teaching programs effectively or consistently. And, finally, when programs have been concluded, some parents are unable to maintain home teaching programs and the educational gains that they have made.

Implications of What We Have Learned

There are several possible responses to the kinds of difficulties just cited. First, one might become so discouraged as to stop working with families and, instead, invest one's time and effort elsewhere. This can happen to teachers who, after a hard day in the classroom, try to work with parents, run into difficulties, feel that their efforts and good intentions are not appreciated, and return to working only with the children. Or, on the other hand, one might decide to "weed out" the potentially troublesome families and work only with motivated parents and "intact" families.

While the above two responses are certainly understandable, they are also counterproductive for everyone involved. Consultants (for example, teachers, clinicians, parents helping other parents) may downgrade their own skills and lose the chance to learn how to help families with difficult problems. Moreover, our understanding of the sources of family problems will remain simplistic. And, in the long run, families that need the most help will continue to get the least.

The position taken in this book, however, is that most of the difficulties encountered when working with some families stem from the larger historical and social conditions within which the parents (along with the rest of us) have been "sweating it out"; for example, job insecurity, the isolation of nuclear families, and the "round" of experiences with professionals. At the same time, our understanding of these conditions and how they produce both problems and strengths, has been limited, as have been our methods for helping families to change. In sum, most "deficiencies" are not in families but are in the larger social conditions of existence and in our methods for helping families.

Let us be more specific about the deficiencies of past programs for families.

Nature of the Consultant-Parent Relationship. The very nature of the parent-consultant relationship can generate problems. If a relationship is too professional, formal, or authoritarian the parents may resist the consultant's offer of help, as well as later suggestions. A relationship that is too informal and friendly may result in a lack of clear expectations and, ultimately, a deterioration in performance.

Inadequate Program. The content of the Program may produce problems. For example, if the educational program that the parents are taught to use in teaching their children does not focus on behaviors that are important to the parents, or does not encompass a wide enough range of behaviors, the parents may feel that their work is not worth the effort and may participate less and less as time goes by. On the other hand, if the instructional methods used by the consultant are not comprehensive enough to help parents to pinpoint and overcome the problems that they face, the parents' efforts to educate their children are likely to be ineffective and inefficient. Moreover, the parents may become dependent on the consultant.

Technological Utopianism. Many behavioral programs (indeed, many social policies) seem to be based on the assumption that human problems can be solved with more sophisticated or powerful technologies (Boguslaw, 1965; Ellul, 1964; Mumford, 1970). Even a cursory look at journal articles, advertisements, and catalogs shows that much money, time, and hope is spent to develop methods for gathering and presenting information and to rearrange the contingencies of reinforcement between parents and children. However, many problems faced by families (e.g., isolation from support services) do not readily yield to technology alone. For example, we might use expensive and sophisticated gadgets, such as videotape, to teach parents to ignore disruptive behaviors and systematically reinforce cooperative behavior. Our initial data might show that the parents have definitely learned the proper teaching methods demonstrated on the videotapes. Two weeks later, however, observations in the home indicate that the parents are back to reinforcing disruptive behaviors. Why? Was the instructional technology not powerful enough to "stamp in" the skills? Must we now develop an even more powerful technology that will provide parents with continuous and instant feedback on their every interaction? More important, what assumptions do we make about people who seem to need such a technology?

The above problem, like so many others, ultimately has little to do with technology. It is more likely that if we examine the parents' beliefs in the efficacy (or even morality) of the educational methods, the division of labor in the home (who does what and how), the patterns of interaction between the parents, and the extent to which the parents get help and support from the extended family, friends and neighbors, we will have a better understanding of why they continue to reinforce problem behaviors. In addition, we will also have a better idea of what we might do to help them.

For instance, perhaps the father's "nerves" are so on edge after work that he simply cannot stand the commotion that is likely to result from ignoring his child's tantrums. And perhaps the mother is simply too tired and too busy to use the methods shown on the videotapes, and receives little support anyway. Clearly, in order to help parents change patterns of interaction with their children, we have to address the issues of marital relations, the roles of mother and father, extra sources of backup support, and the management of tension and anxiety. The solution, in other words, requires teaching people to analyze, understand, and change the conditions of their daily lives, rather than simply using a technology to modify a few behaviors that are the end product of those conditions.

Lack of a Historical/Social Perspective. For the past several decades there has been an apparent conflict between persons in the psychodynamic and behavioral camps. While persons in the two camps may differ in their theoretical propositions (explanations) and in some clinical-educational methods (see Wachtel, 1977, for an excellent comparison), in one way they are similar. By and large, they both tend to focus on the person or persons with presenting problems and on the immediate circumstances in the lives of those persons (Jacoby, 1975). While it is true that both behavioral and psychodynamic workers "take a history" during interviews with clients, a case history is not social history; it is, rather, biography.

I am not arguing that client histories are unimportant. They are important in developing programs that are relevant to persons with whom we are working. Rather, I am arguing that the usual histories do not go far enough in showing us the social nature of what only appear to be individual problems. Indeed, as seen in the next chapter, the historical experiences of families of deviant children are so similar that one is almost forced to conclude that remedies for the problems of individual families, while perhaps benefitting a fortunate few, may be little more than irrelevant anecdotes for the majority, and, moreover, do little to increase our understanding of, or to change, the social conditions within which family problems develop in the first place.

As mentioned, the purpose of this book is to help the reader to plan, conduct, and evaluate successful programs for families of children with learning and behavior problems. As the reader may have guessed, however, the Program described in subsequent chapters attempts to remedy the deficiencies in past work, including my own. In doing so, the Program addresses issues that go beyond the immediate interaction between parents and their children. We begin by discussing the social history (the "career") of families of deviant children. In this way, we can see how the career experiences may produce strengths as well as problems for families.

2 THE CAREER OF FAMILIES OF CHILDREN WITH LEARNING AND BEHAVIOR PROBLEMS

I. HOW TO VIEW THE FAMILY CAREER

From the time parents recognize that their child has serious problems (behavioral or physical) the family is faced with many difficulties, for example, the deviant behaviors of the child, the reactions of strangers, and the frustrating "round" of trying to get help. Most parents try to solve, or at least cope with, their family's difficulties, but few parents of children with learning and behavior problems have been taught beforehand how to help their own children. In fact, few parents of "normal" children have been taught proper parenting skills. Consequently, some of the things parents do to solve or cope with difficulties (for example, the child's disruptive behaviors) may not work well and may be *counterproductive,* that is, make existing problems more severe and harder to change and produce additional difficulties. In the long run, the family situation may go from bad to worse. Moreover, as a result of their career experiences, the parents may never learn of the people who might be able to help (potential consultants), may be unwilling to start working with consultants, and may be unable to conduct or maintain a good home educational program.

Figure 2-1 summarizes many of the difficulties that families face over time in their career. The discussion that follows Figure 2-1 represents a synthesis of a number of sources of information: intensive interviews with approximately fifty families; the responses of groups of parents to the initial ideas; and recent research on families of children with medical and behavioral problems.

While studying Figure 2-1, keep in mind:

1. Each experience or problem in the sequence is not exactly a cause of the next. At least it would be difficult to prove that one directly caused another. Instead, think of the figure as showing what tends to happen to the family as the career goes on year after year.

2. Not all families experience every problem depicted on Figure 2-1. For example, some families receive excellent help from the beginning and never experience many of the problems that are later in the sequence. Some parents are

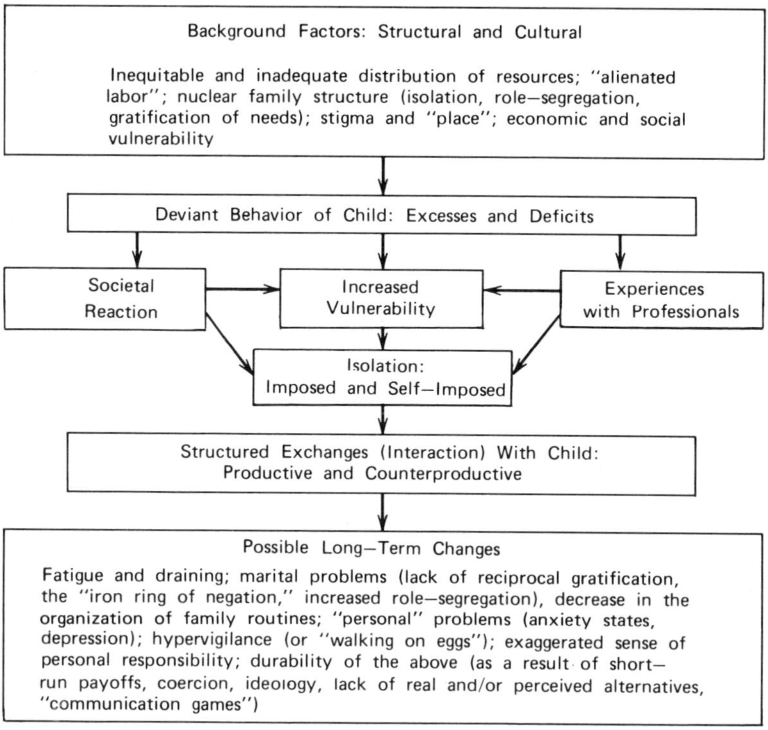

Figure 2-1 Sequence of experiences and problems in families of deviant children (children with learning and behavior problems).

such "cool customers" and have so much "moxie," that the reactions of outsiders (early in the career) do not result in the parents isolating themselves or their child. Or, the parents may have such a strong marriage that, even though their lives are marked with anguish and fatigue, marital problems never develop. Indeed, many parents and many marriages become even stronger as a result of the difficulties experienced by the family. The point is that when families have had the experiences and faced the problems shown on the sequence (Figure 2-1), your understanding of those experiences and difficulties helps to insure a successful Program. Consequently, it is important to learn what families have been through before a Program is started.

3. The family is a small social system within larger social systems such as the community and society (Bott, 1971; Kantor and Lehr, 1976; Buckley, 1967). As a result, what goes on inside the family (for example, the methods the parents use to cope with problems) often reflects what is and has been going on in the larger social systems outside the family.

For example, the way many families of deviant children are isolated from the people and events in their neighborhood and community reflects (and is an exaggeration of) the general isolation of nuclear families (parents and their immediate offspring) in modern societies. In addition, the fact that many parents are at their wits' end reflects (or is a result of) the short supply and inequitable distribution of services. And, finally, the fact that some fathers of "special-needs" children leave much of the child rearing to their wives reflects the general separation of household tasks in modern societies.

Unless we see that what goes on inside the family reflects or is a result of what goes on outside the family, it is easy to infer that families have problems because the parents are "sick," stupid, inept, or uncaring. It is especially easy to begin thinking this way when we are having a hard time helping families. Therefore, we have to see that those who have "normal" children are not necessarily healthier, smarter, more organized, or more caring. They are usually just luckier.

Now, let us look at the career of families of deviant children.

II. BACKGROUND FACTORS: STRUCTURAL AND CULTURAL

It is perhaps easier to understand what happens in families of deviant children when we examine the larger social-structural and cultural conditions within which the families exist. While most of us live out our lives within similar conditions, they pose special difficulties for families of children with problems.

Distribution of Resources. Not only is the overall supply of helping resources inadequate to meet the needs that exist, but many families simply cannot afford available services. The result is that some families go without help for many years, while others spend much money and time trying to find adequate help. As time goes by, problems that might have been avoided or more easily solved often become worse.

Conditions of Work: "Alienated Labor." By "alienated labor" is meant work that, for many people, does not gratify emotional needs, does not enable them to achieve their potentials, and is fraught with insecurities. Many workers have little control over the conditions of work, the production process, or what they produce, and see their work as something alien to them, which dominates and drives them, makes them small, insignificant, ultimately expendable and obsolete (Shostak and Gomberg, 1964; Mills, 1951; Blauner, 1964; Seeman, 1972; Marcuse, 1964, 1966; Henry, 1971).

To the extent that a person regards his or her work in the above way, and believes that the probability of change is nearly zero, the person is likely to see much of his or her life as a treadmill and work as something from which one escapes at the end of the work day and week. At the same time, however, the self-shriveling nature of much work and the emotional draining that results from it, may make it difficult for the worker to return home each day with enough energy and good spirits to gratify the emotional needs of other members of the family (Zaretsky, 1976).

One of the tragic ironies, here, is that some parents may not see that the work life of many professionals who are trying to help them is just as alienating as it is for the parents. Consequently, instead of working together as people with common interests, parents and consultants may be caught in an adversary relationship, or at least one without mutual trust, which weakens their potential strength.

Nuclear Family Structure. By ''nuclear family'' is meant a family of one or both parents and their children. The nuclear family is characterized by at least three factors. First, it is often isolated from members of the extended family (parents, brothers, sisters, cousins, uncles, and aunts) (Goode, 1963; Winch et al., 1967). This is especially true of geographically mobile families. The result is that the parents of a deviant child often cannot count on continual backup support from the extended family. Instead, they must face their difficulties either alone or with the help of strangers who, as the parents may see it, do not understand their problems or needs.

Second, the division of labor within the nuclear family may be rather extreme—what Henry (1971) has called ''role-segregation.'' That is, the husband and father may conceive of his role as involving certain tasks and not others, as may the wife and mother (Mussen, 1969; Oakley, 1975). To the extent that the roles are inflexible, moreover, the child-rearing tasks of the wife and mother may be an even greater burden if the child has severely deviant behaviors. In effect, she may need help from a husband who may regard the giving of such help (e.g., changing dirty diapers) as outside of his role (and ''unmanly''). In addition, if the husband is the main breadwinner, he may simply be unable to come home during the day to give his wife the support she needs. On the other hand, if the wife puts all of her time and energy into tasks and interests that she considers wifely and womanly (e.g., taking care of the house), she may be unable to provide her husband with the time and gratification he needs.

Third, since the nuclear family usually consists of two adults and their children, the situation is often such that each adult is responsible for gratifying most needs of the other. Not only is the task of continually gratifying another person difficult in the best of circumstances, but, given the many factors mentioned above, it may be even more difficult in the family of a severely deviant child.

Stigma and ''Place.'' How does a person develop a conception of self as a member in good standing in society? How does a person acquire a ''place''? On what basis do people accord each other respect and at least a minimum of deferential treatment? An axiom in social psychology is that a person conceives of self and of his place in the social system by interpreting the responses of others to him or her. But on what basis do others provide self- and place-confirming or self- and place-denying messages? According to Jules Henry (1966), the answer is found in "socially significant symbols."

In all societies, certain material possessions, life situations, and behaviors are valued by most, if not all, members of society. These are a society's socially significant symbols. To the extent that a person acquires and keeps many of the socially significant symbols, that person is treated with respect, develops self-respect, and comes to feel that he or she has a place in society as a member in good standing.

In some societies, the highest place (or status) and the most respect are given to those who are the most religiously observant; in other societies, to those who are the most giving of possessions. In America, the major socially significant symbols of membership by which a person gets and keeps a place and respectful treatment, include the following: (1) *for the child and adolescent:* a name given by the legal father, its own blanket, spoon, and toys, shame and disgust for certain bodily functions and smells, "proper" behavior in various settings (speech, bladder and bowel control, self-feeding and dressing), good grades in school, friends, a close friend of the opposite sex, clothes of the right style, possibly a car and other material possessions; (2) *for an adult:* a job, success at the job (whether in or outside of the home), friends, a mate of the opposite sex, children who have a place in society, and grandchildren.

As evidence of the validity of the above argument, ask yourself how people feel about themselves when they lose some of the socially significant symbols (e.g., when they lose a job and cannot find work or when, following a stroke, they cannot feed themselves) and how others feel about people who never acquired or who lost socially significant symbols. To give an extreme (but real) example, how do we act toward, and what do we think of, an adult who walks around with urine stains on his pants or with food on his face?

Such a person seems to be showing us that he does not know how to, or cannot, take care of himself, or that he does not know (or care) that in this society it is important to keep oneself "properly" clean. When we see such a person, we are likely to stare, whisper, consider him odd (if not sick), and avoid him, as though he had a dreaded disease.

What do we usually think of a child who throws tantrums, makes bizarre sounds and gestures, and creates havoc in restaurants or in grocery stores? Do we not stare at the child and think that the child does not know how (or does not care) to behave properly in public? And what do we think of the parents?

> Somebody ought to teach that child to behave in stores. Doesn't that child have any self-control? Don't his parents know how a child is supposed to behave? Don't they

> know how to control (teach, discipline) him? Don't they care? What a screwy family!

Getting and keeping socially significant symbols is the heart of seeing oneself as a member in good standing, and is involved in others' labeling us as normal or valuable and treating us as such. The failure of others to acquire and keep socially significant symbols, on the other hand, seems to set the stage for us to label them as deviant in one way or another (stupid, immoral, sick, strange, disturbed, retarded) and to treat others in ways that we, as members in good standing, would never allow ourselves to be treated—from unkind remarks to institutionalization (Goffman, 1963; Freidson, 1965; Mercer, 1973; Scheff, 1964, 1975; Kitsuse, 1962; Lemert, 1951; Szasz, 1970; Becker, 1963; Garfinkel, 1956; Rubington and Weinberg, 1968).

Vulnerability. In all societies, there are things to which members are vulnerable and which they often fear (Henry, 1971). For example, we are often vulnerable to the opinions others have of us. "Do they think I'm smart? Am I likeable? Am I pretty?" We are vulnerable to the economic system.

> Will I ever make ends meet? Will my boss think I'm a valuable employee? Will I get fired? What will happen to my family if business does not pick up soon? I hate this job, but I can't do anything else!

We are vulnerable (in this society) to time as associated with aging.

> Will I be able to live on Social Security? Will I spend my later years in a nursing home? Will people think I'm ugly, senile, and worthless?

To avoid or escape the things to which we are vulnerable (the opinions of others, the economic system, old age, and many more) we engage in all sorts of behaviors. For example, we buy new clothes, furniture, and deodorant to avoid embarrassment; work hard at a job (sometimes giving ourselves high blood pressure and ulcers) to avoid being poor or losing prestige, respectful treatment, and self-respect; hide our real opinions so as to avoid losing our jobs and friends; and buy life insurance policies as a way of hedging on time.

The irony of our effort to avoid and escape vulnerability is that, while our effort often contributes to the economic system and provides us with short-run or temporary payoffs, it does little or nothing to help us understand and change the conditions that have made us vulnerable in the first place.

Given the above background factors in the lives of many people, let us turn to the first stage in the career of families of deviant children.

III. EFFECTS OF THE CHILD'S DEVIANT BEHAVIOR ON THE FAMILY

A Load to Bear

Deviant behavior is a problem in and of itself. For example, if the child engages in disruptive behaviors (tantrums, self-abuse, making messes, aggression) at a high rate, the parents must try to tolerate, live with, put a stop to, or handle such behaviors. They may have to (or believe that they have to) protect themselves, their property, and others from the child, or protect the child from his or her own behavior (as in self-injurious behavior). On the other hand, the child's behavioral inadequacies (such as a lack of play, self-help, and language skills) mean that the parents have a lot of work to do taking care of the child (even though the child may be so large as to make the caretaking difficult), figuring out what the child wants, and occupying the child's time.

As a result, the parents may feel that each day is a battle, that their lives are grinding work with no end in sight, and that their child is a constant burden. They may feel like the mythical Sisyphus, doomed for eternity to push a huge boulder up a mountain, only to watch it roll back down again and again.

Effects on the Parents' Self-Respect and Place in the Community

The child's deviant behavior affects not only the amount of work the parents have to do, their level of fatigue, and their feelings about the present and future, but it affects their perception of themselves and of how others view and treat them. For example, many parents of deviant children feel like outsiders or strangers in their own land, that they no longer have a place in the community or society. They speak as though they have little self-respect left, and indicate that few have treated them with respect for their feelings and needs.

The child's socially disruptive behaviors and lack of socially appropriate behaviors may adversely affect the parents' self-respect and place in several ways. First, the parents may wonder how they measure up to other adults since having a normal child is one of the socially significant symbols of membership. In addition, the "societal reaction" to the child's deviant behaviors may imply that others question the parents' place. For example, if a child has acquired and displays the socially significant possessions and skills, and shows regard for values and rules, then others assume that the parents, too, are members in good standing because: (1) they seem to know and have regard for what is expected and valued in the culture (for example, that children should learn to move their bowels in bathrooms and not in their pants) and (2) they seem to have the means (such as money, knowledge, and skill) for providing the child with the proper symbols of membership, such as appropriate (culturally valued) behavior.

When a child fails to learn (or fails to perform) culturally valued and expected skills and behaves in a culturally devalued manner (considered bad, taboo, shameful, unacceptable, and unnatural), then: (1) not only is the child seen as less of a member in good standing in society, but (2) the parents' capabilities as parents, and their place as members in good standing, are also questioned. In fact, both the child, his parents, and siblings may be treated in ways that indicate to them that others have a lowered opinion of the place and membership of the family.

For instance, the stares, the whispers that the parents often hear ("I wonder if it runs in the family," "Jeez, what a weird kid"), the callous remarks ("Has he always acted like that?"), and the unasked-for advice ("I know a good doctor who you might see," or "If he were my kid, I'd tan his hide")—all of these convey a message to the parents that they and their child are seen as different. Moreover, the parents may have lost what comfort and security there may be in knowing that, with all the ills they have to bear, at least they are accepted as equal members of society.

At some point, then, the parents may begin to question their competence ("Maybe if I were a better parent, Jimmy would learn better"). They may feel guilty for their child's condition ("Where did we go wrong?"). They may even become somewhat ashamed of their child's deficiencies and problem behaviors, not because they do not love the child, but because the child's (1) public displays of deficiencies and problems produce the disrespectful treatment from others, and (2) private (home) displays are painful reminders of what happens in public (Voysey, 1972).

Given the above, we can begin to predict some ways parents try to handle the pain of knowing that others see their child, and them, as different. For example, they might build walls around the family, shelter their child from the stares of others, become hypersensitive to the manner and possible motives of anyone who offers help (that is, they may be on the lookout for insults, for any messages that they are to blame for their child's problems, and for any indications that those offering help have little to offer).

Increased Vulnerability

The vulnerability of adults is vastly increased when they have a child with serious behavioral or physical problems. The fear of what will happen to their child when they die (vulnerability to time) is not just a passing thought. Furthermore, insurance policies do not lessen the fear because the real issue is "Who will care for Billy?" And the fear becomes more intense, becomes a nagging fear, as Billy grows older (and larger). In addition, the parents may become even more economically vulnerable as they spend time and hard-earned dollars looking and paying for help. They may become more socially vulnerable, too, that is, vulnerable to the opinions of others, as conveyed by the stares and whispers, the insults, the lack of invitations to neighborhood parties, and the lack of children who come to play with their child. And, in their desperate efforts to find help, they become vulnerable to almost anyone (for example, an "expert" or professional) who holds out the hope of an answer or a crumb of information that they can use.

Moreover, in a society such as this one, in which the main breadwinner, usually the male, is away from home for most of the day, the wife and mother is extremely vulnerable—both physically, emotionally, and financially. For, on top of the usual everyday tasks of child rearing and housekeeping, the mother must cope with the time-consuming, energy-draining, and nerve-wracking behaviors of her child. Worse still, if she has no mate, or if she does not get extra help and emotional support from her mate, she may well feel that each day is a struggle to keep some order within herself and in the home. Consequently, the mother may find it hard to interact with (teach) her child in a carefully planned, objective way. And, if she is physically and emotionally drained (and perhaps a little angry in general) at the end of the day, she may be unable to give her mate what he needs and wants. Thus, extreme vulnerability lays the groundwork both for counterproductive ways of interacting with the child and for marital and "personal" problems.

IV. EXPERIENCES AND PROBLEMS IN TRYING TO FIND HELP

When parents begin to worry that their child's problems are serious and will not be corrected by time, they generally search for professionals who they assume can tell them what is wrong, help the child, or refer them to the proper services and give them some idea of what they can expect about their child's future (their child's chances).

When a child has certain physical problems (for example, cerebral palsy), the explanation, help, and predictions (prognosis) given by the professional may be straightforward. It is a different story, however, when the child has learning and behavior problems. It may not be so clear just what is wrong "inside" the child; it is not so easy to say why the child has failed to develop, learn, or behave normally; nor is it clear just what is the best course of action to take. Does the child need psychotherapy for an "emotional problem"? Does the child merely need more time or more love? Does the child need a high-powered educational program? So, the first problem the parents may face in their search for help is uncertainty. Moreover there is often a lack of both people to assess what is wrong with their child, and services that the experts say their child needs.

The result of the parents' (and professionals') uncertainty, and the absence of a comprehensive system of assessment, referral, and remediation in most communities, is that the parents begin to make the rounds—from family physician, to neurologist, psychiatrist, allergist, psychologist, chiropractor, school, and back again (Kvaraceus and Hayes, 1969; Brutten et al., 1973; Lapin and Lapin, 1976; Wilson, 1968; Greenfield, 1972; Park, 1972). Too often, however, parents say that they have spent a lot of money and time and have received little in return. Their child has been given a number of labels (autistic, mentally retarded, aphasic), but the parents have received little practical information as to what they should do to help their child. Moreover, one expert may say that the child's future is bleak, while another may leave them uncertain as to what will happen ("Let's give it another year").

After each costly but unrewarding experience the parents' vulnerability seems to increase, for they do not know where to turn next. Soon, they become desperate. "If they can't help, who can? What in God's name will we do now?"

Some parents have said that their experiences with professionals were more than just a waste of time and money. They felt insulted and that their privacy was invaded. For example, the parents, already sensitized to their "differentness" by the stares of others, felt that by their questions and comments some interviewers seemed to be blaming them for their child's condition.

Dr. X: When Alan was an infant, did you leave him alone in his crib for long periods of time?

Mrs. Y: I don't think so. (Did I do something wrong? Lord, did I do this to my child?)

What is the End Result?

The result of many parents' experiences is hostility toward professionals, a lack of confidence in what professionals have to offer, and sometimes, most unfortunately, an unwillingness to seek (and possibly an unwillingness to accept) help from others who "come off" as experts. One parent expressed his feelings this way:

> All those &%$@**#!! did was ask dumb questions and take our money. They never gave us any help at all! When they told us that we might as well put him in an institution because he would never be able to count money or even talk, I sort of lost my mind. I was so sad that I was in a fog for about a week. Then I heard a voice inside me telling me that I would have to do the job by myself. (The parents taught their eight-year-old son to ask for things and answer simple questions in sentences, in less than two months during a Program.)

Some parents decide that if anyone is going to help their child, it will be them. At the other extreme, some parents seem to give up and live one day at a time, making do. In sum, the wall around the family, already partially built by the insensitive reactions of outsiders, grows higher as the parents come to believe that they cannot even depend on professionals—those who are supposed to have the answers.

Despite the unrewarding and painful experiences many parents have had with professionals, some do get help. The results may then be that they cling to the hope that a new ''pill'' will be found. Thus, even if they enter a program that offers them support and teaching skills, and take on the job of changing the ways they interact with each other and with their child, they may not make a total commitment because they still think that someone, someday, will be able to do it for them.

Either way, the problem for those trying to help parents is that: (1) some may not trust the consultant's motives or skills (and hesitate to participate at all) and (2) some may begin shopping for another source of help when the going gets tough during the Program. This means that consultants may have to make special efforts to contact many families and spark their interest. And it means that consultants have to present themselves and their program in such a way that they establish trust and confidence. Without these, the consultant may not get to first base.

V. ISOLATION

In families of children with physical, learning, and behavior problems isolation is partly caused by what has happened to the family (reactions of outsiders, experiences with professionals) and by the nuclear family structure of industrial societies.

As was noted, the fact that in modern societies grown children often move away from their parents and start a nuclear family of their own, increases the vulnerability of the nuclear family which has a deviant child, because the parents of the child may not be able to count on help (baby-sitting, emotional support, advice) from their own parents and other relatives who no longer live near them and who do not have answers anyway. In addition, relatives may offer conflicting (and sometimes unwanted) advice (Handel, 1967). As a result, the family must cope with its problems by itself.

Not only is isolation built into the social structure of modern societies, but it may be imposed. The parents may not attend neighborhood and community events (such as picnics, parties, carnivals, and circuses). They may not take their deviant child out often into public places. Indeed, they may not even be invited to the homes of others often or invite others into their home.

> *Neighbor:* I hope the Jones family doesn't come. Billy will only make a scene.
>
> *Mr. Jones to his wife:* Let's not go to the neighborhood party. Billy will just spend the day spinning the hamburger buns and rolling the hot dogs on the table.

The difficulty of getting baby-sitters and the parents' concern for what might happen at home even if they could get a sitter (Billy tearing up the house), may mean that the parents rarely go out together, so that what recreation they get must be obtained in the home.

The results of the isolation described above are often the following:

1. The parents are greatly fatigued or drained because they get little outside help and little relief.
2. The more drained parents become, the less effectively they cope with their child and the less they may gratify each other.
3. The child is exposed to few normal (outside) settings in which to learn and perform what he has learned.
4. The family members are seen as even more different because they seem to be loners, even eccentrics (which may lead to further isolation).

In sum, as time goes on, the family may become a "closed system" in which there is little or no energy or additional resource coming into the family from the outside. Now there is nothing wrong with closed systems as such, as long as what is going on between the members of the system generates good feelings and productive behaviors which generate more good feelings and productive behaviors. But if family interaction is producing pain in the parents and even more problem behaviors in the child (which requires that still more energy be spent in trying to alleviate the pain and cope with the child) and if the parents cannot gratify one another so as to replace the energy they are using up, we can predict that some families may run into big trouble. Perhaps the marriage breaks up, the child is "put away," or the parents somehow resign themselves to living a nightmare (Downey, 1965; Korkes, 1955; Farber, 1959; Farber et al, 1960).

Teaching Parents to Educate Their Children Will Not Solve the Long-Term Problems of Isolation. It is true that by making contact and conducting a Program with families, one can help to decrease isolation. However, if families are still isolated once the Program has ended and frequent contact with you has been faded out, many of the beneficial changes that were brought about may be reversed. Without additional sources of information, reinforcement, and backup support, the parents may become fatigued again, encounter problems for which they do not have solutions, experience a decrease in gratification, and, consequently, return to old ways of making do. Thus, it is important to: (1) teach parents methods for maintaining the changes that they have made in themselves and their children and (2) help them to develop and use other outside sources of help.

The following ways of overcoming isolation that may have long-term beneficial effects on families, are discussed in more detail in later chapters:

1. Work with families in groups, so that esprit de corps, an identification with the group, and friendships develop, and so that group processes, such as modeling, group problem-solving, group pressure, and peer reinforcement can be used to motivate, initiate, and strengthen change in each participating family.
2. Build interfamily networks (that is, close working and friendship relationships between families), so that families continue to support, coach, motivate, and reinforce each other once the Program has ended.
3. Help families to become involved in parents' organizations to maintain their identification with something larger than the family, and from which they can obtain new information and can work to get more and better services.
4. Teach siblings, relatives, and even neighbors and high school students to provide inputs to the families (for example, baby-sitting, respite care) to replace the inputs lost at the end of the Program.

VI. PATTERNS OF INTERACTION (STRUCTURED EXCHANGES) WITH THE CHILD

So far, a possible picture of the family looks like this. The parents (and perhaps the siblings) feel something like outsiders as a result of other people's reactions to them and to the child. They may feel unsure of their competence as parents, guilty about the child's condition, and afraid of the future. Moreover, as a result of unrewarding experiences with professionals, they may distrust professionals and feel hostile toward them. Consequently, they may live much of their lives behind closed doors (in isolation). The problem behaviors of the child, which are physically and emotionally draining, the general isolation of nuclear families, and the fact that many husbands do not help spouses with child rearing and household tasks often, may all result in the parents being less able to gratify one another. On top of all this, the parents interact with their children in ways that are repetitive and durable. And some of those patterns of interaction (structured exchanges) may produce changes in the child that are the opposite of what the parents want. That is, some exchanges may be counterproductive.

What is a Structured Exchange?

The concept of "structured exchange" helps to focus attention on the reciprocal influences and changes that take place through repeated interaction (Hamblin et al., 1971; Homans, 1961; Thibaut and Kelley, 1959; Kozloff, 1973; Blau, 1964). It is generally taken for granted that some behaviors are affected by their consequences. For example, behaviors that are consistently followed by rewards or positive reinforcers tend to increase in frequency and skill. Behaviors that are no longer reinforced tend to decrease. And behaviors that are consistently punished tend to decrease.

In social life the behavior of others provides many of the effective consequences for our behaviors. Some people reward or positively reinforce some of our behaviors, ignore or provide neutral consequences (that is, consequences that we do not much care about one way or another) for other behaviors, and punish still other behaviors. And our behaviors generally change accordingly. For example, we generally smile more often at those who return our smiles and speak nicely to us; smile less and less at people who return our smiles with a blank face or who walk right on by; and steer clear of those who return our smiles with grunts and scowls.

So far, we have looked at only one side of social interaction or exchange, that is, the behavior of one person. If we are to understand long-term change, however, we must look at the behavior of the other persons involved in exchanges. What is it, for example, that keeps the other person or persons rewarding, ignoring, or punishing our behaviors? The answer, in part, is to be found in the immediate and long-term changes in our behaviors after another person has responded to us (provided a consequence for our behaviors).

Consider some structured exchanges between a wife and husband. If the husband tells his wife "I love you," she may respond by hugging him. If hugs from his wife are gratifying (positively reinforcing consequences) to him, then he is likely to smile back at his wife (an immediate change in his behavior) and to say "I love you" to his wife more often (a long-term change). In other words, the wife's response (a hug) to the husband's "I love you" produces both immediate changes in his behavior (smiles) and long-term changes (a higher rate of saying "I love you"). Finally, if smiles and "I love you" from the husband are positive reinforcers for the wife, then the wife is likely to continue reinforcing her husband when he smiles at her and says "I love you." In sum, each party is rewarding the behavior of the other party (Patterson and Reid, 1970).

The reciprocal reinforcement built into the above exchange is likely to have three long-term results. First, the behaviors of each person in the exchange are likely to increase. The husband smiles and says "I love you" more often; the wife hugs her husband more often. Second, the affectionate exchange itself is likely to be repeated more and more often. That is, it becomes a structured exchange. It may become frequent and durable, a predictable unit of life in the family. And third, the structured affectionate exchange may produce changes in other exchanges. For example, the husband and wife may spend more time together talking, reading, and going out, and they may punish one another (blame, argue, deprive) less and less.

With the above ideas in mind, let us look at the main types of structured exchanges between parents and children. The exchanges are presented in pairs: a counterproductive exchange followed by the corresponding productive exchange.

Reinforcing Problem Behaviors (Escape): Reacting or "Giving In"

This is a common structured exchange. The parents reinforce (reward) problem behaviors (such as tantrums or head-banging) by cuddling the child, talking to him, giving him food, toys and TV, yelling at the child or chasing after him. The parents, finding the child's problem behaviors punishing (note how fatigue sensitizes them to the disruptive behaviors), are attempting to stop the behavior. Usually, the parents' escape efforts do stop the disruptive behavior for a short time, and this negatively reinforces the parents for their efforts, making it more likely that they will use their escape behaviors in the future.

The tragedy of this exchange is that both the parents and the child are reinforced. The child is positively reinforced by the attention of the parents (and the other "goodies" he may be getting), and the parents are negatively reinforced when the child temporarily stops the disruptive behavior. So, over time, the behavior of both parents and child increases. The child engages in disruptive behavior more often and perhaps more skillfully. The parents try to stop disruptive behavior more often and more desperately. In effect, the exchange itself is repeated more often. It becomes a stable feature of family life. The child is disruptive; the parents react. And in so reacting, the parents are kept on their toes, feel like "live wires," and are exhausted. Every time they react, however, they strengthen the very behaviors that they cannot stand in their child (Patterson, 1971).

Riding it Out, Hanging Tough, or Keeping Cool

This is an alternative to the escape exchange. The parents do not react to and reinforce a problem behavior but, instead, respond in such a way as to weaken the problem behavior and replace it with a more appropriate behavior. For example, they might make statements to themselves, such as "I'm not going to give in to his whining. He'll have to ask for what he wants." And, whenever the child starts to whine, they turn away from the child or calmly stand there and make no response (extinction), or they put the child in his room until he has stopped whining for awhile (time out). Then, when the child makes an effort to engage in appropriate behavior (e.g., asking instead of whining), the parents reinforce the child—"Now that's the way to ask!!"

Placation or Avoidance: "Selling Out"

After repeatedly experiencing events that are punishing to us, we begin to predict when punishment is going to come our way. The same applies to parents and their experiences with disruptive behaviors. They can see that their child's behavior is working up or leading to another tantrum or episode of head-banging.

They also know the situations in which their child is likely to "blow." What do parents do? They do what most of us do. They try to avoid the episodes of disruptive behavior.

For example, the parents may reinforce the child for being quiet, aimlessly wandering around the house, watching TV, or pushing and pulling on them, because these are behaviors that the parents can stand. Moreover, by reinforcing these behaviors with food, attention, and other things that the parents know (or hope) that the child wants or likes, the child does not engage in his worst disruptive behaviors to get what he wants. In effect, the parents are using reinforcers to buy a little peace and quiet. In the long run, however, they are wasting reinforcers that could be used to strengthen proper play, speech, and self-care behaviors.

At the same time, however, they may be accidently teaching the child to threaten or coerce them with behaviors that indicate that unless the parents give the child when he wants now, he will engage in the behaviors they cannot stand! It is as though the child were saying:

> Although I am whining, you had better give me that cookie, because if you don't, I'll start to scream my head off!

Earning Rewards: "No Freebies"

This is an alternative to the placation exchange. Instead of reinforcing the child for unskillful performances of important appropriate behaviors, for aimless and quiet behaviors, or for threats, the parents require the child to earn reinforcers. For example, instead of putting the child's plate on the table so that the child does not drop or throw it, the parents make statements to themselves, such as "She's a member of this family! She can help out" or "If she wants to eat, she'll have to set her own place." They then require the child to set her own place, or to make a good attempt, before they let the child eat.

This does not imply that the parents are hard-hearted. Rather, it means that the parents seem to be aware of the child's capabilities and of what will happen if they fail to expect and reinforce improvements in their child's behaviors. Of course, just as the parents might "sell out" too cheaply (expect too little), as in the placation exchange, they might require too much of their child at the moment. Both extremes must be dealt with during a Program.

Multiple Signals: Wasting Your Breath

In this exchange, the parents give a signal to the child in an effort to change the child's behavior in some way. For example, they ask a question or give a direction or command (to start or stop a behavior). If the child does not comply with the signal, the parents are likely to repeat it, over and over, until either the child finally complies or the parents give up. The latter is usually the case! The problem, here, is that each time the parents repeat the signal, they may reinforce the child's last act of noncompliance (with their attention). Thus, the child becomes even less likely to comply with signals in the future. In fact, the child may appear to be tuning out the parents, and to be aloof, indifferent, and withdrawn. On the other hand, the child's lack of compliance may result in the parents' giving the child fewer and fewer signals (opportunities to respond and learn). The result may be that the child tunes out the parents and the parents tune out the child—until disruptive behavior starts or seems on the verge of starting—and then the escape or placation exchanges may occur.

Single Signals: Making Your Words Count

Some parents are not caught in the multiple-signal (nagging) trap. Instead of repeating a signal over and over, to little avail, they present a signal only when the child is paying attention. If cooperation with the signal is clearly in the child's interests ("Sally, would you like some ice cream?") the parents allow the child to experience the natural consequences of ignoring their signal (Sally simply misses the chance to have ice cream). If cooperation with the signal is desired by the parents ("Billy, put your clothes in the drawer, please"), then the parents might prompt the child through the motions. In either case, there is no protracted conflict over the child's inattentiveness and noncooperation. The child consistently experiences the consequences of attentiveness and cooperation versus inattentiveness and noncooperation.

Lack of Rewards for Appropriate Behaviors

Not only do some parents reinforce problem behaviors a great deal, but they may seldom reinforce appropriate behaviors (except those that "jump out at them"—like a new word). Sometimes, the reason why parents fail to reinforce appropriate behaviors stems from values in the larger culture: "Children should be good and not reinforced (rewarded) for what they should be doing anyway." Usually, however, the reasons are: (1) the parents are so overwhelmed by disruptive behaviors that they do not even see the few episodes of appropriate behaviors that should be reinforced and (2) many appropriate behaviors which should be reinforced are, nevertheless, performed with so little skill that the parents do not recognize these behaviors as reinforceable (for example, when the child makes a half-hearted attempt to occupy himself in a constructive way—(play). The result is that the appropriate behaviors that could replace the problem behaviors as ways of spending time and getting attention are not strengthened. Thus, appropriate behaviors remain weak, while problem behaviors worsen.

Catching 'Em Doing Good

On the other hand, parents may be on the lookout for appropriate behaviors and good tries, and may reinforce such behaviors often. For example, in some families, the parents are sensitive to their child's language behavior and are quick to reinforce it. Other parents are sensitive to and likely to reinforce self-help skills. And still others are generally sensitive to and likely to reinforce appropriate behaviors.

Lack of Opportunities (Occasions) to Respond and to Learn: Child is "Hanging Around"

In some families, possibly in all families at certain times, the parents give the child few occasions to learn and to respond. The parents may have low expectations of the child's ability to learn or of their own ability to teach. Consequently, they may make few requests of their child to do anything and, instead, assume the role of caretakers. On the other hand, their child may have been so disruptive and inattentive when they did try to teach, that they have stopped trying. Consequently, placation has become a predominant exchange. The child changes little in a beneficial direction and the parents may become pessimistic or fatalistic about the future.

Many Opportunities (Occasions) to Respond and to Learn: Child is "Doing His or Her Share"

On the other hand, parents may have high expectations concerning their child's chances and of their abilities to help their child change. Or, they may simply feel that they must "give it our best shot" no matter what the outcome since "nobody else has been able to help." Thus, the parents may generally give their child many opportunities during the day to learn new behaviors and to participate in family life. Or, they may concentrate on several behaviors that are important to them and the child, such as self-help skills. Either way, if the parents' efforts are successful in helping their child to learn, their expectations and self-confidence increase, as do their efforts to teach their child.

Improper or Unnecessary Punishment

We have not found parents of severely deviant children, as a group, to be "punishment oriented." That is, they do not punish problem behaviors often and do not see it as a cure-all. Indeed, the opposite is true; they often reinforce problem behaviors. However, punishment (in the form of spankings, for example) does sometimes occur, but, when it does, it is not usually done correctly.

For example, the parents may wait too long before they finally punish (that is, when they cannot stand the behavior any longer). They may not punish with enough intensity (that is, the aversive stimulus, for example, a slap on the bottom, is so light that it is more likely to make the child smile). In addition, after the punishment has been delivered, the parents sometimes give the child extra attention (for example, they talk to or cuddle the child). In this way, the child may learn to engage in the problem behavior just to get the attention after the punishment has been delivered. Moreover, the punishment may be given infrequently or inconsistently, depending on how tired and aggravated the parents are. And finally, the parents may not be reinforcing appropriate behaviors to replace the problem behaviors they are punishing.

Some parents punish appropriate behaviors (Henry, 1971). For example, they yell at or spank their child for handling certain valuable objects in the home, even though the behavior constitutes the first signs of attention and curiosity. Clearly, this often happens in families of so-called normal children as well.

The long-term results of improper and unnecessary punishment seem to be as follows:

1. Problem behaviors remain unchanged or may increase.
2. The parents decide that punishment is ineffective (and may resist later suggestions that it be used on certain behaviors, such as head-banging).
3. The parents feel even less competent, even less able to control their child and their own feelings ("If spanking Billy won't stop him, what in God's name will?").
4. Certain appropriate behaviors that have been punished become even weaker.

Proper Use of Punishment

Sometimes punishment is used properly. For example, it is used sparingly and only when it seems to be the best choice. And when they punish, parents do so immediately, every time, and with strong punishers, do not reinforce while the child is upset, and reinforce appropriate replacement behaviors. Moreover, many parents encourage rather than inadvertently punish appropriate behaviors. For instance, instead of inadvertently punishing their child's exploratory behaviors, they remove expensive or breakable items and, instead, provide a variety of objects to play with.

Implications of the Above

The counterproductive exchanges just described happen so frequently in some families, involve so many different behaviors, and take up so much time and energy, that teaching parents how to deal with just one or two of their child's behaviors is not likely to produce much change for long. In fact, with so much aggravation from disruptive behaviors that they have not been taught to change, the parents may be unwilling or feel unable to change even the few behaviors you help them with. Consequently, from the beginning, teach parents to see and replace the counterproductive exchanges with productive exchanges, and to accentuate productive exchanges that exist. This may mean reversing many of the ways they have been interacting with the child: becoming insensitive to (ignoring) disruptive behaviors and becoming sensitive to (reinforcing) appropriate behaviors.

By reversing many of the counterproductive exchanges, and by accentuating or strengthening existing productive exchanges, the parents may achieve the following:

1. Produce changes early, and quickly, in many behaviors of their child (such as improving attention and cooperation and replacing tantrums and noncompliance).
2. Become more confident of their abilities.
3. Have more energy (because there will be fewer episodes of disruptive behavior).
4. Learn the general principles and methods for interacting with (teaching) their child, thereby enabling them to conduct good home education programs for specific target behaviors later in a Program.

VII. LONG-TERM CHANGES IN FAMILIES

What happens if problems facing a family and counterproductive exchanges with the child continue for years? The answer is that, in many families, existing problems worsen and new ones develop. For example, the family may become even more isolated; counterproductive exchanges with the child may become more frequent and durable (difficult to change); the parents may become even more fatigued (drained), tense, and hypervigilant; marital problems (such as conflict and withdrawal) may develop; family routines may become less organized; the parents may begin to play communication games with themselves and others in order to avoid further pain; and personal problems (such as anxiety, depression, and self-defeating views of the present and future) may develop (Hannan, 1974; Holroyd and McArthur, 1976; Crain et al, 1966; Birenbaum, 1971; Gambrill, 1963; Downey, 1965; Gordon and Kutner, 1965; Carver and Carver, 1974; Davis, 1963; Farber, 1960).

Let us look more closely at the kinds of changes that can take place over the years, which must be considered when planning and conducting a Program.

Fatigue/Draining

One long-term change may be increasing fatigue. The more the child's problem behaviors rise in frequency, severity, and duration, and the more the parents are kept on their toes trying to anticipate and clean up after their child, the more fatigued they become. More and more energy is channeled into thinking about and reacting to the child. Moreover, if the "walls" around the family decrease support from the outside, and if the spouses are not gratifying (restoring) one another, they may become too drained to stand back and see what is happening, too tired to make the effort to change, and too pessimistic to believe that beneficial change is possible.

Fatigue may make the parents either unwilling to participate in a Program or unable to effectively conduct a home educational program if they do participate. Thus, in trying to interest parents in a Program, convince them that: (1) in the long run they are likely to expend less energy than they are now, and (2) other families will be helping them. During a Program teach parents methods for scheduling and taking "breaks" in efforts to teach their children (for example, for part of each day and for certain days of the week). Without scheduled breaks even the most energetic parents are likely to "burn out" in a short time.

Marital Problems

What happens when parents are forced to work together on a serious problem that they cannot solve, especially one that is draining? What happens if they are unable to gratify each other's needs because they are so tired and on edge? In many cases, various patterns of punishment develop.

For instance, the father, who is usually out of the home most of the day, may return home to find his wife exhausted. Perhaps the wife is a little angry that she has had to cope with the child all day by herself. Wanting a little peace and quiet, the husband finds, then, a wife who is on edge and a child who is "on wheels." Unless he is unusually sensitive and strong, he is likely to return his wife's irritation and anger.

Wife: I'm so tired. I never get any help around here!! (She may not intend to blame him, but he interprets it that way. He is just as frustrated at work as she is at home.)

Husband: What am I supposed to do? Somebody's got to earn a living!

As you can imagine, this exchange, in which each person punishes the other, leads to an evening in which neither gives the other what he or she needs (recognition, understanding, tenderness). And the night of punishment sets them up for a repeat performance on the next day. The wife gets up in the morning knowing that she will be just as alone as before, and the husband knows the situation that he will be coming home to that evening. The pattern of mutual punishment can eventually escalate to the point where each is snipping at the other; "negating," arguing with, and "cutting" what the other says and does; and unwilling to give affection and help.

The roles of mother and father may become extremely segregated (Henry, 1971). That is, the husband may do less and less of the child rearing and housework and, instead, may keep to himself. Such "role segregation," which in part matches what goes on in the larger society (husbands do one kind of work; wives do another), may be more extreme because the father has found that he is unable to be effective in helping his own child (which may make him feel less manly), and because interaction with his wife regarding the child usually ends up in more fighting or friction. As can be seen, such a pattern may make it difficult for the parents to work together during a Program or after it has ended. (See Appendix 7 for a discussion of the single-parent family.)

However, while the patterns of interaction (exchanges) between parents can become punishing, and can lead to extreme role segregation, I am not saying that this is the usual case. Sometimes the marital relationship becomes stronger. Often the parents try to give one another some kind of relief. For example, one may watch the child with learning and behavior problems, while the other is busy with the siblings or with another household task. Moreover, the parents may give one another emotional support (sympathy after a hard day or coming home from work to help out in a crisis). Yet, while giving relief is probably important in maintaining the marriage (and the spouses' sanity), it does not mean that the parents are consistently and effectively working together to carry out a program to educate or socialize their child. Relief-giving, in other words, may turn out to be one more way of making do or getting by a day at a time.

Therefore, in preparing parents to participate in a Progrram, and in helping them to conduct and maintain a home educational program, be sensitive, both to counterproductive and productive marital exchanges. From the beginning of a Program, then, help parents to pinpoint and analyze their own interaction, to accentuate productive marital exchanges (e.g., affectionate exchanges, working cooperatively), and to replace any counterproductive ones (blaming, depriving, withdrawing).

Decrease in the Organization of Family Routines

One of the long-term effects of fatigue, marital problems, the problem behaviors and behavioral inadequacies of the child, and isolation from sources of help, may be a decrease in the organization of certain arrangements or routines in the home. If the mother, for example, spends a great deal of time keeping up with and cleaning up after her child, and if in the process she has become fatigued, feeling that she is barely keeping her head above water, she may be unable to "run a tight ship'' in the home. Meal times may begin to vary from day to day. Chores may not get done or may not be done as well as others expect. The house may be filled with much noise (from other children, TVs, and record players) when the mother is attending to the deviant child or is too tired to make the effort to keep the noise down for long.

A decrease in household organization may add to marital problems. For, if the husband wants a tight ship, he may punish the wife for what he considers her sloppiness and failure to be a good wife (housekeeper), which in turn may affect her self-respect. And the more she is punished (instead of being helped), the less likely she is to give her husband what he wants, leading to more punishment for her.

In addition, if various everyday activities are continually disrupted, and if the parents have gotten out of the habit of living according to certain schedules, it may be difficult for them to conduct a consistent home educational program. If, for example, meals are to be used as a reinforcer in a speech training program, and if meals come at different times each day, the child may be extremely hungry (and fussy) one day, and not hungry (unmotivated) the next. Or, if toys are scattered all over the house, it may be difficult to run an effective program for teaching the child to play. Or, if there is a great deal of noise in the house, it will be hard to run teaching sessions on almost any behavior.

In sum, parents may need help early in their Program to establish more order in home life, making it easier to run teaching programs. (It may also be easier on their nerves.) For example, they may benefit from help on making and keeping to certain schedules (meals, shopping, other chores), on teaching themselves and their other children to keep the house clean and less noisy, and on working together as a team to run the house.

Hypervigilance and an Exaggerated Belief in Responsibility

The longer the family is isolated, and the more counterproductive exchanges in the family are repeated, the more involved the parents may become in the moment-by-moment behaviors of their children (and themselves). They may become hypersensitive or hypervigilant, on the lookout for behaviors that are painful to them, and feel that they are "walking on eggs." In addition, it sometimes seems that exchanges happen so fast that the parents no longer see them. It is as though they are experiencing an event and immediately reacting to it. So long as the parents fail to see what is going on (their exchanges), and unless they can stand back and plan before they respond, it is difficult to help them to change their exchanges, which often leads to failure in a home educational program.

Moreover, the parents may come to believe that they are personally responsible for the moment-to-moment behaviors of their child and for everything that their child might or might not become. In fact, they may believe that the future depends, not on their behaviors, but on the kind of people they are. They may not see that their behaviors have been learned or shaped up through interaction with their child, but, rather, that their behaviors reflect their "essential" personality. Thus, every time the child throws a tantrum or displays his inadequacies, and every time the parents interact with their child in a way that does not work out as they had planned, it is another confirmation of their fear that they are essentially stupid, sick, inept, weak, and guilty.

Some parents who have an exaggerated belief in personal responsibility for their children's behaviors and future, are not likely to enter a Program that involves their actually working with their child. For any perceived failure would be a terrible condemnation of the self. Similarly, perceived failure during a Program may result in their dropping out, so as to avoid more failure.

To be successful with parents, then, help them replace: (1) hypervigilance with a more detached (objective) view of ongoing events; (2) a pattern of experiencing and immediately reacting, with a pattern of waiting, planning, and correcting (that is, following a problem-solving sequence); and (3) an exaggerated belief in personal responsibility for their child's behavior and future, with confidence in more general (less personal) principles and processes. That is, it is helpful if they believe that under the right environmental conditions their child is likely to change. All they are responsible for is trying to make sure that the conditions (including their own teaching behaviors) are there. They need not become different persons (better, smarter, stronger); they perhaps need to change their behaviors.

Personal Problems

Another set of difficulties consists of "personal" problems, each of which can hinder success during and after a Program. For example, a parent may experience the following:

1. Tenseness, especially when the child is engaging in disruptive behaviors (for example, the parent may feel on edge, hypersensitive to changes in his own body and in his feelings, and to changes in his child's behavior).
2. Anxiety (have thoughts of impending doom or of other terrible things that might happen, combined with a state of high arousal—rapidly beating heart and increased respiration, knotted stomach, cold sweat, and periodic attacks of panic).
3. Depression (including fatigue, sleep and eating disturbances, feelings of guilt, crying, and a decrease in the performance of usual activities).
4. Unassertiveness (allow others to degrade or take advantage, fail to assert personal rights, fail to initiate interaction in certain conditions).

All of the above personal problems may be accompanied by self-defeating statements and beliefs regarding incompetence, guilt, a lack of self-worth, an inability to control oneself or one's child, and pessimisim concerning the child's future. For example, a parent might say to himself and/or others:

> I just can't stop thinking that I'm a stupid person. I can't stop feeling sad all the time. Sometimes I feel like I'm coming apart. I think I must be going crazy.

The above personal problems are likely to have an effect on the ways parents interact with each other and their children, their readiness to make a commitment to a Program and its goals (change), and their ability to carry out and maintain effective home programs. For example, the tense or anxious parent may be unable to ignore extremely disruptive behaviors. The depressed parent may not have (or feel that he or she does not have) enough energy or confidence to make changes in the home or to carry out teaching programs. And the parent who makes statements such as "Everything is hopeless," "I can't control myself," or "I'm coming apart" may be unwilling to start working with the child or, later in a Program, if the going gets tough, may use such statements to avoid doing assignments or to excuse possible failure.

Since many parents already feel tense, discouraged, and possibly pessimistic, help them to remedy such difficulties (or come to believe that they can be remedied in systematic ways) from the first contact. Otherwise, you may not spark an initial interest in your Program. On the other hand, during a Program, you may have to help the parents (individually or as a group) to learn how to remedy personal problems (e.g., with assertiveness training, systematic desensitization, progressive relaxation, cognitive relabeling, and medical regimens). Methods for doing so are described in Chapter 10.

Many parents do not develop personal problems. Instead, they become stronger, maintain their resolve to help their child, have an amazing ability to cope with potentially stressful events, and have tremendous energy. Indeed, many who suffer from anxiety and depression have various strengths. Thus, in the same way that you help parents to pinpoint and remedy personal problems, help them to pinpoint, accentuate, and utilize strengths.

Durability of the Above Problems

As time goes by, many of the problems described above (for example, counterproductive exchanges) become durable or resistant to change. The major question that this section tries to answer is: Why do people continue to engage in counterproductive behaviors, which produce more pain and problems?

Short-Run Payoffs. Even when the options and long-run aversive consequences are clear, people are often so "hooked" on the short-run or immediate payoffs (reinforcements) that they continue to engage in behaviors that are likely to harm themselves or others. Overeating is an excellent example. Although it may eventually increase the chances of a heart attack, in the short run it is often reinforcing. Similarly, in the escape exchange talked about earlier, the child is immediately reinforced by the attention of the parents when they try to stop the disruptive behavior, and the parents are immediately reinforced when the child temporarily stops the disruptive behavior. Or, when two people punish one another, each may be immediately reinforced by the pain written on the face of the other. As a result, the exchanges are repeated. The tragic effect is that, while in the short run both parties are reinforced (getting something they want or escaping and avoiding what they cannot stand), in the long run they are piling up a great deal of pain and losing chances to change for the better the ways they interact.

Coercion. Coercion is another source of durability. By "coercion" is meant that a person acts as though he has no choice or but little choice to respond as he does because of the aversiveness of the other person's behavior. For example, even if the parents realize that they are "giving in" to the child (the escape exchange), the child's disruptive behaviors may be so painful that they still do whatever they can to stop them. Similarly, although they try never to reinforce tantrums anymore, the tantrums may escalate in intensity or duration, to the point at which the parents again can no longer withstand them. The increasing severity of the child's behavior, in other words, may coerce the parents into reacting in such a way that the behavior is eventually reinforced (Patterson and Reid, 1970).

On the other hand, the parents may coerce one another into maintaining old behavior patterns. If the husband, for example, is in a position to punish the wife no matter what she does, or if he controls reinforcers that his wife can get nowhere else, the husband can coerce compliance from the wife, forcing her to play the role of sole caretaker for the child or reinforce disruptive behavior ("Can't you shut him up!").

Ideology/Philosophy. A third source of durability consists of beliefs and values (statements made to oneself or to others to justify behavior) concerning what is right, proper, or necessary. If, for example, the wife believes that it is a mother's job to care for the child (sees that role as her place), she continues to play that role although, by doing it alone, she is becoming more and more drained. In addition, she continues to stay married to a man who gives her no help because she tells herself that divorce is not right ("A woman's job is to stay by her man").

Similarly, parents may placate the child and fail to reinforce appropriate behaviors because they accept the more general cultural notions that: (1) "defective" children should be pitied and given tender loving care and (2) children should not be reinforced for what they ought to be doing anyway. Or, finally parents may explain their hesitation to participate in a Program with philosophical statements such as, "Well, that's life"; "I guess some things are meant to be"; or "This is our cross to bear."

Thus, from your first contacts with a family, you may have to help the parents to see that the statements they use to explain or justify their behaviors may be: (1) illogical ("Sympathy for your child does not mean that he should be allowed to do as he pleases, does it?"); (2) not as good for them to believe as other statements (which you will provide); and (3) the kinds of statements that will prevent them from attaining goals.

Lack of Real or Perceived Alternatives. Each time people repeat an exchange, they lose a chance to try another way of interacting or of solving a mutual problem (Watzlawick et al., 1967). Moreover, when "walls" have been built around a family the parents are cut off from the information that they might use to help themselves and their child. The combination of lost opportunities each time an exchange is repeated and the lack of information on how to change, keeps the exchanges in the family from changing much, if at all. Moreover, the longer problems remain, the less people believe that they are anemable to change ("Nothing can be done anyway.")

Communication Games. Like just about everyone else, some parents play communication games (Berne, 1964). The games seem to be the end-result of years of looking for help and not finding it; of making do on their own; of feeling incompetent and possibly guilty for their child's condition. The games seem to have several purposes. They enable parents to: (1) present a good image (both to others and to themselves), so that others treat them according to that image; (2) maintain existing patterns of family interaction because, in the short run (that is, day-to-day), it seems easier, they no longer believe that change is possible, or they want to avoid the pain of another failure; and (3) obtain help.

Some games that may occur, which both you and the parents should learn to avoid, pinpoint, or successfully overcome, are as follows:

Overworked Advocate. This game is sometimes played by a parent who is deeply committed to the welfare of children and who does much work in various organizations (such as the National Society for Autistic Children, the Association for Retarded Citizens, or the Association for Children with Learning Disabilities). However, the parent may have all but given up on changing his or her own child. He may feel that he has tried everything and that nothing more can be done. The game of "overworked advocate" enables the parent to avoid making a strong and genuine commitment to a Program without appearing to be uncaring because, after all, the parent is doing so much good work. Keep in mind that "overworked advocate" is not a type of person. It is a game that a decent (but tired) person may play.

Sometimes, the game of overworked advocate is played after a parent has started a Program. For example, the parent may say that he cannot do all of the assignments because he is hard at work advocating on behalf of the children.

> We weren't able to work with Marty this week because we had to go to meetings of the. . . .

Of course, as time goes on, statements of that sort may become more frequent.

"We've Tried That." This game is also an effort to preserve the public and private image of the interested, caring, and hard-working parent when, in fact, the parents may be unwilling to make a commitment because they have experienced nothing but failure, are drained, know that they do not get along with each other well enough to conduct a good home program, or because, in reality, they would rather leave things as they are. For instance, in response to an invitation to join a Program (that is, before the Program starts), or in response to a suggestion that they try a certain technique (during the Program), the parents might reply: "It won't work" or "We've tried that before."

"It's Not Our Job." This game is often played by parents who have been through the mill and who are probably advocates for children. They may be so angry about their past experiences with certain professionals or about the past lack of educational services that, when some services finally become available, the parents become less willing to participate in the job of educating their children. They want and expect others to do it.

The parents' argument that their child has a right to services does make legal sense, since all states now have laws mandating an education to all children regardless of handicap. But the argument that "It is not (or is no longer) our job" does not make educational sense. The more people who work with their child, the faster the child will learn, the more behaviors the child will learn, and the more the child's behaviors will generalize. And, as stated in Chapter 1, unless the parents help, the child's behaviors may not change much, if at all, in the home.

"So Do Me Something" or "You Can't Make Me Feel Guilty." Some parents "talk" a good home program. They have the right verbal behavior, but do not put in the time and/or effort to carry out a good home program. They may be that way from the start of a Program or may slack off if progress is slow. No matter what is tried (persuasion, demonstration of proper methods, contracts, smaller steps, group pressure), the parent(s) may do less than agreed upon.

For example, when working on toilet training, they might agree to put their child on the toilet every hour and to take data on what the child did. However, their data show that they have been putting the child on the toilet no more than three times a day. Occasionally, a parent may seem proud of his failure to carry out an assignment. He may not say "We did not have the time" or "We were sick." Instead, he might say "Well, some people just can't be trusted" or "Well, I guess I'm just a jerk."

This game usually happens after other methods for trying to help parents have been tried and failed. And it appears to be a difficult game to handle because, in effect, the parent is "putting himself down" and putting words in the consultant's mouth. Unless the consultant effectively overcomes this game, failure to help the parent and child is almost certain.

"Help Me, I'm Stupid." In this game, the parent continues to make mistakes in his or her program despite all the help given. For example, the parent may not schedule teaching sessions properly, continues to reinforce problem behaviors, or fails to properly arrange the physical layout of the house (e.g., by keeping extra teaching materials stored away). The consultant can give demonstrations, role-play proper techniques, show the parent what is happening on videotape, have the parent make appropriate verbal responses to what he sees, and have the parent write schedules and plans on paper, but the parent's behavior does not change much or for long. The parent's response may be: "I guess I'm just stupid" or "I try so hard, but I just can't do it right."

Overcoming and Moving Beyond Games. Games are clearly a roadblock to success in helping families. One method for overcoming games is to show the game player that what he or she is saying contradicts other values and beliefs that he or she holds. For instance, since "overworked advocate" is usually played by persons who do care for children, value their work on behalf of children, and have strong antipathies toward those who do not help families and childen, it can often be overcome by pointing out that statements such as "We just don't have the time" contradict the whole thrust of their advocacy work:

> You mean that you have time for other children, but not for your own? With all that you do for other peoples' children, surely you can find a few hours a week for your own.

Another method has been called "reverse psychology" or "therapeutic paradox" (Watzlawick et al., 1967, 1974; Rabkin, 1977; Haley, 1976; Frankl, 1960). Instead of trying to dissuade the person from playing games ("Look, you are playing games. Let's try to cut it out."), or to convince the person that you are trustworthy and competent ("Have I done anything that you should be hostile toward me?"), or to argue against the persons' statements ("Of course this method works! Try it."), all of which may reinforce the game-playing and escalate "resistance," reverse psychology involves indicating to the person that you see that he or she is playing a certain game, that such games are expected, and that the game is a good sign of potential success or actual progress in the relationship or in the Program. In effect, you define or prescribe the game as a good thing, which may be the opposite of what the game-player expects to hear. Thus, the person may stop playing the game (which is what you wanted anyway), or, if the person continues it, it is no longer the same, since you have given your approval.

Finally, if necessary, you might help the person to go beyond games by talking about why they are being played (lack of proper help from the consultant? fear of failure? unrealistic expectations?) and providing alternative ways of obtaining what he or she wants (self-respect, change in the child).

I'm not implying that parents of children with learning and behavior problems are, as a class, game players, and that one might as well be cynical about working with them. Rather, if the blame lies anywhere, it is in the historical social conditions that lead people to be dishonest with themselves and others, as the only way left to protect their vulnerable selves.

VIII. HOW FAMILY CAREER EXPERIENCES MAY PRODUCE PROBLEMS RELATED TO A PROGRAM

What has been said shows that a family's career experiences may produce problems before, during, and after a Program. Specifically, if the parents:

1. Are isolated from the community, they may not find out about you or your Program.

2. Are tired, pessimistic, and distrustful of professionals; cannot see that their child needs help or that they can and must help; believe in fate ("There's nothing we can do. It was meant to be this way"); and are unwilling to make an effort to change themselves and their children, then they may be uninterested in or uncommitted to your Program—not ready to change.

3. Feel guilty for their child's condition; are tense and hypervigilant, depressed, and pessimistic; so caught up in moment-to-moment behaviors, problems, and events that they cannot think about or plan for the long run; worry so much about the future that they are not satisfied with (reinforced by) small changes in the short run; feel so responsible for changing their child that they are afraid of failure; do not cooperate with one another or gratify (reinforce) each other; and lack organization in everyday routines in the home, then it is unlikely that they will learn much from you or conduct a good educational program in the home.

4. Do not schedule "breaks" in their home educational program (because they feel that they must always be "on"); have not learned to anticipate and handle the many problems that can arise in their home educational program; have not learned enough skills to find (pinpoint) and teach harder behaviors for which their child is ready; remain isolated from sources of information, reinforcement, and help (coaching) besides yourself; and do not work as a team, they may not be able to persist in running a good home educational program during their work with you, or maintain their program once the relationship with you is faded out.

Clearly, provide the parents with more than information. Provide them with a comprehensive program. Otherwise, you and they cannot avoid or overcome the many problems that their experiences are likely to have engendered.

Chapter 3 discusses what it takes to conduct a Program that is successful at all the points in the change process. In doing so, it provides an overview of the Program for families.

3 WHAT IT TAKES TO BE SUCCESSFUL: AN OVERVIEW OF THE PROGRAM FOR FAMILIES

I. A COMPREHENSIVE PROGRAM

A program for families cannot be run ''by the seat of the pants.'' Moreover, even if you have a carefully organized program consisting of excellent lectures, videotapes or films, written materials, and demonstrations, you may still not be successful with more than one of three families. The reason is that all of the above methods primarily provide information and, given the problems that may result from the families' career experiences, information by itself may not be enough to help the parents to change themselves and their child much. Instead, you need a comprehensive program.

What Goes Into a Comprehensive Program?

A comprehensive program for families has three main parts: (1) a comprehensive educational program for the children; (2) a wide range of skills that the parents use in changing their own behaviors and educating their children; and (3) methods that you and the parents can use to avoid or overcome the problems that may be caused by career experiences and by the program itself.

Let us look more closely at each component.

A Comprehensive Educational Program for Children

As mentioned several times, a main goal of a Program for parents is to help them to produce and maintain substantial behavioral changes in themselves, their children, and in the lives of others in the same situation. However, in many cases the educational program which the parents are taught to use with their children is limited in scope and complexity. That is, the parents learn how to change only a few of their children's behaviors—usually those they are the most concerned about changing (such as disruptive behaviors).

What parents need is a comprehensive educational program, especially if their children have severe learning and behavior problems. By "comprehensive educational program" is meant, first, that the curriculum for the children contains many potential target behaviors. Second, the behaviors are arranged and taught in a proper developmental-learning sequence (for example, from easier to harder behaviors and in such a way that there is a lot of generalization or transfer from one behavior to another), so that the children's progress is smooth. And third, it means that there are rules, materials, and methods that parents can use for these reasons:

1. Evaluating their children's educational needs.
2. Planning their children's educational programs.
3. Conducting teaching programs for all target behaviors that need changing.
4. Evaluating their children's progress.
5. Revising the educational program plans as needed.

Here are some specific reasons why parents must be provided with a comprehensive educational program.

1. If there are few behaviors in the educational program, the children may not change much. As a result, the parents may not be sufficiently reinforced for their efforts and may become lax or drop out.

2. If the behaviors are not arranged and taught in a proper developmental-learning sequence, progress is likely to be spotty if the children progress at all.

3. If there are few rules, materials, and methods for evaluating the children, and for planning, conducting, evaluating, and revising the children's educational programs, the home programs are likely to be haphazard, rigid, or limited and the parents will be dependent on you and others to help them to decide what to do next. Moreover, when contact with you has been faded out, the parents may encounter problems they cannot solve, resulting in a deterioration of the home program.

The comprehensive educational program for parents, described in this book, is found in complete form in *Educating Children With Learning and Behavior Problems* (Kozloff, 1974). This book grew out of six years of work with parents and teachers of children having a variety of learning and behavior problems (e.g., autistic, mentally retarded, emotionally disturbed, oppositional, and speech-impaired). The book is used in programs for parents and teachers that I conduct and by others in schools and clinics around the country (Kaufman, 1976). It can be read and used by the parents in the Program described in this book.

What does *Educating Children With Learning and Behavior Problems* offer parents? First, it provides a "Behavior Evaluation Scale" (BES) with which parents can evaluate their child's behavioral strengths and weaknesses. It also provides rules and methods for planning the overall educational program (that is, determining the skill areas for which their child is ready and the sequence to follow when teaching the necessary target behaviors).

The book shows parents how to plan teaching programs for pinpointed target behaviors (e.g., using rewards, shaping, prompting and fading, and chaining). A number of chapters provide rules, methods, and materials for actually teaching target behaviors in seven skill areas: Learning Readiness; Looking, Listening, and Moving; Motor Imitation; Verbal Imitation; Functional Speech; Chores and Self-Help; and Replacing Problem Behaviors. The book teaches parents how to evaluate or keep track of their child's progress and revise the teaching programs accordingly.

However, like all educational programs, the one presented in *Educating Children with Learning and Behavior Problems* cannot satisfy all educational needs of all children. Thus, you might supplement it with materials for parents of physically-impaired, aggressive, reading-deficient, chronically ill, hearing and visually-impaired children (Finnie, 1970; Marks, 1974; Westlake and Rutherford, 1961; Crickmay, 1966; Creer and Christian, 1976; Fredericks, 1976; Kent, 1974; Owens and Harper, 1971; Larson and Bricker, 1968; Patterson, 1971; Becker, 1971; Gray and Ryan, 1973; Rosner, 1975; Patterson et al., 1975).

Comprehensive Range of Teaching Skills

As mentioned in Chapter 1, many fine programs for families have been conducted. However, in most programs the range of skills the parents are taught for changing themselves and their children is small. Here is the usual list of skills:

1. Pinpointing behaviors to change (target behaviors).
2. Breaking down appropriate behaviors into smaller and easier to learn steps, so that the behaviors can be taught a step at a time (shaped).
3. Finding reinforcers or "rewards."
4. Prompting the child to perform appropriate behaviors.
5. Ignoring or timing out the child for engaging in inappropriate behaviors.
6. Counting and charting the number of times or the length of time that the child performs a target behavior, so that the parents can evaluate progress.

While the skills in the above list are certainly important, by themselves they do not seem sufficient to enable parents to maintain a comprehensive and flexible educational program. Thus, in addition to the above skills for teaching specific target behaviors, the parents must learn to accomplish the following:

1. Conduct a comprehensive evaluation of their child.
2. Plan a comprehensive educational program.
3. Pinpoint harder behaviors for which their child is ready.
4. Pinpoint behaviors to teach their child that are not in the curriculum, so that the parents can later operate independently of the consultant.
5. Conduct teaching programs for several target behaviors at once (to facilitate transfer of learning to new behaviors).
6. Chain newly learned behaviors into more complex tasks or sequences of activities.
7. Avoid or handle boredom, satiation, and overprompting (almost inevitable problems).
8. Help their child's behaviors generalize to other people and settings.
9. Move from arbitrary reinforcers (such as food or tokens) to more common reinforcers (such as praise and activities).
10. Of crucial importance, strengthen and maintain their own teaching behaviors (for example, through self-reinforcement, scheduled breaks, cooperation between the spouses and other families).

Methods for Avoiding or Overcoming Obstacles to Success

In addition to a comprehensive educational program and a comprehensive set of teaching skills most parents need to learn how to pinpoint, avoid, or overcome problems that may interfere with their participating in the Program and with their conducting and maintaining a good home educational program.

As you read in Chapter 2, the career experiences of the parents may generate a number of behaviors, attitudes, and relationships: some constitute personal and family strengths, and others constitute problems. An important part of the Program described in this book, then, involves teaching parents both to accentuate their personal and family strengths and to pinpoint, avoid, or change behaviors, attitudes, and relationships that hinder their ability to produce and maintain beneficial change. For example, the Program aims to teach parents to: enter into an open and productive relationship with a consultant (clinician, teacher, another parent); replace counterproductive exchanges with productive ones; solve personal and marital problems; develop and use networks of backup support; schedule breaks; generalize their skills to other settings; and follow a problem-solving sequence.

II. DESCRIPTION OF THE PROGRAM

The overall work with families has three stages: (1) Pre-Program, (2) Program, and (3) Maintenance/Follow-up. Here is a brief description of the activities in each.

Pre-Program

This stage completes five tasks that enable you to conduct a carefully planned Program.

Making Contact. First, parents must be made aware of you and your Program. This can be done through interviews when parents are enrolling their child in a facility, or through brochures, ads, letters, phone calls, and presentations to parents' groups, schools, clinics, physicians, and others. (The important problem of the ethics and legality of what may sound like advertising is discussed in Chapter 4.) Parents can learn of your Program through other parents. Once parents have learned of your Program, it is up to them to make the next response, indicating their interest in learning more.

Assessing and Strengthening Readiness to Change. Earlier, when describing the family career, we noted several reasons why parents may not be ready to change: pessimism, fatigue, distrust of professionals, marital problems, isolation, and fatalism, among others. These may keep parents from learning of your Program, from becoming interested in it, or from making a commitment to work with you to change themselves and their children.

Thus, while you make contact with parents, formalize a relationship, and assess the family's strengths and needs, you are working to assess and, if necessary, increase the parents' motivation or readiness to participate in the Program. Methods for doing this are discussed in Chapter 4. Some of the main ways of increasing readiness to change involve:

1. Present yourself as empathetic, competent, and businesslike; as unlike those with whom the parents have had bad experiences; as willing to work hard for the parents, to reinforce them, and treat them as intelligent, strong, and caring.

2. Give parents hard evidence (e.g., videotape, film, and discussion with other parents) of past successes of parents with whom you (and others) have worked, to show them that they can be good teachers, their child can change, the costs of changing themselves and their child are less, in the long run, than the costs they are now bearing and may continue to bear unless certain changes are made, and to give them high, but realistic, expectations of success.

3. Confront, counter, and replace the many kinds of hesitations and objections (philosophical notions, games) the parents might have:

It won't work.

I don't have the strength.

I have my own life to live.

There's nothing wrong with Billy that time won't heal.

I guess Sally was just meant to be this way.

I just don't have the time.

Show them that such statements and beliefs have probably been learned as a result of the career they have lived and are self-defeating, and they owe it to themselves and their child to at least give it another try, as many other parents have done ("After all, those parents are no more able than you, are they?").

Formalizing a Working Relationship. The relationship is formalized through one or more interviews. When it has been determined that the parents are both interested in and committed to participating in a working relationship, the relationship can be formalized verbally or with a written contract (the major Program Contract) so that the mutual responsibilities of all parties are specified and agreed upon.

As part of the working relationship, a contract-credit system establishes a businesslike orientation, strengthens and maintains productive participation, and possibly helps develop networks of backup support. Chapter 4 describes a number of options for a contract-credit system; for example, participants might earn or even exchange positive reinforcers (baby-sitting, respite care), earn back part of an initial deposit, or avoid having one of their certified checks or money orders mailed to an organization for which they have indicated a dislike.

Assessment. You cannot plan and conduct a successful Program unless you have determined just which behaviors, attitudes, and patterns of interaction or exchange need to be changed and which represent strengths to be accentuated. In other words, answer such questions as: Which behaviors does each parent have to learn to do with more skill, more often, or at the right time and place? Which exchanges between members of the family (parents, child, siblings) and between the family and other persons (relatives, neighbors) need to be changed because they are strengthening inappropriate behaviors or failing to strengthen appropriate behaviors? Which behaviors of the parents (and which exchanges in the family) represent strengths for which the parents should be reinforced and which they can be taught to use in helping each other and in teaching their child? Similar questions must be answered regarding the child. For example: Which behaviors does the child have to learn to do with more skill, more often, and at the right time and place? Which behaviors constitute problem behaviors that must be replaced? Which behaviors represent strengths that can be built upon (that is, used by the child to learn other behaviors)?

Assessment is accomplished both through interviews (that is, the parents answer questions regarding the career of the family, present circumstances, and expectations regarding the future), and through direct, Baseline Observations (conducted by you or your staff, and by the parents) in the home and, if possible, in school or treatment facilities attended by the child.

Organizing Information and Planning the Program. All information collected up to this point should be organized in such a way that it can be readily retrieved and used in planning, conducting, and evaluating the Program. Thus, it is important to have an efficient system for recording and filing data.

Once all of the necessary information has been collected and properly organized, it is used to plan and specify the overall Program:

1. The behaviors of parents and children to work on.
2. The sequence by which behaviors will be changed.
3. The instructional methods that you will use.
4. The methods you will teach parents to use in teaching their children.
5. Tentative agendas for future group or individual meetings.

Once the five Pre-Programs tasks have been accomplished, you are ready to start the Program.

Program Stage

The major components of instruction during the Program stage consist of the following:

1. Meetings (for groups or with individual families) involving review and discussion of weekly activities at home, demonstrations, role-playing, possibly videotape presentations, and individualized planning of home activities.
2. Reading and home teaching assignments.
3. Home visits by consultants (and possibly by other parents).
4. Phone calls to and from consultants and other families.

Just how the above are organized into a sequence of units of instruction depends on several factors, such as how long the Program stage can last, the number of consultants and families in the Program stage, the heterogeneity of the children's needs, the children's rates of progress, and the setting within which the Program is being conducted. Here, then, are several alternative designs.

1. Intensive Program. The bulk of the Program stage might consist of about fourteen two-hour weekly meetings with individual families or a group. Each meeting might begin with a check or participants' performance of agreed upon tasks, with consequences delivered according to a contract-credit system. Each family's home program of the past week is presented, evaluated, and discussed. If possible, videotapes of the parents working in the home are shown, both to illustrate methods that others can use and to provide the parents with objective feedback.

Next, the topic for the coming week is presented (e.g., the next skill area to work on with the children). Teaching methods to be used by parents are taught through brief lecture, film or videotape, demonstration, and role-playing. Prior to each meeting, parents read about the coming week's topic in *Educating Children With Learning Behavior Problems* (and possibly other sources).

At the end of each meeting, the parents and consultant plan the coming week's activities; for example, the details of the teaching program to be worked on and the date and time of any home visit or phone call. The tasks that both parties (parents and consultant) agree to perform during the week are written on a Weekly Contract form, which is signed.

During the week, the consultant or another person makes a home visit to observe, videotape, and coach the parents as they interact with themselves and their child, to reinforce the parents for efforts and successes, to demonstrate proper techniques, if necessary, and to help the parents with any problems they may be having. If videotapes are being made, they can be shown to the parents in the home to provide immediate feedback. They might also be shown at the next group meeting if parents are willing and emotionally ready. Any revisions needed in the home teaching program for the remainder of the week are written on the Weekly Contract form at the end of the home visit.

In the first four to six meetings, parents are taught the basic skills needed to conduct most teaching programs:

1. A behavioral perspective (objectivity and principles of learning)
2. To see, analyze, and replace certain counterproductive exchanges between themselves and their child.
3. To maintain and increase productive exchanges.
4. Basic components of the teaching-learning process (reinforcers and reinforcement schedules; shaping; prompting and fading; how to present signals, handle problem behaviors, run teaching sessions, and plan a comprehensive educational program and the teaching programs in it).
5. How to analyze and begin solving personal, marital, and other home problems.

Most of the remaining units or weekly meetings (that is, after about the sixth meeting) are devoted to planning, conducting, evaluating, and revising teaching programs for various behaviors pinpointed by the parents, using the "Behavior Evaluation Scale" (BES) and chapters in *Educating Children with Learning and Behavior Problems* (Kozloff, 1974). Depending on the severity of the children's problems, home programs might begin with Learning Readiness Skills (such as eye contact, sitting, and cooperating) and progress through the harder skill areas, such as Functional Speech. The educational program is described both in Chapter 4 of *Educating Children* and in Chapter 8 of this book.

Toward the end of the series of weekly meetings, the parents learn to use a higher level problem-solving approach; for example, how to maintain their own and their children's behaviors, to work with less help from consultants and to work with other families and groups, to plan far into the future, and to anticipate and solve the many problems that may arise.

As the series of instructional meetings in the Program stage is being completed, parents are encouraged and helped to find and use other sources of information, reinforcement, and support, such as scheduled and unscheduled phone calls to and from consultants, hotlines and home visits with other families who have been in Programs, written materials, and parents' organizations. In sum, while contact with consultants (meetings, home visits, phone calls) is being faded out, an effort is made to increase the parents' involvements in networks of extended support so as to help them maintain the change process and disseminate information and help others.

This is essentially the way my staff and I have conducted some Programs.

2. Extended Program. This method of organization is used by Dr. Kenneth Kaufman and his staff in some of their Programs at the Sagamore Children's Center. Here, the Program stage lasts for a longer time (for instance, six to nine months), and consists of about twenty meetings for groups of families. Fifteen or so meetings are conducted as described in alternative method 1 above. That is, each meeting focuses on the ideas and methods in one or more chapters of *Educating Children*. During other meetings, the focus is on special issues, such as a review of parents' home programs to date, parents' plans for their children's future, methods for handling problems in the family, and methods for coordinating home and school programs. Home visits, finally, are not conducted each week but, rather, when the parents are having difficulty or when they are beginning a new teaching program.

Data collected by me and by Dr. Kaufman indicate that alternative methods 1 and 2 are equally effective in helping parents and children to change.

3. Additional Possibilities. Further modifications are possible, of course. For example, a Program conducted in conjunction with a school or treatment facility might schedule meetings throughout the school year. During the summer, the Pre-Program stage might be conducted with prospective families and follow-up meetings might be held for families in the last Program. Parents' participation could be reinforced with extra tutoring, baby-sitting, and respite care. In such a program, the consultants for the families might be the children's teachers, therapists, psychologists, or social workers at the facility or in the school system.

At the start of the Program, parents might meet individually or as a group in short sessions with their consultant to discuss early chapters of *Educating Children* (on principles of learning, changing patterns of exchange in the home, evaluating their children's needs, and planning teaching programs). In later weeks, parents might receive some of their instruction on basic and advanced teaching methods in classroom settings, coached by a consultant or another person. Some later meetings with the consultant might be short, individual sessions (for instance, after school) every week or so, during which the consultant and parents would review later chapters in *Educating Children* and would discuss and revise the home program. Other meetings might be more lengthy group meetings in which parents come together to discuss special topics. While home visits might be made occasionally, to help parents to institute new methods or to solve problems, greater use might be made of both: 1) a notebook traveling between home and school and containing current teaching program plans, parents' logs and notes, consultant's notes and comments, and data; and 2) phone calls with the consultant and other parents.

Maintenance and Follow-up

In this stage, parents are helped to maintain and upgrade their home educational programs and to solve problems. This can be done in a number of ways:

1. Periodic meetings (i.e., "boosters"), home visits, and phone calls.
2. Scheduled in-class instruction and practice (e.g., to learn new methods being used by the teachers)
3. Hotlines to consultants.
4. The development of a network of support consisting of other parents, organizations, student volunteers, and specialists, who can provide information, tutoring, respite care, baby-sitting, and emotional support.

How Many Families in a Group?

The group Programs I conducted usually involved four to eight families. Staffing has consisted of three to four part-time consultants, including myself. We worked with so few families and used so many consultants simply to enable us to better evaluate as many aspects of the Program as we could. After three years, we came to the conclusion that fewer consultants could conduct the same Program with perhaps ten families. For example, once materials had been written *(Educating Children with Learning and Behavior Problems)* and weekly agendas and instructional methods had been developed and tested (as described in this book), planning and conducting the Program itself required little time (about 17 hours per week for the entire staff.) Moreover, we found that home visits every week are not necessary (a finding supported by the work of Kenneth Kaufman and his staff, as noted earlier).

However, a larger group poses the potential problem of spreading consultants too thin to give families the attention they need. The following guidelines may help you to avoid such a problem in a larger group:

1. The consultant's major task is to present new information, help solve difficult problems, and teach parents how to conduct their own group programs.

2. After presentations by the consultant, the larger group can divide into subgroups, based perhaps on the similarity of the children's needs. Parents are taught to play the roles of rotating leader and temporary expert (described in Chapter 5) in the small group; they discuss the past week's home programs and plan programs.

3. Consultants and some parents can move among the subgroups to help with difficult problems and to finalize Weekly Contracts.

4. Parents are encouraged and helped to develop a telephone hotline and to exchange home visits and other reinforcers, such as baby-sitting or respite care.

Chapter 4 discusses in detail all of the tasks in the Pre-Program stage.

4 THE PRE-PROGRAM STAGE

I. THE CONSULTANT-PARENT RELATIONSHIP

Before addressing the five tasks of the Pre-Program stage, let us discuss a more general topic, namely, the relationship between the family consultant (you or persons working with you) and the parents because several problems must be overcome and others avoided.

The Dilemma. What kind of relationship should there be between family consultants and parents? Should it be an informal, friendship relationship? That is, should you present yourself as devoting your time and energy to a family because you feel friendly toward the parents? Should parents follow your suggestions and put in the time and energy that your Program involves because they consider you their friend? Or, should the basis of the relationship be strictly that of professional and client? That is, should you assume the role of "expert" who knows more than the parents do, and who is in a better position to analyze the problems of the parents and children? And should you prescribe changes to be made in the family, while parents, in the role of "willing recipients," are expected to comply with the prescription?

The answer to questions about both kinds of relationships is "No." Our past work has shown that when the basis of the relationship between parents and those working with them (consultants) is friendship, it often becomes difficult for each party to hold the other party accountable for his or her actions (Kozloff, 1973). Both parties can appeal, without saying so, to the "friendship" between them in order to excuse themselves from obligations.

Toward the middle of a Program, for example, consultants (such as teachers) may begin to long for time at home. And parents may become tired of the day-to-day work involved in educating their children. Either party may then excuse himself or herself from living up to the obligations of the working relationship because his or her "friend" will understand.

> Gee, it's really been a rough week. Would you mind if we rescheduled the meeting till next week?
>
> Sure. I understand. Next week will be fine.

The likely result is that the parents and consultants remain friends while the quality and quantity of their work quickly deteriorate at the expense of the children. In fact, even the friendship may weaken when each party realizes that the relationship is "empty," that is, nothing much is happening that is benefiting anyone.

On the other hand, if the relationship is strictly one between professional and client (with all of the usual trappings), those parents who have had a history of unsuccessful experiences with professionals may be unwilling to enter another such relationship. In fact, they may feel hostile toward consultants who too quickly assume the role of expert. The parents may feel that they have had enough probing into their family lives, enough advice and questions from people whom they feel do not understand what they have been going through. Or, if the parents have been somewhat successful in getting help from professionals, they may adopt a dependent role and be unwilling or unable to assume responsibility for changing (that is, take an active part in changing) themselves and their children. They may want or expect the professional to do it for them.

A Way Through the Dilemma. You need not choose between being either a friend or a "professional." At the risk of sounding "corny," we have found it satisfying and successful to establish and maintain a parent-consultant relationship based on a businesslike approach to change but conducted with openness, honesty, and warmth. In other words, the relationship can involve a balance between formality (objectivity, accountability, written agreements on expectations and tasks) and informality (friendliness, humor, honesty, expressions of sentiments, and supportiveness). The balance, however, is not always easy to maintain. Here, then, are some tips on how to make it work.

First, instead of beginning the relationship on the basis of friendship (which can easily happen if the consultant, for example, a teacher, has known the parents and children for some time), start the relationship in a businesslike fashion, with the specific goals of the Program, the means to achieving the goals (that is, the Program activities), and the mutual obligations of all parties (that is, expected actions) made explicit and put in writing. In this way, it is easier for all parties to keep track of progress and to judge the other party's performance of agreed-upon tasks. Friendship can later develop on the basis of success. Moreover, the businesslike orientation should remain in effect. If anyone's performance begins to slip, he or she is immediately and objectively informed and expected to work to find solutions to difficulties.

Second, the formal, businesslike orientation is balanced by more personal or informal considerations. That is, consultants encourage parents to express feelings, and respond with empathy and support. Yet consultants try to combine supportiveness with teaching—pointing out ways the parents can (and helping the parents to) change themselves, their child, and possibly even the larger educational system. In sum, the line between empathy, support, and teaching parents to take an active part in the change process on the one hand, and mere sympathy and friendliness (which may mean reinforcing pessimism, dependence, and inactivity) on the other hand, is clearly drawn from the start. Parents who have become pessimistic and drained are encouraged and helped to remedy the problems they face.

Third, consultants should blur unnecessary status distinctions between themselves and parents, since most status symbols are at best artificial and at worst invidious. For example, consultants avoid the unnecessary use of ''four dollar'' words, and do not appeal to the ''authority'' of their degrees or occupations to try to persuade parents to their point of view. Here is an example of what not to do.

Consultant: I think you should let Alan stay in the car if he refuses to get out when you arrive home. Don't tell him over and over to get out. And don't carry him out. (Direct prescription).

Parent: I can't just let him sit there in a hot car. He'll suffocate!(Parent counters prescription.)

Consultant: Look. I've been in this business for ten years! Now please, do what I say! (Appeal to authority.)

Such an appeal to authority amounts to ''brow-beating'' and does not teach the parents to think for themselves. In fact, it may be perceived as another ''put down'' and is likely to produce resentment or to start a vicious cycle of direction-giving from the consultant and resistance from the parents.

Rather, if necessary, the consultant teaches parents (or reminds them of) a set of rules and a body of knowledge (principles of behavior change) that they are encouraged to apply to the situation or problem at hand.

Parent: I can't just let him sit there in a hot car. He'll suffocate! (Nonbehavioral justification for carrying child out of the car.)

Consultant: Do you think that talking to Alan and carrying him out of the car are reinforcers for Alan? (Sets occasion for parent to apply principles of learning.)

Parent: Yes, I guess so.

Consultant: Okay, then. If you talk to him and carry him out of the hot car, which behaviors will you be reinforcing? (Produces contradiction or tension. Parent is to see that her old method is strengthening precisely the behaviors that she does not want.)

Parent: Sitting in the car when we get home. (Recognizes contradiction.)

Consultant: Right! In other words, noncompliance and dependence? (Reinforces her recognition that she is reinforcing inappropriate behaviors.)

Parent: Yeah.

Consultant: I've got an idea that you probably don't want him to get better at being noncompliant and dependent. (Reiterates contradiction.)

Parent: Of course not! He is too noncompliant and dependent as it is.

Consultant: Right again! So can you think of a natural kind of consequence that will teach Alan to get out of the car by himself and not wait for you to carry him out? (Sets occasion for parent to resolve contradiction by trying another method, this one based on a behavioral analysis.)

Parent: Oh, I see. I could let him sit there until he finds out that I'm not going to take him out, and he'll be hot enough to get out himself. (Parent finds solution.)

Consultant: Perfect! Just perfect. You figured out what was happening and thought of a good solution. (Reinforces parent for arriving at solution, and not merely for agreeing with consultant.)

In meetings and home visits, consultants need not wear fancy clothes, but come dressed looking like they are prepared to work. Confidence and respect, in other words, cannot be expected or demanded from parents. They must be earned as the consultant demonstrates expertise and caring.

During meetings, consultants do not present themselves as all-knowing, but are willing to admit that they cannot readily answer some questions, that they can and do make mistakes, and that they expect parents to try to catch mistakes and help to find the answers.

II. MAIN ACTIVITIES AND TASKS IN THE PRE-PROGRAM STAGE

The five tasks in the Pre-Program stage and the general order for working on them are:

1. Making contact with parents and interesting them in working with you.
2. Assessing and strengthening readiness to change.
3. Formalizing a working relationship.
4. Assessing the strengths as well as the needs of the family (through Assessment Interviews and direct Baseline Observations).
5. Organizing the assessment information and planning the program for and with the family or families.

Then, the Program itself is conducted, evaluated, and revised in step-by-step fashion.

Although each task is discussed in this chapter, note that some overlap. For example, while working to strengthen readiness to change, you are assessing behaviors of the parents that can be built on (strengths such as optimism and cooperative marital relations) or which the parents may need to change (such as counterproductive self-statements and exchanges with their children, or marital problems).

The following diagram (Figure 4-1) shows the sequence of activities by which the five Pre-Program tasks are accomplished.

Pulling It All Together: The Assessment and Programming Guide (APG)

All information gathered during the Pre-Program stage is relevant to assessment. In order to pinpoint important events and relationships, make sense out of what is observed, and use the assessment information in planning a Program, ask and answer the following three questions:

"What is it that I assess?" In general, you assess (observe and make judgments about) a sample of behaviors, attitudes, and relationships that have a bearing on success or difficulty throughout the change process (that is, the Pre-Program, Program, and Follow-up stages). Luckily, we have a good idea of what those behaviors, attitudes, and relationships are.

"Once I have assessed behaviors, attitudes, and relationships that affect success, how do I use the information to plan and later conduct the Program?" This book provides specific methods and activities to accentuate the existing behaviors, attitudes, and relationships in the family that constitute strengths and, on the other hand, to help the parents remedy those that pose problems. For example, it is important in conducting a good home educational program to have a cooperative working relationship between the parents. If the assessment indicates that cooperation is weak, then you know that you must help parents on this item. Later chapters tell you how.

Is there anything that lays it all out? The "Assessment and Programming Guide" (APG) in Appendix 1 tells you:

1. Which behaviors, attitudes, and relationships seem to determine success or difficulty throughout the change process. These are the "items" to assess through observations and discussions with parents, and through questions during Assessment Interviews.
2. What problems there may be in the parents' learning, using, or changing each important behavior, attitude, or relationship item.

Using the APG in Another Way. Not only does the APG pinpoint and define the items of behavior, attitude, and relationship (as well as potential problems) to assess, but it can be used to keep track of progress and problems on each item during and after the Program. For example, let us say that during an Initial Interview you find that the parents do not expect to be very successful in changing their child. As shown by the APG, an expectation of success—Item

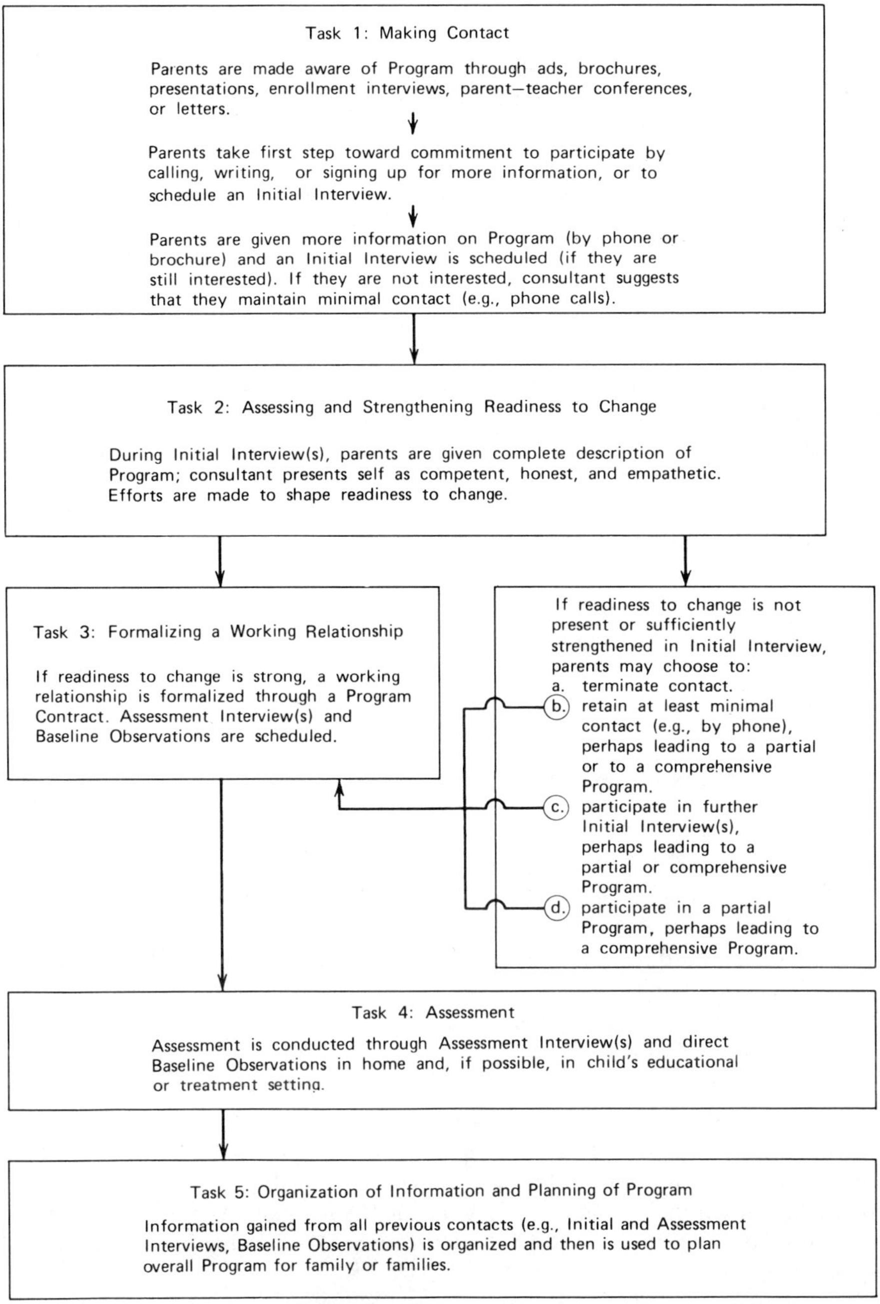

Figure 4-1 Sequence of activities for accomplishing the five Pre-Program tasks.

7—is an important ''attitude'' involved in readiness to change. You can indicate on the APG that the parents are pessimistic (that is, have a low expectation of success) by underlining ''pessimism'' in Item 7 or by writing it in the space provided under the item. Also, you can circle the number of the item. Later, if you have sufficiently increased the parents' expectation of success (Item 7) you might place a check-mark next to the item, along with the date, and underline additional words or sentences that indicate their increased expectations.

Finally, as much as possible, the following sections tell you what to look and listen for, and what to ask, to find out how the family ''stacks up'' on each APG item.

Now let us turn to the first task: making contact. It might be helpful to read the section on Item 1 in the Assessment and Programming Guide before you continue reading here.

III. TASK 1: MAKING CONTACT WITH PARENTS

A major problem that may prevent parents from learning of you or of your Program is the kind of isolation talked about in Chapter 2. Therefore, you may have to make special efforts to help parents become aware of and interested in your Program.

Methods for Making Contact

There are several ways to make contact with parents so as to show them what you have to offer and what they may gain. Ads may be placed in local newspapers, in newsletters of parents' and professionals' organizations, and on bulletin boards in schools, libraries, and other facilities for children and families. Brochures or letters can be sent to parents' organizations (state, local, or school), to administrators in school, clinic, or mental health settings, to physicians, or to families. Moreover, you can describe your work with children or families by giving presentations in meetings of parents' organizations or to groups of parents in educational or treatment facilities. Finally, the importance of parents working with their children at home, and their interest in participating in a working relationship with you, can be broached and discussed when parents are being interviewed prior to their child's enrollment in a facility with which you are associated, when their child is being evaluated, when parents are bringing their child to school or picking up their child after school, or during parent-teacher or parent-therapist conferences.

It is important to discuss the ethics and legality of what may appear to be advertising one's services. Unless some method is used to tell parents that a Program is available, many families that need such a program never learn of it. If a Program is being offered as part of the services of a school or treatment facility, and if the Program is free, then placing ads in local newspapers and sending brochures constitutes public service messages, not advertising for private gain.

In all of the above initial contacts, do not inadvertently coerce parents into working with you, overwhelm them with information, or rush them into a commitment. Even if you could coerce parents into agreeing to participate in a Program (for example, by telling them that their child's entrance into the facility is contingent upon their participating), their attendance at meetings would not mean that they would learn anything or do anything that they learned. If you overwhelm parents with information, or try to rush them to agree to participate (as in "high-pressure" sales tactics), there is, again, no assurance that they will be giving more than lip service.

In sum, it is important that parents want to work with you, because they trust or like you, expect to be successful, and see that the benefits are likely to outweigh the costs. Thus, in all initial contacts, keep the message clear and simple. And, even if parents seem eager to start, give them a chance to think it over before you formalize a working relationship.

Here are some tips on what to say and how to say it when you are making an initial contact:

1. Use simple language (many parents are annoyed by jargon).
2. Spell out the reasons why parents should become involved in their child's education (see Section I of Chapter 1).
3. Briefly describe the goals and major activities of the Program (see Chapter 3).
4. Indicate the many benefits that the parents and their children are likely to gain from your Program (beneficial behavior change in the children, easier to live with their children, increasing their children's educational and life chances, greater control over their own and their children's future, skills for changing themselves and for changing the educational system, self-confidence). If possible, give "hard" evidence of the successes of parents who have worked with their children (through videotapes, films, and concrete examples).

Most important, it is left up to the parents to contact you either for more information or to indicate that they are interested in or committed to working with you. For example, through ads, brochures, and letters you might ask parents to contact you for more information, and provide them with your address and phone number (and possibly with a "tear off and mail" slip). Similarly, at the end of presentations or conferences give parents your address and phone number (or make available a "sign up for more information" sheet). Those who have signed such a sheet may be sent a brochure or letter that describes the Program and tells them to call or write if they are still interested.

In other words, by having parents make the next response, you are giving them time to think it over, reassess their child's problems and future, and find reasons why they can and should start a home educational program. In addition, by taking the next step (rather than being pressured or pursued,) they are making a tentative commitment to working with you.

A copy of a brochure is in Appendix 2.

What to Do if Parents Call, Write, or Sign Up After an Initial Contact

Those parents who call, write you, or sign up because they want more information, or because they already seem committed to working with you, should make an appointment for one or more initial interviews.

IV. THE INITIAL INTERVIEW(S)

As mentioned in the last section, the Initial Interview serves many purposes at once. It is the time to begin the consultant-parent relationship on the right footing—a businesslike approach to change (formality) combined with a warm personal relationship (informality). It is the time to strengthen readiness to change as a prerequisite for formalizing a working relationship. If readiness to change is strong, you can formalize the working relationship through a verbal or written contract. And, finally, you can begin to pinpoint some strengths and needs of the parents and children in preparation for a more comprehensive assessment during later Assessment Interviews and direct Baseline Observations.

Since readiness to change is so important to success in a Program, strengthening readiness to change is the major task of the Initial Interview(s).

What Does it Take to be Ready to Change?

Items 2 through 10 on the Assessment and Programming Guide (APG) in Appendix 1 describe readiness to change as well as types of "unreadiness" or hesitancy. Although readiness to change is important for success, this does not mean that parents must be strong on all nine readiness items before you work with them. For example, if parents are weak on several readiness items, they might be offered a partial Program, during which you may be able to strengthen the remaining items, and then offer the parents a more comprehensive Program.

Using the APG During the Initial Interviews(s), When Assessing and Strengthening Readiness to Change

Use one copy of the APG for each family you are working with. During the Initial Interview(s), use the APG to remind you of the nine components of readiness to change and keep track of (assess) the family's strengths and needs on each component.

This can be done in several ways. The APG describes many components of each item of behavior, attitude, or belief, and lists, in brackets, problems that may interfere with the parents' learning or using the components of the item. Thus, you can underline important words in each item that describe your observations of the parents. For example, regarding Item 2 (trust), you might underline "smile and nod," "seem physically relaxed, joke, make eye contact," and "indicate trust." And, you might not underline any of the words or sentences in brackets (that is, problems) because none were observed. Or, regarding Item 7 (expectation of success), you might observe that the parents did not emit any of the behaviors that indicate high expectations, but they did emit several of the "problem" behaviors listed in the brackets. Therefore, you might underline "find and state reasons why the successes of other parents do not apply to their family. . . ."

If possible, underline while you are interviewing or observing the parents. Also, as soon as possible after the interview or observation, go back over the items, recall what took place, and then underline.

Another way to record observations is to write what you observe during the interviews in a notebook. Later, transfer the important points in your notes either by writing them in the spaces provided under each APG item or by underlining important words or sentences. Or, you can make notes on the APG during interviews and observations. For example, for Item 2 (trust), you might write:

> Parents say that they will try anything consultant suggests because consultant is the first person who ever made them feel that she had their interests at heart (a good indication of "trust").

In addition to underlining and/or taking notes on each of the nine items regarding readiness to change, observe and take notes on:

1. Communication games that the parents may have played and the extent to which you were able to overcome such games.
2. Exchanges between the parents (for example, "hogging" versus sharing the conversation; "negating" versus confirming or elaborating on what the other says; blaming versus supporting the other).
3. More personal characteristics of each parent (for example, timidness, tension, "depressed" mood, and difficulty in communicating versus optimism, calmness, or clarity of communication).

When Is an Item "Passed"? An item is "passed" when the parents no longer need help with any of the components and no longer display any problems that may be associated with an item. You might indicate items and components with which the parents need help by circling (with the date) the number of the item and its components. In this way, you can see at a glance which items and components to work on. Later, as progress is made, place a check-mark (with the date) next to items or components that have been passed.

Arranging the Initial Interview(s)

Atmosphere is important, especially in your first close contact with parents. Possibly for the first time in their career, the parents are going to meet with someone who may be able to give them concrete help. However, they may anticipate that the interview will be "another fruitless (and insulting) experience." Hence, try to put the parents at ease to increase the chances that they will see you in a nonthreatening way and will talk about things that are important to them and that are possibly emotional. Therefore:

1. Schedule the interview at a time that is convenient for both parents. Have both parents attend if possible. If you are dealing with a single-parent family (or if one spouse is simply unable to come), have the one parent bring another person who may become involved in the program, either someone who can also work with the child or who can at least offer backup support to the one parent (for example, an older sibling, a close relative, or a friend).

2. The interview can be held either in your office or in the home of the parents. In either case, try to arrange for the setting to be relatively free of distractions. For example, if the interview is to be in their home, ask the parent(s) (beforehand) to arrange for it to be at a quiet time and in a place where the interview is not likely to be interrupted. If it is held in your office, the decor and lighting should be rather soft, so as to make the parents more comfortable. Wall posters on nature scenes or children are helpful.

3. If the interview is held in your office (for example, in a school), you might offer the parents refreshments to start the session with an everyday routine that can break the ice.

4. Dress and act in a way that expresses your openness and personal concern for the family. This does not mean that you should wear blue jeans and a tee shirt (which may actually offend parents who expect you to be somewhat more professional). Dress in a way that shows that you are not the kind of person who stands on ceremony.

5. Make paper and pencils available to the parents, telling them that it is a good idea if they write down any questions that occur to them during the conversation or take notes on important points of information which they might want to remember. Ask them if it is alright with them if you take notes on important things that are said, so that you can remember them. Encouraging the parents to take notes helps to establish a businesslike context. In addition, the parents become more like partners in the relationship with you, rather than passive recipients.

Strengthening (Shaping) Readiness to Change (Task 2)

The method for strengthening readiness to change has several steps. At each step, you are setting the occasion for the parents to emit behaviors (the components of readiness) which you can reinforce or confirm. As the parents emit readiness behaviors at one step, they become more likely to emit readiness behaviors at the next. All in all, however, you are doing more than merely strengthening a number of isolated behaviors, feelings, attitudes, or perceptions. You are possibly beginning to change the parents' way of looking at and responding to their total career situation. Such radical or higher-level change may be necessary because, as Chapter 3 pointed out, changes in just a few of the parents' behaviors may not be enough to help them produce or sustain significant change in themselves and their children. Many parents may need a new framework (Watzlawick et al., 1974), described in part by the nine components of change-readiness.*

Here are the steps in the process for shaping readiness to change during the Initial Interview(s).

Step 1: Setting the Stage by Talking About the Family's Career and Problems.

In most cases, the parents are likely to want to talk about their child's problems, their own difficulties in trying to get help, personal frustrations, fatigue, and fear, and perhaps their goals. This is good, because it gives you behavior (e.g., parents' expressions of feelings, ways of looking at and responding to their situation) that you can begin to shape, depending on your response (Truax and Mitchell, 1971). Moreover, by allowing (indeed, encouraging) the parents to talk about their child and what they have been through, you can:

1. Present yourself as trustworthy, friendly, competent, and empathetic.
2. Help the parents to pinpoint their strengths and needs and to establish goals.
3. Indicate the ways in which the Program may help them to solve problems and achieve goals.

Here is a scenario of what might be said in the beginning of an Initial Interview, conducted, for instance, in your office:

Consultant: Well, I'm glad to see you Mr. and Mrs. Blake. (Parents are offered and take a seat at a comfortable distance from consultant. If parents seem tense or shy, the consultant encourages a little ice-breaking small talk about the weather, about a funny incident at the child's school, or some encouraging developments in the child's education, and possibly offers them coffee or a soft drink.)

*Additional components of the "new framework" consist of the components of or prerequisites for conducting and maintaining a good home educational program, which are discussed in later chapters, and which are presented on the APG.

Parents: (Return greeting and participate in small talk.)

Consultant: (Make sure to smile at parents as they indicate that they are more at ease; for example, when parents smile at consultant or settle into their chairs.) This is our first meeting. And it may be the first of some valuable meetings to come. I think we can get a lot done together. To get us started, is there anything that you would like to ask me? About (use child's name)? About this Program? (Eventually, you want the parents to start talking about their career problems and experiences. However, the parents may ask specific questions about the Program; for example, fees, if applicable, length of the Program, other parents who might be part of the Program. Such questions should be briefly answered.)

Some parents, however, remain silent when asked if they have any questions, or when they are given the chance to talk about their child. In that case:

Consultant: (Calmly allows parents to remain silent for a short time, say 15 seconds, but is alert for any movements that might be preparatory to speaking, for example, movements of the mouth or eye-to-eye contact, and reinforces such movements by nodding or smiling at parents. If parents continue to remain silent and appear to be apprehensive or shy, raise the issue of their uneasiness.) You seem to be a little uneasy. (Said with a smile and a soft voice.)

Parents: (Give affirmative nod, verbalize agreement, fidget or remain silent.)

Consultant: (Smiles and speaks softly.) It's natural to feel a bit uneasy. I sometimes get butterflies, too, when I first meet parents. I don't know how they feel about things. And, you know, some parents have gotten so little help, that they may not have much trust in new people who offer them help. And I don't blame them at all. If I were you I wouldn't trust me, at least not yet! (Anticipates possible distrust or hostility of parents toward professionals. Remains alert for any movements indicating parents' agreement, such as a smile, nod of the head, or a settling into a more comfortable position, and reinforces such movements by smiling.)

Notice that, by labeling (in a nonthreatening way) what the parents seem to be feeling (uneasiness? distrust?), you indicate empathy with the parents, which is sufficient to get most parents talking. They either laugh or smile and then ask a question, or start talking about their child. Or they talk about their uneasiness. If they talk about their uneasiness, reassure them that it is natural and suggest that it will certainly pass in a few moments as the conversation goes along. If they ask a specific question, on the other hand, it should be answered, as noted above. And if they start talking about their child, then the conversation may proceed in that direction. If they do not start talking about their child, career, goals, or related matters, you might ease the conversation in that direction.

Consultant: (With a smile.) So, tell me, what is Billy like at home? (This question brings the conversation back to the issue of the child in the family, the career, and the goals the parents have.)

This is an extremely important part of the Initial Interview. The ice has been broken and the parents are beginning to open up about their lives. They will be giving you occasions to assess and shape their readiness to change. Note that during a later Assessment Interview, you will be asking the parents to provide a more complete history of their child and the family's career. Now, however, you want them to describe briefly their child and what they have been through as a family—enough so that you can help them to specify some problems and goals, to see you as a businesslike but empathetic person, and acquire most if not all components of readiness to enter a working relationship with you. Thus take notes on what they are saying, using the APG as much as possible.

Here are some tips on what to talk about and how to respond when parents describe their child and their experiences.

1. When specific problem behaviors and behavioral inadequacies of their child are described, be empathetic (but not sickeningly so). Lean forward, nod your head and say "Mm hmm," "I understand," or "That behavior must be hard to live with" to indicate that you are following them and that you understand what they have been going through.

2. If the parents talk about their child's behaviors but do not tell you of their efforts to teach their child or to handle problem behaviors, ask them. Reinforce past efforts. In effect, translate their career into a partial success story. Thus, reinforce them for:

a. spending so much time, energy, and money looking for help. ("Boy, you folks don't give up easily, do you?".)

b. strong marital relations. (Reinforce parents whenever they mention that they have shared tasks in the home, been supportive of one another, or worked together in a home educational program.)

c. any and all indications of "moxie," that is, strength, perseverance, optimism, activism, or independence. For example:

Parent: Well, all in all, we tried hard to teach Billy. I don't know how successful we've been, but we sure tried hard.

Consultant: You sure have tried hard! And more, you've been darn successful. Billy wouldn't be in the good shape he's in now if it weren't for your work. I don't think that I could have done as well in handling what you folks have. And I have an idea that you could learn how to teach Billy much more. (Note: The consultant's prediction "I have an idea that you could learn how to teach . . ." should be reasonable and likely. The consultant should not make glib predictions or offer possibly false hopes, just to "sell" the parents.)

d. spending so much time and energy actually working with their child. (Pinpoint and reinforce specific instances of productive exchanges and of the application of certain teaching methods, such as requiring the child to earn reinforcers, prompting correct responses, or ignoring inappropriate behavior. You can introduce a few behavioral terms to help parents describe what was going on. This is also a way in which to generate an acceptance of the behavioral approach.)

Regarding item "d," here is an example of how to help parents begin to see what has been going on and how to reinforce for their efforts.

Parent: Billy simply refused to walk. He crawled until he was almost four years old.

Consultant: Wow! That must have been a burden. (Empathizes.) If he didn't walk, how did he get around? (Sets occasion for parents to describe what may have been the reinforcement of crawling, which consultant will then address.)

Parent: Well, he would crawl to get some things he wanted, like boxes to tear apart. And if he couldn't reach what he wanted, we would carry him.

Consultant: How come? (Sets occasion for more details of the exchange.)

Parent: Oh, my! He would just whine and yell 'til we couldn't think straight. (Parents indicate that whining and yelling are quite aversive. Consultant makes note of it. Parents may need relaxation training. Also, there may be a pattern of escape exchanges that will have to be replaced.) And besides, Dr. Nink told us that Billy was retarded, and we figured that he couldn't walk. (Parents indicate that they had low expectations which justified reinforcing child's crawling, whining, and yelling. Consultant notes that parents' expectations for child may have to be raised.)

Consultant: I see. So his yelling was so hard to take that, to escape it, you would carry him. (Restates the escape exchange.) And besides, you weren't sure if he could walk, anyway. (Said in a nonthreatening way. The consultant must not imply! "God, you were dumb to reinforce his yelling by carrying him!")

Parent: That's right.

Consultant: So, how did you teach him to walk? (Indicates to parents that they taught Billy to walk.)

Parent: Well, one day we'd just had it. I guess we were fed up with carrying him around and spoiling him.

Consultant: Spoiling him? You figured that carrying him and giving in to his yelling and whining were spoiling him? What do you mean? (Sets occasion for parents to demonstrate their correct behavioral-exchange analysis of child's inappropriate behaviors.)

Parent: Hell, he wasn't a vegetable! He would look right at what he wanted and then back at us, and start whining. I figured that if he knew enough to get our goat, then he could at least try to walk.

Consultant: That's right! So, you thought that he was manipulating you. He knew that if he whined loud enough, you would give in. (Reinforces parent for seeing relationship between parent's behavior and child's behavior. Rephrases situation as an exchange.)

Parent: Yeah. And if we didn't pick him up right away, he would yell even louder and reach up for us to pick him up. So I figured that it was all because he was used to us picking him up when he yelled. (Parent states exchange.)

Consultant: Right! (Reinforces parent's last statement.) So, you figured out what was happening. Good! (Makes parents feel a bit "special.") Do you see what I mean? . . . Every time he yelled and you picked him up, what was Billy learning? (Sets occasion for parents to pinpoint behavior that was being reinforced.)

Parent: I guess he was learning to yell. (Correct answer.)

Consultant: Ah, right on the button! Every time he whined or yelled, and you picked him up, he was reinforced or rewarded for whining or yelling. In other words, he learned that loud whining and yelling got him something he wanted—a reward of being picked up and getting something he was after. (Reinforces parents for pinpointing the behavior being reinforced. Consultant then introduced a more technical term, "reinforcement." Later, helps parents use the term "reinforcement" to describe other exchanges. This helps to generate parents' acceptance of behavioral approach.)

Parent: Yep. He sure had us going for a couple of years.

Consultant: Yes, but you two had the "smarts" and the guts to turn things around. Just how did you teach him to walk? (Sets occasion for parents to describe their method. Then will reinforce them and introduce more terms.)

Parent: Well, he was near his chair at the supper table, whining to be put in his chair for supper. So I stood him near the table and made him try to walk to his chair.

Consultant: Mm hmm. (Smiles.)

Parent: He fussed and fussed, but I just held him up on his feet. And when he started to move his feet forward, I gave him a little help. I just didn't pay attention to his yelling. And we did that all the way to his chair.

Consultant: Excellent job! That's great. I'll bet you'll be naturals.(Reinforces parents for their efforts. Also bolsters parents' morale: "You'll be naturals." And indicates that their participation in the Program is likely.)

Parent: We just kept it up, and made him walk farther and farther and more and more by himself.

Consultant: All I can say is, that's great! You couldn't have done it better. Do you know what that is called? It's called shaping. You taught him in small steps. (Gives a technical term. Again builds acceptance of behavioral approach by indicating that what the parents did was behavioral.)

Parent: Yeah, I guess we did! (Parents smile.)

Consultant: How did it feel to be so successful?

Parents: Terrific. And we started making him do other things, too.

Consultant: Great! Such as? (Sets occasion for parents to describe more of their efforts, which gives consultant the occasion to translate what parents say into exchange terms and to reinforce parents for their efforts, boosting their "moxie," self-confidence, and optimism, and teaching them to see consultant as competent, friendly, and trustworthy.)

3. So far, you will have reinforced the parents many times, shown them that you are empathetic, and given them a bit of insight into what has been going on. That is, they are beginning to discriminate (pinpoint) and label (name) some of the structured exchanges that have existed. In addition, demonstrate to the parents that you are competent, have expertise, and are an insider regarding what they have been through. Here are several ways to do this.

First, as the parents talk about their experiences and efforts to cope, anticipate some of what they might be planning to say and post-dict (offer hypotheses about) the occurrence of some of their past experiences. For example:

Parent: And Jeff was hard to take at bedtime. In and out of bed! In and out of his room! Going to the refrigerator, getting a drink, talking to us from his room, asking for water, asking us what we were doing, knocking on our door.

Consultant: Mm hmm. (Empathizes and encourages parent to continue.)

Parent: And that's not all. He would get up in the middle of the night and do the same thing!

Consultant: Sounds like you didn't get much sleep.

Parent: You can say that again!

Consultant: I bet it was sometimes hard to deal with Jeff in an effective way during the day if you were so fatigued. (Anticipates what parents were likely to say, showing that consultant is an insider.) So, what did you do to handle Jeff's bedtime behavior? (Sets occasion to help parents analyze child's behavior as well as to demonstrate consultant's competence.)

Parent: Well, for a while we tried ignoring his talking to us, coming to our room, and roaming the house. But it didn't work.

Consultant: (Smiles and nods.) Yeah, I think I know what you mean. When you ignored his attention-getting behavior, his behavior went right through the roof. He talked louder and louder and longer and longer, maybe even banged on your door, trying to get you to respond, I'll bet. (Post-dicts what parents have been through, demonstrating some expertise.)

Parent: That's right! I thought I'd go crazy listening to him call "Mommy" a hundred times!

Consultant: I know what you mean. (Empathizes.) What Jeff did is called an "extinction burst." It often happens. When you start to ignore a behavior that used to pay off, the person tries harder and harder to get back the payoff—in this case, attention. But the behavior may gradually decrease if you can stick to your guns. (Gives parents a technical term that they can later use to explain other escalations when child was on extinction.)

Or,

Consultant: So, it sounds like you've been about everywhere trying to get help.

Parent: That's right. And we haven't really gotten any help.

Consultant: After so many years, you must have sometimes felt pretty isolated, frustrated, and maybe even pessimistic about seeing Bobby get better. (Post-dicts some effects of career experiences, showing that consultant is both empathetic and an insider.)

Parent: Yeah. Sometimes we'd get to feeling pretty low. Worried about what was going to happen. I mean, we're not getting any younger and Bobby's not getting much better.

Consultant: Well, I won't pretend that I have felt just like you have felt at times, but I can understand something of what you have been through. (Consultant presents self as empathetic but not presumptuous.) Like I said, you folks have a lot of guts. Many parents would have given up long before. (Reinforces their "moxie".)

Again, the point is to show that you are an insider by post-dicting what the parents have probably experienced. This helps to generate trust and confidence.

Second, point out the difference between yourself (and what you have to offer) and others from whom the parents have tried, unsuccessfully, to get help. This does not mean attacking or degrading the work of others, but point out enough differences so that the parents see you as someone more likely to be of help. Here are examples:

Parent: Well, you know, Seth walked around with a blanket over his head almost all the time, for about two years. (Parent has a disgusted look, so consultant replies as follows.)

Consultant: A blanket over his head? (Gives a look indicating half humor and half disbelief.)

Parent: Yeah, Dr. Quibble told us that it was Seth's security and that we should just let him wear it until he was ready. (Parent continues to look disgusted with the past advice given.)

Consultant: I'm not sure if wearing a blanket for two years would make a child more secure. But it could sure give a child one heck of a rash! (Consultant indicates that she is just about as disgusted with Quibble's advice as the parents were.)

Parent: (Laughs.) Well, what did we know? Dr. Quibble was the expert.

Consultant: And Seth doesn't wear his blanket any more? (Sets occasion for parents to say something with which consultant can agree, establishing difference between Dr. Quibble and consultant.)

Parent: No. We decided that enough was enough, and we just threw it away.

Consultant: And he threw a terrific tantrum, didn't he? (Post-dicts child's behavior.)

Parent: He sure did. But that was too bad! I mean, how many years was he supposed to walk around like that?

Consultant: He calmed down in a few days, though, didn't he? (Again, post-dicts behavior, reinforcing parents for their method.)

Parent: Mm hmm.

Consultant: I thought so! I wish I had been there to help you back then. I might have suggested that you do exactly as you did. After all, if he always had the blanket, how would he learn to be secure without it? (Consultant points out difference between her behavioral orientation and that of Dr. Quibble. Also points out similarity between her thinking and that of the parents, establishing a common ground with the parents.)

Or,

Parent: Jane used to scratch her hands a lot.

Consultant: Um hmm. What did you do about it?

Parent: Well, we were taking her to see Dr. Blither. He told us just to ignore it, that Jane was scratching her hands to get attention. And we did, for weeks!! But she kept it up—no more, no less than before. (Parent looks disgusted.)

Consultant: Did Dr. Blither ever see Jane at home? (Consultant subtly indicates that she may question Dr. Blither's advice, because Blither was not around to conduct a behavioral analysis.)

Parent: No.

Consultant: Well, you see, attention is only one reason why Jane might have been scratching her hands. (Indicates an alternative to Blither's analysis and advice.)

Parent: Oh?

Consultant: Well, she might have scratched her hands because she had an allergy. Or, she might have been turned on or reinforced by the feelings in her hands when she scratched them. You see, before you decide what to do to handle a problem, you have to analyze the behavior and the situation—and that means that you have to examine the child, sometimes medically, and observe the child's behavior before you can really tell why the child seems to be doing the behavior. (Consultant points out that she might have offered different advice.)

Parent: I see. And besides, she scratched her hands even when she was by herself. We never really did think that she did it just for attention.

Consultant: That's a good observation! (Reinforces parents.) And what about her scratching now?

Parent: She still does it. (Gives consultant a chance to offer her own suggestion.)

Consultant: See, there are several reasons why she might be scratching her hands. Allergy, attention, self-stimulation. In fact, they all may be true at the same time. So, we have to check out the possibilities and try to eliminate the ones that do not apply. It might be a good idea to have an allergist see her. If she does not have an allergy, then we can observe Jane's behavior more carefully to see what else might be causing her scratching. And, you know, even if attention has something to do with her scratching, ignoring it does not teach her other, proper ways to get attention. In addition to not rewarding or reinforcing her scratching with attention, we have to teach her alternative ways to get attention. (Presents main features of a problem-solving strategy and points out importance of teaching alternative behaviors.)

And, finally,

Consultant: Sounds like you've gone just about everywhere for help.

Parent: We have. But we haven't gotten much help.

Consultant: But lots of bills! (Empathizes.)

Parent: Yeah. Lots of bills. But they just never told us what to do. They asked all kinds of questions, like "Did you leave Marty alone for long periods of time?" Made us feel real guilty with those questions.

Consultant: I imagine that you have felt frustrated, maybe even angry. (Empathizes.) You're looking for help and you're getting a lot of talk. Well, I like to talk too. But there is also a time to get down to business and change Marty's behavior, despite what may or may not have happened a long time ago. I'd rather help you to change Marty's behavior now. Sure, we can talk about the past, but only if it helps us to help you and Marty now. (Stresses differences between what he has to offer and the way he sees things, and other professionals. Consultant is nonjudgmental, present-oriented, and action-oriented.)

Parent: Well, we're ready to get down to business!

Consultant: So am I!

So far in the Initial Interview, the parents have been:

1. Encouraged to talk about their child's problems and some of their career experiences.
2. Reinforced for all efforts to get help for their child and to work together in the home trying to teach, or at least cope with, their child.
3. Shown that you are sensitive to what they have been feeling and even about any uneasiness they may have had when the interview began.
4. Shown that you are nonthreatening.
5. Encouraged to express feelings. You have nodded and smiled at them, congratulated them, post-dicted what they have experienced, and helped them to analyze and describe what has been going on.

6. Shown important differences between yourself (and what you have to offer) and others from whom they have sought help.
7. Given workable alternatives to the unsuccessful methods others told them to use, or that they tried on their own (Truax and Carkhuff, 1967; Goldstein, 1971; Noland, 1971, 1973, 1975).

At this point the parents should be ready to hear more about what you have to offer.

Step 2: Describing the Program.

If the Program has already been described to the parents (for example, if they attended a presentation) then briefly describe its main features again and answer any questions. If, however, they do not know what the Program entails, give them a more complete description now, perhaps based on what was said in Chapter 3.

There are two important things to do when describing the Program. First, point out the many reasons why parents need to be involved in their child's education. To review what was said at the beginning of Chapter 1, parents should and can be involved because:

1. They spend the most time with their child and have many things at their disposal (such as reinforcers) that generate behavior change. Moreover, they have extensive and intimate knowledge of their child's behavioral characteristics and thus have information that helps in program planning. In effect, the parents are in a perfect position to produce substantial change in their child. Not to conduct home programs would simply be a waste.

2. Unless the parents conduct a complementary home educational program, the behavioral gains that their child might be making in an educational or treatment setting may not generalize to the home.

3. By conducting a home educational program similar to the one conducted in the child's school, the parents may be able to accelerate the rate of change.

4. If the child is not yet in school, or if the child's school provides a poor program, the parents can either prepare their child for entrance or can partially supply their child with the education that their child is not getting. In addition, they will learn what a good educational program consists of, which goals are feasible, and which methods are effective, so that they can work in a cooperative fashion with their child's school or treatment facility.

5. The parents have a right to learn all they can, since they have paid for the research that generated the educational methods.

Second, and most important, provide concrete evidence of progress made by parents and children in past programs. For example, show brief videotapes or films of parents during baseline (pre-program) sessions trying to teach their child or interacting with their child in "the usual way." Such tapes or films might show the disruptive behavior or unresponsiveness of the child and obvious aggravation in the parents. The baseline tapes or films are then followed by tapes or films of the same parents and children in later stages of their Program, showing how effectively they teach behaviors with which their child needed much, how much calmer and attentive the children have become, and how much they have improved in various other behaviors, such as speech, reading, and/or self-help.

Point out how hard it had been for the parents shown on the tapes or films to live with their children before the Program began. Then, in an enthusiastic but realistic way, point out that the parents (on the tapes or films):

1. With time and hard work, began to "turn their children around" by requiring them to earn reinforcers rather than getting them on demand or receiving them for immature or inadequate behaviors.
2. Started to replace their children's long-standing disruptive behaviors with appropriate behaviors, such as good sitting, cooperation, playing, or doing chores.
3. By the end of the Program, had become skilled at teaching, changed the family environment so that their children were easier to live with, were cooperating better with one another and were closer than they had been for years, were sleeping better at night and not dreading each morning, and were more self-confident and prepared to work to produce a future for their child.

If the Initial Interview is being conducted in an educational or treatment facility, you can let the parents observe other parents who have been in Programs, working with children in classrooms. If videotapes or films are not available, however, you might give examples of the success other parents have had. And, you can have other parents who have been in Programs meet with or call the parents you are interviewing to describe the results of their Programs.

Again, while a rather high expectation of success is important for the parents' readiness to participate in a Program, it is neither ethical nor, in the long run, productive to overestimate the child's probable rate or extent of progress, or to underestimate the amount of effort the parents may have to put in, at least initially. Ultimately, you can only tell (and show) the parents what the probable outcomes of their participation may be, based on your own and others' experience.

However, in pointing out some possible difficulties parents may encounter (such as periods of slow progress), stress that:

1. Since you, and now the parents, are aware of the kinds of difficulties that can arise, the chances of avoiding or overcoming them are greater than they were in past years.

2. While some children's progress may be slower than everyone wants during the Program, their progress is likely to be greater than in the past.
3. Continued progress may eventually add up to important improvements in the children's educational chances and participation in family life.

Thus, a child whose neurological impairments are so extensive that he or she makes modest improvements only in attention and self-feeding during the Program, is likely to continue to make progress in those and other areas after the Program, if the parents maintain their own teaching behaviors.

Step 3: Anticipating Hesitations and Stressing Additional Benefits.

At this point many parents are likely to feel that they could become more effective in interacting with their child and may see the benefits of running a home educational program. Yet, they may have a variety of hesitations about working with you. For example, they may:

1. Worry about the confidentiality of the Program.
2. Be wary of opening their home to the eyes of observers.
3. Have outside interests which they fear they will be giving up.
4. Simply feel that the cost of participating (in terms of time and effort) is too high (especially if they are "drained").

One way to handle the above hesitations is to anticipate them. That is, "de-fuse" such hesitations by voicing them before the parents have a chance to. In that way, they may again see you as empathetic and nonthreatening. For example, while describing the Program, or right after, you can say:

> Now you may be uncomfortable about someone coming into your home and making videotapes. And I know there are many things you might like to do besides come here on Wednesday nights. And I know that at the end of a hard day sitting down and teaching (child) how to read may be the last thing you feel like doing. Well, I want to assure you that your feelings are natural. But look. First of all, nobody's going to videotape your personal and private activities. The videotapes are just to help us and you get a record of how your teaching programs are going. You can't believe how great parents feel when they see tapes of a good session. And we don't make home visits to spy on parents, but to help them with problems they may be having, or to reinforce them for doing so well. And, besides, after a few days, the observer pretty much fades into the woodwork. In fact, unless you agree to it in writing, no one outside of this Program is going to know your name or see any tapes or films that you let us make.
>
> You may worry that meetings and working with (child) just about every day may be a drag. And you're right! There have been times when I wanted to stay home on a meeting night and on a night when I was to make a home visit. But those feelings passed when I realized how much progress the parents and children were going to make because of our work together.

> You may be concerned about putting in the time now because in the past your time hasn't gotten you anything but more aggravation. But if you learned how to teach (child), you would start wanting to come to meetings so that you could find out what to do next and show other families how well you had done. In other words, in this program, your time and effort are likely to pay off!
>
> And I know you've got outside interests. There may be lots of other things that you like to do. But surely you can squeeze in half an hour a day to work with (child) on a certain teaching program. And, to be honest about it, your kid worries you and runs you ragged as it is! If you put in some extra time now to get him on the right track, in a few months you'll see that you have much more free time to do what you want to do because you've taught him how to keep himself busy instead of getting into trouble.

Second, stress the additional benefits (reinforcement) that the parents will gain in the program. For example:

1. If the Program is run with a group of parents, "true" friendships, rather than the possible "fairweather" friends which the parents have had, are likely to develop. The group may become a source of strength because each person can count on the others' information, encouragement, and reinforcement. In fact, as friendships develop, the families may begin to provide each other with services, such as baby-sitting or coaching. Indeed, even if you will be working individually with a family, the family can still become part of a network of other families that are now or have been in Programs, thus making them part of a larger group.

2. Rather than the meetings becoming a burden, the parents will find that they look forward to the meetings as a night out because they will be meeting with new friends, will be learning to be successful teachers, and will be displaying and discussing successes.

3. The parents will be learning to understand, change, and control far more than their child's behavior. They will be gaining the skills to help plan, produce, and chart their child's future; to change their other children and even themselves. They will be gaining self-confidence and peace of mind because, at last, they will be able to see what is happening, know how to plan for change and produce change, and no longer be so alone and vulnerable.

If the parents still have hesitations or reservations about making a commitment, those must be handled (and replaced by the components of readiness to change) before you formalize a working relationship. The next section discusses certain obstacles to readiness.

Step 4: Handling Persistent Hesitations, Philosophical/Cultural/Ideological Objections, and Communication Games

Some persistent hesitations result from the parents having missed or not understood what you said earlier. Therefore, handle many such hesitations by repeating, in a different way, what you said. For example:

1. In the long run, you probably will be spending much less time taking care of and keeping up with your child. In fact, instead of being one step behind your child, you will be planning his behavior: He will be coming to you.

2. You will be putting in only about 40 hours in meetings, in return for thousands of hours of peace, quiet, and satisfying interaction with your child. Just think of how many hours you spend each week, each month, each year doing things for your child, cleaning up after him, and worrying about the future. Wouldn't it be easier to put in some extra time now in return for an easier and more helpful future?

3. I (or all of the consultants in the Program) have your interests at heart. I am (or we are) going to be giving our time and energy to help you.

4. The videotapes and home observations that may be made will not be invasions of your privacy. In fact, you may really like to see yourself and your child on tape.

Again, contact with parents from past Programs can help to overcome many hesitations.

In addition to certain hesitations about their relationship with you, the parents may have philosophical/cultural/ideological objections to, or reservations about, the behavioral approach itself (for example, explanations of their child's problems or teaching methods to use). In many cases, you can anticipate and de-fuse those objections by mentioning them, explaining their bases (for example, showing that many objections have been propagated by the very professionals from whom the parents have gotten no help), and showing why the objections are not based on an accurate picture of the behavioral approach. The method of anticipating and de-fusing can be used any time you are discussing behavioral analyses or behavioral methods with the parents; for example, when you are helping them to understand their child or their career in behavioral terms, describing the Program, or suggesting behavioral methods to try.

On the other hand, if the parents raise an objection, empathize with their concern ("Of course you do not want to deprive your child."), help them to analyze and understand the basis of their objection, and show them why the objection is not necessarily based on an accurate picture of the behavioral approach.

Here are some common philosophical/cultural/ideological objections, as noted under Item 10 of the APG.

1. "Reinforcement is Bribery." This objection often rests on a misunderstanding of the nature of reinforcement. That is, the parents may not see that reinforcement is a natural part of daily life for everyone. They may not see the difference between the broader technical definition of positive reinforcement (as a change in the environment following a response, which is likely to increase the strength of the response) and the narrower cultural definition of "rewarding" (as the obvious delivery of things and activities that people want, like, or enjoy in recognition of satisfactory or salutary performance).

To handle this objection, then, explore with parents the dictionary definition of bribery: "inducing a person to commit an illegal or immoral act by offering a reward." Certainly you do not expect parents to teach illegal or immoral behaviors. As to the nature of positive reinforcement itself, give the parents many examples of positive reinforcement in daily life, such as compliments for looking nice, wages or salaries for working, and awards for excellent performance. Ask the parents how long people would work at a job if they were no longer paid or if their hard work were never recognized.

Note that, since the above examples are of positive reinforcement delivered by others, positive reinforcement might still be seen as a "reward." Therefore, make sure to give examples of positive reinforcement that occurs in more "natural" ways, such as the reinforcement for properly shooting a basket (when the ball goes through the hoop), learning how to read (when reading later enables the reader to learn about things that are of interest), or dropping coins in a soda pop machine (when the can comes through the slot).

2. "Children (people) should not be Reinforced for what they Ought to be Doing Anyway." To handle this objection, which is closely tied to the first, agree with the parents' concerns. Then point out that while learning and engaging in some behaviors because they are enjoyable or beneficial in themselves is our goal, sometimes people must first find out that the behavior will pay off for them, or they will not even learn or perform it. For example,

> We all want our children to learn to read because, in the long run, it is good for them and it is enjoyable. And we do not want to have to always reinforce them for reading. But, unless we reinforce our children with praise while they are struggling with the hard task of learning to read, they may not stick to it long enough to find out that it is enjoyable and beneficial.

Stress that their child may have been reinforced for behaviors that are the opposite of what they now want their child to do. Unless the new behaviors are strongly reinforced, their child may not replace the old behaviors.

3. "Bad Behavior Ought to be Punished." This objection may be raised when parents describe their methods for handling problem behaviors, or when you describe reinforcement procedures for strengthening appropriate behaviors to replace problem behaviors. The main method to use here is to point out that punishment alone is not usually an effective way to "get rid of" problem behaviors, since punishment does not teach the child alternative behavior and is so easy to misuse (for example, it must be immediate, consistent, and of high intensity to work best). Moreover, since punishment may suppress a behavior quickly (but only for a relatively short time if it is misused), the parents may be reinforced for using punishment and become the "kind" of persons that they do not want to become (that is, they may start to like using punishment or become insensitive to what they are doing).

In other words, point out that:

1. They must reinforce appropriate behaviors anyway, so as to teach the child behaviors that are alternatives to the ones that are being punished.
2. Punishment may be hard for them to use properly (and its misuse may produce even more problems).
3. Its initial effectiveness may turn them into persons that they may not want to become.

Tell the parents (if you agree, that is) that punishment may be needed in certain cases (extreme self-injury, for example), but that, with most behaviors, it is better to try positive reinforcement procedures first.

4. "How can you Expect me to Deprive my Poor Child?" "It Isn't Fair to Withhold Things These Children Enjoy." This objection has two main components—the parents' perception of their child as pitiable and therefore to be placated, "babied," or given noncontingent reinforcement, and their misunderstanding of withholding reinforcement contingent upon the child's engaging in reinforceable behaviors. This objection may be raised by the parents when you describe methods for teaching certain behaviors (such as paying attention, sitting properly, or speaking) during meals or snack times, when food might be used as a reinforcer.

Help change the parents' perception of their child and clear up their misunderstandings about withholding reinforcement by first, telling them in a straightforward but nonthreatening way that the child's problems are indeed unfortunate, that their protectiveness indicates how much they care for the child, but that protection and pity, alone, are not likely to help anyone in the long run. As much as their child needs their caring, their child needs to learn. This point can be backed up by pointing out ways in which they have been successful in changing their child.

Second, stress that no one expects them to subject their child to pain or starvation, but merely expects them to help their child earn what the child likes, reinforcers that the child may have been getting for nothing or for inadequate behaviors because of their efforts to care for the child. In other words, they will simply be giving their child some of the things the child likes after the child engages in bits of appropriate behavior. As a result, appropriate behaviors will increase, and their child will be getting more reinforcement than before. In other words, your job is to show the parents that, far from being cruel, they can give their child the greatest gift of all—a repertoire of behaviors that enables him to have a voice in the world around him through adaptive behaviors.

Third, make it clear that you will not try to browbeat them into using any method. If you suggest that, initially, their severely impaired child earn all bites of supper by making eye contact, and if they do not want their child to ever be hungry, they are welcome to use praise, or anything else they want to try as a reinforcer. For example, explain that if they decide to use praise and not food, and the target behavior increases a great deal, so much the better! But, if the target behavior does not increase, it is up to them to assess their data and decide what to do next, possibly to try a stronger reinforcer. In other words, they have the right (indeed, the responsibility) to choose their teaching methods and the responsibility for being sensitive to the consequences of their decisions.

5. "All Children Should be Treated Alike." In effect, the parents are saying that they should not handle the one child any differently than they handle their other children, or any differently than other parents handle their children. That is, if the siblings are not reinforced as often, or are not reinforced with food, tokens, or special activities, neither should the child with learning and behavior problems.

Again, agree with the parents that the goal is to teach as many "normal" behaviors as possible and to teach their child to perform those behaviors for the same reasons and in the same conditions as other children(that is, with minimal signals and prompts, and with "natural" or common reinforcers). However, that is the goal. The means, on the other hand, may have to involve, at first, a more powerful or more structured learning environment, or the child may never reach the goals.

For example, one goal may be to teach the child to read without being prompted, and with the reinforcement being that the child's reading brings the child into contact with other reinforcers, such as comic strips and conversations. Yet, to reach the goal the child may have to be started off with extra praise and activity rewards after lessons. Without the extra reinforcement, reading may not increase much. In fact, efforts to force the child to read, and to read because the child "should" enjoy it, may produce escalating conflict in which no one wins.

Second, stress that all children, indeed all people, are not alike! We all have different needs and wants (are reinforced by different things) and have different skills and abilities. To treat people as if they were all exactly alike (that is, to expect the same skills, likes, and dislikes) would be to commit the fallacy of "artificial equality," to deny individuality.

Some people, in other words, need more practice, time, reinforcement, or powerful reinforcers to start them learning. And perhaps some will always need an environment that is somewhat different (more sensitive to their skills and learning problems). To deny them those environmental conditions in the name of equality may mean that they are denied the very conditions that could help them to be more equal in terms of their behaviors and, hence, in their control of their own future.

The next three objections have a common core, namely, the belief that the behavioral approach cannot work with their child.

6. "My Child's Problems Won't be Corrected by Something as Simple as Reinforcement." Knowing that their child has many behavioral inadequacies and engages in many problem behaviors, the parents may argue that reinforcing their child for engaging in appropriate behaviors is not sufficient to produce substantial change, given the enormity of the problem. It is as though the parents are saying that a small amount of an antibiotic cannot do much good if an infection is well advanced.

The parents, of course, are right. And you should agree with them (usually circumvents a debate). Your task, then, is to point out that: (1) Reinforcement is only one procedure, but an important one, among many procedures that they will be taught to use and (2) while their child, indeed, has a lot to learn, no one expects the job to be done in a week! Their child's learning and behavior problems will be handled in step-by-step fashion, sometimes working on one behavior at a time, and sometimes working on several at once. In that way, they will find that in time their child has changed a great deal.

7. "My behaviors have Little to do with my Child's Behaviors." Statements such as this represent problems in relation to APG Item 5 of readiness to change. To help the parents see that parents and children do affect each others' behavior, you can use examples from your own life. Then return to the parents' descriptions (or ask them for descriptions) of their child's problem behaviors and their reactions to problem behaviors. In a nonthreatening way, you might show them how their child has taught them to inadvertently pay attention to (reinforce) precisely the behaviors that they cannot stand. If necessary, show them videotapes of counterproductive exchanges between parents and children during Baseline Observations in past Programs.

Similarly, show them examples of how parents and children teach each other appropriate behaviors. For example, as parents reinforce a child for starting to learn to talk, the child's speech increases in frequency and skill, which reinforces the parents for reinforcing the child, resulting in the parents' reinforcing speech more often and the child's talking more often.

8. "Nothing Much can be Done—It won't Work Anyway." Statements such as this usually represent pessimism and fatigue resulting from a career full of "frustration" (extinction, punishment). As before, empathize with the parents' feelings, but counter their pessimism with examples from their life which demonstrate that their child has changed as a result of their efforts. In giving examples of their successes or partial successes, make sure to translate into behavioral terms the methods they used in teaching their child. The message to convey is:

> You have done it before without help. Think of how much your child will progress with the help you can now get, if you want it.

If this does not work (perhaps because the parents enjoy arguing or proving that optimistic people are wrong), you might try "reverse psychology," as noted in the section on communication games in Chapter 2. That is, agree with the parents that perhaps nothing much can be done, especially since they have worked so hard, seen so many specialists, and so much time has passed. Such a reversal in the usual pattern of consultants' suggesting how much might be done (which results in some parents' finding new reasons why nothing much can be done), may prompt the parents to reevaluate the past and their child's chances of improvement. Indeed, they may begin to pinpoint beneficial changes and suggest that they (and you) are being too pessimistic. For example:

Parent: What you are saying sounds real good on paper, but I don't think that much can be done for Becky.

Consultant: Well, you may be right. Perhaps nothing can be done. (Waits for parent to respond to apparently paradoxical message.)

Parent: What?! Why do you say that?

Consultant: Well, after all, you have told me about all of the places where you have gone for help, and about all of the things that you have tried at home, and nothing seems to have resulted in much improvement. So, what else can I conclude? (Consultant places parent in a position of having to find alternative reasons for past lack of progress, or agree that no change is possible—with all of the implications.)

Parent: Well, maybe it's not Becky's fault.

Consultant: You think not? (Continues to express belief that perhaps nothing can be done, prompting parent to find reasons why something can be done.)

Parent: Maybe the specialists did not try hard enough or did not know enough.

Consultant: Maybe. But could all of them have failed? (Maintains pressure.)

Parent: I don't know. Maybe they didn't exactly fail. These kids aren't so easy to figure out, you know. And I'm sure that we made mistakes at home, too.

Consultant: So, what are you suggesting?

Parent: That maybe if we try again—try some of the things you have been talking about—Becky will improve.

Consultant: I don't know. I guess I'm pretty hard-headed. I'm not sure that you have convinced me that I can help you to help Becky, but I'll give it my best shot. (Consultant now appears to be saying what parents were saying earlier. To prove consultant wrong, parents now might work to change their child.)

9. "What you are Suggesting Sounds so Mechanical." This last objection is complex. Variations of it include statements such as:

> Behavior is more complex than the way you explain it. (Similar to objection 6 above.) Those methods will make my child a robot. But you are talking only about externals. What about things that are going on inside, like "will," "thinking," and "mental processes"?

As you may imagine, such statements go to the heart of the parents' accepting or rejecting the behavioral approach. Therefore, be careful. First, help the parents to see that there is a difference between the terms and principles that are used to describe or analyze behavior and the human behavioral reality itself. For example:

Interviewer: You seem to be bothered by what I have been saying.

Parent: Yes.

Interviewer: Tell me about it. Perhaps I haven't been clear.

Parent: Well, you made Greg and his problems sound so simple. For example, you used words like "reinforcement," "structured exchange," and "ignoring."

Interviewer: Yes?

Parent: Well, I understood what you were saying. I really did. I could see the structured exchanges you were talking about. Like when Greg would throw tantrums and we would give him what he wanted so that he would stop. I understand how that was reinforcing him for throwing tantrums.

Interviewer: (Smiles.) I agree. You do have a good understanding of what we've been talking about.

Parent: But it just can't be that simple! Greg has lots of behaviors that need to be changed. But you are using the same words, over and over again, to explain what he is doing! It can't be that simple. There is so much to change and you are trying to explain it and change it with just a few words.

Interviewer: Ah! Now I see. Well, you know what? I agree with you. It does sound too easy. You are right. I have been using words like "reinforcement," "structured exchange," and "ignoring" to explain a lot of what has been going on over the years, and to suggest methods to use to help change Greg's behaviors.

And you are right in thinking that those few words, or even a dozen words more, do not cover or explain everything there is to know about Greg as a whole person or everything that is happening. But words never do explain and change everything. We are looking at Greg's behavior—some of his behaviors—and we are trying to get a handle on his behaviors, figure out just what the problem is, and trying to figure out how to change some of them—a few at a time. But we are using words that do cover a lot of what is important about Greg, aren't we?

Parent: Yes, I agree that "reinforcement" has a lot to do with Greg's behavior. (Parent still does not look at ease.)

Interviewer: But?

Parent: Well, like I said, there is more to Greg than can be covered by a few words.

Interviewer: You are absolutely right! You see how complex Greg is, and how complex behavior is. Those few words make it seem like we are forgetting that Greg is more than a bunch of behaviors; he is a whole person. Think of it this way. We can get a good picture—not a complete picture—but a pretty good picture of a person by describing that person with certain important words, like "generous," "friendly," and "open-minded." Don't those few words tell us a great deal about a person? How that person behaves? What you can expect them to do in certain situations? And how you might want to treat them?

Parent: Yes.

Interviewer: Yes! They do tell us a lot about a person. But still, they do not tell us everything about that person. They do not reproduce the person. They just tell us some important things about him. This may sound like a strange question, but have you ever gone to anyone for help when you felt ill?

Parent: Sure.

Interviewer: What kind of person have you gone to?

Parent: A doctor.

Interviewer: Medical doctor?

Parent: Sure.

Interviewer: Well, let's look at what the doctor does. You are feeling real sick. Something is wrong. Let's say it is pneumonia. Does the doctor have to know everything about you as a whole person in order to find out that you have pneumonia or to treat you for it?

Parent: Well, no.

Interviewer: And doesn't the doctor pretty much keep away from words like "personality" and "mind"?

Parent: Yes.

Interviewer: Right! But why? You do have a mind, don't you?

Parent: Sure, because the pneumonia isn't in my mind; it is in my body.

Interviewer: Right!! And to find out what is wrong and how to cure you, the doctor takes your pulse, blood pressure, and respiration, checks your throat and lungs, and some other things. In other words, the problem is in your body, and that is what the doctor examines. And just a few words, like ''temperature'' and ''lungs'' have a lot do to with what is wrong in your body.

When the doctor describes and treats your pneumonia, and uses words that have to do with your body, and not with your mind, you don't feel that the rest of you is being neglected, do you? You don't feel dehumanized, do you?

Parent: Well, no. Not unless the doctor is too rough or stern.

Interviewer: I see what you mean. So if the doctor acts like he or she cares about you as a whole person, you don't mind if he talks just about your body, do you?

Parent: No, that would be all right.

Interviewer: Well, just because we are using words like ''reinforcement'' and ''structured exchange'' doesn't mean that we don't care about Greg as a whole person. It's just that his behavior is the most important thing about him that has a problem now. In fact, it is because we care about him as a person, and about his welfare, that all of us are working to help him by changing his behavior. And words like ''reinforcement'' help us to understand Greg's behavior.

Second, the parents may be concerned because, in discussions with them, the interviewer is not dealing with what is supposed to be inside of a person, such as mind, will, and thinking. The parents may really be concerned that the ''whole child'' is being neglected or that the interviewer, by emphasizing externals, is challenging their assumption that behavior is determined by thinking (and other so-called internal processes).

You will probably not be able to change, nor is it always necessary to change, several decades of cultural conditioning that taught the parents to believe that there are internal processes that are almost independent of external events, and that are the ''real'' causes of behavior. Therefore, your task is to place such internal processes in their proper perspective—as being no more important than their child's overt behaviors.

Interviewer: I get the feeling that something isn't sitting just right.

Parent: It's the way you are talking about John's behavior. It's like only his behavior is important to you. And the methods you have suggested for changing his behavior have to do only with what is going on outside of him.

Interviewer: Yes. And that seems to bother you, doesn't it?

Parent: Yes, it does.

Interviewer: Mm hmm. Why is that?

Parent: Well, it makes John seem to be something like a machine. Like there is nothing else about him but his behavior. And like nothing is important in changing his behavior but what is going on outside of him, like the way he is reinforced. What about his mind, his thoughts?

Interviewer: I agree with you. I can see how you might be uneasy since I have been talking about John—describing him and talking about how to change him—using words that have to do only with his behavior and with what's happening outside of him, in his environment. I can see how it might make you think that I see John as some kind of machine, without feelings, thoughts, or a personality.

Parent: You do?

Interviewer: Sure. If I were you, I would be uneasy, too! Here you are, caring for John all of these years. And somebody comes along and makes him sound like a machine. Makes him sound like he is less than human.

Parent: Then why do you make it sound like he is a machine?

Interviewer: Well, it's not that I don't believe in thinking or personality. It's just that the words I am using when I talk about John have to do with things that we can all see or observe. You can see his behavior and you can see the reinforcement that affects his behavior.

Parent: Uh huh. (Parent does not look convinced.)

Interviewer: All I'm saying is that, while thinking and personality may all exist, we can only know about them second hand. What do you have to see in order to say what a person is feeling inside, or what their personality is like?

Parent: What they do, what they say.

Interviewer: Right!! You can only know what is going on inside of them by their behavior—how they act, how they tell you they feel.

Parent: Yes?

Interviewer: Remember, I'm not saying that John has no personality, or that he does not think. I'm just saying that if you want to know how he thinks or feels, all you have to go on is what you can see and hear, and that is his behavior. That is why we talk about his behavior and not about his personality. We can't see his inner personality. We can only see his behavior.

Parent: Okay, but doesn't his behavior happen because of the way he thinks? You always talk about his behavior being caused by what is going on outside of him.

Interviewer: You know why that is? It's because his thinking and his observable behavior are all caused by what is going on in the environment. See, many people talk as though a person thinks something and then their thinking causes the behavior that we can see. But, thinking is a behavior too. In fact, what is personality if not a summary of a person's behavior? All of these are behavior. It's just that you can't see another person's behavior called "thinking."

What really happens when we think? When we think, don't we sort of say things to ourselves inside our heads? Where did we learn how to talk to ourselves? Where did we learn the words to use—the language—when we think? Were we born with it? Or did we learn it?

Parent: Learned it.

Interviewer: Where? How?

Parent: Our parents.

Interviewer: Right. Our parents taught us words to use to talk about our world, inside and outside. And they taught us to see and talk about the way things are hooked-up in the world. Later, we could talk to ourselves. And by talking to ourselves, we could figure out what was going on, and act accordingly. But, again, where did we learn how to think? From our parents. And also, we learned how to think about our world because of what our actions were finding out about the world for us. We found out that certain behaviors produced reinforcement and other behaviors produced punishment. When we found that out, how did our behaviors change?

Parent: We kept doing the behaviors that were reinforced and stopped doing the ones that were punished.

Interviewer: Right again! Well, then, what is causing our behavior? Our thoughts? Or the environment of reinforcement and punishment that taught us how to think about what happens when we behave in certain ways?

Parent: Both?

Interviewer: Very good. You can see that even though thinking affects the way we act, thinking is still learned because of what happens outside of us. And since we can only know about the way a person is thinking from the way they behave, we might as well look at that environment to help us to understand both thinking and acting.

At this point, have the parents examine some of their behaviors, to illustrate how their thinking (for example, planning), which may occur before certain observable behaviors, is itself a reflection of or result of past interaction with the "outside" world. The point to get across is that we need to use our knowledge of the outside world to understand both how we think and how we engage in observable behaviors.

Finally, the parents may be concerned that their child will be turned into a robot.

Parent: I'm worried that if we do the things you suggest, Pam will be just like a robot. She won't be directing or controlling her behavior. We will. Or the reinforcement will.

Interviewer: And you are absolutely right to be worried! But I would like you to keep this sentence in your heads. Our whole purpose in working with Pam is to give her more freedom. The more adaptive behaviors she has, the more independent she will become, the more choices she will have, the less she will be a prisoner of her rituals, her tantrums, and her lack of speech.

Parent: I can see that. I really can! We want the same thing. But you are talking about using reinforcement in a businesslike way. Won't she become a prisoner to the things we will be doing? To the way we teach her?

Interviewer: That is a good question!! And an important one. It has bothered me for a long time. All I can say, for sure, is this. We all agree that reinforcement, for example, affects what we do. But there are many reinforcers and many behaviors. If you set it up so that Pam can get what she wants in only one way, then she will certainly look like a robot. She will only learn to get reinforcers with that one behavior. But that won't be the fault of the reinforcer!! You are the one who set up the exchange that way so that she would learn to behave like a robot!!

Parent: I think I see what you mean.

Interviewer: How does a robot act? It can only do a certain, limited number of things. And it does them the same way all the time and under the same conditions. Well, if you make things so rigid that only a few behaviors work, and they only work in a few situations, then Pam will learn to act just like a robot.

So, if you don't want her to learn to be a robot, which I'm sure you don't, then we must set up the teaching exchanges so that she learns many, many behaviors to get many, many things that she wants in many, many situations. Then she will not act like a robot. She will act like a person who makes choices, a person who can adapt her behavior to different circumstances. That's not a robot. That's a human being.

Parent: I see. That makes me feel lots better.

Interviewer: And yet?

Parent: Well, you talked about teaching Pam in small steps, according to an educational program plan. It sounds like she will be programmed, molded, or trained!

Interviewer: Okay. So, we have two issues here. The first is what happens during any teaching program. That is, will the use of positive reinforcement and other teaching methods make her a robot or limit her freedom? Regarding that issue, we said that it is not teaching methods themselves, but how they are used, that help to give a person more freedom or to limit their freedom, right?

Parent: Right. It depends on how we teach her. Whether we teach her to make choices and teach behaviors that are useful to her.

Interviewer: Right. Now the second issue, the one I think you are raising now, has to do with the overall educational program. Is it going to limit her, program her, mold her to be just one type of person?

Parent: Right. That's it!

Interviewer: Well, the answer is a lot like the answer to the first issue. The educational program can be planned so that she only learns certain behaviors, only learns them when we want her to, and never learns to make choices. But that is not the way we will plan or conduct Pam's educational program. Sure, we will go in small steps, but that is only to insure that she is successful and enjoys learning. In fact, we will be

> encouraging her to learn many more behaviors than are strictly in her curriculum. And we are going to work to help her to be independent.
>
> Not only that, but consider this. As a result of careful planning and teaching, Pam is likely to learn more than isolated behaviors. She is likely to learn a more general skill. She is likely to learn how to learn. Which means that, as time goes on, she will become much more independent in the learning process. And it should take much less effort and programming to help her to learn.

It is not necessary that the parents completely accept the behavioral approach at this point. You are looking for a tentative acceptance. Thus, if parents raised some objections but now are willing to work with you and try using some of the methods you have suggested, that is sufficient. During the Program you can continue to shape their acceptance, based on success.

In addition to certain hesitations about working with you, as well as philosophical/cultural/ideological objections to or misunderstandings of the behavioral approach, the parents may not be ready to change because of certain communication games, some of which are discussed in Chapter 2. They are as follows:

1. "It's Not (or is No Longer) Our Job." Some parents feel that it is the job of the teacher or therapist to change their child. Perhaps they believe this because they are simply unaware of the necessity of their conducting complementary programs in the home. In that case, discuss the various reasons, listed earlier, why they need to work with their child at home.

On the other hand, they may feel that they have a right to expect others to educate their child. Indeed, a legal right. They may, in fact, feel hostile toward people (like you) who suggest that it is still partly their job when, after all, as taxpayers, the school is supposed to do the job.

An approach to try with parents who raise the legal issue is as follows.

a. Empathize with what they have been going through.

b. Demonstrate that you will be working just as hard for them and their child as you will be expecting them to work.

c. Point out that all the laws in the world and all the best schools in the world are not going to "make their child normal" or straighten out their child in the home, unless they learn to help educate their child.

If the above does not work, you may have to help the parents to understand the historical and current relationship between human misfortunes and social services (that is, the "bottom line"). Specifically, while it is now claimed that everyone has a right to educational services, and while there are now laws mandating that communities provide such services, both the belief in a right to educational services and the laws can change. Further, there are no mandatory services for victims of cancer; few people get the best heart specialists; and those who are poor and severely mentally ill are likely to spend the rest of their lives getting custodial treatment in large public mental hospitals. Thus, the availability of services does not seem to flow solely from the existence of misery and misfortune or from natural rights but, rather, from power, prestige, and money.

In sum, in the long run, the reality is that all children can depend on is their parents. To the extent that facilities and specialists are available now, it is in the parents' and children's interests that the parents use those services (including the Program) as much as they can. In that way, the parents will be able to provide their child with needed help. Moreover, in a Program such as the one offered to them, the parents will acquire some degree of power (knowledge, skill, self-confidence) to help their child, themselves, and others, even if services and specialists come and go.

Such an argument is likely to work with most parents; at least it may generate a tentative agreement with your statements about the educational necessity of their working with their child. From that point, you may be able to obtain a complete commitment or at least a commitment to a partial Program.

2. "We've Tried That." This game can occur during a Program (when parents might object to trying a particular method) or at this early point, when the parents, in effect, are saying: "We've tried 'behavior modification,' " or "We've tried to teach our child, but it didn't work."

As you can see, such statements are general, and that is the weak spot that should be challenged. First, you might try to show that there is a contradiction in what they are saying. Then give them an opportunity to resolve the contradiction, but in a way that requires that they at least try to do what you are suggesting—namely work with you to change themselves and their child. Here are some examples.

Parent: Your program sounds good, but we've tried behavior modification and it didn't work.

Consultant: It didn't work? (Stated in a nonthreatening way, indicating that the consultant believes them.)

Parent: No. Sandy's behavior didn't change at all.

Consultant: Well, tell me, just what did you do when you were using behavior modification? (Sets occasion for parents to be specific, which will later give consultant a chance to show why "behavior modification" itself was not at fault, but rather, specific procedures that were used.)

Parent: Well, for example, Dr. Simple told us just to ignore Sandy when he threw tantrums to get our attention. And we followed his advice. We completely stopped paying attention to tantrums.

Consultant: Um hmm. And?

Parent: After two weeks, Sandy was throwing more tantrums than ever. Behavior modification didn't work.

Consultant: I can see that you would be upset! (Empathizes.) I'll bet he threw even worse tantrums, too. (Post-dicts behavior of child, showing that he is an "insider".)

Parent: That's right. They were terrible!

Consultant: Well, you see, there are many ways of doing, or trying to do, the same thing. Ignoring is just one way to try to decrease a behavior. But all of the ways might be called "behavior modification." Just like there are lots of ways to cook an egg. If you cook an egg in motor oil, it will taste terrible, but its still called "cooking." See, it's not that behavior modification didn't work. It's that ignoring didn't work. Other methods, also part of behavior modification, probably would have worked better. (Shows parents that the term "behavior modification" is too vague. Now consultant must show why ignoring did not work and why a different method might have been better. That is, consultant must "put up or shut up.")

Parent: Like what?

Consultant: First of all, ignoring by itself will not teach Sandy proper ways of getting your attention. If ignoring is to be tried, at least it should be combined with lots of reinforcement for playing, talking, and cooperating, as ways of getting attention. Or, perhaps mild punishment, such as putting Sandy in his room every time he throws a tantrum, combined with reinforcement for appropriate behaviors, would work better. (Shows that a different "behavior modification" technique might work better.)

Parent: I see. Well, we never thought that just ignoring tantrums would work, anyway, but we tried.

Consultant: You were right to question the use of ignoring all by itself. (Reinforces parent's partial agreement.) But do you see that behavior modification was not at fault? Ignoring was at fault. (Sets up the differences between the whole—behavior modification—and its parts—a specific procedure.)

Parent: Yes.

Consultant: What about mild punishment plus positive reinforcement for appropriate behaviors? Do you think that might work better? (Note, if parents agree, they are agreeing to another "behavior modification" procedure.)

Parent: Well, certainly better than ignoring.

Consultant: Right. Of course, that would also be behavior modification, you know. (Smiles.)

Parent: Okay, I've got the point. (Smiles back.)

Or,

Parent: Your program sounds good, but we've tried for years to teach Billy. Nothing seems to work. Either he can't learn or we can't teach.

Consultant: So you feel that you've worked hard for a long time and you're not satisfied. (Empathizes. Restates what parents have only half said.)

Parent: That's putting it mildly!

Consultant: Yes? (Encourages parent to continue.)

Parent: He's just no better than he was years ago.

Consultant: I think I know how you feel. But, you know, there are a lot of things that Billy can do. He can feed himself; he's partially toilet trained; he can dress himself; and he communicates with a few sentences. (Nonthreatening challenge to parent's first statement.)

Parent: That's true. But it's not much. (Parent begins to see that her first statement was too general.)

Consultant: I'll agree with you that he has a long way to go. (Indicates agreement with parent's initial perception of little change, but states it in a more positive way.) But surely he didn't teach himself all of the behaviors he can do. Somebody had to teach him. And I think I'm looking at his teachers. (Nonthreatening challenge to parents' statement that they can't teach.)

Parent: Well, I guess he has made some progress. (Begins to recognize progress.)

Consultant: Yes, he has. He would not be in the pretty good shape he's in now if it weren't for your hard work at teaching him. And that's the thing to keep in mind. Billy can learn and you can teach. You've proved it. (Reinforces past work and stresses that both child and parents have "ability.")

Parent: Um hmm.

Consultant: The thing for us to do is figure out just what are the best methods for teaching Billy, and teach you how to use them. Look, you've been doing it alone all these years; you've been persistent and you've been inventive. Well, we've learned a lot about how children like Billy learn. And we've developed some methods for teaching kids much faster and easier. If you've been pretty successful by yourselves, think of how successful you'll be once you are armed with the new methods we've learned, plus people to back you up, to help you on the spot, and show you that Billy is changing. If you will give it another try, so will I. (Shows parents that what they need are better methods, which will be supplied by the Program.)

Parent: Okay, what the hell! What do we have to lose? You're right, he's not going to teach himself.

If the above method does not work, you might address the game itself. For instance:

Consultant: I understand how you feel. You've tried hard. You've been getting the runaround for years. And you may be afraid of failing. I think that you may be tricking yourself into thinking that nothing can be done. It's natural! Nobody wants to feel like a failure. But, it's not you who is the failure. It's the people you went to for help over the years, people who talked a lot but who never gave you anything concrete that you could use.

Parent: Um hmm.

Consultant: You don't look like a quitter to me. Are you?

Parent: No. I'm a pretty strong person, I think.

Consultant: Okay, then, let's not quit now. Let's get down to business and come up with a program for Billy that will work!

3. "Overworked Advocate." This game may appear during a Program (when the parents say that they do not have the time to work this week because of meetings that they have to attend) or now, when you are trying to strengthen readiness to change. They may state that while "your program sounds like a good one," and while they would "love to be part of it," they "just do not have the time" because they "have so much to do" as members of an organization working for children.

It is relatively easy to show many parents that their statements and hesitations are not consistent with their values. For example, you can tell them that their being advocates for other children is wonderful, but it does not necessarily mean that their own child is going to benefit. And that, in working for other children, they inadvertently may be depriving their own child of their talents and energies. However, you do not want to make the parents feel guilty or discourage the good work they are doing! You merely want to point out that working for others and working for their own child are not incompatible, since you are not suggesting that they drop their outside work. That is, you want the parents to see that perhaps, for the time being, they could direct a bit more of their energies and talents to their child. This implies that they adjust their priorities, so that changing the system through their advocacy work becomes a long-term rather than an immediate goal. For example:

> I think that your work on behalf of kids is terrific. And I know that it is time-consuming. But you have a few hours a week, don't you, to learn more about how to work with your child? In fact, the more you learn about how to evaluate children and services, and how to plan programs and teach, the more you will be able to contribute to the long-term process of changing the system for delivering services.

It will be hard for many parents to completely refuse you when you phrase it this way. Most are likely to agree that they do have a bit more time than they thought. And, when they agree with you that they have the time and interest, you should reinforce or confirm their self-image as dedicated and hard-working parents (which they are!) and set the occasion for them to make an initial commitment.

> Great! Now just how much time do you think that you can give? And what do you think you have the energy to do?

If they make a verbal commitment to participate in some way, you can formalize the working relationship for a partial (or comprehensive) Program with a written or verbal contract, planned with them, specifying how much time they will put in each week, and what activities they will perform. Gradually, as they achieve success (for many overworked advocates are parents of older children and may feel that they are unable to help their child), you can encourage them to participate in a more comprehensive program.

Finally, as with other games, if the above method does not seem to work, you might go to the "bottom line." That is, address the game itself. For example:

> You know, sometimes when we are faced with a situation that we do not understand, or with a problem that we can't seem to solve, we trick ourselves into thinking that the situation or problem isn't there, or that it is not what it appears to be, or that we couldn't have solved it anyway. Often, without even knowing it, we play a game with ourselves to make ourselves feel better or just so that we can carry on.
>
> For example, I can't stand it when kids throw tantrums. It drives me up the wall! But if I started pulling my hair out every time a kid started to throw a tantrum, how could I deal with it effectively? And how could I teach and expect others to deal with their kids' tantrums in a cool, effective manner? So, you know what I do? I play the game of "tough guy." The tantrums don't bother me. Oh, no, not me!
>
> Well, I'm kidding myself and others when I play "tough guy." But the little game makes it possible to deal effectively with tantrums.
>
> But I sometimes play games that are not so productive. If I've been working with a kid for a long time—trying to teach the kid to talk, for example—and I think that I've tried everything but the child is just not making any progress, I might play the game of "I've done all I can." See what that game does? It puts the blame on the child! And it takes me off the hook. I can still feel good about myself. Also, if I can get others to play the game with me, then they will keep on thinking that I'm competent.
>
> But look at the unproductive results of the game! Since I have convinced myself and others that I have done all that anyone can do, then there is no reason to invent new teaching methods! So, the child I'm working with, and other children who have a hard time learning to talk, will suffer, while I feel good about myself.
>
> Now, I wonder if you are tricking yourselves; playing a game with yourselves. Is it possible that over the years you have become tired and pessimistic about being able to help your own child? . . . So, you are doing all kinds of good work for other parents and children but may have perhaps resigned yourselves to making the best of the way things are with your child at home?
>
> Well, if that's what is happening, I can sure understand it. But, you know, you're still tricking yourselves. In fact, you may be downgrading yourselves into thinking that you don't have what it takes to work with Barbara or to help her change much. But, from what you told me about the ways that you have worked with Barbara in the past, I do think that you have what it takes to be good teachers! In addition, we've learned a lot in the past few years about how to teach children like Barbara. So, let me get down to the bottom line. I think that your work for children and families is great, but with your skills and dedication, and with what we now know about

teaching children with learning and behavior problems, I think that if you direct a bit of your time and energy into this Program, you are going to be more successful than you think.

If this works (the parents agree to try to help their child and to schedule time for meetings and for conducting a home educational program), formalize a working relationship, as noted in the above paragraph.

4. "I Have My Own Life to Live." This communication game is usually played by frustrated and pessimistic parents. Consequently, they have sought other sources of reinforcement, such as outside activities. Your Program, ironically, gives them another chance to fail and simultaneously cuts off their access (or so they might think) to their sources of reinforcement (the outside activities).

To handle this game, show parents that:

- **a.** they are not failures; rather they might have been failed by others.
- **b.** they have produced change in their child.
- **c.** they have a perfect right to outside activities, but the Program will not cut deeply into these activities. In fact, by changing their child, they will have even more time for themselves.
- **d.** the meetings will become enjoyable activities.
- **e.** they owe it to themselves to give it one more try.

Some parents, however, continue to voice hesitations. That is, as each game is handled (with the parents perhaps agreeing that there was something wrong in what they were thinking and that you made a good point), the parents initiate another. For example, after they agree it is still, in part, their job, they may argue, in effect, "Yes, but we've tried that before;" "Yes, but we have our own life to live;" or "Yes, but we don't have the time." In this case if you are sure that the problem is not a matter of misunderstanding or lack of information, then address the fact that they are playing one game after another; that you recognize the games being played, understand why the parents are playing games or seem to be hesitant about working with you, and expected the games and hesitations and see them as a sign of progress in the relationship.

Consultant: You know, I'll bet that you folks never bought a vacuum cleaner from a door-to-door salesperson. You have so many good questions and raise so many important points. I imagine that when you do buy something, your mind is completely made up, you buy the best, and are satisfied. I think that is great! Too many people are suckers for a pitch and are unhappy later on. So, I'm glad that you have been hesitant to make a commitment. It is a good sign of your honesty and of progress in our relationship. It means that if we worked together, we would always know where we stood, could talk things out and settle any difficulties. (De-fuses implicit adversary relationship.)

Parent: Yup. I do sort of pride myself on being hard-headed. I guess it is pretty hard on some people. I'm not easy to convince.

Consultant: I think that your hard-headedness, as you call it, is refreshing—and challenging. It probably means that you could learn what I have to teach you quickly, and that you could catch any weaknesses in my methods. It would be an asset to any group.

Parent: Think so?

Consultant: Sure. Who wants to work with people who just sit there and eat up everything you have to say? I, at least, like to work with people in an active way. Talking and planning together. You could probably be a leader in a group.

Parent: Well, maybe you're right.

Consultant: Of course, I don't want to rush you. You have to decide for yourself if you think that we can work together.

Parent: Well, why not? You seem like an honest guy.

"Isn't This Going too Far?" We are dealing with important ethical issues here. How far should one go to persuade parents (or anyone) that they should make an effort to change and that you are the one who may be able to help them to change, especially if they seem not to want to change or to work with you? Were we dealing with an individual, the problem would be easier to solve. One might say:

> Okay, you have come to me and I have told you what I will try to do for and with you. So, if you do not want me to try to help you, that is entirely up to you.

In this case, however, a third party is involved, namely, the child. And the child is supposed to be the ultimate recipient of what you have to offer. Indeed, the child will bear the consequences of either choice the parents make (to work with you or not). To whatever extent possible, then, the child should have a voice in the parents' choice, possibly by participating in the interviews. But if the child is so physically or behaviorally handicapped that the child, in effect or in reality, has no voice, then, it seems to me the interviewer is obligated to give voice to the child and to the child's interests. Clearly, the parents have a right not to be emotionally bludgeoned into working with you, but the parents are not and will not be the only ones to experience the unpleasant consequences of their child's problem behaviors and inadequacies.

Simply stated, since more and more work shows that educational methods, if humanely and properly used, can produce substantial and beneficial changes in children with learning and behavior problems, the right not to change the way one interacts with one's children loses its legitimacy. A verbal effort to convince parents of the need to change and to help in educating their children does not seem to be going too far in view of the consequences for themselves and their child if the effort is not made.

Step 5: Nailing Down the Issue of Commitment

At this point, you have done just about everything anyone can do ethically to interest parents in what you have to offer, establish yourself as a person with whom it would be beneficial and enjoyable to work, and strengthen readiness to change. Thus, it is time to (1) set the occasion for specific responses indicating the parents' degree of commitment or readiness; (2) decide if a working relationship should be formalized at this time; and (3) if a relationship should be formalized, decide what kind of program best suits the parents' readiness (partial or comprehensive program).

Some parents may have indicated all along that they are anxious to start. They say that they will try anything. They already want to learn how to change certain behaviors, and want to know when the program starts. Such parents are likely to have a great deal of energy and independence, and to be in the "top one-third" (for whom a little information and coaching go a long way).

Nevertheless, ask parents certain questions before you formalize a working relationship. For example:

> Well, now that you know what the program is all about, do you think that it would be of benefit to you?
>
> Are you ready to give it the old college try?
>
> If you feel that you want to start the program, we can go on to the next step. Are you ready?
>
> You have expressed a strong interest in starting the program, but, tell me, is there anything you can think of that might keep you from coming to meetings or from conducting home educational programs? And what could you do about it? Is there anything that we can do to help you over the rough spots?

If your discussions have indicated that the parents are "ready" in terms of the nine components of readiness to change, and if the parents are emphatic that nothing will prevent them from coming to meetings or from working with their child, that they will take steps to reschedule certain activities, and that only illness would stop them for a short time, then formalize the working relationship, either during the first interview or during the next interview.

On the other hand, if the parents had expressed many hesitations (which you were able to overcome, but with a lot of effort or time), it is not a good idea to formalize a working relationship at this time. Instead, tell the parents that you do not want them to rush into something that they are not completely sure about. Tell them that you would like them to take a few days to think it over. Then if they call or write saying that they want to work with you, another interview can be scheduled and a working relationship can be formalized. During the cooling-off period, in other words, the parents will either find reasons why they can and should work with you or why they cannot. Again, leave it up to them to make the commitment response.

Finally, as to the comprehensiveness of the program, if parents are very committed to working with you but have unavoidable conflicts, such as a job or other important activities, or if they still have hesitations, you can try to interest them in participating in a more limited way, gradually increasing the comprehensiveness of the Program as they experience success. For example, you can ask if they would like to:

1. Sit in on a meeting of an ongoing Program.
2. Read one or two chapters of *Educating Children With Learning and Behavior Problems* and do short teaching assignments relevant to certain behavioral inadequacies or problem behaviors.
3. Keep in phone contact with you so that you can give them valuable suggestions on how to work with their child, making sure that further suggestions are contingent upon their calling you periodically and keeping data.
4. Make one or two minor changes in the ways they interact with their child (ways that will produce rapid change); for example, reinforcing spontaneous eye contact, timing out the child each time the child throws a tantrum, or requiring the child to put his plate on the table before he gets to eat).
5. Count one or two behaviors (as the first step of a behavioral analysis), which may lead them to ask you how to change the behaviors they have been counting (which leads back to any of the above).

The availability of partial participation may result in an initial commitment from many parents. If so, offer to help them with one of the above simple tasks for the next week. If the parents are enthusiastically praised as they do these tasks over a period of a few weeks, and if they seem more confident and more interested in home teaching, you can again offer to work with them in a more comprehensive Program.

In sum, the above method is designed to shape parents into doing more and more by first finding out what little bit they are willing to do; helping them to do that; reinforcing them for their efforts and success; and then encouraging them to do still more (that is, other items on the above list) until, perhaps, they are prepared to work in the full Program.

If parents remain uninterested in participating in any way, the interview can be ended. However, do not end it in such a way as to imply that: 1) you feel that the parents have failed you, their child, or themselves, 2) you are no longer interested in working with them, or 3) all channels of contact between yourself and the family are now effectively closed. Instead, one last way of slowly shaping some parents' readiness is to provide them with periodic, nonthreatening, and noncontingent expressions of your interest in their welfare. For example, you can say that you are interested in the welfare of themselves and their child, and that you would like to be able to phone them now and again. If they indicate that it is alright for you to phone them, you can do so, perhaps every few weeks, to find out "how things are going," give simple suggestions for handling "things" around the house, provide emotional support, and chat. To the extent that you become a continual and nonthreatening source of support, indicating your noncontingent caring, the parents may become more willing to re-open the possibility of working with you. If so, you might offer them a partial Program, leading perhaps to a more comprehensive one.

Step 6: Both Spouses, Partners, or a Substitute

The last issue to cover in the Initial Interview(s) is the involvement of both spouses or partners. It is important that both partners participate because the tasks involved in conducting a home educational program are new to most parents and, consequently, may seem like much work. In addition, people usually need another person to give them objective feedback and emotional support, as well as to share the tasks of carrying out the home programs and other household and child-rearing tasks.

Some fathers already help the wife and mother a great deal. Others say that they are willing to become involved—and mean it. Others merely give lip service when the issue of father's involvement is raised. And still others hesitate to give much of a commitment, if any, because: they have become passive or withdrawn over the years (as noted in Chapter 2) or they are strong believers in (or at least live) the notion that child rearing is the wife's job.

In either case, try to convince fathers that their child needs their help. Empathize with the frustration they have experienced over the years when they tried to help or get close to their child, only to feel ineffective or rejected. Stress that the Program is likely to help them, at last, to be effective and that there can be nothing more "manly" than producing beneficial change in their child. Indeed, argue that the skills that they will acquire for changing behavior may make them even more manly since they will be acquiring tools for changing themselves and part of the world around them (not only their child but schools and service delivery systems).

To confirm the necessity and manliness of the father's participating, have a father with whom you have worked before meet with or call the hesitant father to discuss his own initial reservations and present feelings.

If a father simply refuses to give complete commitment (that is, to participate in the full Program), try to at least obtain a commitment to participate (help) in some way. For instance, to: perform certain household tasks; take care of the other children while the wife is working with the one child; coach the wife; read the materials; give the wife emotional support; take data; call you (or allow you to call him) at specified times to discuss problems and progress; provide special reinforcement to the wife (nights out, for example).

It may even be possible to shape more complete participation as the father is reinforced (by the wife, other fathers, and yourself) for performing the simpler tasks noted above.

If the father or partner will not participate in any way (or drops out later), or if you are working with a single-parent family, have the participating parent arrange for one or more other persons to help, either complete co-participation or performance of some tasks mentioned above. For example, the participating parents might enlist cooperation from a close friend, neighbor, relative, or older sibling of the child. Appendix 7 discusses methods for working with the single-parent family.

V. TASK 3: FORMALIZING THE WORKING RELATIONSHIP

This task establishes a businesslike orientation in your work with a family. Specifically, before a Program starts: 1. The parents must know just what they are expected to do during the course of the Program and what you, in turn, will be doing (that is, mutual goals, responsibilities, and expectations must be established). 2. The parents' right to privacy and to leave the Program are recognized and insured. 3. An objective method for assessing each party's performance of agreed-upon tasks is made available (and perhaps a method of providing consequences for performing or failing to perform agreed-upon tasks). 4. All of the above are agreed upon. 5. If agreeable, all of the above are put in writing.

Although a verbal agreement is satisfactory in many cases, the major vehicle we have used to establish and maintain a businesslike orientation and businesslike behavior is a written Program Contract (Appendix 3).

The contract in Appendix 3 was used in Programs I conducted with co-workers.*

Explaining the Contract to the Parents

The parents may wonder why a written Program Contract is suggested. Therefore, its purpose must be explained and many of its terms must be worked out with the parents.

Discuss with parents how a written Contract (combined with consequences for performance) both starts the relationship on a businesslike footing and makes it possible to maintain businesslike behavior (productive participation) since "it is

*Greg Hudson, Virginia Hudson, John Peters, Shelley Leavitt, Joel Vatter, Dr. Barbara Bruno-Golden, Barbara Cutler, Agnes Myles and Martin Sawzin. There can be many variations of the Contract, depending on the kinds of consequences that will be delivered contingent upon performance. The point is that any Program Contract that you and the parents write should cover as many details of the Program as possible.

all there in black and white." That is, the Contract can be referred to if questions later arise about responsibilities and consequences.

The parents can be informed that, no matter how much they are gratified by behavior change in their children, such change is not always going to be enough to maintain their hard work, nor is change in their behaviors enough to keep consultants motivated at all times (for example, to prepare and conduct the best meetings possible). The reason is the schedule and quality of reinforcement (Kozloff, 1973). That is, early in a Program, consultants are teaching parents simple but important skills which the parents are likely to learn quickly. Similarly, in early home teaching programs, parents may be working to change easy behaviors, such as cooperation, which they perceive to be important.

Later in the Program, however, when the parents are trying to teach hard behaviors to their children (such as reading), the rate of change in their children is likely to slow down temporarily. Indeed, as their Program progresses, the parents may have to work even harder and longer to produce change in behaviors they may see as less important. And, from the consultant's point of view, teaching parents how to strengthen cooperation is generally easier than teaching them how to teach their child to read.

For both parties, then, the probability and quality of reinforcement (in the form of behavior change in the other with whom they are working) may decrease. Consequently, the consultants' teaching behaviors (with parents) and the parents' teaching behaviors (with their children) may begin to weaken. Clearly, alternative sources of reinforcement are needed to keep consultants and parents working until the next short-term behavioral goal is reached.

Would Social Reinforcement Between Parents and Consultants be Enough?

The answer is "maybe." Although parents and consultants praise each other, the real issue is behavior change. And if behaviors are not changing fast enough, social reinforcement in a group or between parents and consultant may lose its value. The mutual praise may become a ritual. For instance:

Consultant: How did the program go this week?

Parent: Fine. Just fine.

Consultant: (To himself.) Baloney.

And as praise becomes ritualized (just words said at the expected time), the game of "Everything's just hunky-dory" may begin, meaning that objectivity about progress and the quality of everyone's effort begins to deteriorate.

One solution is the Program Contract, which can specify various additional positive reinforcers (such as money, baby-sitting time, respite care) which can be earned contingent upon each party living up to his or her agreed-upon responsibilities.

Note that the consequences for the parents, as specified in the Contract, are not made contingent upon the parents actually changing the child, but upon their properly working at the task. Similarly, if reinforcement is arranged for the consultant, it is not made contingent solely upon change in the parents or child, but upon the consultant's engaging in proper, agreed-upon parent-instructing behaviors.

This may sound strange—reinforcing people for proper effort(that is, "on-task behaviors"), rather than for producing change in the people with whom they are working. The reasons, however, are simple:

1. Since behaviors change at different rates, if parents, for example, are reinforced only when each target behavior of their child has changed sufficiently, the flow of reinforcement to them will be uneven. Reinforcing them for working at producing change, however, ties the reinforcement more closely to their own behavior (namely, good teaching).

2. It often takes several tries before the right combination of methods (either for teaching a parent or a child) is found. If reinforcement depends solely on behavior change itself, the consultant or parent would not be reinforced until they had hit upon the right set of methods. This would mean that all of their previous tries would go unreinforced. While they might learn something through their unsuccessful tries, they might give up before hitting the right combination of methods.

3. Most important, a major philosophical position in the Program is that change takes care of itself. Behavior change is described by various laws. If the right conditions are in effect, behavior changes automatically. So, all the parents and consultants have to do through their behavior is try to insure that the right conditions are in effect. And that is the behavior for which they should be reinforced.

Examples of Contract-Credit Systems That Can be Built Into the Program Contract

There are at least three variations of a contract-credit system by which consequences can be provided to participants, based on their performance from week to week. In fact, parents are given a choice (e.g., show them a "Credits Earned" sheet like the one in Appendix 4).

Option 1: Positive Reinforcement. Here, the parents (and perhaps even consultants) earn various positive reinforcers if or when they accumulate enough credits earned for satisfactorily performing agreed-upon tasks. For example:

1. Baby-sitting services (with sitters coming from other families, from service organizations, junior high and high schools, or from colleges).

2. Extra tutoring for the child or siblings (again from the above sources).

3. College credit or tuition for adult education courses.

4. Passes to movies, plays, restaurants, or amusement parks, perhaps paid from a "pool" established by the families and consultants at the start.

5. Respite care arranged with group homes, clinics, other facilities in the area, or with other families from past and present Programs.

6. Special items, such as personalized tee shirts, coffee mugs, books, magazine subscriptions.

7. Clothing and food (while food and clothing have been used as reinforcers in behavioral programs, there are, I think, important economic, political, and moral implications here. Such reinforcers might be powerful to "low income" (a euphemism for "poor") families. It is not clear, however, that poor families should have to educate their "special child" in order to earn what is in such abundance in this society and that the consultant—or anyone—should be in a position to control such reinforcers.

8. Extra home visits provided, for example, by another parent in the Program or by a highly skilled parent from a past Program.

In this option, the more valuable a backup positive reinforcer is to a participant, the more credits it costs. Thus, a person might choose to earn relatively inexpensive backup reinforcers after each week or meeting, or save credits so as to acquire a more expensive reinforcer later. This option also means that consultants and parents must arrange, perhaps with outside agencies or groups, to acquire the backup reinforcers—for example, high schools and respite care facilities. Parents themselves might act as a group to make such arrangements. For instance, they can work to organize a baby-sitting pool or a tutoring program. Indeed, by giving their group a name, they might acquire passes to movies, baseball games, and other facilities.

Option 2: Deposit. A participant deposits a certain amount of money to a group bank or with a consultant (Kovitz, 1976). A portion of the deposit is returned each meeting or when a certain number of credits has been earned.

Option 3: Negative Reinforcement. This option is adapted from Programs conducted by Dr. Leopold Walder (1968) and has been used in several Programs conducted by me and my staff. In this option, once the working relationship has been formalized, each family (and perhaps each consultant) writes three certified checks or money orders to organizations that they do not like. The checks are written in increasing amounts; for example, ten ten-thousandths; fifteen ten-thousandths; and twenty-five ten-thousandths of the annual income. Of course, the percentages could be more or less depending on the relative income of participants, since twenty-five dollars is worth a lot more to a person whose annual income is six thousand dollars than it is to a person whose annual income is thirty thousand dollars.

Every week, each family and each consultant has to earn a minimum number of points or credits for having fulfilled the terms of the original Program Contract (for example, coming to the meeting) and to the terms of a Weekly Contract written at the end of the previous meeting (for example, carrying out a specific teaching program in the home). Take a look at the "Credits Earned" sheet in Appendix 4.

Notice that each family can earn a maximum of 18 credits each week. The most important behaviors are worth the most credits. And the minimum needed to avoid a check being sent is 16 credits. Similarly, each consultant can earn 8 credits per week, with the most important behaviors worth the most credits, and the minimum needed being 7.

This means that each participant has some leeway. But if even two of the behaviors are not performed (for example, one parent misses the meeting and the other is late), a check would be mailed. Of course, the minimum number of credits required can be less.

Also notice that credits do not add up from week to week. When a participant comes to a meeting, he or she begins again at zero and starts to earn credits for coming to the meeting, being on time, participating, and so on.

Checks are mailed starting with the one written for the smallest amount. Each time a check is sent, the participant must replace it with one written in the largest value of the three (that is, twenty-five ten-thousandths). If a participant drops out, all checks are sent. Remaining checks are returned at the end of the program.

How the Contract-Credit Systems Work During a Program

Once the Program has started, one family (or parent) can be responsible for keeping track of credits earned by the consultant(s), and one consultant keeps track of credits earned by parents. Procedurally, the "credit-checkers" (at the start of each group meeting) go around the room with a "Credits-Earned" sheet (like the one in Appendix 4) for each person (or family) whom they are checking. The parent who is checking on a consultant, for example, marks the sheet if the consultant is on time. Then the checker turns to the family with whom the consultant was supposed to make a home visit during the week, and asks if the consultant made the home visit, was on time, and had performed other agreed-upon tasks (as written on a Weekly Contract, by the family and consultant at the last meeting).

If participants have earned enough credits, they either earn backup reinforcers (e.g., five hours of baby-sitting over the weekend), earn part of their deposit (which might be returned at that time), or prevent one of their checks or money orders from being mailed. If a participant or family has not earned enough credits the credit-checker informs them of it, indicates why credits were not earned, and, if Option 3 is being used, tells the participant that a check will be mailed.

Variations

Of course, there are a number of variations on each of the above contract-credit systems, which you may want to try depending on the situation. Moreover, different families in a group or individual Program may want to use different options. For example, one family in a group might want the threat of a check being mailed to ''keep us on our toes,'' whereas another family might want to earn backup positive reinforcers. One family may choose to earn the same backup reinforcer week after week; another may choose to switch reinforcers from time to time. Indeed, one parent in a family might want one type of option (or reinforcer) while the other may want a different one. Therefore, in the Program Contract, if possible, specify:

1. The contract-credit option chosen by the parents.
2. Alternative reinforcers that are requested and will be made available (as in Option 1).
3. The number of credits that must be earned in order to acquire various reinforcers or to prevent a check from being mailed.

Note that the same Credits-Earned sheet found in Appendix 4 can be used no matter which option a family chooses.

Which Option is best? Frankly, I do not know the answer. While I sometimes used the third option (negative reinforcement), I have no evidence that the method is essential in strengthening and maintaining performance. It may be that the threat of a check's being mailed merely helps to establish and maintain a businesslike orientation. Yet, the written Program Contract alone might produce the same orientation. Moreover, not only might participants' behaviors quickly deteriorate once the negative reinforcement contingencies are terminated (at the end of the Program), but the loss of certified checks or money orders may be too much for some families to bear and may be irrelevant to persons who can afford it. The same might be true of the deposit option.

In sum, I prefer to use a written Program Contract (which may be important in itself) and the positive reinforcement option because it:

1. Offers a variety of reinforcers.
2. Provides parents with reinforcers which, themselves, constitute important inputs to the family system (e.g., respite, extra coaching).

3. Is more likely to facilitate the development of networks of backup support (e.g., families exchanging respite care and home visits) and thus help parents to maintain home programs.
4. Is simply more in keeping with the overall philosophy of the Program.

Signing the Contract

After explaining the Program Contract to the parents, discussing the various contract-credit options (if you are going to use one), letting them choose one (or more), and answering any remaining questions, the Program Contract is signed. The parents keep one copy and the consultant keeps another. The consultant's copy is then filed in a special folder for the family.

If certified checks, money orders, or cash are to be used (as in Options 2 and 3), ask the parents to obtain their checks. Any further contacts with the family (such as Assessment Interviews or Baseline Observations) are contingent upon their calling or writing to indicate that they have the checks ready. On the other hand, if Option 1 is to be used, the consultants and parents begin to arrange to acquire the backup reinforcers.

If the working relationship is formalized at the end of an Initial Interview, an Assessment Interview can be scheduled. If the working relationship is formalized at the beginning of an additional Initial Interview (because the first Initial Interview took so long), begin the more formal assessment during the same interivew.

Developing a Contract-Credit System During the Program

Instead of presenting parents with ready-made contract-credit systems, parents can develop their own system after the Program has started. For example, in a group Program, parents and consultants can discuss the need for, plan, and institute a contract-credit system as one of the first projects.

VI. TASK 4: ASSESSMENT REGARDING ITEMS IMPORTANT FOR CONDUCTING, PERSISTING AT, AND MAINTAINING A GOOD HOME EDUCATIONAL PROGRAM

By this time, you have assessed and strengthened the parents' readiness to change using the Assessment and Programming Guide (APG), and formalized a working relationship through the Program Contract. Now, in order to plan the activities for the Program stage, describe the family with regard to the items of behavior, attitude, and relationship having a bearing on success in conducting, persisting at, and maintaining a good home educational program. We are still talking about an initial assessment. During the Program itself, however, continue to assess the family on all APG items (even the readiness to change items because problems can arise) so as to keep track of progress and problems.

Just as it did with ''awareness of you and of what the Program has to offer'' (AGP Item 1) and ''readiness to change'' (Items 2 through 10), the APG lists the behaviors, attitudes, and relationships that seem to be important for success at conducting, persisting at, and maintaining a good home program, as well as potential problems in the parents learning or using the important items (11 through 27).

''How Do I Assess the Family on the Behaviors and Relationships Needed to Conduct, Persist at, and Maintain a Good Home Program.'' The family is assessed by: 1) Assessment Interview(s) and 2) direct Baseline Observations in the home and, if possible, in the child's school (or other educational/treatment setting). The Interview Schedule at the end of this chapter suggests questions to ask of and discuss with parents regarding many items important for success during the Program stage. In addition, direct Baseline Observations provide more detailed information on a number of items, some which cannot be sampled easily by interviews.

''But, Surely Not Everything Can Be Learned During Assessment Interviews and a Few Baseline Observations.'' That is correct. However, in the first place, you are not trying to reproduce the family's past and present circumstances. You are trying to obtain a sample of behaviors and relationships that are important for success. Second, it is not necessary to learn everything, even if you could. Assessment helps in making decisions about what to do in the Program (for example, what methods to use to teach the parents certain skills). Since the assessment indicates if the family needs even a little help on certain items, you will know that you must plan to work on those items during the Program. The idea is to err on the side of caution.

For example, cooperation between spouses or partners (Item 19) is important for success. If parents in a certain family were at each others' throats all the time, naturally you would plan to work on cooperation during the Program. But even if you saw only a little marital conflict, either because you were not in the home long enough or because there was little conflict, you would still plan to work on cooperation.

Finally, during the Program itself, you can obtain more of the detailed information you could not get during Assessment Interviews and Baseline Observations. For example, after working with a family for a while, problems (as well as strengths) that you simply did not see will become evident.

Tips on Planning and Conducting the Assessment

1. Arrange for the Assessment Interview(s) in the same way that you arranged for the Initial Interviews. This is described near the beginning of Section IV above.

2. Complete the Assessment Interview(s) and Baseline Observations (may take about a week). Conduct the first Assessment Interview by itself. That is, schedule the first Baseline Observation for a later date, especially if the Assessment Interview is to be conducted in the home. (You don't want to be intruding on the family much at this point.) If additional Assessment Interviews are needed to complete the Interview Schedule, you can complete it the same day of a later Baseline Observation session.

3. If additional information is to be obtained, such as the results of past tests the child has been given or reports from past programs in which the child was enrolled, arrange with the family to obtain it if they consent. Try to obtain such additional information before the Program starts, so that it can be used in planning.

4. Before conducting the first Assessment Interview, any certified checks or money orders that were to be part of the contractual working relationship should be ready.

Assessment Interview(s)

Assessment Interviews are conducted much like the Initial Interviews. You ask parents questions that allow you to: 1) sample important behaviors, attitudes, and relationships and 2) begin to change the parents' way of looking at and thinking about their behaviors, attitudes, and relationships. Questions can come from the "Interview Schedule" at the end of this chapter.

The Interview Schedule. This schedule consists of questions to ask parents. Some are general. That is, they set the stage for the parents to talk about a broad topic in their lives, such as efforts to find help. Thus, general questions give both the interviewer and the parents leeway—to elaborate upon, clarify, interpret (or reinterpret) an experience, to see how one experience (such as "giving in" to disruptive behavior) is connected to, perhaps caused by, other aspects of family life (for example, hypervigilance and tension).

Other questions are specific. That is, the interviewer is interested in learning about an aspect of family life that is important in itself and relevant to a particular APG item, such as the availability of people who can offer the parents backup support (Item 25).

The questions in the Schedule are organized into topic areas, which represent the different stages in the sequence of career experiences of families of children with learning and behavior problems. You might glance at Figure 2–1, Chapter 2, to refresh your memory of the career sequence.

Not only are the questions organized into topic areas, but the Interview Schedule presents the topic areas in the same sequence as they are arranged in Figure 2–1. The result of asking questions in that order is hopefully that both the parents and the interviewer will develop a meaningful, coherent, and comprehensive picture of what the family has been through and what the family situation is like now. In other words, although the interviewer is seeking information to use in planning and conducting a Program, an extremely important by-product of the Assessment Interview(s) may be that the parents begin to make sense out of what they have been through and understand their specific beliefs (such as "I am not competent"), behavior patterns (such as structured exchanges with each other and with their children), and feelings (such as anxiety) in terms of the overall picture. To the extent that the parents come to see and understand their career, they may be able to change it, not as passive recipients of information but as agents.

An understanding of their career may help parents to become agents of change because: (1) developing an understanding of the factors that have shaped their lives is itself an active process, (2) understanding their career may at the least show parents that they are survivors (which imputes a certain strength), and (3) by developing an understanding of their career with the help of the interviewer-consultant, the consultant and parents become partners in the process of change.

Since the purpose of assessment, at this point, is to help plan and conduct a Program tailored to the needs and strengths of the family, the questions on the Interview Schedule are related to the items on the Assessment and Programming Guide (APG) in Appendix 1. Most of the numbered questions are accompanied by additional questions (probes) which help to "flesh out" the parents' answers.

Now turn to the end of this chapter and read the Interview Schedule.

Tips on Using the Interview Schedule.

1. Make copies of the Interview Schedule for use in your work. Add important questions, subtract questions that you feel are not important or that are covered in other sections of the Schedule and reword those that are not as clear or phrased as well as you would like them to be.
2. In making copies of the Interview Schedule, leave space under each question to take notes.
3. The interviewer takes notes on: (a) parents' answers to the interview questions; (b) parents' behavior during the interview(s) (for example, exchanges between the parents; personal characteristics, such as tenseness, calmness, effectiveness of communication; and the quality of the interviewer-parent

relationship, such as openness or defensiveness, apparent honesty, communication games); and (c) parents' statements of goals regarding the Program, which can be written in Section G of the Interview Schedule.

4. Use the Assessment Interviews (as well as Baseline Observations) as an opportunity to begin changing behaviors of the parents. The Assessment Interviews (like the Initial Interviews) give you a chance to shape certain behaviors both by the way you respond to answers and by the questions you ask. As in the Initial Interviews:

a. Present yourself as warm, open, and friendly, but businesslike.

b. Reinforce the parents for their efforts, correct use of basic teaching methods, patterns of cooperation, correct behavioral analyses of various behaviors and exchanges in the family—in other words, for any and all behaviors, relationships, and ways of looking at and analyzing their situation that are important to success.

c. Help the parents begin to understand various family events and processes, indeed the whole career, in behavioral terms. For example, if the parents say that, over the years, they have become more and more depressed, help them to see their "depression" as a result, possibly, of their child's increasing learning and behavior problems (relative to the child's age), their fearful recognition of fewer chances of finding outside help, and a vicious cycle of the parents gratifying one another less and less often.

d. Without lecturing or trying to cover too much, help the parents see (pinpoint) some behaviors and relationships that need to be changed, and how. For example, when the parents are describing some of their ways of responding to problem behaviors, it may be obvious that they are responding in a counterproductive way (that is, a counterproductive, structured exchange). In a nonthreatening way, help them to see, in behavioral terms, why the exchange is counterproductive and how they might change their behavior. Or, if the parents indicate that one of the couple does most of the work with the child, point out, as you did during the Initial Interview, that they may have to learn to work together more often if they are to be successful. Shaping behavior during Assessment Interviews may sound unscientific. Perhaps it is. The choice is yours. If you simply ask questions and record answers, you will have a purer Pre-Program stage with which to compare the results of the Program stage. However, it is probably impossible to avoid shaping some behaviors, anyway, by the questions alone, the slightest eye contacts, other body movements as the parents are talking, and even your silence. In addition, as far as I am concerned, not to start helping parents would be an unnecessary waste of perfect opportunities. Besides, if you had to help the parents on certain behaviors and relationships during the Assessment Interviews, that, in itself, would be data.

e. For purposes of keeping down the interview time, try to have parents stick to the questions at hand, but in a nice way. For example, "I think we are getting off the subject. Now, about your method for handling tantrums. . . ."

5. Stop the interview before the parents are fatigued (no more than an hour or so), and take a break in the middle. At the end of the interview, you can engage in small talk. Then, the first Baseline Observation, or an additional Assessment Interview, can be scheduled.
6. At the end of the Assessment Interview(s), summarize the notes that you made. To do this, use the same copy of the APG that was used when you assessed readiness to change. Simply transfer the information from the Interview Schedule to the APG, either by underlining relevant words or phrases on the items or by making notes in the spaces provided under the items of the APG. Remember, circle the number of any item for which the parents need help, even if they have "passed" some components.

For example, several questions on the Interview Schedule concern marital relations. Parents' answers to these and other questions are relevant to APG Item 19: cooperation. Thus, when summarizing the parents' answers to the Interview Schedule questions that have a bearing on marital cooperation, underline words or sentences on APG Item 19 that represent the parents' responses, or make notes in the spaces provided. More specifically, during the interview the mother might make statements such as:

> Bill always gets up—even in the middle of the night—to handle our son when our son goes on the rampage. He's real helpful that way. He even comes home from work to help me handle our son.

Such a statement corresponds to component "e" for APG item 19: "share household tasks, such as childrearing and housekeeping." Therefore, you can either underline "share household tasks, such as child-rearing . . .," or write what the mother said in the spaces under that item. Note that even though the parents might fare well on this item, they may need work on some components of it. If so, circle the number of the item.

Again, the idea is to transfer the information gained from parents' answers to questions on the Interview Schedule to the relevant items on the APG.

After the first Assessment Interview, schedule the first Baseline Observation. Again, if a second Assessment Interview is needed to complete the Interview Schedule, you can conduct a Baseline Observation session and an interview on the same day.

Using the Interview Schedule as a Questionnaire. There are clear advantages and disadvantages in both interviews and questionnaires. During interviews, you can ask probe questions, begin the behavior change process, and observe the interviewee's verbal and nonverbal behavior. However, the interviewee may be: uncomfortable, may take more time than he wishes to give that day, and may think of additional points after the interview. Therefore, in some Programs we give the Interview Schedule (with reworded probes) to parents for use as a questionnaire. They work on it together or separately at their convenience. In some cases, we seem to obtain much more detailed information. We collect the Interview Schedule-questionnaire during Baseline Observations and make a copy for the parents.

Baseline Observations in the Home and, if Possible, in the Child's School

We conduct at least three Baseline Observation sessions with a family. At least two families can be observed in the home per day by one person; each session lasts about two hours.

Which Is Better? Home or School Observations? The answer depends on where the parents will be performing the behaviors they learn in the Program. Most children live with their parents. Naturally, then, you should observe interaction in the home. If parents will also be working in classrooms, it would be a good idea to observe them there, too. However, if parents will be working with their children at home, and if it has to be a choice between Baseline Observations in the home or in the classroom, conduct Baseline Observations in the home because the stimuli in the classroom, such as lighting, sound, materials, and furniture, can be controlled. For purposes of research, that is fine. But, if the thrust of your work with a family is to change the ways the parents interact with each other and with their children in the home, such control (and the fact that the classroom setting is different from the home setting) means that parents and children may act differently in the classroom then they do in the home. They may look good in the classroom (especially if you are observing them working with another child) but may actually need much help in the home, or vice versa. Finally, even if you will be teaching parents to work in a classroom setting (e.g., as aides), you need to help them generalize their skills to the home (assuming that their child is at home). Again, then, observe in the home to see if or to what extent their behaviors have generalized.

Purposes of Baseline Observations.

1. Depending on observer-parent interaction during and after sessions, the Baseline Observations can be used to continue to build the parents' confidence in themselves, in the future, and in the consultants who will be working with them.

2. The Baseline Observations can be used to check the validity of what the parents said during the Assessment Interviews. For example, during the Assessment Interviews, the parents might have said that they hardly ever give in to their child when their child demands things by whining, pushing or pulling on them, or by throwing tantrums. The Baseline Observations may show, however, that the parents, perhaps without recognizing it at all, give in (reinforce such behaviors) almost all of the time. In other words, Baseline Observations may provide a more accurate picture of what is going on in the home.

3. Some behaviors and relationships cannot be sampled well, if at all, during Assessment Interviews, but can be sampled during Baseline Observations. For example, the parents' description of how they try to teach certain appropriate behaviors may simply leave out certain items of "basic teaching methods," such as how the parents reinforce or prompt. By giving the parents concrete opportunities to try to teach certain behaviors, you can observe and assess the parents on basic teaching methods (Item 18).

4. In general, the Baseline Observations allow you to pinpoint behaviors (of parents, the child with learning and behavior problems, siblings, and others) and exchange relationships (between parents, between parents and children and, possibly, between family members and others) that represent strengths to be built upon or that represent weaknesses to be corrected during the Program.

The next few pages suggest what and how to observe and record.

Videotape. Although assessment information can be collected well with pencil and paper, videotaping is also an excellent method. In addition, videotapes can be used for instructional purposes during the Program, as well as for Program evaluation. Portable videotape equipment is easy to use and relatively inexpensive. Of course, the parents must give permission beforehand. Thus, it is well to explain the benefits of videotaping before and during the time you are formalizing the relationship with parents who have given consent but seem distressed. Introduce taping slowly, perhaps by teaching them to tape you and later by your taping something rather innocuous in the home.

Observing three kinds of situations. They are presented starting with the most important. All three, however, can be observed either during the same observation session or during different sessions.

1. Teaching Sessions. The observation (and, if possible, videotaping) of teaching sessions is important. Before the series of observations starts (for example, at the end of the prior Assessment Interview), the observer discusses with the parents the child's performance in various skill areas to determine how much skill the child has with Learning Readiness; Looking, Listening, and Moving

(Motor) skills; Motor Imitation; Verbal Imitation; Functional Speech; and Chores and Self-Help skills. The different skill areas and the target behaviors in them are described in Chapter 4 and Appendix 2 of *Educating Children With Learning and Behavior Problems*. In addition it may be useful to have various specialists (e.g., speech, language, physical and occupational therapists) suggest behaviors to assess at this time. Thus, when going to the home (or classroom) to observe and/or videotape teaching sessions, the observer has a standard set of tasks for the parents to give their child in each of the skill areas. All of the tasks might be written on a piece of paper or on a 3 × 5 card, one card per skill area.

For example, to assess the child on Learning Readiness (and the parents' efforts to teach it), the 3 × 5 card might list five to ten simple cooperation tasks for the parents to ask the child to do; for instance, turning on a light or picking up a sock from the floor. In addition, the card might specify that the parents try to get the child to make eye contact with them or to sit down, and remain seated for several minutes.

To assess Looking, Listening and Moving (Motor) skills, the observer might bring to the home (or have available in the classroom) three or four puzzles (a few of which the child has never worked before) and several other Small Motor tasks, such as beads to string or blocks to stack (or these should be provided by the parents). In addition, the 3 × 5 card might list five or six Large Motor tasks for the parents to try to teach the child or have the child perform (e.g., raising both arms over the head, rolling a ball).

To assess Motor Imitation, the card should list a number of small motor, large motor, mouth position, and object placement models for the child to imitate. To assess Verbal Imitation, the 3 × 5 card might list a number of sounds, syllables, words, phrases, and sentences for the child to imitate. Naturally, if it is known that the child is nearly mute, there is no need to have the parents try to have the child imitate sentences. Thus, a general rule to follow in selecting tasks is: Select tasks that include those which the child can already perform and some which are slightly beyond the child. For example, if the child can imitate only some isolated sounds (''Ah,'' ''M''), the list should include those sounds the child can imitate, some which the child does not imitate, and a few simple syllables composed of sounds that the child can imitate (''Mah'').

To assess Functional Speech, the card might list various objects to name or colors to identify. The objects and colors can be obtained from the parents (for example, spoons, forks, knives, cups, types of food, articles of clothing, or pictures) or can be brought by the observer. Of course, the more skilled the child, the higher the level of language which should be assessed. Finally, to assess Chores and Self-Help skills, the card should list chores and self-help skills for the parents to give the child.

Here is what one of the 3 x 5 cards might look like

MOTOR IMITATION—Blake Family			
Large Motor	Small Motor	Mouth Positions	Object Placements
Stand up Raise arms Jump	Pat head Pat tummy Clap hands	Open mouth Close mouth Stick out tongue	Stack 3 blocks Roll ball Fold paper in half

At least three of the skill areas can be sampled at each session. Give the parents three or more skill area cards and let each parent work on several skill areas, 5 to 10 minutes for each card. Then switch to a different parent and to different skill area cards. In this way, in about three sessions, all skill areas are sampled several times and each parent has had the chance to work on almost every skill area several times. It is also helpful to have both parents work together with the child (e.g., on a Self-Help task) for part of one or two sessions to assess patterns of interaction between the parents.

Before you begin the teaching sessions, make a schedule of skill areas and parents, such as the one below.

Day 1.	Mr. Jones:	Learning Readiness (eye contact on request, cooperation tasks); Small Motor; Motor Imitation.
	Mrs. Jones:	Chores and Self-Help; Verbal Imitation; Functional Speech.
Day 2.	Mrs. Jones:	Small Motor; Learning Readiness; Motor Imitation.
	Mr. Jones:	Functional Speech; Verbal Imitation.
	Both Parents:	Chores and Self-Help.
Day 3.	Mr. Jones:	Motor Imitation; Verbal Imitation; Learning Readiness.
	Mrs. Jones:	Functional Speech; Chores and Self-Help.
	Both Parents:	Small Motor.

There are only a few instructions to give the parents regarding teaching sessions. Tell them that they are not being tested: "I just want to see how you go about trying to get Agnes to perform the tasks." Also tell them you "want to see how well Agnes performs the tasks or cooperates with instructions" and that they should "try and teach Agnes the way they usually do." Do not give them instructions on how to teach tasks, for that would distort the information you get on their teaching skills.

During sessions, do not give the parents specific feedback. For example, do not make comments, such as "That was good, the way you rewarded her." And, of course, do not criticize them or make suggestions as to what they should do instead. For example, if the child becomes disruptive, let the session continue for a short time to see how they handle it (unless, of course, the situation is dangerous). If the disruptions continue, you might end the session for that day. But be sure to record the conditions under which disruptive behavior occurred and what the parents did about it.

At the end of the session, you can comment to the parents on what you think their child needs to learn. In other words, start helping them to pinpoint target behaviors. Also, give lots of general praise on how hard they try, as well as an optimistic, but honest, appraisal of expected progress.

If videotape is being used, the person operating the camera, or a second observer, writes down on a 3 × 5 card the footage on the tapes for each skill area that the parents are working on. In this way, the information can be retrieved and the different portions of each tape can be shown at a later time. Whether or not videotape is used, the observer writes down:

1. Specific behaviors of the child that need to be changed (e.g., attention, cooperation, hand/eye coordination);
2. Teaching skills that parents need to learn (as listed on the "Guide" for Item 18);
3. Behaviors that the parents should no longer engage in with their child, such as paying attention to disruptive behavior;
4. Patterns of interaction between the parents to be maintained (e.g., praising one another) or to be changed (e.g., criticism).
5. Observations of other relevant items on the APG (e.g., household organization, parents' feeling-states, behavior of siblings).

These notes can later be summarized on the APG to help plan the Program for the parents and children.

2. Selected Short Subjects. This consists of observing or taping brief exchanges between parents or between parents and children and recording episodes that illustrate important principles of teaching or learning. That is, the camera is turned on (or the observer starts writing) when an interesting exchange begins.

Examples of episodes you might tape or write down are: 1) The child begins to whine and the parents, at first, ignore it, but the whining gets louder and louder, turning into a tantrum, at which point the parents go to the child and pick him up.

2) The child makes an effort to cooperate with a request and the parents reinforce the child. 3) The child is throwing a tantrum, and one parent blames the other parent for it (or, conversely, helps the other parent to tolerate and ignore it). "Selected shorts" can be recorded for about 10 minutes each session, before or after a teaching session.

The observer makes a note of each selected short subject that is being videotaped (that is, a brief description and the tape footage) and indicates the principles of learning or teaching which are illustrated. These portions of tape can later be used in meetings, especially early meetings, to present examples of the kinds of exchanges in the family which either need to be changed or which can be accentuated, and to give examples of principles of learning and teaching.

3. Free Interaction. This can be observed and recorded for 30 minutes during one or two Baseline Observations. This kind of recording shows what the child and the parents do when they are on their own. Just tell the parents to go about their business and not to pay any attention to the observer.

The observer stands in the corner of a room or around a corner of a doorway and simply writes down or tapes what is happening. If videotape is being used, either the person operating the camera or, better, a second observer, makes notes on important events, the footage being recorded, and the behaviors of the child or the parents (or specific exchanges) that may be of interest. For example, it might be noted that the parents pay attention to the child when the child is disruptive and fail to pay attention to the child when the child is quiet.

The videotapes of free interaction can later be used both for instruction during meetings (for example, to show parents the ways they interact with their child), or to point out possible changes that have occurred (by comparing a free interaction tape made during the baseline with one made toward the middle or end of the Program).

The weakness of free interaction recording, however, is that the sample of behavior is small and may be biased. Hence, you cannot legitimately compare observations for purposes of evaluation. Moreover, nothing much may happen (the child may watch TV for 30 minutes).

Pencil and Paper Data. If videotape equipment is not available, or if the parents have not given permission, a good substitute is to use paper and pencil to take data during the same three segments: free interaction, teaching sessions, and selected short subjects. During free interaction, the observer merely writes down as complete a description as possible of what is happening, noting the frequency and duration of appropriate and inappropriate behaviors of the child; for example, cooperation with requests, speech, episodes of playing, and episodes of tantrums. Moreover, the observer notes when the parents give the child requests to cooperate, when they try to "occasion" speech from the child, the frequency with which they prompt the child to respond, and the frequency with which they reinforce the child.

During teaching sessions, on the other hand, data can be taken on a recording sheet. It is best to make up your own recording sheet. Here is one way of doing it.

Each time the parents start working on a certain task, write it in a column on the left-hand side of the page. The tasks are those on the 3 × 5 cards. Then, regarding each task, record what the parents do to teach it, and what the child does in response. Thus, for each task, record the number of times the parents give the child an occasion to respond (''Here, put this piece in''), or prompt and reinforce the child. Also, for each task, record each time the child's response to an occasion is incorrect, prompted, an approximation, a correct response, or no response. After each session, determine the percentage of occasions that resulted in each kind of response (e.g., on session 1, there might be 10 percent correct responses). Finally, keep track of how long and how often the child engaged in different problem behaviors (tantrums, noncompliance, head-banging) and how often the parents reinforced, ignored, timed out, or punished the behaviors.

Table 4-1 on page 116 is an example of such a recording sheet.

The observer also takes extra notes on behaviors of parents (and children) that are either ''good'' or that need changing—with reference, of course, to APG items (such as ''basic teaching methods'' or ''planning rather than reacting'').

Selected short subjects can be recorded by writing down important events or exchanges as they occur, e.g., exchanges that illustrate principles of learning or teaching. While not as effective as videotape, these lists of exchanges can at least be read and role-played with the parents during meetings or home visits.

Using Data. Numerical data taken from the videotapes or recording sheets can be used to evaluate the progress of parents and children (as described in Chapter 11). The pencil and paper data taken by the observer (and all notes) on the exchanges can be used to plan the Program and, later, to help parents change patterns of exchange.

Self-Recording by Parents. Baseline Observations can also be made by parents in the home. After practice with the equipment, parents might videotape teaching sessions, selected short subjects, or anything they feel is interesting or useful. They might write logs on daily events (e.g., a description of a typical day) or record the frequency or duration of certain behaviors. Self-recording may be useful in several ways. It may reveal differences in behaviors or interaction patterns when the family is alone and when being observed. Moreover, logs written by parents (or siblings) may provide evidence of how family members perceive their situation.

The last major task in the Pre-Program stage is to organize the collected

Table 4-1. Example of Pencil and Paper Recording Sheet

Blake Family   Baseline Session 1   10/1/78   7:30-8:00 PM

Motor Imitation (Father)

	1	2	3	4	5	(Trials or occasions to respond)	
Clap hands	I	I	P	I-R	N		
Pat head	I	N	N	I	N-R	4 correct responses / 20 occasions	= 20% correct responses
Stand up	C	C	C	A	N	0 reinforcement / 4 correct responses	= 0% reinforcement for correct responses
Open mouth	C	P-R	N	I	N		

Verbal Imitation (Mother)

	1	2	3	4	5	(Trials or occasions to respond)	
Ah	C	C-R	C	A	A		
M	C	A	A	I	I	5 correct responses / 20 occasions	= 25% correct responses
Uh	I	I	P	P	N	1 reinforcement / 5 correct responses	= 20% reinforcement for correct responses
MAh	N	I	C	A	A-R		

1 Tantrum for 30 seconds. Reinforced 2 times.

Suggestions

Child: Sitting behavior is strong, as is eye contact. Motor and Verbal Imitation are weak. Start educational program with Cooperation.

Father: Needs to prompt and reinforce more often and faster; needs to learn various types of prompts; needs to require eye contact before giving occasion to respond. Reinforce father for good pacing of trials and for good coaching of wife.

Mother: Needs to wait longer between trials; needs to prompt and reinforce more often; good at requiring eye contact before giving occasions to respond; needs to ignore tantrums; needs only a little help on prompting verbal imitation; needs to praise Father more often.

I: Incorrect response
N: No response
A: Approximately correct response
P: Prompted response
C: Correct response (no prompt)
R: Reinforcement

Each entry represents one trial. The type of response made by the child following the parents' signaling (occasioning) the child is indicated. Responses followed by "-R" were reinforced.

assessment information and to plan the Program for and with the family or families. The task may be started at the end of the last Baseline Observation session.

VII. TASK 5: ORGANIZING THE ASSESSMENT INFORMATION AND PLANNING THE PROGRAM

This last task consists of several steps which might best be done in the following order:

1. Establishing and discussing goals with the parents.
2. Pointing out how the Program may help them to achieve their goals.
3. Summarizing the assessment information and using the summary to plan the Program.
4. Developing a system for keeping records.
5. Making arrangements for the first meeting.

Establishing Goals and Reaching an "Understanding"

The parents have come to you for help; you have described the Program for them; and for about one week, through Initial Interview(s), Assessment Interview(s), and Baseline Observations, you have been observing the family and talking with the parents about their past and present situation, focusing on behaviors, exchange relationships, perceptions, and attitudes that represent either strengths to be built upon or shortcomings to be remedied by the Program. The emphasis, throughout, has been on changing themselves and their children. Therefore, it is time to help the parents to specify goals, that is, state what they would like your program to help them to change.

Section G of the Interview Schedule is for the specification of goals. At the end of the last Baseline Observation, take out the Interview Schedule and review with the parents the goals they stated which you wrote in Section G. Ask them to revise or add to the list of goals. At the same time, however, you and the parents must be aware of the following:

Goals, Reasons, Costs, Feasibility, and Consequences. Several times I have stressed that during the Pre-Program stage you are in a possible dilemma. If you do not emphasize the likelihood of the parents achieving their goals (e.g., producing what to them is significant change in their child), they may not participate in a Program with you; if, on the other hand, your claims for the efficacy of the Program are too optimistic, some parents simply will not believe you, and others, while participating in the Program, may become disillusioned when they find out, either during or after the Program, how much work it requires to change their child and/or how slow or minimal the child's progress is. Consequently, as suggested several times, be "cautiously optimistic" in presenting the potential benefits of the Program.

Even if the parents seem to be cautiously optimistic, they may have a number of long-term goals for their child and reasons for wanting to achieve those goals, which they are only partially aware of or willing to admit. In addition, at this point, there remain several unknowns with which the parents may not have come to terms but which they have to face during the Program and certainly after it; for example, the costs (time, effort, emotion) of working to achieve their goals and the feasibility of reaching their goals. To the extent that the parents are unprepared for what happens (not just minimal and difficult change but significant change as well), several unpleasant, even tragic, consequences may result. Therefore, at this time, you and the parents must examine, come to an understanding of, and develop a workable solution to the following issues:

What are the Parents' Goals for Their Child? First, we must distinguish short- and long-term goals. Short-term goals are changes in the child and themselves that the parents would like to see take place during the Program and in the near future. Long-term goals are changes that the parents would like to see take place later in the child's life; for example, when the child has grown up. Note that the parents' goals may range from specific to nebulous or ill-defined. Their expectations for achieving goals may range from certainty ("No question about it. I will definitely toilet train her!" or "My Jerry is going to be normal one day!") to what even they may see as wishful thinking ("I would like her to be able to talk").

The parents may or may not see the connection between achieving short- and long-term goals. For example, while some may understand what it will take for them to help produce short-term changes in their child's behaviors (e.g., toilet training), they may not see the further changes in their child and in the larger social environment which will be required to achieve long-term goals (e.g., that their child lead a more independent life). Other parents, however, may have a detailed picture of what it will take, in terms of their child's behaviors and social opportunities (e.g., jobs and living arrangements), to achieve long-term goals.

Examples of parents' goals for their child are to:

1. Become "normal" (that is, to be indistinguishable from other children or adults).
2. Eventually function in more normal settings outside the home (for example, sheltered workshop, at a job, in a group home).
3. Continue living in the home (for example, to become easier to live with, less of a burden, participate in family life).
4. Learn and perform specific skills or appropriate behaviors (for instance, to

talk, occupy time in a constructive way, express affection, become toilet trained).

5. Stop performing specific inappropriate behaviors (for example, tantrums, self-injury, bizarre behavior).

Parents' Reasons for Wanting to Achieve Goals. By "reasons" I mean the way in which the achieving of a goal constitutes a reinforcer for the parents. Note that achieving a goal may be a reinforcer in several ways at the same time. In addition, the parents may or may not be aware of(that is, be able to state) how the achieving of a goal is a reinforcer for them.

Some reasons for wanting to achieve goals are to:

1. Make life more enjoyable for their child (in the home and in later life).
2. Increase the parents' feelings of self-worth.
3. Reduce (escape) the guilt stemming from a belief that they may have had something to do with their child's condition or from a belief that they have not done enough for their child.
4. Avoid the guilt which they may anticipate experiencing if they do not work with their child or do not succeed in helping their child.
5. Relieve themselves of some of the effort of taking care of their child or some of their worrying about the future.
6. Enable the family to lead a more normal life (less stigmatized and isolated, freer).

Feasibility and Costs of Goals. Both the costs and feasibility of attaining goals depend on: 1) the nature and severity of the child's problems (e.g., oppositional behavior, severely "mentally" impaired, mild to severe cerebral palsy); 2) the family situation (defined in terms of most, if not all, of the items on the Assessment and Programming Guide); and 3) the availability of high-quality learning, living, and working opportunities for the child. Thus, the child's progress may be rapid and even; moderate overall; rapid or moderate up to a point, and then uneven or slow; or slow and limited overall. At the same time, the costs required of parents and siblings (in time, effort, and emotion), both in working directly with the child and in working to create future opportunities for the child, may range from relatively light, to moderate, to extensive.

Consequences or Outcomes. Combinations of the above factors may yield a number of consequences during and after the Program. At one extreme, the parents may see that, indeed, their goals may be attained. Their child makes satisfactory progress in the short tun, and it seems that future living and working opportunities are becoming available. At the other extreme, the parents may see that their short-term goals are not being attained (their child's progress is slow perhaps), their long-range goals may not be attained (e.g., even if their child is making satisfactory progress, no future living arrangements seem available); or the costs of change are simply too high, whether or not their goals may be attained. Let us examine several possibilities or scenarios in more detail.

1. The child is making progress which the parents perceive to be satisfactory (in terms of their goals). They become excited, hopeful. They begin to invest more and more time and effort. However, they realize that they cannot continue to work at such a high rate and must give more of themselves to the siblings. Hence, they begin to work at a more moderate, but steady, pace. Consequently, the change process continues fairly smoothly, while cautious optimism and self-worth are high.

2. The child, as in 1, is making satisfactory progress. The parents work harder and harder ("He'll be fine any day now!!" or "Well, it wasn't so hard to teach her to work puzzles. Now I'll teach her to talk!"). The result? The parents may begin to "burn out" and/or the siblings may suffer. But if the parents, now burned out, spend less and less effort working with or for the child, what else happens to them? Do they begin to feel guilty? ("We are letting Anthony down.") Are their feelings of self-worth weakened? ("If only we could have kept at it. If only I were a stronger person.") Do marital problems develop? ("If only you had helped me more.") Do the parents' hopes for the future crumble? ("Lord, after all this, we may end up putting him away.")

3. The child's progress is moderate or seems to slow down. The parents adjust their expectations or goals somewhat. They appraise the likely consequences of "killing themselves" trying to produce a higher rate of progress, but work with the child slowly, steadily, and effectively. They begin to work to provide the child with opportunities for the future. Overall, then, the change process is rather smooth; cautious optimism and feelings of self-worth remain high.

4. The child's progress, as in 3, is moderate or seems to slow down. The parents become frightened ("My God, what's happening!"), disillusioned ("But I thought . . . ."), desperate, their hopes begin to crumble. Now what happens? Perhaps they work harder and harder, in a frantic effort to salvage their hopes and feelings of self-worth, leading either to further despair or to a burnout (which may then lead to guilt, marital problems, and a life in which the child is a constant reminder of their hopes and their "failure"). Or, perhaps they simply work less and less with their child, which may result in a deterioration in the gains they have made and, possibly, in guilt, self-doubt, and extensive and durable communication games ("It's not my job" or "If it weren't for you").

A Strategy for Helping Parents to Examine, Understand, and Develop Workable Solutions to the Above Potential Problems

Frankly, it is impossible to predict exactly what will happen given various combinations of goals, reasons, costs, and degrees of feasibility of achieving goals. Nor can it be said exactly what to tell parents in every situation. There are simply too many unknowns. For example, if parents have been properly using certain speech training methods but their child is just not making much progress, at what point should the parents realistically lower their expectations (change their short-term goal) concerning their child's learning to communicate? For, in just the past few years, many methods have been developed for teaching non-vocal (sign) communication, which has sometimes led to children learning vocal communication as well. Similarly, at what point should parents change the long-term goal that their child be able to live outside of the family, if alternative living arrangements are not yet available in their area? Recently, many persons have been developing alternative, family-style living arrangements for behaviorally impaired persons. Thus, all that can reasonably be suggested is a strategy that might be used, both at this point and during the Program. In particular:

1. Help parents to become aware of and to specify their short- and long-term goals. Help them to see what may be required in order to achieve their goals (changes in the child, changes in the larger social environment, and possible costs). Also discuss the feasibility of achieving goals. Most important, help them to see that there are a number of possible goals and that there is nothing wrong with altering their goals in light of a reasonable appraisal of costs and feasibility, as they keep track of progress.

2. Help the parents to examine, become aware of, and specify their reasons for wanting to achieve goals, some of which may be in the list presented earlier. One way to help parents to become aware of reasons is to ask them how they would feel if certain goals were—or were not—being achieved. For instance:

Consultant: So, one of your goals is to help Sally to learn to talk. How would you feel if you found that she was making progress?

Parent: Oh, I'd feel real good about it!

Consultant: Mm hmm. It would make you feel good.

Parent: Yeah. I would know that one day Sally was going to benefit from it.

Consultant: So, achieving that goal would make you feel good because it was helping Sally?

Parent: Right.

Consultant: And you? (Consultant slightly shifts parent's attention to how she might feel about herself but does not put words in parent's mouth.)

Parent: Oh, if Sally were making progress, it would make me feel real good about myself. I wouldn't become snotty about it! I'd just feel that I was doing a good job. You know, that I had skill and was doing my part.

Or

Consultant: Let's say that Sally were making progress in learning to talk, but you started to become too tired. Maybe you had been working too hard and not getting enough outside enjoyment. So, you slowed down on working with Sally—and then she talked less and less.

Parent: Gee, after all that work and all that progress? I don't know. I guess I would feel like I was letting her down.

Consultant: Mm hmm.

Parent: Yeah, I wouldn't feel good about it. I'd get nervous. You know, feeling guilty.

At this point, then, the consultant could review his or her impressions of what the parent's underlying reasons are for wanting to achieve goals. For example, in the above discussion, the parent seems to be motivated, or anticipates being motivated, by the benefits to the child, increased feelings of self-worth, and the anxiety or guilt of not doing for the child what is in the parent's power.

Help parents to see that, while their reasons for wanting to achieve certain goals are understandable and humane, some of their reasons may be counterproductive. For example, if parents begin to work very hard to teach their child, in part because they have been taught to believe that they are guilty for their child's condition, and if progress in their child will both reduce their feelings of guilt and increase their feelings of self-worth, what will happen if, despite their hard work, the child's progress is minimal? Guilt may increase and feelings of self-worth may decrease.

Thus, help parents to confront and debunk (expose, criticize) the following counterproductive and erroneous notions that: (1) they are guilty for their child's condition, (2) they are personally responsible for changing their child and for everything that their child becomes or does not become, and (3) feelings of self-worth should be tied to the child's progress. Instead, help them to see that: (1) there is little or no evidence that they are responsible for their child's condition, (2) they are neither personally nor solely responsible for change in their child, and (3) feelings of self-worth should be tied to their reasonable efforts and not to change in their child.

In sum, a reasonable framework within which parents can evaluate themselves is "Doing what you can." It is your job, then, to help parents acquire skills and to see when they can reasonably do more and when they are doing as much as anyone can do without injuring themselves and others.

3. Help parents to examine the possible costs and feasibility of working to achieve their goals. For example, a father might want his mute, 10-year-old autistic son to learn to carry on conversations. While achieving that goal may be possible, it is not certain. Moreover, working to achieve that goal may be costly. Thus, it is important that the father see that a number of short-term subgoals are possible; for instance, that his son learns the prerequisites for learning speech, to communicate some of his wants in less disruptive ways, and to imitate and use several words and phrases. In this way, the father can put his long-term goal on the "back burner" and concern himself with subgoals. In addition, by doing so, the father avoids being in a perpetual state of high arousal, waiting and hoping for his son to suddenly carry on a conversation. In sum, parents have to begin to see that if they (and others) work properly on the short-run goals (with an occasional glance toward the future), the long-term goals are more likely to be achieved. At least the change process will be much easier on everyone.

4. Help parents to examine several scenarios of consequences or outcomes, as was done above. For example, what might happen in their family if the child makes rapid progress? Will they escalate their effort to the point that they burn out (and then feel guilty)? Or will they recognize that they are beginning to escalate, anticipate the consequences of trying to maintain a "killing pace," and then work at a more moderate pace? And if their child's progress slows down, will they maintain their high expectations of achieving dramatic, long-term change (perhaps leading to desperate effort, burnout, and guilt), or will they appraise the situation, keep an eye open for more effective teaching methods, and moderate their efforts and their goals?

By examining possible scenarios now and during the Program, you can help parents to anticipate the kinds of problems that may arise during and after their Program and provide them with a strategy for avoiding and solving the problems.

All of the above issues are dealt with again in later chapters on weekly activities when potential problems can arise.

Pointing Out How the Program May Help

You have indicated some of the general ways in which the Program may help the family. At this point, since you have had a number of opportunities to observe the family, discuss some of your observations and assessments with the parents, generally following the items on the APG. For example, you might point out things of which the parents were not aware, such as that it would be a good idea to make arrangements with neighbors and relatives to give the parents some backup support during and after the Program. If they agree, making such arrangements can be added to the list of goals. Make sure to pinpoint for the parents the various strengths you have observed and how they increase the parents' chances of achieving goals.

An APG for the Parents

It is a good idea to give the parents a copy of the list of goals that has been drawn up. In this way, both you and the parents can keep track of the parents' achievement of goals. It may be beneficial to provide parents with a copy of the APG. At this time, it can be used when reviewing with parents your observations of their strengths and needs.

> Now, you see this item, here, on general teaching methods? Here are my impressions of your strengths and of what I think I can help you to improve. First of all, the physical layout of the house is real good. You've got a special place for Winston's toys; the TV is out of his reach. . . .

During and after the Program stage, on the other hand, they can use the APG to keep track of progress and problems, that is, to maintain the home program. However, it may be wise to revise the APG so that it is easier to self-administer and so that potentially threatening or irrelevant comments can be deleted.

Summarizing the Assessment Information

The next task is to summarize all of the information so that you can plan the Program. Remember, the main contents and sequence of the Program are generally the same for all families. Therefore, you want to find out what needs to be emphasized or modified in a Program, depending on your assessment of a family's particular situation. The steps for summarizing the assessment information and planning some details of the Program are simple.

1. Place in front of you the Assessment and Programming Guide (APG) used with the family. You will have made notes under some items, underlined important words describing your observations, and circled items with which the parents need help. You should also have reports and assessments from others from whom the parents sought help.

2. Also place in front of you the Interview Schedule containing notes on parents' answers to questions, as well as notes of some of your observations of parents' behaviors during the interview(s).

3. Notes made during the Baseline Observations should also be in front of you. In addition to notes made during and after Baseline sessions, you (as well as certain specialists and co-workers) should watch some of the videotapes and take notes on what you see; for example, strengths and needs of the child, structured exchanges with the child, cooperation between the spouses, basic teaching methods, response pattern involving planning (versus reacting), and personal problems.

4. Now, with all data in front of you, carefully review it. Read what you underlined or wrote for each APG item, your notes on the Interview Schedule, and all notes or data taken during Baseline Observations. Now simply transfer all of the information to the APG, item by item. This may sound like a huge order, but it is not.

For example, starting with the items for Readiness to Change, do the observations you made during the Assessment Interviews and Baseline Observations lead you to change your rating of the parents on any readiness item (Items 2 through 10)? If so, change or add to your underlinings or notes for those items.

Then continue through the APG for the items relevant to the Program stage (Items 11 through 27). For example:

> How objective are the parents (Item 12)? Have they given any evidence of skill at pinpointing and describing behaviors? Do they use any basic princi-

ples of learning to analyze behaviors? Are there any potential problems that will interfere with objectivity?

Do the parents seem to have confidence in general principles of learning (Item 13)?

Do they seem to have any of the skills in planning an educational program (Item 14), such as determining the behaviors with which their child needs help?

Have the parents given any indication of willingness to try certain behavioral methods (Item 15), such as requiring their child to earn reinforcers?

How do they respond to problems? Do they react? Or do they wait and plan (Item 16), as observed during Baseline Observations and as described by the parents?

What are the structured exchanges like in the family (Item 17), as observed during Baseline Observations and as described by parents?

To what extent do they have skill using general teaching methods (Item 18), as observed during Baseline sessions, especially teaching sessions?

To what extent do the parents cooperate with one another (Item 19)? To what extent are there problems of marital cooperation? Must cooperation be worked on immediately?

What is the household organization like? Are schedules generally followed and chores done relatively efficiently (Item 20)? Are there problems in household organization?

Do the parents have personal problems, as indicated in discussions and through observations (Item 21)? If so, how do they handle them? Are there any other problems that might interfere with their learning to pinpoint and solve personal problems? Should you begin to work on personal problems right away?

To what extent are the parents honest, accurate, and open (Item 22), as indicated by comparing what they say with what you observe, or by comparing what they say at different times?

Do the parents seem willing and able to take scheduled breaks (Item 23)? What would help parents to take breaks?

To what extent do the parents reinforce themselves and each other (Item 24), as observed during interviews and Baseline Observations, and as described by them? Are there problems which might interfere with their reinforcing themselves? What resources might be made available?

Are the parents integrated in any networks or organizations offering resources of various kinds (Item 25)? Or, are they rather isolated, apathetic, fiercely independent? What potential is there for integration (parents' willingness, organizations, acquaintance with other parents)?

To what extent do the parents involve others in their child's life, take their child into public places, enlist the help of others (Item 26)?

Finally, how do the parents handle problems (Item 27)? To what extent do they use a problem-solving strategy?

Remember, circle all items with which the parents need any help.

Using the Assessment Information to Plan the Program

The curriculum for the Program stage, which is described starting with Chapter 5, is detailed and is based on the assumption that most parents need help with many of the items relevant to conducting, persisting at, and maintaining a good home educational program (Items 11 through 27). The purpose of summarizing all of the assessment information gathered so far and transferring it to the Assessment and Programming Guide (APG) for a family is to: 1) enable you to tailor some details of the Program to the individual strengths and needs of each family and 2) provide you with a Pre-Program rating of the family so that you can make comparisons through time, as a way of evaluating the Program's effectiveness. It is also important to update your rating of the parents on each item periodically during the course of the Program stage. Parents can be doing the same thing. For instance, as they learn more of the basic teaching methods (Item 18), you can underline or make notes to that effect under Item 18, check-marking and dating those components which are passed. Naturally, you would indicate any differences between individual parents of the same family.

If the Program is to be for a group of families, one last planning step is needed. Consultants meet to plan the Program for the group. All of the assessment information is on hand for each family when consultants discuss each family's (and each parent's) needs and strengths. The consultants decide:

1. Which problems are so unique to a family that they should not be part of the group curriculum but should be handled in the consultant-family relationship (for example, a personal problem that should be kept out of group discussion).

2. What problems or needs are common to the group and, therefore, should be part of the group's curriculum (for example, tension to be handled by progressive relaxation).

3. How the children were rated on the various skill areas of the education program found in *Educating Children with Learning and Behavior Problems,* so that a tentative sequence for teaching the parents to work on the skill areas can be developed.

Finally, whether the Program is to be for individual families or a group of families:

1. Copies of *Educating Children* are obtained, one copy for each family.
2. The agenda for each meeting is tentatively planned, based on the assessments of the family or families. The agenda for each week's activities is detailed briefly in Section VIII below.
3. Any equipment or supplies are obtained, such as note pads for parents to use during meetings, wrist-counters, stopwatches.
4. The roles to be played by consultants are established; for example, who will make certain presentations, handle refreshments, or take data during meetings.
5. Arrangements are made regarding backup reinforcers that parents might be earning, such as respite care, baby-sitting or tutoring services, passes to movies.
6. All other materials are available, such as Weekly Contract forms, Credits-Earned sheets, behavior count tables and charts, teaching program plans. As discussed below, all such materials are placed in a weekly folder for each family.

Developing a System for Keeping Records

Conducting programs for families can be hectic, indeed, unless parents and consultants have a system for keeping accurate records of what has happened. A record-keeping system helps both parents and consultants: (1) maintain a businesslike approach, (2) plan programs for the parents and children, (3) keep track of or evaluate the progress of parents and children during the Program, and (4) evaluate the Program when it has been completed. The message is simply this: try to keep accurate records on all aspects of the Program. While this might seem troublesome, it decreases confusion and maintains efficiency.

Luckily, all records can be grouped into three files: (1) folders for each family, (2) folders for each meeting, (3) videotape, film, slides, and other instructional materials.

Folders for Each Family. Before the Program starts, each family (in a Program for groups) has one person assigned to it as a consultant. Part of the consultant's job is to maintain a complete, accurate, and up-to-date set of folders for his or her family, with one folder for each week. Each folder is labeled with the name of the family, the Program week number, and dates for which the folder is relevant.

The first folder includes copies of all Pre-Program materials, for example: (1)

the Program Contract, (2) the Interview Schedule, (3) the family's certified checks (if used),(4) the Assessment and Programming Guide (APG) scored by the consultant, (5) any notes made by the consultant, and (6) any data taken by the parents, consultant, or observers during the baseline period.

Once the Program is under way, a new folder is kept for each week. Each weekly folder includes:

1. A copy of the Contract written during the weekly meeting.
2. A copy of any Contract or teaching program written during the home visit.
3. Notes made by the consultant during the home visit.
4. A copy of any logs written by the parents concerning daily activities.
5. Notes on phone calls to and from the parents.
6. A copy of behavior count tables and charts (from *Educating Children*) made by the parents.
7. Copies of any additional teaching materials, teaching programs, or data produced by parents during the week.
8. Copies of assignments at the end of chapters in *Educating Children* completed during the week.
9. A copy of the sheet of Credits Earned for the week.

Examples of Weekly Contracts are in Table 6-3 and in Appendix 5 of this book.

Educating Children with Learning and Behavior Problems also contains teaching programs which are filled out by the parents each week (page 146), behavior count tables and charts (pages 150–153), and written assignments at the ends of Chapters 1 to 5, 7, and 8. The chapters on the different skill areas contain various record-keeping and progress sheets to be filled out by the parents. These are also copied and inserted into the files for the week when they were filled out.

Folders for Each Meeting. One consultant keeps a folder on each group meeting. The folders are clearly marked with the meeting number and date and contain such things as:

1. A detailed agenda for the meeting (especially a group meeting).
2. A set of notes made by one of the consultants on events that took place during the meeting.
3. Any data taken by consultants during the meeting (for example, on the number of suggestions versus complaints made by parents).
4. A list of the instructional materials and methods used (for example, the reel

numbers, footage, and contents of videotapes; role playing; or demonstrations).

5. Copies of Credits-Earned sheets for all consultants.

The file of meeting folders can be used by consultants or persons in other Programs to plan future meetings.

Videotape. An important part of the Program for instruction and evaluation, the use of videotape is discussed in more detail later. To make the best use of videotapes, records are kept on them, so as to allow quick access to relevant portions. Have a small box with one filing card for each videotape (or audiotape). Each filing card contains: (1) the number of the tape, (2) the number of the Program (for example, if Programs are being run in a series), (3) the name of the family being videotaped, (4) the date and week number, and (5) a list of what is shown on the tape, along with the footage. The information on such a card might look like the following:

Tape No. 40	
Program 2	Blake Family
Week 4	October 2-9, 1978

First session on "eye contact on request."
0–15 min. (Mother works on cooperation.)
16–30 min. (Father works on eye contact on request.)
Good tape. They need to reinforce faster.

Most important, each tape is clearly labeled. The box is labeled on the outside with the number of the Program, the number of the tape, name of the family, Program week, and date. The reel itself is labeled just in case the boxes get mixed up! And a small filing card within each tape box duplicates the one kept in the filing box.

The person recording the videotape makes the card for each tape, either during the taping or as soon as the taping is finished. In fact, while the tape is running, the person operating the machine, or a second observer, can make notes of the footage when interesting events are happening, and the footage when the parents are working on different activities. This information is then put on the filing card so that consultants, when planning the next meeting, can quickly find just which tapes and which portions of these tapes are most relevant to the meeting.

Before starting the Program, have all folders for all families and all weeks prepared and labeled. And copies of Weekly Contracts, Credits-Earned sheets, behavior count tables, assignments, and other written materials are ready.

As stated, it is a good idea to make copies of many things (Weekly Contracts, notes, agendas). How do you make copies? Each consultant and family can have a clipboard with a pad of writing paper and carbon paper. Then, when an agenda is written down, one copy is used and one copy is filed. Or, when a Weekly Contract is written, one copy is filed in the family folder for that week and one copy is kept by the parents.

Making Arrangements for the First Meeting

A final task is to arrange the time for the weekly (or bi-weekly) meetings. Naturally, it should be convenient for participants in the family or families. When the first meeting is scheduled, the parents are reminded to bring their certified checks or money orders (if used). One consultant is responsible for bringing coffee, cookies, or any other snacks to be had during the break in the meeting. Other consultants are assigned the responsibility of bringing videotape equipment, films, and projectors, note pads and pencils for all participants, and any other written materials to be handed out during the meetings. Lastly, give the parents their first assignment: to read and do the written assignments in Chapter 1 of *Educating Children With Learning and Behavior Problems* before the first meeting. Remind them to bring their copies of *Educating Children,* their written assignments, and, if provided, their copy of the APG.

VIII. TENTATIVE AGENDAS

Since there are several Program variations, the following agendas are tentative. Each entry is for a unit of work, which takes one or more meetings to complete.

Unit One. Introduce the Program (needs for and goals of). Discuss Program Contract and, if used, contract-credit system. Review Chapter 1 of *Educating Children*. Make effort to build esprit de corps in the group and self-confidence of parents. Present briefly principles of learning and exchange. Assign reading and homework in Chapter 2 of *Educating Children*.

Unit Two. Present, discuss, and review videotapes on principles of learning and structured exchanges. Discuss implications for changes in family interaction. Present briefly rewards. Assignment: to begin instituting productive exchanges and to read and do assignments in Chapter 3 of *Educating children,* on rewards.

Unit Three. Review and discuss home programs. Present and discuss at greater length ideas in and implications of Chapter 3. Revise or update program to institute productive exchanges. Assignment: to read and do assignments in

Chapter 4 of *Educating Children* (evaluating child and planning an educational program).

Unit Four. Review and discuss children's evaluations and educational program plans, rewards, and programs to institute productive exchanges. Briefly present measuring behaviors (pinpointing, defining, recording). Assignment: to read Chapters 5 and 6 in *Educating Children,* take Baseline on first target behavior(s), and read portion of chapter in *Educating Children* on how to teach first target behavior.

Unit Five. Review and discuss Baseline Observations. Presentation, role-playing, and videotape or film on general teaching methods and Program planning (signals, prompts, rewards, shaping, running sessions). Stress cooperation, self-reinforcement, scheduled breaks, and linkages with other parents. Assignment: to read pages 143–145 in Chapter 6 as well as Chapter 7 in *Educating Children,* and to conduct first teaching program.

Unit Six. Evaluate first teaching program and present problem-solving sequence. Review main ideas and methods for conducting advanced teaching programs. Describe and practice methods for teaching next target behaviors. Assignment: to continue first teaching program, possibly start one on the next target behavior(s), and to read Chapter 8 of *Educating Children.*

Units Six through Twelve (or more). In these units focus on the next skill areas and target behaviors for home teaching programs as well as on special topics from the APG (e.g., progressive relaxation training, assertiveness training and advocacy, the development of networks of extended support, generalization of children's skills, general review of the Program and progress in the families). Toward the end of the Program stage, prepare parents for maintenance (e.g., discussions of long-term planning and problem-solving).

Give assignments from later chapters in *Educating Children* and from other relevant materials.

Follow-up and Maintenance

When the series of instructional units (the Program stage) has been completed, schedule maintenance meetings and home visits, review and upgrade home programs, and solve problems. The length of this stage depends on the type of Program and its setting. For instance, if conducted in association with a school or treatment facility, this stage can run indefinitely, with consultants and other parents continually available.

IX. INTERVIEW SCHEDULE FOR FAMILY ASSESSMENT

Date____________________

Interviewer____________________

A. General Information

1. Parents, guardians or other who will be participants (partners) in the Program.

Name____________________Relationship____________________Age______

Address____________________Occupation ____________________

Schooling______________________________Phone __________
(highest grade completed)

Name____________________Relationship____________________Age ______

Address____________________Occupation ____________________

Schooling______________________________Phone __________
(highest grade completed)

2. Child(ren) who will be the focus of the Program.

Name	Date of Birth	Sex

3. Siblings.

Name	Date of birth	Sex

4. Are there any pets in the family? (Can be useful for training.)

Name(s) ____

B. Questions Regarding Effects of Child's Deviant Behavior and Development on the Family

Questions in this section are designed to give the parents a chance to trace their career experiences, with a focus on the child with learning and behavior problems, from the time they noticed something was wrong to the present. The questions are general, enabling the parents to connect many topics. For example, when describing their child's behavior over the years, they might also indicate their feelings and their efforts to change their child's behavior. Probes (in parentheses) help in obtaining information.

1. Tell me how you came to find out that something was wrong with (child)? (First suspicions, your reactions, child's development, what made you sure.)
2. Please give me a general idea of what (child's) behavior has been like over the years (Acceptable and unacceptable behaviors, how you taught child or controlled problem behaviors.)
3. What are (child's) behaviors like now? For example, what does (child) do in a typical day? (Present skills, problem behaviors, how child spends time, how child communicates, what child does to get what he wants.)
4. How have (child's) siblings been affected by having (child) as a (brother, sister)? (Their feelings, needs for attention, problems with peers, their strengths.)
5. Please tell me what stands out in your memory when you think of how other people have reacted to (child). (Strangers, friends, relatives, neighbors, your feelings, extent to which they have cooperated.)
6. In general, how does having a child with special needs make you feel?

C. Questions Regarding Experiences and Problems in Trying to Find Help

(Introductory remarks to parents.) When many parents realize that something is wrong with their child, they start looking for help. So, I'd like to ask you some questions about efforts you might have made to find help, what help you have gotten, and how you feel about your experiences.

1. Please tell me where you have gone over the years for help with (child). Start with the first place or person you went to.

Name or Place	*Date*	*Specialty*	*Help Sought*
a.			
b.			
c.			
d.			
e.			

2. I'd like to know about the kind of help you got from each place or person. (Tests, diagnoses, prognosis, treatment methods used, effects of treatments, advice or suggestions given to parents, parents' evaluation, effects on parents' feelings about themselves and expectations for the future.)

a.

b.

c.

d.

e.

3. Please tell me what schools or other kinds of programs (child) has attended. (Dates of attendance, educational or treatment methods used, results, parents' evaluations.)

a.

b.

c.

d.

D. Questions Regarding Isolation

This section obtains information on sources of reinforcement, information, and backup support services that parents might use during or after the Program and the parents' willingness and opportunities to generalize their own and their child's behavior changes to other persons and places.

1. Are there any persons you could or do count on for help, such as information or advice on what to do with (child), or for emotional support if you are feeling down, or for special help, such as babysitting, taking (child) for a few days, lending a helping hand?

Actual Sources of Help *Type of Help Given*

a.

b.

c.

d.

e.

2. Are there any persons from whom you have not gotten help but from whom you might get help if you tried?

Potential Sources of Help *Type of Help That Might Be Given*

a.

b.

c.

d.

e.

3. Does anyone come to you for help? To whom do you give help? What kind of help do you give to each person? How often? (Explore the chances of developing a structured exchange of services as a way of helping parents to conduct and maintain their home educational program.)

Persons Parents Help	*Type of Help Given*	*Frequency of Help*	*Possible Exchanges of Services*
a.			
b.			
c.			
d.			
e.			

4. Where else have you gotten or do get help? For example, organizations for parents, conferences, parent training programs, parent-teacher meetings? How involved were you (are you) in such groups, programs, or relationships? What benefits did you receive (information, support, backup services)? Did both of you participate?

Organizations, Programs, Relationships	*Who Participated*	*Extent of Involvement*	*Benefits*
a.			
b.			
c.			
d.			
e.			

5. Please tell me about the whole issue of taking (child) out in public. (Homes of neighbors and relatives, stores, movies, restaurants.)

Where do you Take Child?	*How Often?*	*Child's Behavior*	*Your Response*
a.			
b.			
c.			
d.			
e.			

6. How often do you get out, together or by yourselves, for recreation of some kind? (Where do you go? Do you go to these places alone or together? How often do you get out? Are you satisfied with how often or where you go out? What prevents you from going out more often? What do you need in order to get out more often? If you are not satisfied with how often or where you go out for recreation, how do you get enjoyment, satisfaction, or a break?)

E. Questions Regarding Patterns of Interaction (Structured Exchanges) With the Child

(Introductory remarks) Now, I'd like to find out what it is like to live with (child).

1. Please describe some of (child's) problem behaviors and tell me what you usually do to handle them. (Try to determine the typical response you make to problem behaviors, i.e., the basic exchange. Also, try to determine the immediacy of your response. For instance, if you use punishment, do you do so immediately or wait until you cannot stand the behavior any more? Do you consistently respond in one way or do you try one method and then another? Further, how well do you feel you handle problem behaviors; and what are you referring to when you judge how well you handle problem behaviors, e.g., long-term decrease, temporary cessation, feeling of relief? Finally, do you respond in the same way?)

Problem Behavior	*Your Typical Response*	*Immediacy/ Consistency*	*Your Evaluation of Results*
a.			
b.			
c.			
d.			
e.			

2. Can you tell when (child) is working up to doing one of his problem behaviors? If so, what does (child) do to "tell" you that he is working up to it? What do you usually do about it? (Placation exchange?)

3. What do you usually do if (child) demands things by whining, pushing or pulling you, or throwing tantrums? (Escape exchange?)

4. Now, please tell me how (child's) problem behaviors make you feel. (Try to determine if you feel the way you do only after a problem behavior has started, or gone on for too long, or if you feel the way you do much of the time, as though you were often hypervigilant, tense, or anxious. Do both of you feel the same way?)

5. What do you think are your biggest problems or needs in controlling or changing (child's) problem behaviors? (Need to learn teaching methods? Cooperate more? Organize household? Be more relaxed? Be more self-confident?)

6. We have been talking about problem behaviors for a while now. So let us talk about the behaviors or skills you would like to see (child) do better, more often, or in more places. At this time, do you try to teach or get (child) to perform certain good or important behaviors, such as cooperating with you, doing chores (talking, playing, etc.)? If so, please give me examples of what you do and how well it works.

Appropriate Behaviors Worked on	*General Description of Methods*	*Results*
a.		
b.		
c.		
d.		
e.		

7. How much time would you say each of you spends every day actually working on teaching (child)? (Do you work on certain behaviors? At certain times or places? Do you have teaching sessions or work with child when opportunities arise?)

8. What do you usually do when (child) is sitting quietly or spending his time in ways you like? Please give me some examples. (Extent to which you reinforce appropriate behaviors.)

9. Now, I'd like to know how you feel about certain ways of teaching children. For example, how do you feel about rewarding children for doing or learning certain appropriate behaviors, for instance, giving a child a treat when the child does a chore for the first time? How do you feel about punishing a child for certain problem behaviors, for instance, spanking a child?

10. What do you think are your biggest problems or needs in teaching or getting (child) to do appropriate behaviors? (Need to learn teaching skills? Cooperate more? Organize household? Be more relaxed? Be more self-confident? Any differences between you?)

F. Long-term Changes in the Family

The purpose of questions in this section is to sample possible problems and strengths that have developed over the years of the family's career.

Marital Relations (Introductory remarks.) As you know, trying to live with, cope with, and teach a child with special needs is not the easiest job in the world, and it makes special demands on the parents. So, I'd like to ask you a few questions about the ways you work together.

1. Do you help each other when one of you is trying to get (child) to do or learn something, or when (child) is doing one of his problem behaviors? Please give me examples.

Ways Help is Given	*Frequency of Help*
a.	
b.	
c.	
d.	

Do you feel that you may need more help from each other?

2. Can you think of any ways that you recognize or praise or do nice things for each other, either because of the tough jobs you each have or just for general purposes? Please give me examples.

3. In general, tell me if the problems of living with (child) over the years have affected your own relationship—not only ways that your relationship might have been strained, but ways that it might have gotten stronger, too. (Probe for specificity.)

Durability

4. Have you ever tried to make big changes in the ways you do things in the home, such as trying to become more strict with (child), trying to ignore certain problem behaviors, or making a big effort to teach (child) something? If so, please tell me about it. (What were the results of any such efforts? Why did you think that you got the results you got? How did your efforts—perceived success or failure—make you feel about yourselves or about your child's future? If you have not tried to make significant changes, try to pinpoint the sources of durability, e.g., short-run payoff, ideology, coercion, lack of knowledge of what to do. To what extent do you see yourselves as willing or able to rise above the obstacles to change?)

Hypervigilance and Exaggerated Sense of Personal Responsibility

5. Do you ever feel on edge, tense, sort of waiting for the next problem or problem behavior to happen? If so, how often do you feel that way? How strong are the feelings of tension? Do you do anything to control the feelings?

6. This question is a little different from the others. How much do you feel that what (child) will do next, or will become in the future, depends on you? In other words, in what ways do you feel responsible for your child's behavior and future?

Organization in the Household

7. Please give me a brief description of the round of daily life in your family, from getting up in the morning through going to sleep at night. (Try to determine the extent to which your family life is organized in terms of time schedules, e.g., meals and bedtimes; the arrangements of objects; the noise and activity level; the regular and efficient performance of chores. Also, try to determine the reasons if there seems to be a lack of order, for instance, fatigue, disruptive behaviors of child or siblings, lack of help, lack of concern for more order.)

Personal Problems. (Introductory remarks.) Sometimes all that parents have gone through can upset them. So, I'd like to ask you a few questions about yourselves as individuals.

8. Have you ever felt so upset or confused that you thought that you needed help? If so, what seemed to be troubling you? How did you feel? Did you try to get help? What were the results?
9. Do you ever feel blue or depressed, get headaches, have trouble sleeping, feel tense, anxious, panicky? (Try to determine what you feel, how often, how strong the feelings are, what seems to set off the feelings, how the feelings affect other behaviors and relationships, what statements you make to yourselves, how you try to control the feelings, and how successful your efforts are.)
10. This is another general question. How much control do you feel you have over the course of your lives or over the lives of your children?

Expectations and Needs

11. What personal qualities, and what qualities as a family, do you feel that you have that will help you to be successful in this Program?
12. How much confidence do you have in your ability to change your child?
13. Are there any ways that you, as individuals and as a family, feel that you need help in order to be better able to participate in the Program and change your child. (Skills? Baby-sitters? Respite? More marital cooperation? More household organization?)

G. Goals

At the end of the Assessment Interview(s) and/or Baseline Observations, have the parents specify what they would like the Program to accomplish, that is, their goals. Ask the parents in what specific ways they would like to change themselves, their child, and the family. Help them to break down long-term goals into short-term goals. Discuss ways that the Program may help. List long- and short-term goals, and provide parents with a copy.

5 UNIT ONE: THE BEHAVIORAL-EDUCATIONAL APPROACH

I. INTRODUCTION

It has certainly taken many pages to arrive at this point. Since we are about to start on the first unit or week of activities, a few introductory comments are in order:

1. Remember that while this book is written as though you were working with groups of parents, it can be used just as well in one-to-one relationships. Whether in a Program for a group or for an individual family, the substance of your interaction with the parents remains the same (specifically, what you discuss each week, the reading assignments, the activities in the home, and most of the methods used to teach the parents).

2. The word "consultant" refers to whoever is working with the parents, either giving a presentation during a meeting, talking with parents during an Individual Consultation, or making a home visit. As noted, the consultant might be a clinical psychologist, teacher, therapist, another parent or, indeed, anyone who is conducting a Program using this book to help parents to help themselves, their children, and other parents.

3. Use this book along with *Educating Children With Learning and Behavior Problems*. While other books are available, *Educating Children* was written precisely because others were not comprehensive enough to help parents to conduct more than a few simple teaching programs. However, you might wish to supplement *Educating Children* with other materials, some of which are listed in Chapter 3.

4. Each remaining chapter describes one or more units of instructional activities, each unit taking about one week to complete. Feel free, however, to add to, modify, or replace any of the suggested activities in the units. Indeed, remove those that you feel are unnecessary or simply inapplicable to the families with which you are working. Moreover, if you are unable to complete a unit of instruction in one week, continue the instructional activities into the following week before starting on the next unit of instruction. During a meeting, if you do not complete all activities, try to complete at least the "main business" portion of the meeting, skip the "introduction to the next week's activities," and end with the Individual Consultation. Then, during the home visit or at the start of the next meeting, pick up where you left off.

5. Most of the chapters on units of instructional activity begin with a section on goals. The goals (and activities for reaching the goals) are related to items on the Assessment and Programming Guide (APG) in Appendix 1. It is helpful if you read those items in the APG before you continue reading in the chapter.

Strengthening Productive Participation in Meetings

As indicated by APG Item 11, productive participation in meetings involves: (1) making statements or asking questions which are behavioral, optimistic, and prescriptive, (2) speaking up and taking one's turn, and (3) encouraging and reinforcing the productive participation of others. In sum, productive participation in meetings involves the creative use of behavioral terms, principles, and educational methods to describe, analyze, and find solutions for a variety of problems. However, the structure and communication process in a group can impede productive participation. For example, problem-solving groups traditionally have a leader who defines the problem and goals, guides communication (encouraging participants to contribute, responding to suggestions), and acts as an expert regarding the problems to be solved and the feasibility of suggested methods. Too often, the results are as follows:

1. The leader is in a defensive position regarding his or her control over communication and expertise, resulting in a failure to encourage or reinforce the creativity of other participants.
2. In an effort to protect their ideas and self-esteem, some participants become blatently or subtly aggressive, attacking, or downgrading, or simply fail to encourage or reinforce the contribution of others.
3. A few persons withdraw.
4. Others may become bored and aggravated with the group and with unproductive communication ("I thought we were here to find out how to educate our children! But we seem to be spending a lot of time picking on each other's ideas or going in circles!")

Yet, by altering the traditional structure of problem-solving groups, and by paying careful attention to communication, it is possible to avoid these problems and to facilitate productive, creative participation. Many of the following suggestions stem from my work and that of my staff but are presented in detail in *The Practice of Creativity* (Prince, 1976) which is recommended reading.

Rotating Leader. Instead of consultants being the sole leaders for the group, it is beneficial to have rotating leaders, with parents gradually assuming more and more tasks of leadership. In this way, they can become more independent of consultants and may be able to conduct, or at least play important roles in, other Programs for families. In addition, the role of leader can be more circumscribed, the main task being to guide the communication process, so as to help the group (and individual parents) to define problems and goals, generate solutions, determine the feasibility and costs of various solutions, and plan how to implement what seems to be the best solution. Thus, the leader encourages other participants to take part in the discussions, handles differences of opinions, relates alternative suggestions to the problem at hand, and helps move the group through the various items on the agenda.

The Temporary Expert. While the rotating leader guides communication, the temporary expert provides a background and understanding of the problem and its solution. The consultants have expertise regarding many of the problems faced by the families and the solutions that might be used. However, parents already have expertise in many matters and will soon acquire expertise in others as a result of the Program itself. In addition, parents from past Programs have expertise relevant to a present Program. And, there are many outside specialists whose expertise is valuable to a Program; for example, physical therapists, social workers, physicians, speech and language therapists, persons who specialize in progressive relaxation, assertiveness, and cognitive behavior modification, and persons involved in the development of various forms of community organization.

Thus, parents from past Programs and outside specialists might be invited to participate as temporary experts when certain topics become relevant. In addition, at certain times in their own Program, parents can temporarily assume the role of expert. For instance, if one parent has developed considerable skill in teaching reading, that parent can assume the role of temporary expert when reading is focused upon.

Instituting the Roles of Rotating Leader and Temporary Expert. It may be possible to help parents assume the roles of rotating leader and temporary expert by moving in a series of small steps, such as the following:

1. In the first or second meeting, you can discuss the issues of productive participation, group processes, and the importance of parents learning to be leaders and experts.

2. In early meetings, consultants themselves can rotate through the roles of leader and expert. For example, one might present information on learning and development (the expert) and another lead communication (for instance, encouraging the parents and the expert to apply the principles presented by the expert to certain problems). In addition, consultants pinpoint for parents just what they (the consultants) are doing. In other words, the consultants present themselves as model leaders and experts, which the parents later have the opportunity to imitate. Consultants might also provide parents with a short list describing the main points of each role. Those are presented in the next section: Facilitating Effective and Creative Communication.

3. During the third meeting or so, parents might volunteer to play the role of rotating leader during portions of the next meeting. During the Individual Consultation prior to the meeting in which a parent will be a leader, the consultant can review with the parent how to be a leader, as well as the issues to be focused upon. For example, a parent might be a leader in reviewing and discussing answers to questions at the end of a chapter, in parents' descriptions of their home teaching programs, in reviewing the past weeks' work of the group, or in introducing the next week's main topic. Instead of being the sole leader during a portion of a meeting, the parent, at this early time, might be a co-leader with one of the consultants.

4. Gradually, parents might assume responsibility for leading larger portions of meetings. In this case, during the Individual Consultation, the consultant might help the parent(s) to develop an agenda for the next meeting. Similarly, a parent or parents might volunteer to play the role of temporary expert; for instance, on how to measure behavior, teach a certain target behavior, or how to use a particular teaching method. As with the parent-leader, the consultant can help the parent-expert to develop a set of notes to use during the meeting.

5. Later still, parents who have already served as leaders and experts can help others who will be playing those roles to develop agendas.

6. If possible, parents can be encouraged and helped to serve as leaders or experts in other Programs, so as to disseminate what they have learned.

Facilitating Effective and Creative Communication. The following tips may be helpful for anyone playing the role of leader or expert:

1. Any lecturing is kept short. Participants should have already been introduced to the topic (for example, in a past meeting) and read relevant materials.

2. The leader or expert is not in competition with the group, but strives to facilitate the development of ideas and their application.

3. All participants should learn not to put others, or allow others to be put, on the defensive. For example, participants should learn to listen to what others are saying, to put their own prejudices and critical urges on the "back burner" and try to understand what others are saying from the others' perspective. Similarly, ideas and suggestions should be seen in terms of a spectrum (Prince, 1976, p. 46), with most ideas (even those that appear to be ridiculous) having both strong and weak points. Thus, the strong points of an idea are pinpointed and reinforced. One way of doing this is to ask others what they like about a suggestion that has been made. Similarly, instead of pinning a person down (''How could that possibly work?!''), the leader can ask questions of the group (''How might Mr. Clark's suggestion be used?'')

Ideas or suggestions that are faltering or that do not seem to be useful are not merely dropped or inadvertently condemned. Rather, the leader or expert can emphasize the generality of an idea and ask for help as to how or where it might be applied:

> Okay, so it may be that ignoring Tommy's whining is not exactly the answer. But ignoring is certainly a useful method. When might it best be used?

Or, the leader can temporarily set aside an idea or suggestion:

> So, when all is said and done, that was a good idea, but perhaps we ought to let it sit for a while because that particular method might be more useful later in a teaching program.

Finally, if two participants disagree, the leader or expert accepts both persons' ideas as being potentially useful. For example:

Mrs. Stone: I need help with Gary's yelling. He yells whenever he doesn't get his way.

Leader: Anybody got an idea?

Mrs. Wince: How about time out? Every time he yells, put him in his room. That was one of the methods we read about.

Mr. Borgia: Yeah, but that doesn't teach Gary a better way to get what he wants!! (True, but said in such a way that Mrs. Wince's suggestion is attacked, as is her competence.) We have to replace yelling, not just try to get rid of it. (Also true, but to completely agree with Mr. Borgia implies an agreement with his attack on Mrs. Wince.)

Leader: Mr. Borgia, Mrs. Wince does seem to be on the right track, doesn't she? Time out is certainly a method that can help to decrease problem behaviors. (Protects Mrs. Wince by showing the generality of her suggestion.) But you are also right about the importance of replacing problem behaviors with more constructive ones. (Protects Mr. Borgia's idea.) We seem to need a way of pulling together all our ideas and applying them to the problem at hand. How might we both decrease a problem behavior and replace it with a more appropriate behavior? (Presents a more general problem within which both parents' ideas are relevant. Asks group for suggestions.)

4. Parents might be encouraged to develop as many specifics as they can, even if not clearly feasible or related to the "big picture" (i.e., long-term goals and consequences, an educational program plan, or a problem-solving sequence). This "brainstorming" method can be applied to a variety of problems and situations; for instance, alternative ways to increase a child's attention span, make a bed, prompt motor imitation, or replace a particular problem behavior.

5. However, the leader or expert must also help parents to look for the generalities behind the specifics. For example, the consultant helps parents to: examine the possible feasibility, consequences, and costs of various suggestions; discover less apparent intermediate steps which must be considered in a good solution (e.g., food reinforcers are not effective unless they are withheld contingent upon the appropriate behavior); and make choices among the alternatives.

6. During discussions and presentations, parents are informed that they are free to ask questions and to make comments. Moreover, the leader can encourage parents to participate by:

a. Asking questions of specific parents.

b. Simply turning toward or smiling and nodding at specific parents.

c. Remaining silent for 5 or 10 seconds after an important idea has been presented.

d. Making statements or asking questions directed to the group as a whole, such as: "Well, what do you think?"; "How does this apply to you?"; or "Somebody help me on this point, please."

Of course, to strengthen productive verbal participation, the leader or expert praises parents and pinpoints for them just what it was about their statement or question that was noteworthy, such as implicit optimism ("You are optimistic, aren't you! That's great. You have every reason to be optimistic."); prescribing methods to try ("Hey, that's a good idea. Sounds like it's worth a try. Anybody else think that they can use that idea with their child?"); the proper use of behavioral concepts and principles; and encouraging, praising, confirming, showing regard for or offering help to another parent ("I'm sure that my saying this will embarrass you half to death, Mrs. Daring, but it was nice to hear you support Mr. Wince's idea that way.").

7. Finally, one of the consultants (and, later, possibly a parent) can take data on parents' and consultants' verbal participation and on possible indicators of their feelings—for example, how often each parent talks; possible tension, anxiety, fatigue, or unhappiness versus relaxation, energy, and hopefulness; and optimistic/prescriptive statements and questions versus pessimistic and generally unproductive statements and questions. Consultants also note the behaviors of the individual parents with whom they are working. All of the above information can be used during Individual Consultations and home visits, to praise parents for their productive participation or, on the other hand, to think about plans for helping parents to strengthen it.

II. GOALS FOR THE FIRST WEEK OR UNIT

There are five goals for the first week. One is to lay the groundwork for a working group. By "working group" it is meant that the parents, often isolated within their career experiences, develop esprit de corps, consisting of an awareness of common histories, interests (in the sense of knowing what is to their advantage or benefit), and goals, as well as the will or motivation to work together to achieve goals. In addition to esprit de corps (which is the cultural side of the working group), the working group operates on the basis of a relationship which is both businesslike, friendly (involving mutual encouragement, support, reinforcement) and open (that is, honest or "up-front"). Of course, a working group is not established during the first week, but many activities during the meeting get it started.

The second goal is to provide the parents with an overall view of the Program so that they have a framework within which the activities of future weeks will not only make sense, but will be expected. Now, you might be saying to yourself, "Why describe the Program again? That was done during the Pre-Program stage." The reason is that by briefly describing the main components and activities of the Program to the group, you set the occasion for the parents to talk about common experiences that make the Program relevant. In addition, they begin to see the Program as a program for a group—their group.

The third goal is to further strengthen or restrengthen some behaviors and attitudes related to various items on the APG. For example, regarding Readiness to Change, reaffirm and increase the parents' trust and confidence in you, recognition of the need to conduct a home educational program and to change their own behaviors, expectations of success, willingness to give up some time and outside interests so as to participate in the Program, and acceptance of the behavioral approach.

Regarding conducting and maintaining good home educational programs, on the other hand, help the parents to become more objective, give them reason to have confidence in more general principles of learning, stress the importance of productive participation, planning, cooperating with one another, being honest about progress and problems, taking breaks, reinforcing themselves, and establishing linkages with others, and give them some hints as to how to start changing their own and their child's behavior.

A fourth goal is to provide the parents with several of the most important key ideas which recur many times during the Program. Key ideas are statements that summarize the message of certain items on the APG. For example, the key idea behind Item 16 is "Plan, don't react!" Not only are key ideas repeated many times during the Program, but they are often found in materials with which the parents may be provided at various points.

The importance of key ideas is that: (1) they serve as a focal point around which many methods can be organized and (2) parents can use key ideas to govern their own actions, possibly even replacing less productive statements which they might have made to themselves in the past (Mahoney, 1974; Skinner, 1957). For instance, when their child suddenly throws a tantrum, the parents might say to themselves, "Remember! Plan, don't react!" instead of, "Oh, God! I'm going to break her neck!!"

The final goal for the first week or unit is to set the stage for the major task of the second unit, which is to begin to institute productive exchanges in the home. Specifically, during the first week, parents learn to be more objective (Item 12), receive a few hints on ways of instituting productive exchanges (17), and learn several general teaching methods (18) which they might be able to use during the second unit of work.

III. STARTING THE MEETING

Arriving

Naturally, the consultant(s) arrive at the meeting place ahead of the parents so as to greet them. Consultants dress rather casually, as during the Pre-Program stage. As each family arrives, consultants can engage them in small talk until everyone is present. Also, it is helpful if all participants wear a name tag, at least for the first few meetings. Everyone's name tag includes the first name. Chairs are arranged so that parents can easily interact with one another; for example, around a large table. A traditional classroom arrangement, in which one person (the teacher) does most of the talking while the students look at the backs of the heads of people in front of them, is not suggested. Moreover, consultants do not sit together, but spread themselves around among the group. In this way, they become part of the group, rather than above it. Finally, paper and pencils are available for parents or it may be suggested that they bring their own in the future.

In later meetings you can start the meeting on time. Since this is the first meeting and people might have had problems with routes and parking, you might start about 10 minutes late. If you do, point out in a nice way that future meetings will start on time.

Introductions

When everyone is present, the consultant(s) subtly start the meeting by turning their attention from the few parents with whom they might be chatting to the group as a whole. As the small talk dies down and parents look at the consultants, one consultant (the leader) opens the meeting with remarks such as the following:

> Well, it took a long time for all of us to finally get together. Frankly, while I know how important all of the activities of the past few weeks will be in helping us to work together, I got impatient to start the Program. I sure hope you feel the same way.
>
> Now, you have talked about very personal matters with us—your hopes and fears, successes and hardships, your strengths and, as you might see them, your needs. You have let us into your homes, answered our questions, signed a contract with us, and done an assignment. So, if you have started asking yourself "That's all well and good, but what am I going to get out of this?" we can sure understand. Well, starting now, and hopefully for the rest of your lives, you are going to find out what you will get out of all this!

The parents might have a few comments or questions relevant to the above remarks, which should be answered before continuing.

Next, either the same consultant or another consultant might follow the initial remarks by saying something like:

> Okay, to get the show on the road, let's introduce ourselves. If you happen to feel a bit shy about doing that, it's fine. I often feel the same way. Let's tell each other our names and give each other a little information about our children, where we've gone for help, and how things stand now.

The consultant who is speaking can lead off the introductions by giving his or her name and then briefly describing his or her past work with children and parents. Then, the person to the speaker's right or left introduces himself or herself, and so on around the room.

Note that each family need spend only a few minutes describing themselves. More time is given to each family later in the meeting. At this point, you are simply after some names to go with the faces, and a background of some common experiences and problems.

When the introductions are over, the parents, as a group, are praised for speaking up.

Establishing the Contract-Credit System

At this point, you might firm up the operation of any contract-credit system being used. The three options noted below might have been discussed with parents during the Pre-Program stage, and one might have already been chosen. Here are some suggestions of what to say:

> And now for the first item of business—the contract-credit system. You all know about the contract-credit system. Let me repeat the reasons why we use it. First of all, it establishes a businesslike orientation. We know what to expect from each other and we know how well we are doing in meeting our obligations.

> Second, even though we would like to be friends, and no doubt that is what we will become, friendship is not enough to keep us working hard. In fact, even when you are making progress with your children, that progress may cost both you and us a lot of time and effort, and sometimes may not seem like it is worth it. So, to keep us going when the going gets tough, or when we feel pooped, or when we would rather go bowling than run our teaching programs or make our home visits, we use the contract-credit system.
>
> As you also know, we earn credits for doing what we have agreed to do, that is, for productive participation, which means coming to meetings, being on time, making home visits, doing all written and teaching assignments, as well as doing anything else that we have agreed and contracted to do during a certain week. This goes for both parents and consultants.

If a Program Contract alone is being used, most of the above remarks still apply.

The last thing to do is to put the contract-credit system into operation. Or, at this time the parents might develop one. As you recall from Chapters 3 and 4, there are at least three options. In Option 1, a participant or family might earn credits toward certain backup reinforcers, such as baby-sitting or respite care. In Option 2, a participant might earn back portions of a deposit. And, in Option 3, a participant might earn at least a minimum number of credits each week, so as to prevent a certified check or money order from being mailed. The option chosen will affect the operation of the system. Here, then, is one way to institute the contract-credit system depending on which option is chosen.

First, one parent and one consultant might assume the duties of credit-checker (perhaps by asking for volunteers). Thus, if Option 3 is used, consultants turn over their checks to the parent who is their credit-checker, and the parents turn over their checks to the consultant who is their credit-checker. If Option 2 is chosen by the group or by some parents, a ''bank'' is established; a consultant or parent serves as banker. Those using Option 2, then deposit their escrow with the banker.

Next, the credit-checkers can go around the room to determine how well each participant has performed his or her agreed upon tasks during the week. Of course, this week consultants can be assessed only for coming to the meeting and arriving on time, and parents can be assessed only for coming to the meeting, arriving on time, and satisfactorily completing their reading and written assignment (Chapter 1 in *Educating Children*). Thus, this week's check might be considered a trial run with everyone given credits for the remaining items on the Credits-Earned sheet.

In later meetings, however, the consultant who is the credit-checker for the parents examines the parents' written work, as well as asks the consultant for each family how the parents performed agreed upon tasks for the week. Similarly, the parent who is credit-checker for the consultants asks the parents who are working with each consultant how well the consultants performed agreed upon tasks.

At each stop around the group, the credit-checkers fill out a Credits-Earned sheet for each family or consultant and inform the participants of how they fared on each item. A carbon copy of each Credits-Earned sheet is made: one copy is kept by the participant and the other is filed in the family folder.

Finally, consequences can be delivered according to the option chosen and the number of credits earned. For instance, a participant might earn a backup reinforcer or learn how many credits are still required; earn back or fail to earn back a certain portion of the deposit; prevent a check from being sent or be informed that in the future a check would be mailed. In all cases, the credit-checker pinpoints the satisfactory or unsatisfactory nature of the performance on each item. Consultants and parents can discuss each other's performance in more detail during the Individual Consultation and home visit.

Stressing the Importance of Productive Participation. Once final arrangements have been made, stress the importance of productive participation (Item 11). Emphasize that you would like the group to develop esprit de corps and cooperative working relationships, both during and outside of meetings. Then, using the list of behaviors for Item 11 on the Assessment and Programming Guide (APG), briefly review what it takes to participate in a productive way. Note that the Program Contract which each family has may serve as a handout which describes all the components of productive participation. Thus, they can use the Program Contract to assess and manage their participation.

This is a good time to discuss the roles of rotating leader and temporary expert, as well as the basic methods for facilitating effective and creative communication (described above). Here is an example of remarks made by a consultant at this point:

> Now, you may be thinking that (the contract-credit system and) all this talk about productive participation, rotating leaders, and communication is complicated and has little to do with why we are here. Well, these are means to an end. We are all here to help our children, ourselves, and others. And the contract-credit system, plus attention to group processes, will help us to achieve our goals.
>
> As to the contract-credit system (and/or the Program Contract), we simply do not know if it is absolutely necessary. But we do know that other families have welcomed it, said that it did help them over the rough spots, that it was nice to have all their tasks down in black and white, and helpful to know just how they were doing at all times. At any rate, it can't hurt.
>
> As to rotating leaders and temporary experts, this is not going to be forced on anyone. Slowly but surely, as we become a group, feel more comfortable with one another, and start closing in on particular problems, then we will start working to help you to take over the running of the meetings.
>
> One last point, and an important one! It is to your advantage to learn how to do for yourselves everything we are doing with you. For example, if you learn how to run part of a group meeting, you are likely to be able to help in other groups working to

> get or improve services, or to help families. And if you learn how to assess yourselves, your children, and the family—just as we were doing during interviews and observations—then you are more likely to accentuate your strengths, avoid potential problems, and pinpoint and solve problems that do occur. Finally, we want you to learn how to evaluate us, for instance, how effectively meetings are being run, the adequacy of the educational methods for your children, the adequacy of the materials we give you. We want you to provide us with feedback on how well we are doing in the same way that we will be providing you with feedback. In that way, we can all maintain high standards and a high-quality Program.
>
> Now, let us get down to the main business of this meeting. . . .

After discussing the contract-credit system and productive participation, which takes no more than about 15 minutes, begin the main business portion of the meeting.

IV. MAIN BUSINESS

In this portion of the meeting, parents are provided with a fairly detailed description and explanation of the overall Program and what it means, both to you and to them. By briefly reviewing the five goals of this unit, you can see that all of them are being worked on here. In general, you are helping to generate esprit de corps among the parents and close working relationships in the group. In addition, you are touching upon several of the key ideas and basic teaching methods.

The presentation and discussion during this portion of the meeting has five parts.

Why We Are Here

The following remarks convey the goals of the Program. They are substantively the remarks that I and my associates make at this point of the first meeting:

> Basically, we are here so that together we can help you to take charge of your children's future. We will help you to learn and to use important skills for planning, running, and keeping track of a home educational program which may change your children in a big way. Make no mistake about it, though. This means learning new skills on your part. It may even mean changing some basic ideas of yours and some habitual ways in which you deal with your children, yourselves, and with other people.
>
> Now, individually, we have already talked about the many reasons why it is important for you to conduct programs for your children in the home. In fact, we have agreed on most, if not all, of the reasons. If not, we wouldn't be here. Let me repeat them briefly so that we can start on common ground.
>
> Well, first, your kids do a lot of things that are driving you up the wall and that do, or will, get your children into trouble and keep them from enjoying many of the good things in life. We can teach you how to reduce and replace those problem behaviors

with behaviors that are helpful for your children to learn and do, which are considered appropriate, normal, some of which may even be expected or demanded if your child is to have a place in this society.

The second reason has to do with the relationship between home and school. Even if your children are in a terrific program and are learning all kinds of things, that does not mean that they are going to do any of them, or do them well, in the home. You have to learn some of the skills your kids' teachers have, if it is a good program, or else a lot of the progress they are making in school may have no effect on your child at home. On the other hand, if you are not satisfied with your children's school program, this program teaches you not only how to provide your children with a partial substitute, but how to evaluate your children's school program and to make important comments on how it can be improved. In fact, imagine what a group of motivated and skillful parents could do to help change the school programs their children are in!

And, if your children are not even in a program anywhere, you certainly need to learn how to teach your children in the home.

Third, many of you have said that you've had a rough time getting help over the years. And you may be pretty bitter as a result of your experiences. Well, we can't make excuses for others, but the truth is that many people and many facilities have just not been geared to meet your needs and the needs of your children. Some, as you know, have not seemed to be interested in the particular problems of your kids.

But things have been changing and can be changed even more. One benefit of this Program, then, is that it can help to prepare your children for evaluations because, as you know, if your children are screaming their heads off or do not pay attention, it is hard to pinpoint their strengths and weaknesses. In addition, we can help you to use available services such as physicians or speech therapists, and to seek outside help when it is needed.

Finally, the Program will help you to establish networks between families, so that you all can maintain your efforts and home programs, and can help others to do what you will have learned.

This is also a good time to have the parents, as individuals and as a group, discuss their own short- and long-term goals, specifying what they want the Program to do for them. They can be using the list of goals written at the end of their Assessment. During the discussion, help parents to:

1. Break down long-term goals into smaller, short-term steps.
2. Examine the possible costs and feasibility of attaining certain goals through the Program and in the future (cautious optimism).
3. Become aware of some reasons or motives behind their goals.
4. Become aware of some possible consequences of achieving or, as they may see it, not achieving their goals.

The presentation and discussion can follow some of the suggestions made in Section VII, Chapter 4.

Finally, you might conduct an exercise used by Dr. Kenneth Kaufman in his programs. All parents simply write five problems which they would like to be able to correct. You need give no instructions as to the kinds of problems they might list. The exercise should take no more than 10 minutes or so. Each family keeps a copy of its list and files it away. Consultants also keep a copy and file it in the families' folders for this week. Later in the Program, the parents' lists can be reviewed to help them gain a perspective on their past and on their progress for, by the time they read their list again, they should be able to solve many of the problems or no longer see them as problems.

At this point, the group might take a 10-minute break. When the group returns, continue with the second part of the main business.

Reviewing Ideas in Chapter 1 of *Educating Children*

For a change of voice, tempo, and style, this part of the presentation might be handled by a different leader-consultant. When everyone is seated, have parents open their copies of *Educating Children* to Chapter 1. The speaker can stand in front of, but close to, the group, so as to give quick demonstrations and use the blackboard. Here are the ideas to convey and some of the statements which the leader-consultant might make. It is a good idea to write the headings, as well as key ideas, on a blackboard. Key ideas are in capital letters below:

> The ideas in Chapter 1 are simple but are the foundation for everything else that we will be learning and doing. So, please ask questions if you are even slightly unsure of anything.
>
> First, no matter how many special tests your kids (and you) have been given, no matter how many theories explain why your child never learned like some people say children are supposed to learn, and no matter what kinds of expensive machines have been built, pills have been invented, and therapies are being tried, you get to the bottom line and start trying to answer the questions, What, underneath all the talk, is the problem? What needs to be done? The answer, every time, is: THE MOST IMPORTANT PROBLEM OF YOUR CHILDREN NOW IS THEIR BEHAVIOR. The reason you are here, the reason why you have spent so much time and money looking for help, and the reason why your kids got into trouble was the behaviors they were not doing often enough or well enough and the behaviors they were doing too often or should not have been doing at all.
>
> Sure, we can still try to find out what went wrong inside of them, maybe in their nervous systems, that kept them from learning properly. But even if we knew why, that would not solve all of the problems. We would still have to focus on their behaviors. And we have to do a lot more than just look at their behaviors. WE HAVE TO CHANGE THEIR BEHAVIORS.
>
> LABELS. Your kids have all kinds of labels, sometimes as many labels as people you have seen for help. The labels aren't much help, are they? Sure, it's better than nothing, I guess. If people told you, "Well, I don't know. I never saw anything like this child in my whole life!" that would scare you plenty. Okay, so you've got labels. You know that your child's problems are not unheard of. That's cold comfort at this point, though. Because behavior change is the problem, not label change.

Look, IF YOUR CHILD'S BEHAVIOR CHANGES SUFFICIENTLY, THEN THE LABEL MAY CHANGE. If a child plays, cooperates, concentrates, and doesn't run around all day, then he should no longer be called "hyperactive." If he talks like anyone else, plays, cooperates, shows affection, and so on and so on, then he should no longer be labeled "autistic." And when he can and does read like other people his age, then he should no longer be called "dyslexic." More importantly, as your children's behaviors improve, people's attitudes toward your children are likely to change.

So, again, let the researchers do the needed research. Let the theorists find the explanations. And let the labelers make the right diagnoses. We're not going to knock anybody's work on behalf of the kids. But OUR JOB IS CHANGING BEHAVIOR!

By the way, when you change your children's behavior, but still don't know what started your children off on the wrong foot way back when, will you care that you still don't know? (A good time for comments.)

BEHAVIOR IS MOVEMENTS. Well, then, just what do we mean by "behavior"? In a nutshell, behavior means . . . (give parents a chance to answer) movements! Watch me! Some of what I'm doing is called verbal behavior or talking. Just what is it? Look! Look at my movements that go together to make up verbal behavior. I move my jaws, chest, lips, tongue, vocal cords.

Do any of your kids throw tantrums? Engage in tantrum behavior? (Wait for a parent to respond affirmatively, then call on the parent. If no one responds, pick another behavior.) Okay, what movements does (child's name) do when he (or she) throws a tantrum? Remember, try not to use words like "angry" or "frustrated," because those words don't tell me what he actually does any more than the word "tantrum" does. (These last lines are said with a smile. When the parent gives a good behavioral description, the parent should, of course, be enthusiastically praised for "catching on" to the use of "observables" so quickly.)

At this point, to continue the discussion of behavior-as-movement, have the parents turn to page 9 of *Educating Children,* where they were assigned the task of observing their child for five minutes. Ask several parents to describe briefly what their child did. Make sure to praise them for describing behaviors in terms of movements. If they make any mistakes (for example, inferring intentions, feelings, or causes, which may be valid but are not what they were asked to do), prompt them to redescribe the same behaviors in terms of what they actually saw—namely movements. Do not spend more than 10 minutes on this task, though. There is plenty of time during the next week. You can then continue with the following remarks:

BEHAVIOR CAN CHANGE IN FOUR WAYS. Well, if the problem is to change behavior, in what ways does it need to change? Most behaviors can change in at least four ways. For example, your child might need to learn to do certain behaviors better or with more skill or more efficiently, that is, with fewer unneeded movements, or in a way that is considered the "right" way to do it. (Ask for examples.)

Or, your child may need to learn to do some behaviors more, that is, more often or more times, or for a longer time. (Ask for examples.)

Third, your child may need to learn to do some behaviors at the right times or places, with more people or in more places, or only with certain people or in certain places. For instance, your child may learn how to ask for things that she wants with great skill and enough times during the day, but if she asks only you or asks only people in the house, then her asking behavior is not yet up to snuff. (Ask for additional examples.)

Finally, your child may need to learn to do some behaviors less often or for less time. For instance, it's okay, I suppose, to cry a little when you scrape your knee, but not for an hour. And a tantrum every once in a while is to be expected. But twelve tantrums a day is a bit much! There are better ways to pass the time and get what you want. (Again, ask for examples.)

REPLACE. One more basic idea we need to stress is, always think about replacing your children's problem behaviors with appropriate behaviors., Why? First of all, your children need to learn appropriate or good behaviors (like cooperating, playing, and doing chores). And if we only think about getting rid of problem behaviors, we may completely forget about the good behaviors that your children need to learn. Second, it simply works faster and easier when we increase good behaviors and decrease problem behaviors at the same time.

Ask the parents to turn to page 16 of *Educating Children*.

The last part of your assignment was to make a list of behaviors to change, as well as behaviors that you think do not need to be changed. Well, in what order did you list behaviors to change? Did you put good behaviors or problem behaviors at the top? (Again, stress the importance of teaching appropriate behaviors.)

In this Program we begin by talking more about increasing good behaviors than decreasing problem behaviors. In the next few weeks, you will see how fast you can replace some problem behaviors with good behaviors simply by catching your kids when they are doing good—by ignoring the problem behaviors as much as you can and by focusing on and rewarding the good behaviors. If certain problem behaviors do not yield to that method, then we will talk about decreasing them in a more direct way.

The third part of the presentation involves basic steps and ideas in planning a comprehensive educational program. The bulk of work on this item (14), however, occurs during the fourth unit (Chapter 8). Here is what you might say at this point.

Now, in order to properly go about changing your children's and your own behaviors, you need to know "principles of learning," or how people learn. You will be finding out about how people learn and teach each other next week. Anyway, before you actually conduct a teaching program to change a behavior, you have to plan your children's educational programs. I want to tell you briefly how that is done. During our third and fourth week, we will be discussing this in detail.

Planning an educational program, a comprehensive educational program, means finding answers to three questions. We, the book *Educating Children,* and your own efforts will give you the answers.

The first question is something like this: WHAT ARE MY CHILD'S STRENGTHS AND WEAKNESSES? In other words, you want to find out which behaviors you need to help your child to change and just which ways each of these behaviors needs to be changed. For instance, does your child need help with cooperation? If so, in what ways does he need help? Does he need to learn to cooperate more often? With more skill? With more people?

To answer this question, you evaluate your child's behaviors. The Behavior Evaluation Scale (BES) and Behavior Evaluation Table (BET) at the back of *Educating Children* tell you exactly how to do that. The BES shows you how to evaluate ninety-nine behaviors to find out if your child needs help with each and, if so, which way each behavior needs to be changed. Let's take a look at the BES and BET for a few moments.

Quickly skim through the BES and BET (and, if used, other behavioral assessments) with the parents, making sure to point out: (1) the seven skill areas, (2) how target behaviors are arranged from easier to harder in each skill area, and (3) how each item of the BES asks various questions which help the parents to figure out if their child needs help with that behavior, and what kinds of help the child needs. Then pick one or two BES items and have the parents read the items while you discuss them.

After you evaluate your child, the second question is, WHERE DO I START MY CHILD'S EDUCATIONAL PROGRAM AND HOW DO I FIND OUT WHICH SKILL AREAS I SHOULD WORK ON? This is an important question. Even if it is obvious that your child needs help in the skill area called Functional Speech, for example, you can't just start working there. Why? Because your child might not be ready.

By "ready," we mean that a child has learned the basics that are needed to be successful in a skill area. Remember, you have to walk before you can run. In the same way, before your child is going to be successful at learning to talk, he has to learn such "basic behaviors" as eye contact, cooperating, and motor imitation. Notice that the basic behaviors for a certain skill area are from the other and easier skill areas.

To figure out just which skill area to start with, we use the Table of Basic Behaviors on pages 84 and 85 of *Educating Children*. (Have the parents turn to the above-mentioned pages.) You see, the Table of Basic Behaviors tells you just which behaviors, basic behaviors, your child needs to learn before he is ready to work in each skill area. If you check this table and then check the BES that you filled out, you will know if your child has learned all of the basic behaviors needed to work in each area. Then, you simply find the skill area for which your child is ready. If he is not ready for any of the other skill areas, you simply start with Learning Readiness skills. Later, when you want to find out if your child is ready for any of the harder skill areas, you again check the Table on pages 84 and 85 and your scoring of the BES, which you will update to show that your child has learned new behaviors.

The last question is, WHERE DO I GO NEXT? In other words, in what sequence do you move from one skill area to the next? You remember from your reading of Chapter 1 that we work in a sequence of small steps. We teach target behaviors in small steps; we work through a skill area in small steps; and we conduct an educational program in small steps.

Now turn to page 82 of *Educating Children*. This is called the Skill Sequence Table. It shows you how to move from one skill area to another.

Here, briefly describe the skill sequence and answer any questions. Before you go on to the fourth part of the presentation, however, make sure that the parents realize that they are not expected to understand how to plan and conduct an educational program at this point. They are only supposed to see the step-by-step planning process and how they will be using various tables to help them. In sum, you want them to see that the job will not be as complicated as they might have thought.

At this point, begin the fourth part of the presentation.

Hard Evidence of (and Some Key Reasons for) Success

Parents may be thinking that what you have been talking about sounds nice, but does it work and can they do it? This, then, is the time to give them hard evidence of the effectiveness of Programs in teaching parents to teach their children, as well as some of the key ideas that have guided parents in their successful work. If possible, show portions of videotapes of several families from past Programs, both during Baseline Observations and at several points during and after their Program. If videotapes are not available or if this is your first Program, films, such as "Reinforcement Therapy" (Smith, Kline and French); "A Social Learning Approach to Family Therapy" (Research Press); "One Step at a Time" (CRM Films); "Teaching Children New Behavior" (Behavior Technics, Inc.); the "Step Behind" series (Hallmark Films and Recordings, Inc.) are good substitutes, as are descriptions of Programs others have conducted. (See references in Chapter 1.)

While describing the work of other parents, make sure to pinpoint and stress the following:

1. The parents and children are similar to the parents and children in the present Program. Thus, drive home the point: "If they could do it, so can you!"

2. The lives of the parents (as well as siblings) are easier now, and the parents are more hopeful and confident, despite the fact that at one point they were not sure if they had "what it took" to be successful.

3. The children changed during the Program, many a great deal, and are still changing, because many parents, siblings, and others are still working at it. Be specific in describing gains in the different skill areas. For example, many long-standing patterns of disruptive behaviors were replaced with attentiveness, cooperation, playing, and doing chores; the children learned to imitate the appropriate behaviors of others, were learning to talk and to take care of themselves.

4. Successful parents:

a. Worked on hard behaviors, reinforcing their children for trying hard and for making correct responses; they "caught 'em doing good."

b. Required their children to earn rewards (no freebies).

c. Reinforced their children immediately at first.

d. Were confident that when they finally found out the best way to teach, their child would make progress.

e. Were satisfied with small changes leading to big ones.

f. Did not immediately react when problem behaviors occurred. Instead, they waited and planned what to do.

g. Cooperated and worked together as a team ("We're in this together").

h. Took scheduled breaks and reinforced themselves as progress was made and as goals were achieved.

Emphasize the above points throughout the showing of videotapes or the discussion of past parents' work. For example, if a portion of videotape or film shows a child throwing a tantrum and the parents calmly waiting until the child stops before going on with a teaching session, point it out to the viewers:

> Watch this again. See? When the tantrum starts, they don't talk to the child. They wait and think of what to do next.

Afterward, encourage parents to comment about the videotapes, films, or descriptions. Reinforce them for making optimistic statements and generalizing from what they have seen to their own families. Do not reinforce pessimistic statements! Get parents thinking and talking in a positive, prescriptive way. For instance, if parents indicate that they do not think that they have the skill, again stress that they are probably no different from other parents, either in their abilities or in their feelings; that other parents soon found out just how competent they could become.

If parents assert that their child is somehow different from the children seen on the tapes or films (implying that the methods might not work with their children), ask them to be specific. Then, explain that no two children are alike! It is not that one "type" of child can learn whereas another "type" cannot, because the principles of learning and of good teaching are the same. Rather, the details of the teaching programs might be different for each child. In sum, using the videotapes, films, or descriptions, do your best to help the parents believe that they may well do the same thing with their children that the other parents have done (again, cautious optimism).

It might be helpful to have a few parents from past Programs, especially those on videotapes, enter the meeting at this point. Then, consultants and parents can listen as the "old hands" describe their experiences before, during, and after the Program. Parents from the present Program are encouraged to ask the "old hands'' some questions. It is a good idea for the ''old hands'' who attend this portion of the meeting to have backgrounds and children similar to parents in the present Program. Both successes and the overcoming of difficulties are stressed.

The final part of the presentation concerns the behaviors of the parents.

What it Takes to be Successful

This part of the presentation is to bring a sense of closure to what has been discussed so far. You began by discussing goals; then spent a lot of time discussing the behavioral approach to understanding children's problems and needs; outlined the educational program for the children; and gave hard evidence of success. In concluding the main business of this meeting, then, bring the discussion back to the role of the parents. In particular:

1. Provide each family with a copy of the Assessment and Programming Guide (APG) (if you have not yet done so).
2. Present some APG items that spell success (asking parents to skim over the items on their copies of the APG at the same time).
3. Note the kinds of problems that can occur during and after the Program.
4. End on a prescriptive note by describing methods that parents (and their consultants) can use to avoid or overcome problems.

Here is what we have said at this point:

> We've been talking about what your children will gain. What will you gain? A great deal! When you have completed this Program, you should be more confident, optimistic about what can be done, full of energy and ideas, and skillful. And, if that is not enough, you will also have made good friends (some of whom are the people sitting here with you) whose help you can count on, people who have been through much the same thing that you have and who will have acquired the same skills as you, people with whom you might be able to work to change the way society deals with children with problems.
>
> Does this sound like a large order? Well, I hope it does! Large order maybe. Tall tale, no! We have run this Program too many times for it not to work. There is only one catch, and I think you know what it is. You are going to have to work at changing things, and you are going to have to work together, but it is important that you see that the work you put in now will be no more, and possibly less, than the work you have been putting in for years. In other words, the work you put in now should pay dividends for years to come!
>
> Not only does it take plain work (or productive participation), such as doing assignments, but it takes working in a certain way. You see, to be successful we have to do things right. Luckily, we have a good idea of what that way is. Here is a quick look at what you might call the ''keys to success.''

It is a good idea to write the key ideas on a blackboard.

First of all, be OBJECTIVE. You have to be able to: describe what is going on in your own behavior and in your children's behavior carefully; explain why things are the way they are; and learn how to keep track of progress.

Second, strange as it sounds, you have to have CONFIDENCE or faith. You have to see that change takes place not because of the kind of person you think you are, but because you have helped to set up a situation that has just what it takes for your children to learn. If you can have confidence in principles of learning and make sure that you create the right setting for your children, it will be a lot easier to plan, conduct, and evaluate your teaching programs.

You also have to plan a COMPREHENSIVE educational program, which we will be doing a few weeks from now. As you know, if the educational program is not planned out, there is no telling what your child will learn, or if your child will learn much at all.

Then, as discussed earlier, you need to become a cool customer, that is, to develop a pattern of waiting and PLANNING before you try to handle a problem that comes up, whether that problem is one of your children's disruptive behaviors or even uncomfortable feelings and thoughts inside of you.

Along with learning to wait and plan, rather than react to what bothers you, you need to learn how to interact with your children in ways that will generally increase good behaviors and decrease problem behaviors. In other words, you need to institute PRODUCTIVE EXCHANGES. Next week we will be talking all about this.

And, along with interacting in a productive way, you have to learn the methods for TEACHING specific behaviors with which your children need help.

Now all of the things that I just mentioned have to do with skills of actually teaching your child. In addition, certain conditions help you to be a good teacher and to keep on being a good teacher.

First, you need to work as a TEAM in the home. You have to cooperate. Now there are all kinds of ways of cooperating: teaching at the same time (co-teaching) or splitting up tasks (for instance, one person teaching and another person coaching). In later meetings, we will talk about different ways of working together.

Second, you need some ORGANIZATION in the home. For example, to make sure that things like meals and bedtimes are regular, that chores are done on time, and that the noise is kept down. I know! We all have our bad days! But you have to work a little to keep things organized in the home or else your teaching may be all disrupted.

Third, you need to learn how to handle what you might call PERSONAL PROBLEMS, such as anxiety and tension, pessimism, fatigue, and even depressed moods. Many people get these bad feelings now and then, and they may keep you from participating as you know you should, or keep you from conducting the kind of good educational program that you know you could be conducting. We can teach you ways to handle these kinds of problems, if they ever happen.

Another condition that helps you to conduct a good home educational program is taking SCHEDULED BREAKS, as well as REINFORCING yourselves. You just can't be teaching all the time! You just can't be having your child's needs on your mind all the time! You deserve and need to take breaks on a scheduled basis. Also, you need to learn how to gratify yourselves, as individuals and as a couple, through pleasant activities, kind words, favors, and so on. These will help to keep your mood up and your motivation high.

You need to become involved in what you might call NETWORKS and organizations outside of the family, from which you can get help and information. You can also make important contributions to others that way.

Then, you have to learn how to GENERALIZE your child's gains to other places and to other people. For example, to teach your child what to do in various public places. And you need to get others, such as brothers and sisters, grandparents, and store clerks, to interact with your child in the right way.

Finally, to help you keep things afloat all the time, you will learn how to pinpoint and SOLVE PROBLEMS that might come up, whether they are in your child's educational program or in your own behavior. That way, you never lose what you have worked so hard to achieve.

Yes, indeed, it is a large order! But, no one said that the job has to be finished next week. We work one step at a time on all of what we have been talking about. You have materials to read that will remind you of what to do to avoid and handle all kinds of problems. You will have other parents to help you. We will be with you, not behind you and not on the sidelines watching, but with you every step of the way.

Well, as they say, "There's no time like the present." In fact, if this isn't the time to start, then when is? And if we aren't the ones to do the job, then who is?

At this point, again explain that the parents use the Assessment and Programming Guide (which, perhaps, should be revised for self-administration) both to pinpoint strengths and needs, pinpoint and solve potential problems, and evaluate progress. As the Program goes on, then, consultants can help the parents to assess themselves using the APG; for instance, during Individual Consultations and home visits. In other words, the parents will now have been provided with four sets of materials which they can use to change and maintain their behaviors—the book *Educating Children,* the Program Contract, the list of goals that was written down at the end of the family assessment, and the APG. Have the parents keep their materials in one place; for instance, in a folder or notebook.

V. ACTIVITIES FOR THE NEXT WEEK

At this time, briefly describe the main business for the coming week and the parents' assignment. The main business involves principles of learning; how principles of learning apply to the home situation (for example, effects of career experiences on the parents and various patterns of interaction—structured exchanges—between parents and children); and, finally, how to institute productive exchanges.

The reading assignment is Chapter 2 (and all written assignments) and pages

186–189 of Chapter 9 in *Educating Children*. Chapter 2 presents basic principles of learning and uses them to analyze exchanges in family and school settings. Pages 186 to 189 discuss methods for instituting productive exchanges as the first step in an educational program. If the parents have been supplied with a copy of the APG, they can also read Items 16 and 17.

VI. INDIVIDUAL CONSULTATION

After briefly describing the activities for the next week, the group can divide into small groups: parents sit down with their consultants. Here, the consultant and parents briefly review some of the main ideas discussed during the meeting.

A weekly Contract should be written (using a form such as the one in Appendix 5) which specifies the reading and written assignment for the next week, the date and time of the home visit, and any tasks that the parents might wish the consultant to perform during the week. For instance, as a result of what has been discussed during the first meeting, the parents want the consultant to help find solutions to some problems.

Since the consultant will be focusing on structured exchanges during the home visit, it is helpful if the parents complete reading and written assignments before the home visit. Thus, the home visit is scheduled three or four days after this meeting. And, parents might agree in writing (that is, on the Weekly Contract form) to finish their assignment before the home visit.

VII. HOME VISIT

The home visit for the first week is an introduction to the main business of the second unit, which is to see (pinpoint) and understand the major patterns of exchange in the family, and perhaps try to institute productive exchanges. Bring a copy of the Weekly Contract for the first week, as well as a list of exchanges noted during the Baseline Observations. Remember, business before pleasure. If the parents offer coffee when you arrive for the home visit, tell them that you would enjoy sharing some with them, but after the business of the visit has been completed. Here is what you might do during this home visit.

First, review Chapter 2 of *Educating Children*. For example: (1) discuss some of the major ideas presented in that chapter, (2) discuss the parents' answers to several of the questions at the end of the chapter, and (3) answer any questions they may have.

Next, give the parents the opportunity to analyze various structured exchanges in the home, in the same way they analyzed the vignettes in Chapter 2. They can analyze exchanges involving the following behaviors of their child: those listed by them at the end of Chapter 1, those that concern them, and those noted during

Baseline Observations. Analyze behaviors of both children and parents in productive and counterproductive exchanges.

To give the parents more practice in analyzing exchanges, you might show them portions of videotapes made during their Baseline Observations, presenting both productive and counterproductive exchanges. (This is optional since it will be done at the second meeting.) While showing a particular exchange, the parents should be coached to pinpoint signals (presented by the parents), the behavior of the child, and the consequences (delivered by the parents), and to predict the direction in which the behaviors in the exchange can be expected to change. It is helpful to run each portion several times, stopping the action at each segment of an exchange to help the parents to pinpoint each behavior.

When analyzing the exchanges, help the parents to draw out the implications of what they are seeing or describing, as found in pages 186 to 189 of Chapter 9 in *Educating Children*. For example, parents should:

1. Not react immediately when problem behaviors occur, but wait, plan what to do, and then respond in a constructive manner, a manner designed to replace the problem behavior.
2. Respond to problem behaviors by completely ignoring the behavior, immediately timing out the child, or, if necessary, punishing the child—for instance, for self-injurious behavior (if necessary, parents can read Chapter 15 of *Educating Children*).
3. Not talk themselves blue in the face trying to get the child to perform a behavior (e.g., a simple task) but wait until the child is attending, then present a simple, clear signal, and, if necessary, prompt the child through the behavior.
4. Not reward the child for aimless behavior or for mild whining or pushing or pulling, but require their child to make an effort to earn rewards for cooperating with simple directions, playing, asking for what the child wants, or for performing self-help routines.
5. Be on the lookout for behaviors to reward, and reward those behaviors immediately, often, with enthusiastic praise, and with the reinforcers they are requiring their child to earn.

Moreover, they must begin to see that the principles for instituting and managing productive exchanges apply to all behaviors and not just the few that concern them at this time.

Finally, on the basis of what has been discussed so far with parents, help them to specify how to change some of the ways they deal with certain problem behaviors and what they can do to strengthen certain appropriate behaviors. Then, you can role-play with the parents just how to institute the new exchanges and coach them to do so when interacting with their child. For instance, if their child often pushes and pulls on them to get things, and if the parents (with or without your help) have decided to require their child to make some effort to ask for what the child wants, you can role-play and coach parents on the method for instructing or prompting the child to make an effort to ask.

Note that the parents are not yet expected to institute all of the pinpointed exchanges. That is the topic for the next week. However, indicate to them that they are free to institute whatever changes they wish. If they do intend to start making changes in a few exchanges (the easiest being more opportunities to respond and more reinforcement for appropriate behaviors), have them call you the next day to give a progress report and take notes on the results of their efforts. These additional assignments should be written on the current Weekly Contract.

When the main business of the visit has been concluded, share some refreshments with the parents, if they have offered. Whether or not you have refreshments, make sure to reinforce the parents for their work of the week, pinpointing just what they did well; for instance, productive talk during meetings, their assignments, and the way they are picking up the ideas and methods. Reassure them about the likelihood of successful outcomes of their Program.

VIII. PLANNING THE ACTIVITIES FOR THE SECOND (OR NEXT) WEEK

As soon as possible after the meeting and home visit, consultants discuss the past week's work, using notes made during and after the meeting, home visits, or phone calls. Consultants then pinpoint areas of progress, as well as problems or potential problems. For instance, it might be noted that one parent seems timid, that another is already using many behavioral principles, that another may have a hard time learning to plan rather than react, and that another seems to be a "natural" at using basic teaching methods as indicated by her changing the way she interacts with her child, solely on the basis of what she read in Chapter 2 of *Educating Children*. Specific plans are then made to deal with potential problems during the coming weeks. Also, indicate progress and problems on each parent's Assessment and Programming Guide; for example, Items 2 through 10 on readiness to change: 11 (productive participation); 12 (objectivity); 13 (confidence in principles); 15 (agreeing to try certain behavioral methods); 16 (planning rather than reacting); 17 (instituting productive exchanges); 19 (cooperation); 20 (organized home life); and 21 (personal problems).

Consultants plan the agenda for the second meeting. For example, portions of videotapes to be used, role-playing exercises, demonstrations, presentations to be made, and materials to be distributed should all be prepared. Chapter 6 describes the activities and materials for the second meeting or unit.

6 UNIT TWO: INSTITUTING PRODUCTIVE EXCHANGES

This long chapter describes in detail every step of the work in this unit. Later chapters are shorter since, except for some reminders, I give the details only on what is new. The material for this unit of work takes at least three hours to complete. If you run out of time in a meeting, a good place to end the main business portion is after the section titled "Analyzing the Families' Careers, Parents' Behaviors, and Certain Family Problems." During the Individual Consultation and home visit, though, you can still follow most of the suggestions provided in this chapter. For instance, if there is simply not enough time during the Individual Consultation for the parents and consultant to write a fairly detailed plan to institute productive exchanges, that can be done during the home visit. At the next meeting you can pick up where you left off, for example, with the section titled "Instituting Productive Exchanges."

I. GOALS FOR THE SECOND UNIT OR WEEK

The main goal is for the parents to institute productive exchanges in the home: Item 17 of the Assessment and Programming Guide (APG). This first step in their child's educational program is described on pages 186 to 189 of *Educating Children With Learning and Behavior Problems*. By instituting productive exchanges at this early point, the parents will become more skillful with some of the basic teaching methods and give their child a head start, possibly reducing some problem behaviors and beginning to replace them with appropriate behaviors such as attending or cooperating with simple requests. In addition to instituting productive exchanges, during this unit of work, help the parents to learn other skills described in the APG, which are:

Item 11. Productive participation: attendance, doing assignments, group participation.

Item 12. Objectivity: describing and pinpointing target behaviors; using principles of learning to analyze behaviors and exchanges and to describe or explain major aspects of family career; writing logs or taking notes on daily events.

Item 13. Confidence in learning principles and long-term perspective.

Item 15. Agreeing to try certain behavioral methods.

Item 16. Following a problem-solving sequence rather than reacting.

Item 18. General teaching methods: arranging the physical environment; using signals, prompts, and rewards properly.

Item 19. Cooperation of spouses or partners: working toward agreement; working together at instituting exchanges; supporting and reinforcing one another; sharing household tasks.

Item 20. Organized home life: especially maintaining a low enough level of noise and activity.

Item 21. Pinpointing and solving personal problems: if necessary, pinpointing and starting to analyze personal problems.

Item 22. Honesty: accurately describing behaviors, progress, problems, feelings.

Item 23. Scheduling breaks: learning to schedule and take off a few hours each day and a day a week.

Item 24. Reinforcement of each other: scheduling and delivering reinforcement to themselves and each other.

Item 25. Linkage with networks and organizations: establishing the beginning of telephone network among families.

Item 26. Generalization: enlisting cooperation from and coaching siblings and others living in the home.

Item 27. Pinpointing and solving problems: using materials to remind themselves of what to do during the week (e.g., how to institute exchanges, scheduling breaks, self-reinforcement, cooperation) and to assess performance.

Although this looks like a large order, keep in mind that you are not working on all of the components of the above items. Moreover, the parents are not expected to become completely competent in one week. Actually, you want them to learn just enough to be generally successful. Over the next three or four weeks, by continuing to work on the same items, the parents will become more and more proficient until, by the time they conduct their first formal teaching program (around the fifth week), they will have mastered many of the items listed above. Consequently, it is important to use the APG to keep track of progress and potential problems in a family.

But how do the parents and consultants keep track of what is supposed to be learned and done each week? The answer is that everything that you and the parents are supposed to do during the week regarding the APG items is written on the Weekly Contract form at the end of each meeting, for example, the reading, written, and teaching assignments; scheduling breaks; reinforcement for oneself and for each other; enlisting cooperation from others; and working to solve personal problems. In that way, everyone knows what he or she is supposed to do and, at the end of the week, can evaluate performance.

II. STARTING THE MEETING

Checking Performance

As was begun during the first meeting, if you are using a contract-credit system, the parents and consultant who are the credit checkers go around the room and find out from the other parents and consultants how well each person has satisfied the terms of the main Program Contract (e.g., coming on time) and the last Weekly Contract (e.g., completing the assignments).

Both checkers write down on a Credits-Earned sheet the number of credits earned by the consultants or parents they are checking. Each family and consultant is given one copy of his or her Credits-Earned sheet for the week. A carbon copy is filed. Parents and consultants are then congratulated for earning or coming closer to earning backup reinforcers, gaining back some of their initial deposit (which might be returned at this time), or preventing a certified check from being sent. For example:

Consultant to parents: Good job Blake family: You've earned back five dollars of your deposit.

Mr. and Mrs. Fernandez, you are now within two credits of six hours of baby-sitting time!

On the other hand, if a participant has not earned enough credits to prevent a certified check from being sent, to earn back a portion of the deposit, or to earn a backup reinforcer for that week (e.g., baby-sitting time), the participant is informed of it in a businesslike way. That is, the checker privately points out just what the participant failed to do well enough. For example:

Consultant to parents: Well, you earned only 14 credits this week. You both were late, which is two points that you did not earn. And you did not complete the written assignment, which is worth two more credits. You need 16 credits to earn back 10 dollars of your deposit. So, during the Individual Consultation, let's work on a method for helping you to earn those credits. I'm sure that you'll do fine next week.

Parent to consultant: Sorry, Jim, but according to Mrs. Fernandez you forgot to make last week's home visit and you were late to tonight's meeting. So you earned only five credits out of eight. Looks like you lose one certified check. I hate to have to mail it, but you know the rules.

Problems that individuals or families are having in satisfying the terms of Contracts, however, are discussed in more detail, both during Individual Consultations at the end of the meeting and during home visits. And, of course, methods are employed to help the participants fulfill their agreed-upon obligations. See Chapter 10 for details of methods that can be used.

Strengthening Productive Participation During the Meeting

As noted in APG Item 11, productive participation consists of more than just coming to meetings, being on time, and doing assignments. It also includes participating in meetings in a productive way. For example, making positive, optimistic, prescriptive statements; using proper behavioral terms and principles; speaking up and taking one's turn; and encouraging and reinforcing the productive participation of other parents. Consequently, three things strengthen productive participation during meetings.

First, to encourage or set the occasion for participation: (1) ask questions of specific parents, (2) turn toward or smile at specific parents, (3) remain silent for a few seconds after an important idea has been presented, and (4) specifically ask the group for help or for an answer to a question.

Second, systematically pinpoint and reinforce productive participation in a variety of ways, for instance: (1) verbally:

> I'm glad to hear you speaking up and describing your home programs. You have a lot of important things to offer the group.

(2) through group recognition:

> I think Jan and Bill should be congratulated for starting to teach Junior to ask for what he wants rather than pushing and pulling on them to get what he wants. How about telling the group what you did?

(3) through the contract-credit system:

> Well, you earned two credits for speaking up so much during the last meeting. You made eight prescriptive statements—statements that suggested specific methods to try.

Third, handle counterproductive verbal behaviors when they occur. These include complaining, making nonprescriptive statements, using nonbehavioral terms and principles, attacking or degrading others, or engaging in excessive off-the-subject talk. When such behaviors occur, remind the group in a nonthreatening way of the ground rules for effective participation. For instance:

Parent: Boy, what a week this has been. Charley threw so many of his tantrums that I thought I'd go crazy! (This is the second meeting in which the parent said this.)

Consultant: Okay, I think we can imagine that Charley's tantrums are hard to take. But what do you think you might do in a teaching program to replace them? Or, can you describe the tantrums in another way—in terms of movements? How else do his tantrums make you feel or what things do you tell yourself during or after his tantrums? When do the tantrums occur? (Emphasizes objectivity and behavioral analysis.)

Or, after the group has gotten off the subject for 30 seconds or so, a consultant might say, "Well, these little breaks are needed now and then, but let's get back to business again."

If counterproductive verbal behaviors continue to occur in meetings (for example, continual complaining about a child or a lack of participation), you can discuss the behavior in private and help the parents to develop and try various methods, such as a special contract for counting complaining versus prescriptive statements, with a certain number of credits to be earned for decreasing the complaints and increasing the number of prescriptive statements.

To keep track of productive versus unproductive participation, a consultant might take data on all participants, noting the number of complaining versus prescriptive statements, educationally-relevant versus irrelevant questions, the number of times parents reinforce other parents, and the number of times parents take their turn in discussions. In addition, when possible, the actual statements made (at least the notable ones) should be written down, for instance, "But I don't have the time to do that!" or "That sounds like it will work. We'll do it!" Note that parents can later assume the role of temporary data-taker.

By taking data in this way, consultants and parents have an objective basis for pinpointing and solving potential problems as well as for reinforcing one another. For instance, having noted parents' behavior during the meeting, the consultant, during the Individual Consultation at the end of the meeting, might say:

> That was a great idea of yours—you know, when you suggested that Mr. Jones remove his daughter's plate when she leaves the supper table!
>
> You seemed a bit shy tonight, Mrs. Blake. I counted only two times that you spoke up. From our own talks, I know that you have a lot of good ideas. How about setting a goal of speaking up three times during the next meeting?

Brief Review

After the performance check, review the main ideas presented at the last meeting. Like all information, the review should present the ideas in a logical sequence, leading up to the ideas and methods that the parents will be learning during the present week. Here is what we have said in our Programs.

> Let's start with a quick review. We are all here because your children have problems. Now there are all kinds of labels for your children's problems and all kinds of

theories to explain why they have problems. But, as you know, when all is said and done, the main problem now is not labels and not an explanation of how your children's problems started. The main problem now is behavior. And what do we mean by "behavior"? (Give parents an opportunity to answer—"Movements.")

Yes, behavior is movements. And we give names to different combinations of movements. One combination of movements is called "brushing your teeth." Another is called "speech." And another, "head-banging." But they are all movements of the body.

Now the difference between the way your children are now and the way you want them to be, is a difference in behavior. Isn't that so? If we gave Jimmy a different label, would he be any different? Would his future be any different? Or, if someone could tell you tomorrow why Sarah never learned to talk, would this make her life much different? No! Because labels and theories do not touch the real problem now, which is behavior. What we need to do now is teach your children to talk, if they don't talk; teach them to dress themselves, if they don't dress themselves; teach them to play, if they don't play. This does not mean that physicians have nothing to offer!! Your children may certainly have physical problems, and may need various medical treatments. What we are saying is that we have to help them learn.

But now that we are looking at behaviors—at movements—your children may be even more confusing to you than before, because you may see so many behaviors that need to be changed! Well, you can decrease the confusion if you keep in mind that there are only about four ways that a behavior can be changed. What are those four ways? (Give parents the opportunity to list the four ways—increase in frequency or duration; increase in skill; change in setting; and decrease in frequency or duration.)

A few weeks from now, you will be evaluating your children and planning a comprehensive educational program for them. You will be using the Behavior Evaluation Scale to find out just which behaviors need to be changed and just which way(s) each behavior might need to be changed. And you will be using the Skill Sequence Table and Table of Basic Behaviors to find out which skill area to start with and where to go next.

But before you start working on specific behaviors, it is a good idea for you to get your children changing in a beneficial direction right now. And it is a good idea for you to get some practice at changing your children right now, before you start specific teaching programs. In other words, we want you to make some changes in the ways you deal with your children. The result of those changes is that your children's behaviors start to change and you start to change. For example, your children start to settle down, to cooperate, to pay attention. And you become more relaxed, more confident, and more optimistic.

Now to be successful in making some basic changes in the ways you deal with your children, changes in what we call "structured exchanges," you have to see what is going on when you interact with your children; and you have to understand some basic principles of how people learn from one another.

The above presentation lasts about 10 minutes. Parents have the chance to ask questions during and after the presentation.

III. MAIN BUSINESS

The three main items of business are: (1) presenting and reviewing elementary principles of learning, (2) applying elementary principles of learning to the home, specifically, to certain behaviors of the child and parents, structured exchanges, and career experiences (for instance, how marital relations can be affected by years of frustration in trying to help the child), and (3) planning a program to institute productive exchanges during the coming week. Here is what we have said when working on each main item of business.

Elementary Principles of Learning: Signals, Behaviors, Consequences, and Behavior Change

First of all, on a blackboard, sketch the framework of the "Signal, Behavior, Consequence, and Behavior Change" table on page 26 of *Educating Children*. Then, as examples of combinations of signals, behaviors, consequences, and behavior changes are presented, write them on the blackboard. It is also a good idea to role-play several combinations. You might introduce the "Table" with something like the following:

> The question now is, What things or conditions change behaviors in the four ways that you have read about and that we talked about last week? Well, as you can see from this table, behaviors are surrounded by things or events called signals and consequences. Signals are events that seem to start a behavior off, such as questions, instructions or requests, timers that tell us that it is time to do something, or even thoughts and feelings inside of us that tell us to do some behavior. And behaviors are always followed by consequences. Something always happens after we do some behavior. For example, we might be praised, get money, or a pat on the back for what we have done; we may simply finish a task, or we may go on to another activity we may enjoy. Or, we may somehow be punished for what we have done. Or, we may be ignored. (Encourage parents to give more examples of signals and consequences. Put them all on the blackboard.)
>
> Now, depending on the kinds of consequences that usually follow our behaviors, our behaviors change in the ways we have talked about. Also, the consequences of our behaviors teach us about signals.

Reviewing Main Ideas in Chapter 2 of Educating Children. At this point, review the main ideas on pages 20 to 25 in Chapter 2 of *Educating Children*. Emphasize the following:

1. Behaviors that are rewarded quickly, often, and with strong rewards increase in frequency and possibly also in skill and duration. That is, they happen more often, for a longer time, and are done better or more efficiently.
2. Behaviors that are no longer rewarded tend to decrease, especially if other behaviors are being rewarded to take their place.

3. Behaviors that are punished quickly, often, and with strong punishers decrease quickly.

Generally, the punishing consequences are more effective if other behaviors are being rewarded to replace the punished behaviors. However, punishment may have a number of counterproductive results (see pages 311 to 312 in Chapter 9).

4. Events that regularly occur before (precede) a behavior that is consistently rewarded tend to become signals for the person to do the behavior.

Events that consistently signal that a behavior will not be rewarded, or that a behavior will be punished, tend to become signals for the person not to do the behavior, but instead to do other behaviors that will be rewarded.

Discussing Review Questions. Now have the parents turn to the end of Chapter 2 to answer and discuss the review questions. Additional discussion may be needed if parents are having any trouble. When all of the parents have satisfactorily answered the review questions, introduce the concept of "structured exchange."

Teaching Parents About Structured Exchanges. We talked about structured exchanges in Section VI, Chapter 2. Introduce this concept now to give the parents a way of seeing:

1. How the principles of behavior apply to both parties (parents and children) when they are interacting.
2. That there may be differences between the short-run (or immediate) and long-term changes in behavior.
3. That the long-term changes may be exactly the opposite of what is good for the people who are interacting.
4. That to alter the long-term direction of behavior for both parties, the exchanges should be changed now.

In presenting the concept of structured exchange, you can move back and forth between presenting examples from Chapter 2 of *Educating Children*, writing the examples on the blackboard and role-playing them, and discussing examples from the parents' and consultants' experiences. Here is what might be said during the presentation, which might be conducted by a different consultant.

> Now, I want to introduce a new term—"structured exchange." This term covers about all of the combinations of Signals-Behaviors-Consequences that there can be. What is going on in all of the examples of Signals-Behaviors-Consequences that you read about? . . . People are exchanging behaviors with one another! For instance, look at example 1 on page 25 of *Educating Children*. . . . Eric makes all kinds of

messes in the bathroom. What does he get in exchange for making messes? (Give parents a chance to answer that he gets attention.) That's right! In exchange for making messes, he gets attention. He's getting a good deal, isn't he? Not only does he have fun making messes, but he has the fun of seeing his mother get upset! Do you think that the attention he gets is a reward for him? Yes! It probably is a reward when his mother chases after him and hollers at him. So what will happen to his behavior of making messes? (Give parents a chance to answer that he will make messes more often.) Right. He will make messes more and more often!

Now, what is Eric's mother's behavior in this exchange with Eric? She is giving him attention. What does she get in exchange for giving Eric attention? (She gets a little peace and quiet!) So, she feels better when she finally gets Eric out of the bathroom, and that is her reward. And that is why she keeps on giving him attention after he makes messes.

This, then, is called a structured exchange. It is an exchange because the behavior of both people has consequences for them. Eric does something and his mother does something in return. She gives him attention. And her behavior is followed by a change in Eric's behavior. Namely, he stops for a little while. And we call it a structured exchange simply because it is not an accident. The exchange occurs over and over. It is predictable. It is a real part of the pattern of life in the family.

Now, here is the problem. In the short-run, Eric is rewarded, and so he keeps on making messes. And his mother is also rewarded in the short-run. Eric stops making messes for a little while. But in the future, what is going to happen? (Give parents the chance to answer that Eric will keep on making messes and his mother will keep on giving him attention.) So, in the long-run, his mother will be spending lots of time and energy chasing after Eric and cleaning up messes. Do you think that the little peace and quiet that she gets after she rewards him with her attention is worth it? (Give parents a chance to ask questions and discuss the example, and possibly to offer prescriptions of what Eric's mother can do—one of which is presented on page 30 of *Educating Children*).

Now have the parents read another example, such as number 4 on page 27, and analyze it. For instance:

What is happening in the case of Frankie and his father? (Frankie whines and whines for water.) And what does Frankie get in exchange for his whining? (He gets attention and water.) And what does Father get for giving Frankie attention and water? (Father gets peace and quiet for the rest of the night.) So, we have an exchange. Frankie does something and also gets something in return. In this case, in the short-run they are both getting rewards, aren't they? Just to make sure, what are the rewards each one is getting in the short-run? (Attention and water; a little peace and quiet.)

Okay, then, if they are both rewarded immediately in this exchange, what do you predict will happen to both of their behaviors in this exchange in the long-run? (Frankie will whine more and more often, and probably for longer and longer. Father will be giving Frankie more and more attention and water.) In fact, the exchange itself will be repeated more and more often! This little bit of interaction in the family will be a durable feature. It will happen over and over again, just as if it were supposed to. It will be a structured exchange.

You know what is worse? Frankie is doing more than learning how to get attention and water. What else is he learning? (He is learning how to control his father; to get his father to respond to him.) And what else is Father learning? (He is learning a general way of escaping from the situations that he cannot stand.) So, Frankie is going to be whining for more than water. He is going to be whining for food, music, TV, and rides in the car. And what is his father going to do about it, since his father has learned to shut Frankie up by giving in to Frankie's whining? (Father will also pay attention to Frankie and give Frankie other things that Frankie wants.)

This is terrible, isn't it? Frankie is learning all kinds of problem behaviors and his father is learning the wrong way to handle problem behaviors. But why does his father keep on rewarding Frankie for whining? Surely, it is not because he likes to hear whining! (He rewards whining, and other problem behaviors, because by rewarding such behaviors he is rewarded in the short-run when those behaviors stop.) So. Father accidentally teaches Frankie to do just the behaviors that Father cannot stand. And by temporarily stopping his whining, Frankie teaches his father to reward Frankie.

What do you think would be a better way of dealing with Frankie's whining? A way that has good results in the long run! (Give parents a chance to discuss various possibilities, such as giving Frankie water before he goes to bed, teaching Frankie to get his own water, leaving a night-light in the hall, and ignoring any and all whining.) The important point, here, is that in the short-run, it may take more effort to teach Frankie to get water by himself. In fact, for a week or so, Frankie might whine more than ever, trying to get back the attention. But if the program is sound and if Father sticks to his guns, in the long-run it will be better and easier for everyone!

Do you think that just telling Frankie's father what he should do would be enough? Maybe not. You see, he must have faith or confidence that the methods you just prescribed will eventually work. He also has to learn to wait and plan what to do, rather than react when Frankie starts whining. And it would help if he wrote down exactly what he is going to do. Finally, it would really help if he set it up so that he rewards himself, or has his wife reward him, for carrying out the teaching plan and for being successful in teaching Frankie to get his own water instead of whining for it.

Now it is a good idea to have the parents analyze other examples on pages 27 to 30 of Chapter 2 of *Educating Children* in terms of structured exchanges, for example, number 7 on page 29, as an example of a productive exchange. Make sure to help parents:

1. Pinpoint the behaviors of each party.
2. Pinpoint the consequences of each party's behavior in the short run.
4. Predict long-term changes.
5. Prescribe methods to alter counterproductive exchanges so that they produce beneficial changes.
6. Understand that in order to institute productive exchanges, they may have to learn how to relax, plan instead of reacting, coach and reinforce one another, and have faith or confidence in the principles of learning.

Describing and Analyzing Specific Types of Counterproductive and Productive Exchanges in the Home

After covering the basic principles of exchanges, begin to apply those principles to the home. It is helpful to describe and analyze a number of counterproductive exchanges and the alternative, productive exchanges, using Table 6-1 below (Productive and Counterproductive Exchanges.) Hand out one copy of Table 6-1 to each parent or family. While discussing each type of exchange, consultants and parents can role-play the exchange; parents are encouraged to generalize to their own experiences; and consultants help parents to use principles of learning to explain what is going on in each exchange and to predict the short- and long-run changes.

Particular behaviors are discussed in the context of abstract classes of exchanges (as on Tables 6-1, 6-2, and 6-3) so that parents can observe the common conditions that are affecting, or could be used to change, the strength of many behaviors. If we only focused on specific behaviors now, the parents might not learn the general principles by which physically different behaviors can be understood. In sum, it is more important that the parents see that behaviors such as tantrums, noncooperation, and whining may be under the control of similar events in one type of exchange or contingency of reinforcement, for instance, the escape exchange.

Discussing Family Exchanges. A good way to start the discussion of both counterproductive and productive exchanges in the home is for the speaker either to give examples of exchanges from his or her own daily life, like some of those on Table 6–1, or to ask the parents to give examples of their own. For instance, referring to Table 6–1,

> Does any of this sound familiar? Do any of the exchanges on Table 6-1 happen in your home? Some of the counterproductive exchanges sure happen in my home! For example, after a hard day, if my son asks me in a nice way to tell him a bedtime story, I am likely to put him off and ask him to wait. In other words, I accidentally ignore good asking! Pretty soon he will again ask nicely and I may again put him off. After a while he may start to nag. Of course, after a hard day, I don't want to be nagged. So, I may finally tell him a story. Unfortunately, I have rewarded the wrong behavior. I rewarded the nagging instead of the nice asking. And how is he likely to ask after a few days of being rewarded for nagging? . . . Of course, he is not going to waste his breath asking nicely! He is going to start right off nagging, because that is the behavior that has been rewarded the most often lately. This is the escape exchange.
>
> Now, am I sick or stupid because I accidentally ignored "good asking" and rewarded nagging a number of times? Well, I may be stupid, but that is not why I rewarded nagging! It was because I was tired, very tired, that I failed to think about what was going on, failed to notice my son's good behavior, and finally reacted to

Table 6-1 Productive and Counterproductive Exchanges

Counterproductive Exchanges (to replace)	*Productive Exchanges (to institute or increase)*
1. *Escape (Reacting or "Giving In")* Child engages in a problem behavior that is hard for parent to take (such as a tantrum, bizarre behavior, yelling, whining, making messes, hitting, biting himself or others). Parent runs after child, talks to child, cuddles child (gives child attention); cleans the mess; gives child food, toys, or other things child seems to "want" or "like." *Short-run Changes.* Child is rewarded by attention and other rewards. Parent is rewarded when child temporarily stops the problem behavior. *Long-run Changes.* Child engages in problem behaviors even more often and problem behaviors may be even harder to replace. Parent "gives in" to problem behaviors more often, becomes more fatigued, irritated, desperate, and perhaps more likely to react.	1. *Riding it Out, Hanging Tough, or Keeping Cool* Child engages in a problem behavior. Parent waits, plans what to do to replace the behavior. Parent either completely ignores the behavior, times out the child immediately, or, if necessary, uses punishment procedures in a carefully planned way. Parent also frequently rewards appropriate behaviors to replace the problem behaviors. *Short- and Long-run Changes.* Child is not rewarded for problem behaviors, but is rewarded for appropriate, "replacement," behaviors. Child engages in problem behaviors less and less and appropriate behaviors more and more. Parent is rewarded for waiting, planning, not reacting to problem behaviors, using "corrective" methods, and for rewarding appropriate behaviors. Parent becomes calmer, more confident, and optimistic; calmly handles problem behaviors more and more, rewards appropriate behaviors more and more.
2. *Placation or Avoidance (Selling out)* Child "threatens" to engage in a problem behavior, seems to be "working up" to a problem behavior, is engaging in rather aimless behavior, or is engaging in problem behaviors that are easier for parent to take. Parent gives child attention, food, and other things that direct child away from engaging in a disruptive behavior, or that keep the child rather quiet. *Short-run Changes.* Child is rewarded by attention and other "goodies." Parent is rewarded by avoiding more-	2. *Earning Rewards (No Freebies)* Parent ignores mild problem behaviors; requires child to earn rewards by engaging in appropriate behaviors (such as playing, cooperating with directions, performing chores, talking); parent institutes policy of "No Freebies," at least until problem behaviors are greatly replaced by appropriate behaviors. Parent uses "Grandma's Law" (natural, activity rewards), for example, "As soon as you put your plate on the table, you can eat supper." Child is allowed to experience the natural consequences of not cooperating. For example, if

continued

Table 6-1 *(Continued*

Counterproductive Exchanges (to replace)	*Productive Exchanges (to institute or increase)*
disruptive behaviors or by a little peace and quiet. *Long-run Changes.* Child threatens, engages in mild problem behaviors or in aimless behaviors more often. Child misses many opportunities to learn and to be rewarded for engaging in appropriate behaviors. Parent misses many chances to learn to properly handle problem behaviors.	child refuses to put plate on table by the time the meal is over, child misses meal. *Short- and Long-run Changes.* Child learns that threatening and aimless behaviors do not pay off, and that rewards can no longer be taken for granted. Threatening and aimless behaviors are replaced by cooperative and constructive behaviors. Parents learn not to be frightened or upset by problem behaviors, to be on the lookout for appropriate behaviors, to be confident.
3. *Multiple Signals (Wasting your breath)* Parent gives child a signal (for instance, a request or direction, a model to imitate); child ignores parent, runs away, or does the opposite of what the signal intended. Parent repeats signal over and over; child may or may not finally cooperate with signal. Or, parent may talk to child a great deal, whether or not child is paying attention. Or, parent may present signals fast, one after another. *Short-run Changes.* Child is rewarded for ignoring parent's signals or for not cooperating. If child finally cooperates, parent is rewarded for presenting multiple signals. If child does not finally cooperate, parent's efforts to signal child to do something are ignored. *Long-run Changes.* Child learns that parent's voice does not "count." Child may seem "out of it," does not pay attention, wanders around, becomes	3. *Single Signals (Making your Words Count)* Parent waits until child pays attention (for example, is standing still and making eye contact) or prompts child to pay attention; presents a simple and clear signal; gives child a few seconds to start to cooperate; if child cooperates, parent rewards child; if child does not cooperate, parent prompts child through the motions (perhaps a number of times). In other words, when a signal is given, child is taught to cooperate. *Short- and Long-run Changes.* Child is not rewarded for ignoring parent or for not cooperating. Attention and cooperation are rewarded, and they become more and more likely to occur when signals are given. Parent is rewarded by child's increasing attention and cooperation; gives signals (opportunities to learn) more and more often; feels more optimistic and self-confident.

continued

Table 6-1 *(Continued)*

Counterproductive Exchanges (to replace)	*Productive Exchanges (to institute or increase)*
uncooperative. Parent learns either to give signals over and over ("Talking yourself blue in the face") or may give up trying to get child to do much of anything.	
4. *Lack of Rewards for Appropriate Behaviors* Child engages in an appropriate behavior or an approximation (a "try"); parent does not reward behavior because parent does not notice the behavior or does not think that it should be rewarded (that it was "good enough"). *Short- and Long-run Changes.* Appropriate behaviors of the child remain weak. Child remains dependent; problem behaviors are not replaced by appropriate behaviors. Parent becomes fatigued, pessimistic about chances of child's changing for the better.	4. *Catching 'Em Doing Good* Parent is on the lookout for appropriate behaviors (even gross approximations or "tries") to reward. Parent rewards appropriate behaviors as well as "tries" often, quickly, with strong rewards, and with a variety of rewards. *Short- and Long-run Changes.* Appropriate behaviors of child become stronger—increase in frequency, duration, and skill. Child's problem behaviors begin to decrease. Parents are rewarded by changes in child's behavior; reward child more and more often.
5. *Lack of Opportunities (Occasions) to Respond and to Learn (child is "Hanging around")* Parent gives child few occasions to learn and to respond. Parents may have low expectations of child's abilities to learn or of their abilities to teach; make few demands on child to participate in home-life or to take care of himself; do things for child or leave child alone (perhaps for fear that child will become disruptive). *Short- and Long-run Changes.* Child changes little in a positive direction.	5. *Many Opportunities (Occasions) to Respond and to Learn (child is "Doing his Share")* Parent expects child to take part in family life and to learn to take care of himself. Parent requires child to earn rewards and not to take them for granted; gives child many occasions during the day to cooperate with requests, to perform chores and self-help routines, to play, talk, socialize. Parent uses "Grandma's Law" (natural, activity rewards), for example, "As soon as you put on your coat, you can go outside."

continued

Table 6-1 *(Continued)*

Counterproductive Exchanges (to replace)	*Productive Exchanges (to institute or increase)*
May become more dependent (require more care). Parents come to believe that child is not able to learn much. Parents have even more work to do, become pessimistic and drained.	*Short- and Long-run Changes.* Child learns appropriate behaviors to replace aimless, dependent, and disruptive behaviors as a way of getting attention, passing time, and getting other things that child "wants." Parent becomes more relaxed, self-confident, optimistic; gives child more occasions to learn.
6. *Improper or Unnecessary Punishment* Parent punishes appropriate behaviors (for instance, when child touches certain objects). Parent punishes problem behaviors when less aversive methods would work just as well and perhaps better. Parent does not use proper punishment procedures (for example, waits too long, does not punish every time, follows punishment with rewards, does not use effective consequences or punishers, does not reward appropriate "replacement" behaviors, does not keep track of the child's behavior change). *Short- and Long-run Changes.* If parent mistakenly punishes appropriate behaviors, they may be suppressed; other problem behaviors may develop (such as withdrawal). If parent uses punishment methods when they are not necessary, parent may fail to learn or use less aversive methods, and fail to focus on teaching child appropriate behaviors; child may become "overcontrolled" and dependent. If parent does not use proper punishment methods, the problem behavior being "punished" may not decrease and may actually increase; appropriate behaviors may not increase to take the place of the "punished" behaviors; child may become aggressive.	6. *Proper Use of Punishment* Parent does not punish appropriate behaviors (for example, teaches child to touch or explore objects, rather than merely punishing the child for touching certain—the wrong—objects). Parent uses punishment methods only when punishment is the best choice. Parent uses proper punishment methods (for example, punishes immediately, every time, with effective consequences, rewards appropriate "replacement" behaviors, keeps track of the child's behavior change). *Short- and Long-run Changes.* Problem behaviors are replaced by appropriate behaviors; parent does not become "punishment-oriented"; child does not become overcontrolled or dependent; parent focuses on building appropriate behaviors through the use of rewards.

> the behavior that I could not stand—nagging. Also, correcting the situation does not require that I change my personality or become smarter. It requires that I think about what is happening, analyze the exchange in terms of signals, behaviors, consequences, and behavior changes, and plan the right way to respond when my son asks nicely and when he asks by nagging.
>
> So, let's spend a little time talking about exchanges that you have now pinpointed in your own families—both counterproductive and productive exchanges. . . . .

While parents are describing exchanges in their families, it is important to:

1. Help them to pinpoint the signals, behaviors, consequences, and expected behavior changes in each exchange;
2. Reinforce their openness or honesty about counterproductive exchanges, their good analyses of exchanges, the productive exchanges they describe, and generalizing from Table 6-1 or from other parents' descriptions to their own families;
3. Help parents to see that it is very unlikely that they were the cause of their child's deviant development (problem behaviors and the lack of appropriate behaviors), that they have been doing the best that anyone could do in their circumstances, but that nevertheless they have to institute new productive exchanges, continue to manage (or even increase) existing productive exchanges, and replace the counterproductive exchanges, in order to conduct a good educational program;
4. Help parents to prescribe ways to replace counterproductive with productive exchanges and to pinpoint the existing productive exchanges which they should maintain or accentuate.

Analyzing Videotapes. If possible, supplement the description and analysis of exchanges in the home by showing portions of videotapes, some from past Programs, but most from Baseline Observations of families in the present Program. The portions of videotape illustrate both productive and counterproductive exchanges described on Table 6−1, as well as those described by the parents in the preceding discussion. Baseline videotapings of teaching sessions and selected short subjects (see Section VI of Chapter 4) are a good source. Note that less than a minute of tape on each exchange is needed, as long as each portion shows a complete exchange. Of course, videotape is used only if parents have given permission. If parents have expressed reluctance, you can perhaps increase their willingness by first showing them portions of their Baseline videotapes during home visits, stressing the benefits of a group discussion of tapes.

While analyzing each exchange, show the portion of tape several times—once or twice straight through and then several times during which the tape is stopped after each segment of the exchange (after the signal, behavior, and consequence).

The goal is to run each sample of an exchange until all of the parents can pinpoint and describe the signals, behaviors, and consequences, predict short- and long-run behavioral changes, and correctly state which exchange on Table 6-1 is being illustrated. For example:

> Parent: Oh, yeah. There I go again! He made a weird noise and I paid attention to him. The good old escape exchange. I should be ignoring those noises and paying attention to him when he is speaking properly.

If parents express an interest in why counterproductive exchanges exist, refer to the ideas presented in the next section. In addition to discussion, it is a good idea for consultants and parents to role-play several exchanges that are being shown, even the counterproductive ones. Moreover, during the analyses and role-playing, encourage parents to prescribe changes in exchanges—for example, ways to increase the use of specific productive exchanges and to replace specific counterproductive exchanges, as outlined on Table 6-1.

Like the earlier discussion of exchanges in the home, showing and analyzing videotapes can be risky because some parents already may be rather pessimistic or feel guilty for their child's problems. Thus, make sure to: (1) stress the productive exchanges that are taking place in each family which they should maintain or even increase, (2) point out that the counterproductive exchanges in their homes are the same as exchanges in families all over the world, including your own, but that with a child who already has learning and behavior problems, counterproductive exchanges may have more serious effects, and (3) since the parents are already managing productive exchanges (as shown on the tapes), it is not impossible for them to replace the counterproductive ones. In other words, during the showing of videotapes, the tone should not be, and the parents should not feel, "My God! What have I done to my child?!" but rather, "Boy, my child and I have each other on the run. We'll have to correct that."

Another way of using videotape, which can be used either in addition to or instead of the above, is described in Section III of Chapter 11, on evaluation.

If videotapes are not available, a film by Robert Mager entitled "Who Did What To Whom?" (Research Press) can be used to illustrate various types of exchanges.

At this time, the group can take a break for refreshments.

Analyzing the Families' Careers, Parents' Behaviors, and Certain Family Problems. As mentioned, a technology for educating their children is often not enough for parents to be able to conduct, persist at, or maintain a good home educational program. As discussed in Chapter 2, partly as a result of their career experiences, problems in the family may interfere with the parents' efforts to change themselves and their children. While an understanding of how the organization of society afffects one's life-course may not be sufficient to enable one, alone, to change society, it may help the parents to change themselves and their life-course, and to help others to do the same thing.

Throughout the Program, you will be helping the parents to understand their career experiences, to overcome problems that may have resulted, and to help them pinpoint and build on their strengths. Now is a good time to start. Here is what you might say to introduce the topic:

> We've done a lot of talking about your children's behaviors. And you have all been doing a great job learning to analyze and understand your children's behaviors, as well as some of the exchanges between yourselves and your children. Let's see if we can use some of the same principles to understand our own behaviors. Do you remember how irritated Eric's mother was in example 1 on page 25 of *Educating Children?* Do you remember how much Frankie's father (example 4, page 27), wanted a little peace and quiet? How tired he was? And do you remember that it was her irritation, her tension, that made Eric's mother so likely to react to Eric's making messes, which meant that she would reward him? And do you remember that it was because Frankie's father was so tired that he would finally give in to Frankie, which meant that Frankie's whining for water would be rewarded? In other words, the way they felt was connected with the exchanges they had with their children. Well, then, if Eric's mother was not so tense, and if Frankie's father were not so drained at the end of the day, they might be able to stand back from what they are doing and deal with their children in a different, more productive way. So, the question is, why were they tense, irritated, and drained of energy? (Give parents a chance to answer this question, using principles of learning and persistent conditions in the lives of parents, for example, work, years of frustration.)
>
> Have you ever been tense, ready to explode, oversensitive to your child's behavior, your spouse's behavior, or even to your own feelings? Have you ever been pessimistic, thinking that the future might be pretty dim? Have you ever found yourself reacting quickly and without thinking? Are you and your spouse ever on the "outs," angry with each other, fed-up?
>
> Are you ever so tired that you get behind on your chores or have a hard time getting supper ready on time? Well, if you have felt like this, then welcome to the club!
>
> Well, perhaps we can smile now, but you know as well as I do that sometimes the things I just mentioned become problems once we are back home and faced with the realities of trying to make a living, raise a family, and get some enjoyment out of life. Why are these things problems? Because by themselves they make us feel rotten and because they may make it hard to conduct and maintain a good home educational program. For example, arguments between ourselves can become vicious cycles that go on for days, affect the ways we interact with our children, and make us feel plain miserable. Not only that, but arguments may make it hard to work together to run home programs.
>
> You remember that last week we talked a bit about problems that people have. Not just you folks, but everyone! For example, when I first started teaching, there were times when I would get so tense and anxious before a class that I had to force myself to walk into the classroom. It was lucky that I already knew the material that I was going to talk about, because if I hadn't known the material, I would have been anxious throughout the class and would have done a terrible job. But why was I so

> anxious? Well, there are probably many reasons. But one reason is that I had to stay up half the night to prepare for the next day's classes, and I had to get up early and teach after only a few hours of sleep. Well, if you do that for a couple of years, you get pretty drained; you get oversensitive, you become a live wire; and soon you start to feel anxiety. And then a vicious cycle starts. You are so anxious that you are afraid of getting anxious, and your work suffers, and you become even more anxious. Somehow, you have to break the vicious cycle. I broke the cycle by making sure that I did not have to teach so early, so that I could get enough sleep. And I made sure that I had some breaks between classes so I could wind down and rest up for the next one. And I learned how to relax my body and how to think constructive thoughts. Instead of thinking: "If I become anxious again, I will make a fool of myself!" I learned to think: "So what! Anxiety always goes away. It never killed you. And if it happens, just relax." And I'm telling you the truth. It worked like a charm, at least after awhile.
>
> Well, does any of this sound familiar? Have you felt like Eric's mother or Frankie's father must have felt? Have you ever had the so-called problems that I mentioned before?

Here again, you may be dealing with an emotionally-loaded issue. If the parents do have personal or family problems (such as marital conflict), they may not feel that they know you or the other families enough to talk about them. Some parents may be insulted by the suggestion that they have problems. So, introducing the issue of career experiences and problems at this early time is risky. However, if you wait until some parents' productive participation and home educational programs have suffered because of family or personal problems, it may be more difficult to remedy the problems.

A way out of the potential dilemma is as follows. First, encourage parents to describe career experiences and problems in relation to exchanges with their child. For example, instead of encouraging parents to describe anxiety or marital problems in general, ask them what has happened in their career experiences that may have affected the way they interact with their children. Second, if with a little encouragement the parents begin to describe career experiences and personal and family problems, then you can continue with an analysis of such experiences and problems (as is described below). If the parents seem reluctant to discuss personal or family problems, tell them in a nonthreatening way that you understand why they might be hesitant at this time, and that perhaps it would be better to wait until everyone knows everyone else better. Then, go on to the next item of main business. Later, during the home visit, you can again raise the issue of potential problems and discuss it with parents.

Let us assume, though, that some parents open up and describe problems such as anxiety, hypervigilance, unhappiness, marital problems, lack of household organization, pessimism, or lack of self-confidence. In that case, help them to pinpoint and describe: (1) the specific behaviors, attitudes, feelings, and thoughts (self-statements) involved, (2) the conditions under which the problems are likely to occur, and (3) the consequences of the problems for other aspects of their personal and family life. For example, if a parent tells the group about his "depression," help the parent to pinpoint and describe just what he means by "depression," when it occurs, and how long it lasts, what he does about it, and how it affects his work, relations with his wife, and relations with the children.

Note, however, that you are not after a detailed description and analysis at this point. Rather, you want parents to recognize the existence of problems, see that their own problems can be analyzed and understood, and learn that methods can be used for remedying the problems. Later, during Individual Consultations, home visits, or in the case of some problems shared by the group, in meetings, problems might be analyzed in detail and methods for avoiding and solving them presented and practiced.

After the parents have briefly pinpointed and described various problems, help them to see how they can begin to analyze or understand their problems using the ideas presented in Chapter 2. For example:

1. Show the parents that many of their problems (as well as strengths) are not unique to them as individuals or as families, but are shared (as they have just seen) by many parents of children with learning and behavior problems. Moreover, many of their problems and strengths are, in part, a result of common experiences they have had from the time they noticed that their child had serious problems. A good way to communicate the above ideas is to draw the sequence of career experiences (Figure 2-1) on the blackboard or to give each family a copy of Figure 2-1.

2. While the parents examine the career sequence, describe what seems to happen at each stage—both problems as well as possible benefits (such as stronger marital relationship, increased activism in the movement to obtain services for children, or effective efforts to teach their child in the home). Regarding problems, show parents how many of their problems seem to be part of vicious cycles resulting from career experiences. For instance, if they sought help and did not get it, if others avoided them, gave them bad advice, or insulted them, and if they tried to teach their child, without much success, then they may have become more pessimistic, isolated, less self-confident, fatigued, hypervigilant, and tense. Moreover, pessimism, fatigue, isolation, diminished self-confidence, and tension might have led to a pattern of quickly reacting to their child's problem behaviors (the escape exchange), accidentally ignoring appropriate behaviors, trying to buy a little peace and quiet (the placation exchange), or even to the improper use of punishment. Later still, the continued worsening of their child's problem behaviors and the failure of their child to learn appropriate behaviors (or to progress at a fast enough rate), may have worsened their pessimism, isolation, self-confidence, fatigue, hypervigilance, and tension, which might have led to the parents' becoming irritated at one another, unable or too tired to gratify one another, to feelings of depression and anxiety, and perhaps to a decrease in the organization of certain household routines.

While discussing the overall career sequence and its effects, use principles of learning and structured exchange to analyze the specifics of the parents' experiences. For instance, a decrease in the parents' efforts to systematically teach their child may represent extinction, resulting from the actual or perceived unresponsiveness of the child. Similarly, a decrease in the organization of certain aspects of home life may have resulted from a combination of fatigue, too much to do, and too little reinforcement (gratification, recognition) given to those who are responsible for performing certain routine activities.

3. Also, try to show parents that many of their career experiences result from the way the larger society is organized. For example, the fatigue of the mother may result, in part, from the load of trying to rear the children mostly by herself, because the economic system is organized in such a way that the main breadwinner (usually the husband) is away for most of the day and because people often live in nuclear families and can not count on day-to-day help and support of relatives who may live far away. The parents' pessimism and anxiety about the future may flow, in part, from the structured economic and social vulnerability of many persons in our society. Yet, the pessimism and anxiety bred by vulnerability may have negative consequences for the marital relationship. That is, to the extent that the husband is often worried about his job security, he may be unable to give his wife the help and attention she needs.

4. Enthusiastically reinforce the parents for being open and honest about their experiences and problems, and for handling them as well as they have. Indicate to the parents that by understanding many pesonal and family problems as consequences not of their own inadequacies but of the organization of the social system of which they are members, they should begin to feel better about themselves as persons and as a family. Moreover, since they see that they are no longer alone in their experiences, more than ever they must work together, within the family and with other families, to understand and change the social conditions that have shaped their careers. Toward that end, the Program teaches them concrete methods to use in helping themselves and each other, both as individual families and as a group.

5. If parents express bitterness regarding past lack of help from certain professionals and facilities, empathize with them, as in earlier interviews. Also, help them to see that bitterness alone cannot help them or their child. Many professionals and facilities can help them. Thus, they need to learn when they need the services of certain kinds of specialists (e.g., an evaluation of their child by an optometrist or speech pathologist), how to obtain services, and how to work with the specialist so as to gain information that they (and their child's teachers) need in order to provide the child with an effective educational program.

If time is short, this is a good place to end the main business portion and move to the Individual Consultation, during which you can still follow many of the suggestions made later in this chapter, and assign the same reading. Anything not covered in the Individual Consultation can be be covered during the home visit. The next meeting, then, completes the unfinished work in this unit and most, if not all, work for the third unit or week (Chapter 7).

Here is the third and final item of main business.

Instituting Productive Exchanges

Actually, you have been helping the parents to work up to this point. For example: (1) last week, having read Chapter 2 and pages 186 to 189 of *Educating Children,* they might have tried to make some changes in structured exchanges between themselves and their child, (2) during this meeting, they have discussed principles of learning and behavior change, and (3) various structured exchanges have been discussed and analyzed through videotapes and role-playing. Thus, it is time to help parents to plan and practice what to do to increase their use of existing productive exchanges in the home and to replace counterproductive exchanges with productive exchanges.

A good way to help the parents to plan and practice what to do, is to deal with each of the six types of structured exchanges on Table 6-1, one-by-one. While focusing on each type of exchange, do the following.

1. Have the parents give examples of the exchange, with most examples coming from the previous discussions as well as from the analysis of videotapes. For instance, there are many examples of the "escape" exchange. Some parents might reward crying and whining with attention. Others might react by giving the child both attention and snacks. Similarly, parents may reward different kinds of problem behaviors—tantrums, bizarre gestures, making messes, and self-injurious behaviors. Consequently, the details of the parents' plans for replacing the escape exchange may differ, depending on the specific combinations of signals-behaviors-consequences.

2. Consultants can demonstrate how to replace each type of counterproductive exchange and how to institute each productive exchange. In other words, consultants can demonstrate proper ways of responding to various problem behaviors, rewarding appropriate behaviors and approximations, providing the child with occasions to respond (for example, signals) and prompting correct responses. After demonstrating specific methods, parents can briefly discuss what they have observed and role-play the specific methods. For example, consultants can demonstrate (and then parents can role-play) methods for dealing with crying and whining for snacks (perhaps by ignoring the crying and whining until the child stops for awhile, providing the child with an occasion to ask properly or an occasion to earn a snack by doing a simple task). Similarly, consultants can demonstrate many examples of the use of ''Grandma's Law.'' For instance, ''As soon as you put your plate on the table, you can eat.''

3. In addition to describing and role-playing methods for replacing counterproductive exchanges and instituting productive exchanges, discuss ways in which the parents can alter the physical environment so as to avoid certain problems and facilitate their child's learning (as described in Item 18B on the APG).

4. Parents can be provided with a blank copy of a table similar to Table 6-1, with perhaps a page for each exchange. Then, as each type of exchange is discussed, demonstrated, and role-played, the parents can write down in the space provided for each exchange, examples of both counterproductive and productive exchanges which have been taking place (as well, perhaps, as similar exchanges in the other families), tentative methods for replacing the counterproductive exchanges, and examples of existing productive exchanges to maintain or even increase. In addition, parents list the types of tentative changes they will make in the physical environment. Table 6-2 below shows what parents from one family might write for several types of structured exchanges. This is the basis for the parents' home program for the coming week. The final plan is worked out during the Individual Consultation and/or home visit.

How Detailed Should the Discussions, Demonstrations, and Plans Be? At this early point in the Program, you want the parents to be able to pinpoint and objectively describe exchanges in the family. And you want them to learn some general teaching methods (described by APG Item 18) which, if used, enable them to begin to generate beneficial changes in themselves and their children. The general teaching methods to teach the parents now, as listed in Item 18, concern changes in the physical environment, signals (all components), prompts (overview of different types), rewards (finding strong rewards; saving rewards for use with appropriate behaviors; rewarding immediately and as often as possible; giving social rewards in an enthusiastic way; telling child why child is being rewarded; and pairing social rewards with other rewards), and replacing problem behaviors (waiting and planning, rather than reacting; ignoring as many problem behaviors as possible; using time out if necessary).

Naturally, the details (or parameters) of the plan for using the different teaching methods depend on the child's likes and dislikes, the severity of the child's problem behaviors, the strength of the child's appropriate behaviors, and the skills and energy of the parents. Such details (for example, whether to use ignoring or time out, how many minutes to keep the child in time out if time out seems the better method, and which rewards to use) can be worked out during the Individual Consultation and home visit.

Emphazing Positive Reinforcement (Rewards). As much as possible, the emphasis is on teaching parents to strengthen appropriate behaviors by giving

Table 6-2 Portion of Parents' Tentative Plan for Changing Exchanges

Counterproductive Exchanges	*Productive Exchanges*
1. *Escape (Reacting or "Giving In")* Sally screams and we go over to her, sit with her, talk softly to her and ask her what is the matter, cuddle her, and sometimes turn on the TV or record player for her or give her a snack.	1. *Riding it out, Hanging Tough* Sally screams and we will either: a) completely ignore it and just go about our business, wait until she has stopped screaming for at least one minute, and then quickly reward her with smiles, hugs, TV, or record player, or a small piece of fruit or cereal. Or, b) immediately put her in her room (time out) without saying anything to her, wait until she has been quiet for at least one minute, and then let her out. When she is out, we will reward her with smiles, praise, hugs, TV, or records, or healthful snacks every few minutes that she is quiet. We will repeat the above method every time she starts to scream.*
4. *Lack of Rewards for Appropriate Behaviors* Sally sits quietly, sometimes follows simple directions, makes eye contact, tries to say words, sometimes cooperates when we are helping her to dress herself, wash herself, and brush her teeth, and sometimes tries to play with toys. We usually do not reward her because we do not notice it often when she is doing "good" behaviors or is making a good try, or we do not know that she should be rewarded.	4. *Catching 'Em Doing Good* We will be on the lookout for the times when Sally is quiet, cooperating, trying to talk, play, dress or wash herself, and when she is making eye contact. We will also be on the lookout for other "good" behaviors that she is doing or trying to do, such as imitating us or her brother, picking up her toys, or watching the behavior of other people. We will reward her as fast and as often as we can (nearly every time) when she is doing a good behavior or is trying. We will reward her with smiles, praise, hugs, TV, or record player, healthful snacks in small bites, and almost anything that she likes to do (activities).

Changes in Objects and Materials in the Home

We will: 1) put all of Sally's toys in a box in the den, where we would like her to learn to play, 2) put a lock on the kitchen cabinets, 3) buy Sally pants with elastic waist-bands, 4) move the portable record player to a high place, where Sally cannot reach it.

*The methods suggested by the parents at this point may or may not be entirely appropriate. The final plan for the home program would be worked out with the consultant and would depend on a more careful analysis of the child's behavior and the parents' past efforts to manage it.

their child many occasions to respond (for instance simple tasks to perform during the day), rewarding their child as often and as quickly as possible for appropriate behaviors, with a variety of rewards, and replacing problem behaviors with appropriate behaviors. However, as noted on Tables 6-1 and 6-2, methods for replacing problem behaviors may involve decelerating consequences such as ignoring, time out, overcorrection, or even punishment. The question, then, is, how much should parents learn about the use of decelerating consequences at this point?

The answer, at least the answer that we have used in our Programs at this time, is to briefly discuss, demonstrate, and role-play the less aversive methods, such as ignoring, time out, and the use of certain natural consequences (such as losing a chance to eat any more of a meal if the child leaves the table). In the case of children with severe problem behaviors (behaviors that are violent and/or self-injurious), the parents are given an assignment to read relevant portions of Chapter 15 of *Educating Children*. Then, during the Individual Consultation and home visit, the more aversive and difficult to use methods, such as overcorrection, or, if it is clearly necessary, punishment, can be discussed, demonstrated, role-played, and incorporated into the parents' plan for changing patterns of exchanges in the home. In sum, the amount of time spent on decelerating consequences at this point in the Program depends on the severity of the child's problem behaviors. In addition, if certain problem behaviors develop, or if long-standing problem behaviors prove resistant to methods such as ignoring or time out, additional methods can be discussed as the Program goes on. (See Section III of Chapter 9 below.)

Acceptance of or Hesitations About Behavioral Methods Suggested. As described in Chapter 4 in the section on establishing readiness to change, it is important that parents generally accept the behavioral approach. At this point, however, they need to do more than merely accept the overall approach; they should agree to try certain teaching methods, as noted in Item 15 of the APG. Yet, now that you are talking about actually using certain methods, some parents may hesitate to try them, specifically to:

1. Withhold, save, or require their child to earn various rewards (especially if they pity their child and/or have been placating their child or giving away many rewards so as to be kind).
2. Let their child experience usual consequences of noncompliant and disruptive behaviors (such as missing a meal because the child kept leaving the supper table).
3. Ignore certain problem behaviors (especially those that they feel are hurting the child) or use what they consider to be inhumane methods (such as time out).
4. Use strong rewards (such as food).

While it is important that parents agree to try certain behavioral methods, it is more important that they evaluate the situation objectively and decide for themselves. Thus, in our Programs, when suggestions to try certain methods meet with hesitation, we: (1) encourage parents to express their hesitations and to be specific about the reasons; (2) are careful to weigh the parents' reasons, both to communicate that we indeed take their ideas seriously and because they might well be right; and (3) leave it up to the parents to prescribe, plan, and try an alternative to the methods that had been suggested, but to be responsible for both evaluating what they plan to try and changing their plans if necessary. For instance, when a father did not want to use food rewards because it reminded him too much of training a dog, and because he simply did not think that food rewards were necessary, we indicated our understanding of his feelings, explained why we felt that food plus social rewards would be more effective for the child at that time than social rewards alone, and left it up to him to decide. However, he still chose to use social rewards alone to try to strengthen various appropriate behaviors of his child, but he took data on his child's progress. After a week, he concluded that social rewards were not strong enough, and decided to use food plus social rewards for the time being.

In the case of stronger hesitations, or even refusal, to try certain methods (e.g., a parent refuses to ignore problem behaviors, or continues to talk to the child even when using time out), you may have to discuss the hesitations in more detail during Individual Consultations and home visits. It may be that the parent feels that he or she would be injuring the child in some way and, by talking to the child, is implicitly communicating to the child:

> I'm not sure that this method is any good, and I feel guilty about causing you any discomfort. So, I will begrudgingly use the method, but tell you that I am sorry.

Here, try to help the parents to state the feelings and thoughts that are maintaining their hesitations and seeming inability to use a certain method. Then help them to see that their feelings and thoughts ("I don't want to hurt my child"; "I want to see myself as a good parent and person.") are perfectly legitimate, but that the methods being suggested do not contradict the parents' thoughts and feelings, and may actually be more consistent with them than the parents' present behaviors. To back-up the effort to alter the parents' "attitudes," you can show "before" and "after" videotapes of parents using ineffective and effective methods with their children, and can have other parents who have felt the same way talk to the hesitant parents.

After discussing, demonstrating, and role-playing methods parents can use to institute productive exchanges during the coming week, bring the final item of business to a close by discussing what else it takes to be successful in actually carrying out their plans.

How to be Successful at Instituting Productive Exchanges

Knowing how to institute productive exchanges (APG Item 17) and knowing some general teaching methods (Item 18) does not insure that the parents will actually be successful in conducting their program to institute productive exchanges. For, as listed on the APG, they may need additional skills, attitudes, and constructive relationships, and many problems can interfere with their efforts. So, in closing the main business portion of the meeting, help the parents to start learning the additional skills, attitudes, and relationships that are needed, and to anticipate and plan how to solve potential or actual problems. During the home visit, you can firm-up the ideas presented below. Here is what you might say to introduce this topic.

> Okay! So you all have a tentative plan of action, a plan of how to institute productive exchanges during the coming week. In fact, you have many of the skills for being successful at carrying out the plan. For example, you are much better at observing and analyzing behavior, and you know many of the general teaching methods, such as how to present signals, how to prompt, and how to reward. Well, everything that you have learned seems to be necessary for success, but it is not sufficient or enough! To actually be successful in conducting your home programs, now and in the future, you need to learn more skills, perhaps new ways to look at your child, yourselves, and the future; new ways to relate to yourselves and others; and ways to prepare for, pinpoint, and solve problems that exist or that may come up.
>
> Now please don't think that there is so much to do that you will never be able to do it. Remember, everything in small steps! Tonight we just want to briefly go over some of the "extras" that you may need to learn to do. The goal is not for you to learn everything by the end of next week, but by the end of the Program. So, here is what it seems to take to be successful in conducting your home programs.

Now you can briefly discuss each APG item that will help the parents to be successful. Certain items can be assigned reading for the next meeting.

Confidence in More General Principles of Learning and a Long-Term Perspective (Item 13). As you know, if the parents are afraid of failure or feel personally responsible for their child's behavior and future, they may be constantly plagued with self-doubts and tension, afraid even to start instituting a home program, or quick to give up. What they may need now is a way of looking at themselves in relation to their child, and a way of looking at the future, that will help place their feelings, behaviors, and "basic personalities" in the proper perspective.

In particular, they may need to see that they are not personally responsible for changing their child. They are responsible only for their own behavior. So long as they are receiving consultation and help for any medical problems of their child, and are conducting their teaching programs according to a carefully-worked-out plan, they are doing about as much as anyone can do. And when they finally develop a teaching program plan that specifies the right conditions for their child (conditions that might include a special diet or even medication), then it is likely that their child will eventually change.

During this meeting (and whenever it is needed in future weeks), the "garden metaphor" can be used to instill the above message. For instance, here is what we have said in our programs.

> Tomorrow you will be starting to change your child's behavior. But don't start thinking that at every moment your child's behavior and your child's future depend on your every movement or on the kind of person that you may think you are. It is not you as a person, at each and every moment, that changes your child's behavior. Rather, it is what is going on in the teaching programs that you use—it is the conditions of learning—that help to change your child's behavior. If the teaching program specifies conditions that are appropriate for your child—such as the right kinds of rewards, the right way of delivering rewards, the right kinds of prompts, and so on—and if you follow the teaching program plan and make sure that the right conditions are there, then your child's behavior eventually changes—maybe not in five minutes, but eventually!
>
> You see, if you feel that you are totally responsible for your child's behavior and future, you would hardly be able to get started, and you would be on edge all the time. I mean, who could accept such a responsibility or carry such a load?
>
> Look, it is like planting a garden. You don't keep digging up the plants to see if they are growing. All you have to do as a gardener is to make sure that you follow the instructions on the back of the seed package. Why? Because the gardening program on the back of the package tells you the conditions that are needed for plant growth. So, if you just make sure that the right conditions for plant growth are there, the growing takes care of itself. At least the growing is out of your hands.
>
> Does it take a special kind of personality to be a successful gardener? Not really. All types of people can be successful gardeners. All they have to do is make sure that they follow the right gardening plan.
>
> The same goes for teaching! All you as a person have to do is make sure that you help to find the right conditions for your child's learning, help to write a teaching program plan that specifies the right conditions, and then follow the plan. In other words, you are not responsible for changing your child. You are only responsible for your own behaviors, namely, making sure that the conditions your child needs in order to learn are there.
>
> Here are some statements that you might make to yourselves and to each other whenever you start thinking that it is all up to you personally:
>
> The laws of learning are universal.
> The teaching program does the job.
> Behavior change takes care of itself.
> I'm only responsible for my own behaviors.
>
> Or, if you are religious,
>
> If we do our work, God will do the rest.

Note that the parents can be encouraged to write down the above statements. Then, at home, they can display the statements in appropriate places (such as on the refrigerator) and even practice saying them to themselves and to each other before teaching sessions and whenever they begin to feel tense or anxious about their child's future and their role in it.

In addition to a feeling of personal responsibility, parents may be overanxious for change to take place. They may be looking for the "big breakthrough," may not be reinforced by short-run gains, since their eyes are fixed on the long-term goal, and may be upset by what they perceive to be slow progress or a plateau. Of course, such problems may occur at any given time during or after the Program. Yet, now is a good time to start helping the parents to acquire a long-term perspective.

You can do this by emphasizing that it may take several tries, even several false starts, before the right learning conditions for their child are discovered. Good statements, key statements, that can help the parents are "Try, try again" and "Well, at least now we know what not to do (or what doesn't work)." To help parents remind themselves to plan, work, and be satisfied with small steps, teach them to use key statements such as "You have to walk before you can run"; "Rome wasn't built in a day"; and "He may have a long way to go, but look how far he has come in such a short time."

Waiting and Planning, Rather than Reacting (Item 16). Learning to wait and plan what to do, rather than react quickly when problems occur, is important if parents are to be successful at conducting teaching programs and at changing their own behaviors and relationships. As you recall from the APG and from Chapter 2, however, a pattern of quickly reacting to problems occurs because parents:

1. Are distressed by the problems (for instance, certain disruptive behaviors of their child).
2. Have learned that by reacting quickly they may get temporary relief.
3. Do not know what else to do.
4. May be so tense or anxious that they are unable to assess the situation objectively or stop themselves from reacting.

Here is what we have said to parents when discussing the importance of learning how to wait and plan rather than react.

> Remember what you saw on the videotapes and what we talked about when we were analyzing exchanges in the home—the problem of quickly reacting to problems, rather than waiting and planning what to do to solve the problems. It's fine and dandy to have a plan that tells you to ignore your child's screaming and to wait for him to stop for at least a minute before you pay attention to him. But, it's another thing to be able to do it—and do it consistently! The question is, how can we learn to wait and plan? How can we teach ourselves to stand back from what is going on, even if what is going on is painful to our eyes and ears and guts? How can we learn

> to change our habits and put our emotions on the "back burner," even in a stressful situation? Well, hard as it may sound, we can do it! And here is how.

At this point, give the parents some time to brainstorm—to think of methods that they might use to stop themselves from quickly reacting, for example:

1. Counting to ten before doing anything.
2. Taking notes on or recording the occurrence of problem events while they are in progress (this includes problem behaviors of the child and even personal problems of parents, such as anxiety).
3. Going to another room and doing something else when a problem event occurs (for example, leaving the kitchen where the child is screaming and either taking data on the screaming or planning what to do next).
4. Placing signs around the house. For instance: WAIT AND PLAN, DON'T REACT! Another sign might state the essential ingredients of a teaching program: FOR SCREAMING, TIME OUT IMMEDIATELY, EVERY TIME, AND WITHOUT TALKING. Or LOTS OF PRAISE WHILE SHE STAYS. IF SHE LEAVES THE TABLE, NO MORE FOOD 'TILL THE NEXT MEAL.
5. Coaching one another to wait and plan, and reinforcing one another for doing so:

> Okay, Honey, he's about to yell. Relax . . . That's it. Just relax . . . Count to ten . . . Good! I'm proud of you!

Cooperation of Spouses or Partners (Item 19). During the first meeting, the importance of cooperation was stressed. Now follow-up on the earlier discussion by describing ways in which the parents can cooperate. Here is what we have said in Programs.

> We have talked about the importance of cooperation before. Many people in this field have found that cooperation is important to success in conducting and maintaining a good home educational program. It simply boils down to the fact that we can all use help, encouragement, gratification, and expressions of appreciation to help us to do a good job. In addition, you are in this together. So, it simply makes sense to work together in ways that are satisfying to you as couples. And third, patterns of cooperation bring people closer together emotionally, and make life more enjoyable. Now, we are not saying that you don't cooperate with one another at home! We are simply saying that it is a good idea to pinpoint the important ways of cooperating so that you can keep these patterns of cooperation as strong as you can.
>
> Well, here are some of the kinds of cooperation that you can begin to focus on . . .

In describing methods for cooperating, simply refer to the components of Item 19 as listed in the APG. Of course, during the coming week the parents are not expected to do everything listed under Item 19. Rather, you want them to:

1. Begin setting aside time to discuss progress, problems, and plans.
2. Specify how they will work together in instituting productive exchanges during the coming week (as a team and/or splitting up teaching tasks).
3. Specify how they will reinforce each other and themselves as a couple.
4. Specify how they will share household tasks.

Later, during the Individual Consultation and home visit, you can help the parents to plan how they will cooperate during the week and to write their plans on a Weekly Contract form.

Organized Home-Life (Item 20). As noted in Chapter 2, if everyday household routines are done irregularly or inefficiently, it may be difficult for parents to conduct good home educational programs. Irregularities may contribute to problems in their children's (and their own) behaviors. Consequently, reemphasize the importance of household organization. This can be a touchy issue, however. That is, parents may be insulted, and have every right to be insulted, by the suggestion that there is any disorganization in the home. Therefore, make yourself clear. For example:

1. You are not saying that anyone actually is disorganized, but that everyone should be sensitive to the importance of organization.
2. Disorganization in anyone's home-life may not be the result of personal incompetence; it is likely the result of fatigue, tension, and the large amount of work to do in the home.
3. By organization you do not mean spotlessness and rigidity, but enough organization to conduct a good program.
4. The kind and amount of household organization that seems to be needed to run a good educational program, can be maintained easily with some simple methods.

At this point you can describe some of those methods.

1. Lindsley's (1966) "Sunday box" method, for example, can be used to teach people to clean up after themselves. Specifically, anything that family members leave laying around the house and out of the proper place (clothes on the floor, for example), is put in the Sunday box, and is not returned until the next Sunday.
2. During a weekly family conference, family members can discuss priorities and the scheduling of routine events and chores, and decide who is responsible for doing each one. The schedule of duties is written and displayed in an appropriate place.

3. Family members can decide on consequences to be attached to their performance or nonperformance of agreed-upon chores. For instance, if necessary, siblings' allowances might be made contingent upon their performance of certain chores. Similarly, family members can agree to reinforce the father (e.g., by washing the car) for his performing the agreed-upon task of washing supper dishes every other evening.
4. Special rules can be established for the behavior of younger siblings during teaching sessions, when a certain level of quiet and noninterruption are necessary. For instance, siblings can be taught to either participate in sessions or to stay in another room, with the TV turned down. Of course, as is noted again later, special efforts are made to give siblings the attention and recognition that they need and deserve.

As with cooperation between spouses or partners, the details of a plan for increasing household organization, if such a plan seems necessary, can be worked out during the Individual Consultation and home visit.

Pinpointing and Solving Personal Problems (Item 21). As indicated on the APG, this item includes: pinpointing and describing, analyzing, and jointly planning and working to solve personal problems. During this meeting, you have mentioned (and parents may have volunteered examples of) the kinds of personal problems that can interfere with conducting a good home educational program, which are often the result of career experiences. Consequently, it is not necessary to discuss personal problems in detail at this time. Instead, you can: (1) briefly list again the kinds of personal problems that parents may have or that may develop; (2) remind parents that such problems can result from career experiences and can often be understood in terms of principles of learning and structured exchanges; and (3) indicate that while it is important to work toward solving personal problems, like almost anything else such work is best done in small steps over the coming weeks.

Any work to be done on personal problems during the next week, then, can be planned during the Individual Consultation or, better, during the home visit, when you have more time to talk to parents. Parents' only assignment regarding personal problems would be to pinpoint and describe in logs or notes what they consider to be personal problems that they may have (the first component of APG Item 21). In later weeks, you and the parents can discuss the "problems" that the parents have pinpointed and described, and can begin to work on the next components of the method for solving personal problems. (See Chapter 10 for details of such methods.)

Honesty (Item 22). Unless parents are honest with themselves and with you, it is not likely that problems in the home programs will be pinpointed and solved before they become serious. For example, if parents do not honestly report that their child is failing to make much progress in a teaching program, weeks may go by with the parents becoming more frustrated and pessimistic and perhaps using counterproductive teaching methods. Consequently, now is the time to stress the importance of honesty. In doing so, however, the reasons why parents (and consultants) might be tempted to be less than honest are openly discussed. They seem to be the following:

1. Fear of failure (in the eyes of others and in the parents' own eyes).
2. Fatigue (for example, it may seem easier in the short-run to continue a rather ineffective teaching program than to admit a problem, which implies that a change of plans, and possibly a decrease in hope, is indicated).
3. Fear of being dropped from the Program.
4. Guilt at less-than-satisfactory performance of tasks and assignments.
5. Slow progress of child (or consultant's perception of slow progress with a family).
6. Desire to please the consultant or to help the consultant "save face," if the consultant's suggestions have not worked.

In briefly discussing honesty, parents are told that if things are not going well in their teaching programs, or if they are becoming tired and less motivated than before, the fault is less likely to be found in themselves as persons than it is in the Program itself (that is, in the teaching behaviors of consultants), in inadequacies in the teaching program plans they are using, or in a family relationship—all of which can be corrected, but only if everyone is honest about what is happening.

Like other APG items, you are not working on all components of honesty at this time. Rather, for the next week give parents an assignment to record some simple observations on how "things" are going in their efforts to institute productive exchanges. For instance, parents might write logs for certain periods of time during each day. You can later discuss the logs with them and raise the issue of honesty in a frank but nonthreatening fashion. This is discussed in the section on the home visit.

Scheduled Breaks (Item 23). Few people can sustain an intense involvement for long. To attempt it may produce the all-too-familiar consequence of "burning out," that is, an almost complete loss of energy and motivation. Moreover, if parents believe that they are expected to be intensely involved in (that is, actively) teaching their child and think about their child's education at all times, they may be reluctant even to start. So, it is very important to explain to parents that they are not expected to be "on" all of the time; that they could not be "on" all of the time anyway; and that remaining "on" is not necessary. They deserve and need breaks from teaching or even thinking about it, as does their child.

Describe methods that the parents can use for taking breaks—scheduled breaks. The major methods for scheduling breaks in a constructive way are as follows:

1. Parents write a weekly schedule of their breaks, specifying hours off during the day and a day or so off each week, how they will maintain their child's gains, and what each parent will be doing or how they will reinforce themselves during breaks (e.g., a night out, reading, and other activities the parents enjoy).
2. Parents take notes on (log) what they and the child did during breaks, or parents telephone their consultant to describe what has been going on during breaks.
3. Consultants can make home visits before (or if necessary, during) several scheduled breaks so as to coach parents in methods for maintaining gains in a relaxed way.
4. Parents volunteer problems that they might be having in scheduling and taking breaks, or in maintaining their child's gains during breaks. The consultant then helps the parents to solve the problems.

During the Individual Consultation at the end of this meeting, you and the parents write on the Weekly Contract when and how scheduled breaks will be taken.

Self- and Mutual Reinforcement (Item 24). Not only do parents need scheduled breaks, but they also need to gratify or reinforce themselves and each other. Therefore, explain the importance of such self- and mutual reinforcement (for example, to keep up their spirits and motivation, to increase each other's self-esteem, and to bring parents even closer together). Then briefly describe methods the parents can use to reinforce themselves and each other. (See APG Item 24 for details.)

During the coming week, of course, the parents are not expected to institute a complex system of reinforcement among themselves. But they can begin to specify and schedule how the will: 1) individually reinforce themselves each day (for example, during a scheduled break or after successfully ignoring a tantrum); 2) reinforce each other (for example, kind words to express affection and recognition of effort; favors or special treats); and 3) reinforce themselves as a couple (for instance, a night out, a special meal that they both like). In addition, in the same way that they can post a sign telling themselves "PLAN, DON'T REACT" and plan for instituting productive exchanges, the parents can post a few signs as reminders to reinforce themselves. For example:

REINFORCE YOURSELF FOR DOING A GOOD JOB. YOU DESERVE IT!
WHAT HAVE I DONE TO SHOW HIM (HER) THAT I CARE?
AS SOON AS I (WE) . . . , THEN I (WE) WILL . . ."

All plans regarding the above are written on the Weekly Contract form during the Individual Consultation at the end of the meeting. Later, during the home visit, check to see if parents are following their plan, coach them (if necessary), reinforce them for following their plan, or help them to revise it.

Linkage with or Integration in Networks and Organizations (Item 25). As explained earlier, linkage with and integration within networks and organizations offering resources of various kinds, can have several benefits; for example, helping parents to:

1. Reduce the isolation of the family.
2. Conduct a good home educational program.
3. Persist at and maintain their home educational program once the Program has been faded out.
4. Work together and with others to increase the availability and improve the quality of services to families and children.

At this time, then, stress the importance and benefits of linkages and integration, encourage parents to describe any contacts they have had with organizations for parents or professionals, describe the ways that they might become integrated within networks and organizations, and start to establish the beginnings of a helping network among the families in the Program and, if possible, with available specialists (e.g., speech therapists). For instance, you can describe the sequence of steps by which parents in the Program might work together, beginning with telephone calls, and, if successful, gradually adding more extensive relationships, such as coaching one another, providing one another with (exchanging) backup services (such as baby-sitting), and possibly working together (and with organizations) to evaluate and make contributions to schools and other services for children and families.

If parents are agreeable, initiate a helping network between the families by distributing a list of the families' telephone numbers, including, if possible, available parents from other Programs. Encourage parents to call one another during the week to pass on information about methods they are using and to help pinpoint or solve problems in instituting productive exchanges. For example, each family (preferably each parent) might agree to call at least one other family at a specified day and time. Indeed, all parents might set aside a certain hour (the "call hour") one day per week, during which they can make and receive calls from others. Unless parents would consider it an imposition (especially since they hardly know one another yet), parents might even write on their Weekly Contract whom they will call and when.

Generalization (Item 26). During the course of the Program, you will be teaching parents to generalize their child's educational gains to many places and persons. For the coming week, you can begin the generalization process by teaching parents to request cooperation from, coach, and instruct the child's siblings (as well as others who may come in contact with the child, such as relatives or neighbors). The parents can discuss and describe with others the behaviors of the child that are to be worked on during the week, and instruct and coach them to interact with the child in productive ways.

For instance, if the plan for instituting productive exchanges calls for consistently ignoring yelling and instead, reinforcing the child for intervals of quiet or for proper speaking, the parents should:

1. Have the siblings (and others) read the plan for instituting productive exchanges.
2. Demonstrate what they want the siblings to do.
3. Coach the siblings at the proper times (e.g., when yelling occurs).
4. Enthusiastically reinforce the siblings for helping.

It is important, however, for the parents to make the siblings feel that they are part of the family program and not merely as though they are potential sources of problems. Consequently, parents must make sure to give the siblings the extra attention that they need and deserve, since it is easy to inadvertently pay less and less attention to the siblings once the Program starts. Siblings can be invited to attend meetings and be encouraged and helped to meet with one another to discuss their feelings and possible involvement.

Problem-solving (Item 27). As you have seen, most APG items are followed by a list of potential problems. Although later chapters of this book, especially Chapter 10, describe methods to help parents anticipate, pinpoint, and solve such problems, a major goal is to teach parents to use a general problem-solving sequence to anticipate, pinpoint, and solve problems more on their own. That is what Item 27 is all about. Therefore, at this time, tell parents about the importance of their learning to follow a problem-solving sequence in which they:

1. Pinpoint and objectively describe a problem.
2. Analyze the problem using principles of learning and structured exchange.
3. Plan how to solve the problem using principles of learning and structured exchange, as well as various methods they have learned, and list a number of alternatives.
4. Choose which seems to be the best first alternative.
5. Implement the plan (make sure to reinforce themselves for carrying out the plan.
6. Evaluate the result.
7. Continue the plan, revise it, or select another alternative.

During the coming week, the parents can do several things to start them using a problem-solving sequence. First, they use their copy of Table 6-1 (Productive and Counterproductive Exchanges) to pinpoint and describe exchanges in the family, and use their plan for instituting productive exchanges (which will be written on their Weekly Contract form) as well as Items 16 and 17 on the APG to remind them of how to interact with their child during the coming week. Second, they use their copy of the Weekly Contract (to be written during the Individual Consultation) to remind them of the rest of their weekly assignment (for instance, the reading assignment from *Educating Children*, scheduled breaks, reinforcement for themselves and each other, and telephone calls). Third, they post signs in the home, again to remind them of some of the main tasks in their assignment. Fourth, they take data on events in the home during the coming week, for instance, a written log noting progress and problems in efforts to institute productive exchanges, scheduling and taking of breaks, efforts to reinforce themselves, cooperation between the spouses, and feelings and thoughts about their work. And fifth, they read over their copy of the APG to keep track of progress and to pinpoint potential problems.

The last thing to do before the Individual Consultation is to briefly describe the main business for the next week: rewards.

IV. INTRODUCING THE NEXT WEEK'S WORK

A long discussion of rewards is not necessary. However, show how the next week's topic—rewards—will help the parents to achieve goals. Here is what we have said in our Programs.

> During the coming week, you will be taking an important step. You will be making some basic changes in the ways you interact with your children. The result is going to be that your children will start to change in the right direction. At the same time, you will be gaining confidence and skill at teaching.
>
> Of course, you want to be working on specific behaviors and skills with which your children need help, such as speech, self-help skills, playing, and imitation. Soon you will be learning how to teach your child those skills. What do you have to know in order to teach specific skills? Well, you already know that consequences are an important condition of learning. Behaviors change depending on the kinds of consequences those behaviors consistently get. Now what kind of consequence helps a person learn to do a behavior more often, for a longer time, and with more skill? . . . REWARDS! Well, since rewards are so important for learning the behaviors and skills you want your children to learn, our next main topic is rewards.
>
> So, your reading assignment for the next meeting is Chapter 3 of *Educating Children*. When you know what kinds of rewards there are, how to use them to help your child learn new behaviors, and how to find rewards in the home, you will be one step closer to starting teaching programs.

Before dividing into small groups of parents and their consultants for the Individual Consultation, you can end the group portion of the meeting with a "rousing" statement such as the following.

> Okay, folks. We're going to split up now for Individual Consultations, so we can plan the details of the work for the coming week. In other words, this is it! So follow your plans, work together, reward yourselves, observe what is happening, take notes, call us and call each other, and try, try again if you have any problems. You will all be at least fifty percent successful, which means half-way there. . . .

V. INDIVIDUAL CONSULTATION

There are three things to do during the Individual Consultation. First, encourage questions about what was discussed during this meeting or about the coming week's work. In general, parents ask two kinds of questions. Questions regarding the intellectual and practical content of the Program thus far (e.g., principles of learning and exchange or methods for changing specific behaviors) can be answered in a straightforward fashion. Questions regarding the future (e.g., your expectations for the child or problems in the family which they fear may hinder their program) are best answered so as to strengthen confidence in learning principles and a long-term perspective. In particular, remind the parents that: the Program moves in small steps; their child's education also moves in small steps; and the parents will be learning to handle potential or actual problems in small steps. In other words, convince parents to focus attention and energy on weekly activities rather than long-term goals. If they are successful each week, many of their long-term goals are likely to be achieved. Moreover, at certain points in the Program, many of their major concerns about the future will be addressed.

Second, pinpoint and praise parents for productive participation. If they have had problems with productive participation (such as not taking their turn during discussions, not completing assignments, or making pessimistic, nonbehavioral statements) pinpoint such behaviors, discuss them, and suggest that you and the parents, during the home visit, work on a plan for improving participation.

Third, help the parents fill out a Weekly Contract for the coming week, specifying what they and the consultant are to do. For example:

1. *Reading assignment.* The parents are to read and answer all questions in Chapter 3 of *Educating Children,* and reread APG Items 16 and 17 (as well as other items).

2. *Plan for instituting productive exchanges* Help the parents to complete the "Tentative Plan for Changing Exchanges" which they started earlier in the meeting. (See Tables 6-1 and 6-2.) You and the parents discuss the behaviors of the child and the exchanges to work on, as well as the behaviors of the parents in each exchange. Thus, the written plan is rather specific. Point out that the plan may have to be revised during the week, which is why the parents follow the plan and take notes or logs on what happens. The plan is either written on the Weekly Contract form in the space for "Teaching Program Plan" or is written on separate pages and attached to the contract.

3. *Cooperation.* With your help, parents specify and write down how they will cooperate with one another during the coming week. How will they work together to institute exchanges? Will they split-up certain household tasks?

4. *Organization in home routines.* If, as a result of the earlier discussion, the parents pinpoint problems of organization, they can specify what they will do to start correcting them. For instance, they might have a "family council" to decide on who will do which chores, and when. Or they might use Lindsley's "Sunday box" to teach family members to clean up after themselves.

5. *Scheduled breaks.* The parents specify and write down which few hours each day, and which day during the week, they will be "on break." In addition, they specify what they will do to maintain the major outlines of their teaching program. For example, one parent can be on break while the other is still implementing the plan.

6. *Reinforcement for themselves and each other.* Parents specify when and how they will reinforce themselves, as individuals and as a couple (e.g., generally increasing expressions of affection and recognition for effort and success; doing favors; a night out together).

7. *Linkages.* If parents were agreeable to exchanging phone numbers, they specify a time to call at least one other family during the week to discuss home programs.

8. *Generalization.* Parents write down how they will involve others in their home program to institute productive exchanges. For example, they might agree to sit down with the siblings and describe the plan, the importance of the siblings' help, and the siblings' feelings. Later in the week, they coach the siblings in how to interact with the child.

9. *Problem-solving.* As to following a problem-solving sequence, the parents agree to post their plan for instituting productive exchanges and to post signs, such as those described earlier. In addition, they might review their Weekly Contract together each evening.

10. *Objectivity and honesty.* The parents agree to call the consultant at a specific time or a certain number of times, to report on progress and possible problems. They take notes or write logs on both novel or major events as well as some important typical incidents each day, both positive and negative (including their feelings and thoughts). Note that parents might also videotape important events as well as their efforts to institute productive exchanges.

11. *Home visit.* Finally, the day and time for your home visit is specified in writing. Note that the home visit is scheduled for a time of day when both parents are present and the child is awake, so that you can coach the parents. Any special assignments that the parents would like you to perform, such as finding an answer to a question of theirs or how to teach certain behaviors, are specified.

Whenever parents are performing different tasks during the week, they note this on the Weekly Contract.

Table 6-3 is an example of a Weekly Contract for the second unit.

The Weekly Contract is lengthy, since it lists most of the details for the coming week's work. While specificity enables all parties to know what is expected of them, there may not be enough time at the end of the meeting to discuss or write everything. The section on "Teaching Program Plan" leaves many questions unanswered. For instance, it does not say which of the two methods the parents should use for handling Sally's screaming. Nor does it say how many times per day the parents should provide Sally with occasions to brush her teeth, perform chores, or learn to work at small motor activities.

Actually, the solution for lengthiness or for a lack of specificity is the same, namely you and the parents can discuss as many details as possible during the Individual Consultation. Later in the week, however, additional details can be worked out over the phone and during the home visit, and then written on the contract. As to the alternative methods for handling certain behaviors of the child, you and the parents can discuss alternatives, write them on the Weekly Contract, and then decide to try only one method during the week. At this point, instruct parents to conduct the program as written, at least until you can help to evaluate it. This may help parents to evaluate and revise their programs according to a problem-solving sequence. When the Weekly Contract has been written, the family should receive a copy. The meeting can then be adjourned.

VI. HOME VISIT

Several tasks are accomplished during the home visit:
1. review the parents' work thus far in the overall Program. 2. help the parents to do all of their assignment for the week by answering questions, directly coaching and demonstrating, providing immediate feedback and reinforcement for parents' efforts and progress. 3. evaluate the work done so far during the week. 4. decide either to continue the plan as written, update it because so much progress has been made, make it more detailed, or revise it so as to handle potential or existing problems or shortcomings.

Remember, after preliminary small talk get down to business and leave any socializing until the business has been completed. In addition, take notes on what you are observing (both progress and potential or actual problems). Encourage parents to take notes on what is discussed.

Table 6-3 Example of a Weekly Contract for the Second Unit

CONTRACT FOR WEEK OF: 10/5/78–10/12/78

Mr. and Mrs. Lawrence agree to complete all parts of the following assignment for the coming week.

1. READ and DO ANY WRITTEN ASSIGNMENTS in Chapter 3 of *Educating Children with Learning and Behavior Problems;* reread APG Items 16 and 17.
2. TEACHING PROGRAM PLAN FOR: *Instituting Productive Exchanges*

Counterproductive Exchanges	*Productive Exchanges*
Escape Sally screams and we go over to her, sit with her, talk softly to her, and ask her what is the matter, cuddle her, and sometimes turn on the TV or record player for her or give her a snack.	*Riding it out* Sally screams and we will either: a) completely ignore it and just go about our business, wait until she has stopped screaming for at least one minute, and then quickly reward her with smiles, hugs, TV, or record player, or a small piece of fruit or cereal. Or, b) immediately put her in her room (time out) without saying anything to her, wait until she has been quiet for at least one minute, and then let her out. When she is out, we will reward her with smiles, praise, hugs, TV, or records, or healthful snacks every few minutes that she is quiet. We will repeat the above method every time that she starts to scream.
Sally stares at her fingers, flaps her hands over and over. When we can't stand it any more or when we are out in public and are embarrassed by her strange hand movements, we gently put her hands down, ask her to stop, or hand her something to hold on to. But this does not stop her or teach her to do something else with her hands that is more productive.	For the next week, we will completely ignore it when she is making strange hand movements, as though we don't even see it. But whenever she has been keeping her hands still, or has been using them in a more productive way (for example, playing with toys, using her tooth brush) for at least one minute, we will quickly reward her with praise, smiles, hugs, or small bites of healthful snacks.
Placation Sally goes to the kitchen drawer, opens it, and takes out food and eats it.	*Earning Rewards* We will put a lock on the kitchen drawers. When Sally tries to get in, and if she screams or has a tantrum, we will com-

continued

Table 6-3 *(Continued)*

Counterproductive Exchanges	*Productive Exchanges*
	pletely ignore it. But during the day, we will keep a small dish of healthful snacks in a special drawer and will give Sally many occasions during the day to earn the chance to open the drawer and eat the snacks. For example, we will give her many simple tasks to do (cleaning up a bit of her room, putting on her shoes, pushing a chair under the table, working a puzzle). If she cooperates, we will quickly praise and hug her, and let her into the drawer. If she does not cooperate, we will completely ignore it.
Multiple Signals We often ask Sally over and over to do a simple task. Sometimes she finally cooperates, but most of the time she does not. Also, we give her signals, such as requests, when she is not looking. And, we often talk to her too much, even when she is not paying any attention.	*Single Signals* From now on, we will only give signals when Sally is looking at us. For now, we will prompt her to look at us by gently calling her name and chucking her under the chin. We will only give her a signal once. If she cooperates, we will praise her, hug her, and give her a bite of healthful snack, some roughhousing, TV, or a record. For now, if she does not cooperate, we will just ignore it and she will lose her chance to earn a reward.
Lack of Rewards for Appropriate Behaviors Sometimes Sally is sitting quietly, keeping her hands still or using them in a constructive way, trying to help around the house or following simple directions, and we do not reward her as often as we should.	*Catch 'Em Doing Good* We will be on the lookout for the times when Sally is sitting quietly, cooperating, keeping her hands still or using them in constructive ways, or helping around the house, and we will reward her as fast as we can and nearly every time that she is doing these behaviors, with praise, smiles, hugs, TV, records, small bites of healthful snacks, and activities, such as roughhousing and going for a ride.
Lack of Opportunities to Respond Sometimes we are so tired that we just leave Sally alone as long as she is quiet.	*Many Opportunities to Respond* During the day, we will give Sally many chances to learn and to earn rewards. For

continued

Table 6-3 ***(Continued)***

Counterproductive Exchanges	*Productive Exchanges*
And we often do things for her, instead of giving her a chance to learn to take care of herself.	example, we will give her simple tasks to do (such as chores), will expect her to help to dress herself and keep herself clean (for instance washing, brushing her teeth), and will require her to at least make a sound before we get things for her or let her do activities that she enjoys, such as going outside or going for a ride.
Improper Punishment Sometimes, if we are aggravated we slap Sally when she is uncooperative, making strange hand movements, or screaming. When we slap her, it is on the behind, not very hard, and not often, and we often talk to her or cuddle her after we slap her bottom.	*Proper Use of Punishment* For the time being, we will try to replace Sally's problem behaviors by using ignoring or time out, plus lots of rewards for appropriate behaviors.

Changes in Objects and Materials in the Home: We will 1) put all of Sally's toys in a box in the den; 2) put a lock on kitchen cabinets; 3) buy pants with elastic waist; 4) move record player to high place.

3. COOPERATION. We will cooperate in the following ways during the week: a) coach each other to institute the productive exchanges according to the plan—for example, reminding each other how to handle problem behaviors, reminding each other to be on the lookout for appropriate behaviors to reward, reminding each other to relax and to wait and think when a problem behavior starts; b) help each other to institute productive exchanges, for example, Mr. Lawrence will put a lock on the kitchen cabinets by Wednesday evening; both parents will institute productive exchanges; and if one parent is busy, the other parent will continue to follow the plan for instituting productive exchanges; c) Mr. Lawrence will do the supper dishes every other night.

4. ORGANIZATION. A family council will be held on Tuesday evening to decide on who will do which chores and when.

5. SCHEDULED BREAKS. Mrs. Lawrence will take a scheduled break between 6:00 and 8:00 each evening. At that time, Mr. Lawrence will institute the plan. Mr. Lawrence will take a scheduled break from 8:00 to 9:00 each night, while Mrs. Lawrence is putting Sally to bed. Both parents will take a break on Sunday, but will

continued

Table 6-3 *(Continued)*

continue to reward Sally for appropriate behaviors and will try not to reward her for problem behaviors. In addition, siblings will give more help in instituting the plan on Sunday.

6. REINFORCEMENT. Mr. and Mrs. Lawrence will praise each other for their efforts, will increase the number of times that they express their affection and appreciation for each other. Saturday night, the Mr. and Mrs. will go to the movies.

7. LINKAGES. Mr. Lawrence will call Mr. Fernandez on Tuesday evening at 7:30. Mrs. Lawrence will call Mrs. Fernandez Tuesday morning at 11:00.

8. GENERALIZATION. At the Tuesday night family council, the plan for instituting productive exchanges will be described to the siblings. We will ask for their advice and support, but will not push it. We will make sure to express our affection for them several times a day. If they are agreeable, we will demonstrate the proper ways to interact with Sally, and will coach them when the time arises.

9. PROBLEM-SOLVING. Mr. Lawrence will make signs saying "PLAN, DON'T REACT"; "YOU DON'T HEAR HER SCREAMING"; and "CATCH HER DOING GOOD BEHAVIORS." He will post them in the kitchen and on the door to the livingroom by Wednesday night. We will read this contract each evening together and evaluate how well the plans are working.

10. OBJECTIVITY AND HONESTY. We will phone our consultant Tuesday night at 8:00. We will each write a short log of each day's events. We will each have a note pad and will keep it handy. We will write down what happened during important exchanges, and we will summarize the day's events each evening, including how we feel about the plans and ourselves.

11. HOME VISIT. Consultant will make a home visit Thursday evening at 7:30 P.M. In addition, consultant will have prepared a tentative plan for teaching Sally to pull up her pants.

Date ______

Mr. Lawrence ______________________________

Mrs. Lawrence ______________________________

Consultant ______________________________

Review

A good way to begin the business of the home visit is to ask the parents to describe how they feel about the Program, their participation in it, and, in particular, their efforts to do the assignments on the Weekly Contract. While the parents are describing their work, you can read their logs or notes, ask for elaborations, reinforce them for honesty and work, and help them to pinpoint and voice potential problems. For example, regarding the Program in general, a parent might state:

Mrs. Lawrence: Well, we think that we are doing pretty well. We're learning an awful lot. And we're already getting results with the new exchanges with Sally.

Consultant: That's great. But do I hear right? I seem to hear a bit of a question in your voice. (Asks for clarification.)

Mrs. Lawrence: Yeah, you're right. Oh, I think the Program is great! I really do. It's the first time that we've gotten any practical advice on what to do. It's just that there is so much for us to learn. We're afraid—or at least I'm afraid—that I won't learn it all fast enough, that I'll make big mistakes because I won't learn fast enough. (Expresses a more specific concern.)

Consultant: I see. Mr. Lawrence—Bill—do you feel about the same?

Mr. Lawrence: Yeah. Things are going great. But I feel like the wife does. You've talked about so much! Breaks, cooperation, getting Sally's big sister involved, and all the methods for teaching Sally.

Consultant: Okay. Let's make sure that we are thinking about the same thing. How do you feel about the way you are participating so far? I mean learning what we are talking about and what you are reading about, learning the teaching methods, and so on? How do you feel that you both are doing? (Asks for more clarification.)

Mr. Lawrence: No problem, there! Right dear? . . . We understand what we're reading and seeing. And you know that we are not shy. We talk a lot in the meetings.

Consultant: Yes, you both make valuable comments. So, it's not your participation, but the long haul that you are concerned about? (Voices parents' concern.)

Mrs. Lawrence: Right! Whether we can learn it all, and what will happen in our home programs each week until we learn it right.

Consultant: Alright. I've got it now. Yes. I agree. There is a lot to learn and do. Was the load too much this week? Were there too many things to do on the Contract? Because if there was just too much, we might be able to go in smaller steps. (Provides alternative.)

Mrs. Lawrence: Oh. No. There wasn't too much to do. We're afraid of mistakes. That's it. We don't want to mess it all up.

Consultant: What would be a mistake? How are you afraid of messing up?

Mrs. Lawrence: Like rewarding Sally when she screams. You know, reacting instead of waiting and planning.

Consultant: Hey! Great example. But since you already know that it would be a mistake, you would quickly correct it, wouldn't you? (Shows parents that their objectivity decreases the likelihood of making mistakes they are worried about.)

Mr. Lawrence: Sure, I'd catch it right away, I think.

Consultant: Then it would only be a minor mistake, wouldn't it? In fact, it would be a good idea to make a few mistakes like that! Because if you catch yourself, you are less likely to make it again, right? (That is, making and correcting mistakes is likely to facilitate discrimination of their own behaviors.)

Mrs. Lawrence: Yeah, you are right! In fact, we did make some mistakes until we just about had the plan memorized. But I doubt if we'll make them again.

Consultant: Great! So the mistakes that you know about are not worth worrying about, because you already have the solution. So, maybe you are still concerned about the mistakes that you don't know about?

Mr. Lawrence: That's it! What happens if we keep making a mistake and don't know about it? Won't we mess Sally up?

Consultant: Well, that's what I'm here for (said with a smile). I expect that there may be one or two things you don't know about yet. (Again said in a friendly way.) You don't see me being too concerned do you? There's no way that you could learn everything in two weeks. We are only teaching you what you need to learn in order to work on a few of Sally's behaviors, a little at a time. (Helps parents to change their time perspective.)

Mrs. Lawrence: Uh, huh.

Consultant: It usually takes a couple of weeks to nail down the methods you will be learning each week. Until you have them down, I and the other parents will be helping you to nail them down and to pinpiont possible mistakes. For instance, a few weeks from now, the methods you are using this week to institute productive exchanges will be second-nature. Then we will work on different methods. Don't worry too much about making mistakes. Until you get better at learning to pinpoint your own mistakes, let me worry about them.

And about your concern for all that there is to learn, remember that we are all going in small steps. To be successful each week, you don't need to know everything about educating Sally. What's the use of knowing all about how to teach her to talk, when she isn't ready to learn how to talk? Everything in small steps. Okay?

Mrs. Lawrence: Well, that makes me feel lots better. I just didn't want to be a failure, not after all these years, now that we're finally getting some help.

Consultant: Whenever you get the jitters like we've just talked about, why don't you remind yourself of what we've been saying, that everything is in small steps? (Provides parents with a statement they can make to themselves.) In fact, why not give another parent a phone call for a little moral support?

Mr. Lawrence: Okay.

At this time, again pinpoint and reinforce the parents' productive participation in the Program (as specified on Item 11 of the APG), for example, talking up during meetings, encouraging and reinforcing productive verbal behavior of other participants, their own productive verbal behavior, completing reading and written assignments, cooperating with and supporting one another in meetings. If, on the other hand, certain needs in the parents' participation have been pinpointed and described, this is the time to address them.

Style is obviously crucial here. Be honest or frank, and yet supportive and prescriptive. That is, help the parents to pinpoint needs, see that they are common, relatively easy to explain and correct, and help the parents to develop methods for improving. For example, if completing reading assignments was a problem (which, you recall, would be noted on the parents' Credits-Earned sheet), the parents might schedule specific times to do their reading, and follow their completion of a reading assignment with reinforcing consequences.

This does not mean that all weaknesses in participation are pinpointed and brought to a parent's attention at this time! In fact, to do so may lower some parents' confidence or damage the parent-consultant relationship, which should involve as much positive reinforcement for appropriate behaviors and progress as possible. Thus, instead of discussing it now, you might remedy a low rate of speaking up in group discussions simply by increasing the parent's opportunities to participate and by reinforcing their responses with nods, winks, and smiles. Similarly, tardiness might be handled through the contract-credit system. At this point, then, problems that are likely to hinder the parents' home program itself are addressed, such as not completing the reading assignment or missing a meeting.

Of course, carefully observe parents' participation during the next several weeks, for unless shortcomings are remedied early in the Program, they may become worse and/or more difficult ot correct.

Helping Parents with Specific Assignments on the Weekly Contract

When the issue of participation in the Program has been discussed, the focus of the home visit can shift to the parents' efforts to do the assignments on their Weekly Contract. A good place to start is with the plan to institute productive exchanges, which includes both their interaction with the child and changes to be made in the physical environment.

Helping Parents to Institute Productive exchanges. Here is an example of the kind of discussion that takes place in our Programs.

Consultant: According to the contract, you were going to work on Sally's getting into the kitchen drawer and eating food from it. I see here from your logs that locking the drawers, ignoring Sally when she screamed to get into them, and giving her many opportunities during the day to earn the chance to open the special drawer and eat the snack inside is working. How about some more details? Just what did you do and just what happened? (Sets occasion for parents to describe their use of the plan for instituting productive exchanges.)

Mrs. Lawrence: Well, Bill put the lock on the drawers the next day after the meeting.

Consultant: Hey, great! That was fast. (Reinforces parent.)

Mrs. Lawrence: Well, we just acted like there was nothing unusual. And Sally, well she kept trying to get into the drawers as always. When she found out that she couldn't open them, she did her screaming bit. But we just coached each other to ignore it. We went to another room and let her scream.

Consultant: Fine. So you coached each other not to react. And you think that you have a lot to learn?! You just learned some of the biggies! Learning to be calm and to cooperate are important. (Pinpoints and reinforces important behaviors.)

Mrs. Lawrence: (With a big smile.) And it seemed to work for her and for us. We felt clamer than ever, and after a while Sally just gave up.

Consultant: How long before she gave up? What do your logs say?

Mr. Lawrence: About 45 minutes the first time. Thirty minutes the second. And about 10 minutes the third time.

Mrs. Lawrence: When Sally would come out of the kitchen, and when she quieted down, we would get her to look at us, and when she did we would talk to her and cuddle her. Then we would give her a simple task to do.

Consultant: Great. You followed the plan to the letter. You're both doing fine. What did you ask her to do? (Reinforces parents and set occasion for more description.)

Mr. Lawrence: Oh, like put a book on the book shelf, turn on the light, or open the door. You know, little things around the house.

Consultant: And?

Mrs. Lawrence: Well, by Heaven, she refused a couple of times, but we just ignored that, too. Then she cooperated once, and we cuddled her and ran her right into the kitchen and opened the special drawer and let her eat a few pieces of fruit in the cup.

Mr. Lawrence: Of course, she tried all the drawers a few more times that day, ran through her screaming number, but we held firm, like the sign says (points to sign on wall saying "PLAN, DON'T REACT"), and when she was quiet for a while, we gave her a simple task to do.

Consultant: Fantastic! Sounds like you are working as a team, too. That's important. So, how do the two of you feel about it?

Mrs. Lawrence: Feel great! Both of us. Why Bill was saying that this is the first time that he's felt like he could help Sally. I feel good, too. I mean, all those years of her screaming and me feeling that I was losing my mind. Now I know that she's got brains and that we can help her to learn a lot.

Discussion such as the above can continue for a short while, with you encouraging the parents to describe their efforts to institute other productive exchanges on their plan. As in the above, do more than merely praise parents for efforts and successes. Pinpoint specific teaching behaviors or skills, attitudes, and relationships, and remind parents how important they are. For example:

> So, you are learning to wait and plan, instead of react. That is great. You remember that we talked about it during the meeting. It is an important habit to develop.
>
> I hear you saying that you are working as a team in several ways. You are coaching one another and working together to institute the productive exchanges. Keep it up.
>
> You said that you required Sally to look at you before you gave her a signal. So, you are doing what we suggested in the meeting. And you found that it worked I'm glad! You learn fast.

Moreover, you might help parents to suggest ways that they can generalize specific teaching methods to other situations and behaviors.

> You seem to be doing very well on a basic method—ignoring a problem behavior (at least one that can be safely ignored), consistently giving Sally a chance to learn alternative behaviors, and reinforcing her for doing the alternative behaviors. Can you think of others of Sally's problem behaviors with which you can use that method?

After discussing the parents' efforts to institute productive exchanges, you can ask for a demonstration of the parents working with their child. If the parents have given their approval, videotape the demonstration. If not, you can at least take notes on the exchanges.

As much as possible, let the parents work with the child on their own. However, provide feedback shortly after each important exchange has occurred. In doing so, pinpoint just what it was that the parents did correctly. For instance,

> That was terrific the way you waited until Sally was looking at you before you gave her a signal. And your signal was clear and simple. You also rewarded her very, very well. You did it quickly and with enthusiasm.

If problems occur, however, first try visual (e.g., gestures) or verbal coaching, such as:

> Okay, just walk away from her (or a hand wave). Don't say anything (or finger on lips). That's it!

Or,

> Okay, telling her to look at you may not be enough. Try gently chucking her under the chin while you tell her to look.

If coaching does not seem to be working, either because the parent is having trouble using a certain teaching method or because the child is just not responding to a method, demonstrate the proper method or work with the child for a short time in order to find out what method(s) might work better. Explain what you have done and then turn the session back to the parents.

Note that you should not inadvertently ignore siblings who are present, but talk to them and, if they interact with the child in a productive way, praise them.

After the demonstration session, which might last about 30 minutes, review the session with the parents, either by showing the videotape over their own TV or by discussing your observations and notes. Videotapes made by the parents can also be viewed at this time. As much as possible, encourage parents to pinpoint their proper use of methods as well as those methods with which they need help. The method of stopping the tape and having parents analyze the preceding portion can be used here. Naturally, praise the parents for their objectivity and for their proper use of methods. In addition, help the parents to compare their behaviors during the Baseline Observations, which were discussed at the last meeting with their behavior this week, stressing improvements.

If the parents needed help on some basic teaching methods (e.g., they gave signals when the child was not looking, asked questions rather than stated directions or requests, or rewarded too slowly), describe your observations. In doing so, tell the parents how close they are to having mastered a method, how much they have improved, and, as much as possible, indicate what they should do rather than what they should not do. For example:

> You've just about got the basic method for rewarding target behaviors. You are catching Sally just about every time. That's great. Now, just reward her a bit faster.

To further strengthen proper methods, you and the parents can role-play those with which the parents were having difficulty, as well as any changes or new methods that have been suggested.

What if the parents have a hard time instituting productive exchanges? There seem to be two reasons for such a problem. First, personal or marital problems may interfere with following the plan, such as anxiety, tension, self-defeating thoughts, or lack of help. For example, a parent may be so tense that he or she cannot tolerate problem behaviors, and so reacts as usual. In this case, you might discuss such possibilities (or observations) with the parents in the last portion of the home visit, and suggest that certain methods (described in Chapter 10) be tried.

Second, the parents may simply have a hard time observing the behavior of their child or themselves or remembering the methods to use. In that case, although it is costly, you might either make additional home visits during this week or arrange to stay in the house longer to coach, demonstrate, and role-play proper methods until the parents can enact them reliably. While costly in the short-run, extended coaching is likely to pay off in the long-run.

Helping Parents with the Remaining Weekly Contract Assignments. Having dealt with the parents' current teaching program plan (instituting productive exchanges), you can review each assignment item on the Weekly Contract, for instance: the portions of Chapter 3 of *Educating Children* that have so far been read (especially the assignment on finding rewards, at the end of the chapter); the plan to cooperate; methods to improve household organization; scheduling and taking of breaks; parents' reinforcing themselves and one another; calling other parents and receiving phone calls from them; efforts to involve the siblings; the posting of signs and rereading of the Weekly Contract; honesty and accuracy in logging and reporting events and feelings; and your own performance of any task that you agreed to do for the parents.

Evaluating Progress and Revising the Weekly Contract

To bring the home visit to a sense of closure, the family's progress thus far during the week can be evaluated. Specifically, you and the parents try to reach an agreement on the progress of the child's behaviors and on the progress of the parents in applying what they have been learning. Work toward an agreement on problems or potential problems, and make initial plans to solve them.

First, problems in the design of the educational program (at this point, the plan for instituting productive exchanges) can be dealt with. For example:

1. Ignoring certain problem behaviors may not seem to be effective, in which case the existing plan might be continued for the remainder of the week and then revised, or, if it is already clear that the original method is not suitable, the parents might try a different one for the remainder of the week, for example, time out. (Our rule of thumb is to make sure a method is being used properly and to allow one to two weeks before instituting a problem-solving sequence and trying another method, unless the first method is clearly inappropriate).

2. Ambiguities and unanswered questions in the plan can be worked out; for instance, how long to leave the child in time out if the child starts a problem behavior again, soon after returning from time out, or how many times during the day the parents should give the child occasions to respond to certain signals (such as Grandma's Law).

3. The reinforcers used by the parents may be too few or may not be powerful, in which case additional reinforcers would be specified.

4. The parents may be attempting to work on too many behaviors or, on the other hand, the plan might be revised to include additional behaviors for which the same methods are relevant.

If it is clear that certain problem behaviors are posing a difficulty, the parents might be assigned portions of Chapter 15 in *Educating Children,* on replacing problem behaviors.

Second, problems that the parents may have had in instituting productive exchanges, such as reacting rather than waiting and planning, or shortcomings in the use of general teaching methods, can be discussed briefly again and remedial methods can be suggested. For instance, the parents might coach each other more or might role-play certain methods.

Third, problems with other assignment items on the Weekly Contract can again be discussed and specific methods planned. Some problems are shortcomings that simply require a bit of advice and practice. For instance, with so much to do the parents may have forgotten or may have put off writing a daily log, taking a scheduled break, or reinforcing one another as often as they should have. In that case, stress the importance of such assignment items and suggest methods that the parents can use to remind themselves, such as writing a daily schedule of assignment items or posting additional signs around the house. All such methods to be used by parents should be written on the existing Weekly Contract.

Other problems, however, may be more difficult. Examples include personal problems, lack of marital cooperation, lack of household organization, less-than-complete honesty (which may mean communication games), lack of cooperation from siblings, and failure to use a problem-solving sequence. Of course, if it is clear that there is only one of the above problems to contend with, then you and the parents can discuss the problem and (using the methods suggested in Chapter 10 as well as other sources) begin to plan how to solve the problem. However, we have found that many of the above problems occur together. For instance, one parent may be anxious or depressed; there may be tension if not conflict between the spouses; the parents may not follow a problem-solving sequence at all, but rather, react to moment-by-moment aggravations; there may be some problems of household organization; and, perhaps to save face, the parents may play communication games (such as "Everything is just fine").

Luckily, you can help the parents to solve many of the above problems at the same time, precisely because they are interrelated and because you can work on them in small steps. In dealing with such problems, help the parents to pinpoint the problems, indicate that it is important to work on them, and stress that they can be solved in small steps. As noted, Chapter 10 presents a number of methods that can be used at this point for helping parents to face and work toward solving special problems.

Finally, in evaluating their work, help the parents to score their copy of the APG so they can pinpoint their own strengths and needs, and can keep track of progress.

Backup Reinforcement

If parents are using the option that involves earning credits in exchange for certain positive reinforcers, the delivery of any reinforcers earned this week is discussed (for instance, baby-sitting time earned for the weekend). In addition, the parents can specify their choice of backup reinforcers for the coming week so that you can begin to make any necessary arrangements.

When the business of the home visit is completed, you can again engage in small talk. Before leaving, remind the parents to bring the Weekly Contract, all logs or notes that they have written, their APG, and their copy of *Educating Children* to the next meeting. Finally, if a videotape recording has been made, ask the parents for permission to show a portion of it during the next meeting. If they are reluctant at this time, empathize with them and discuss their reluctance, but do not try to force them to allow the tape to be shown. As time goes by in the Program, the parents are likely to ask that their tapes be shown.

VII. INSTRUCTING IN A SCHOOL SETTING: AN OPTION

In the home visit for this week, the parents will have received instruction and practice on objectivity (Item 12), instituting productive exchanges (Item 17), and general teaching methods (Item 18), along with other items on the APG. As noted in Chapter 4, it is important that parents receive instruction and practice in the home, since in most cases that is where they will be using their skills. However, the parents may also be given instruction and practice on the same items in a school setting, either as a temporary substitute for work in the home or as a supplement.

There are several good reasons for working with parents in a school setting. First, they may be able to use that experience in the future, for example, in working cooperatively with teachers or in volunteering their services as classroom aides. Second, to the extent that parents work with other children, their skills may become even more durable, they will have encountered additional and perhaps novel problems to solve, and with a larger background of experience they may be better able to help other parents.

The method for working with parents in a classroom setting is described in detail in *Reaching the Autistic Child* (Kozloff, 1973). The main features are as follows.

1. After reading introductory materials (for example, Chapters 1 and 2 in *Educating Children*), the parent observes a teacher working with the child in school, for example, from behind a one-way mirror. While the parent is observing, a second person (consultant, another teacher or aide, another parent) helps the parent to pinpoint important events and processes, such as signals, behaviors, consequences, and various types of exchanges.

2. After several coached observation sessions, the parent records his or her observations, either with pencil and paper or onto a dictating machine or tape recorder. The coach either makes the same kind of recording or videotapes the teaching session. After the session, the parent and the coach compare notes, or better, watch the videotape and compare the parent's recording with the videotape recording. The coach helps the parent to pinpoint events and processes and describe them in terms of observable movements. It is also important that the coach help the parent to use basic principles of learning to explain why certain teaching methods might be used and to predict behavior change. This is also a good opportunity to teach the parent to name and understand certain teaching methods, such as shaping, prompting and fading, pairing secondary reinforcers (e.g., praise) with primary reinforcers, and continuous versus intermittent reinforcement.

3. When the parent can satisfactorily pinpoint, describe, and explain what is going on in teaching sessions, he or she and the coach plan and write a simple teaching program for the parent to institute in the classroom. The teaching program plan can be substantially the same as the plan written on the parent's Weekly Contract regarding the instituting of productive exchanges in the home. Thus, the parent is primarily learning to institute the same productive exchanges, and to replace the same counterproductive exchanges, in a classroom setting. If necessary (e.g., the parent is "nervous" about going into the classroom), the parent and coach can first role-play the methods written on the plan.

4. The parent then goes into the classroom. Here, the parent might work one-to-one with a child (in which case the parent will be using many methods) or the parent might work as an aide along with a teacher, with a number of children (in which case, the parent might be learning to use only a few methods, e.g., to ignore problem behaviors and to reinforce appropriate behaviors that have already been pinpointed).

The parent might be coached directly or immediately either by the teacher in the classroom or by another person observing behind the one-way mirror (e.g., via a wireless hearing aide or "bug-in-the-ear"). In coaching the parent:

a. Emphasize "positive" rather than "negative" aspects of the parent's performance (e.g., "Good! That was good the way you reinforced her immediately and with enthusiastic praise. Keep it up.").

b. Set the occasion for the parent to emit an appropriate teaching response, rather than waiting for the parent to make error after error (e.g., "Okay, now, the next time she stands up, look over at another child, and quickly reinforce that child for sitting").

c. Help the parent if he or she runs into trouble and seems unable to correct it (for example, have the parent "backup" and work on a simpler target behavior or have the parent, in a group situation, use fewer teaching methods; provide "step-by-step" instructions; or, as a last resort, have the coach enter the classroom and serve as a model for a short time).

d. Gradually fade out the coaching as the parent acquires expertise.

In sum, it is important that the parent's initial teaching experiences be successful and gratifying.

5. The above methods can be used for several days in a row, or even longer, so that the parent obtains intensive practice and expertise in a relatively short time. It is likely, in other words, that if the instructional sessions are spread out over a long period of time (e.g., once a week), the parent might make a number of "errors" in the home between sessions, resulting in a partial reversal of progress by the time of the next session.

6. As the parent acquires some of the basic methods for instituting and managing productive exchanges, as well as basic teaching methods, the parent can gradually be given instruction and practice on using special skills for teaching harder behaviors and for managing a class. In other words, in-school instruction can be continued throughout the Program or can be re-introduced periodically as the parents begin to work on more complex target behaviors in their home educational programs.

7. Finally, videotape can be used during in-school instruction the same way as in home visits.

VIII. PLANNING THE ACTIVITIES FOR THE THIRD WEEK

As soon as possible, use notes written during the last meeting, home visit, and/or in-school instruction to update the APG for the families you are working with, indicating progress and problems by underlining illustrative words or phrases, or by making notes in the spaces by each item. In addition, you can write plans for handling problems. For instance, those parents who rarely talked during the last meeting might be given extra occasions to respond and extra reinforcement for doing so at the next meeting. Or, those who made many complaining or otherwise unconstructive statements at the last meeting, might be reminded of the rules for productive participation before the meeting starts, and are given extra occasions and coaching to make optimistic, prescriptive statements. On the other hand, use Chapter 10, as well as other sources, to plan special programs to handle personal, marital, and other problems discussed during the home visit.

You might use the notes written during the home visit to suggest possible changes in the parents' plan for instituting productive exchanges. In addition, you can write your best guesses as to the first target behaviors of the children to work on when teaching programs for strengthening appropriate behaviors are planned, which will be in a few weeks.

Finally, plan the third unit of work, deciding who will make which presentations, give various demonstrations, show videotapes, and be on the lookout for certain behaviors of the parents which are to be systematically changed. Prepare all materials, such as Weekly Contract forms, Credits-Earned sheets, and videotapes from the last home visit that are to be shown.

7 UNIT THREE: REWARDS

I. GOALS FOR THE THIRD UNIT OR WEEK

So far, the parents have learned some principles and methods of behavior change, and have instituted productive exchanges in the home. As a result their children may have changed in a beneficial direction and the parents may have become more confident of their abilities and perhaps more optimistic about the future. The major goals for this unit, then, are to:

1. Help parents acquire a basic knowledge of rewards, for use in both their program to institute productive exchanges and later teaching programs.
2. Help parents review, evaluate, and update or revise their program for instituting productive exchanges.
3. Continue to strengthen components of other items on the Assessment and Programming Guide (APG) in Appendix 1.

Note that there is no problem if you were unable to complete in one week all of the activities suggested in Chapter 6. For example, if you were unable to discuss career experiences or "How to be Successful at Instituting Productive Exchanges," you can discuss such topics during the main business portion of this meeting.

APG Items to Work On

Although many items were addressed during the past week, in most cases you only focused on a few of the easiest components. Here is a list of the items and the components to work on now:

Item 11. Productive participation: Continue working on attendance, doing assignments, and group participation. Institute special plans to strengthen productive participation, if necessary. (See Chapter 10, Section I.)

Item 12. Objectivity: Continue working on pinpointing, describing, and analyzing behaviors, exchanges, and aspects of family career; parents continue writing logs or taking notes on daily events. Work on pinpointing small, fleeting, or subtle movements; teach parents to use their logs or notes to evaluate progress and pinpoint problems.

Item 13. Confidence in general principles of learning and long-term perspective: Continue to encourage parents to believe that they are only responsible for their own behavior, that behavior change will take care of itself if the conditions are appropriate for their child, that they do not have to be a certain "kind" of person. Continue to strengthen their use of "key statements," such as "Rome wasn't built in a day."

Item 14. Planning an Educational Program: Teach the parents to use some of the terms and ideas relevant to planning and conducting a comprehensive educational program.

Item 15. Agreeing to try certain behavioral methods: Continue to strengthen the parents' agreeing to try certain behavioral methods, not by appealing to authority, but by teaching them to analyze behaviors, come to their own conclusions about which methods might be used, and be responsible for changing their minds and their methods, if their initial efforts do not seem to work.

Item 16. Planning rather than reacting: Continue to strengthen a pattern of planning rather than reacting. Plan and start to institute a special program on relaxation if tension and anxiety interfere with parents' efforts. (see Chapter 10, Section II.)

Item 17. Instituting productive exchanges: Continue to strengthen the parents' efforts and skills at instituting productive exchanges (though coaching, videotape feedback, praise, contract-credit system); use direct observations, videotape, and parents' logs or notes to evaluate program to institute productive exchanges; continue with, update, or revise plans regarding specific exchanges; if possible, add new exchanges to work on.

Item 18. General teaching methods: Continue to strengthen parents' changing the physical environment and their proper use of signals, prompts, and rewards. In addition, teach them some of the basics of planning a teaching program (pinpointing a target behavior and setting goals); setting up teaching sessions; shaping; signals (especially using Grandma's Law); prompting (describing different types and using them as needed); rewards (as described in Chapter 3 of *Educating Children*); replacing problem behaviors; and evaluating and, if necessary, revising their plans.

Item 19. Cooperation of spouses or partners: Continue to help parents work toward agreement, work together at instituting productive exchanges, support and reinforce one another, and share household tasks. In addition, if relevant, help parents to work together at solving personal problems. (See Chapter 10, Section II.)

Item 20. Organized home life: Continue to emphasize the types of organization that will increase the chances of success. If problems of organization were evident during the home visit, help parents to institute a plan to increase organization.

Item 21. Pinpointing and solving personal problems: Continue to help parents to anticipate, describe, and analyze personal problems. If parents have described personal problems, begin to plan and conduct a program to solve them. (See Chapter 10.)

Item 22. Honesty: Continue to stress the importance of honesty; reinforce parents for honesty and accuracy in describing events in the home and for writing logs and/or notes. If necessary, deal openly (through privately) with possible lack of honesty.

Item 23. Scheduled breaks: Continue to stress the importance of scheduling and taking breaks; teach the methods for doing so in a way that maintains children's beneficial behavioral changes; teach parents to use their logs and notes to evaluate what is happening during breaks.

Item 24. Reinforcement for each other: Continue to teach parents how to schedule and deliver reinforcement for themselves and for each other. Emphasize the importance of communication, respect, regard, and affection, and coach parents to increase the frequency of such communications.

Item 25. Linkage with networks and organizations: Continue the use of a telephone network between the families. If successful thus far, begin to plan home visits or backup support services between the families.

Item 26. Generalization: Continue to stress the importance of including others in the home educational programs. Discuss their past week's efforts to include siblings and others (such as grandparents) and help parents to solve any problems they encountered. In addition, begin to plan on generalizing their efforts to settings outside the home, for example, grocery stores. (See Chapter 9.)

Item 27. Pinpointing and solving problems: Reinforce parents for using handouts, signs, and their Weekly Contract as reminders of what to do during the week. Help them to apply a general problem-solving sequence to any sort of problem (for example, in their educational program, marital relations, themselves, or relations with the siblings).

II. STARTING THE MEETING

Checking Performance

As was done during the first and second meetings, the parent and consultant who are serving as credit-checkers make the rounds to assess each participant's performance (as specified on the Weekly Contract) and write the number of credits earned on the Credits-Earned sheet. Again, participants are praised for their good work and, if possible, backup reinforcers (such as the return of a portion of a deposit) are delivered. Problems in meeting the terms of the contract can be briefly noted at this time, but discussed in more detail during the Individual Consultation.

Strengthening Productive Participation During the Meeting

Chapters 5 and 6 describe methods for strengthening productive participation during meetings. Naturally, continue to provide parents, individually and as a group, with occasions to talk, and systematically reinforce productive verbal behavior. During the last meeting, however, you (and parents) may have noted some problems regarding productive verbal behavior. For example, some parents may have:

1. Been timid, not taking their turn or speaking up.
2. Made complaining and self-pitying statements, rather than taking an active part in finding and using solutions to problems.
3. Engaged in comic relief (telling jokes, making a number of irrelevant side comments) a bit too much.
4. Failed to support or reinforce productive participation of other parents.

Such potential or actual problems should have been pinpointed and openly discussed with parents during the last Individual Consultation and home visit, and simple plans should have been written for replacing unproductive with productive verbal behaviors. Thus, at the start of this meeting, parents, perhaps in private, might be reminded of the behaviors they have contracted to try to change. In addition, both you and the parents take data on the verbal behaviors that have been targeted, for purposes of evaluation and discussion during the Individual Consultation.

Brief Review

After the performance check, review what has been accomplished during the past two weeks or units. For example:

> Okay. Where are we and how have we gotten here? First of all, you knew that your children had problems, and that many of their problems concerned their behaviors. What was wrong with their behaviors? Some of their behaviors were considered problem behaviors. They were behaviors that were harmful in some way, disruptive, painful to your children or to others. Basically, they were behaviors that happened too often or for too long, or should not have been happening at all. Will someone please give me some examples of problem behaviors? (Give parents a chance to briefly list some problem behaviors.) These, then, are behaviors to replace with appropriate behaviors.

Now, as to appropriate or constructive behaviors, there were many behaviors that your children did not do well enough or with enough skill, did not do often enough or for long enough, or did not do at the right time and place or in enough places. These, then, are behaviors to increase or to teach your children to do at certain times and places. May I please have some examples of constructive behaviors that your children need to learn to do more often, for a longer time, with more skill, or at the right times and places? (Give parents a chance to offer examples and write them on a blackboard.)

Notice that the appropriate behaviors you just listed are the ones that can replace the problem behaviors. How? Well, the answer is fairly straightforward. Everyone has to be doing something, and everyone wants, or at least goes after, gratification or rewards of some kind. So, if your children are engaging in some problem behavior for lack of anything else to do, you can teach them a better way of spending their time. Or, if your children are engaging in some problem behaviors because they get something out of it, some kind of reward, then you can teach them other, better, ways of getting the things or rewards that they want.

Okay, so you know that some behaviors need to change, and you know the directions or ways in which they need to be changed. How do you go about changing them? That is the second thing you have learned. You have learned some basic principles of behavior change. For example, you know that behaviors that are rewarded consistently, quickly, frequently, and with strong rewards, tend to increase. You know that behaviors that are no longer rewarded tend to decrease, especially if other behaviors, replacement behaviors, are being rewarded instead. You know that punishment can sometimes cause more problems than it is worth, but that if it seems as if it is the best choice, you still have to be rewarding replacement behaviors. And finally, you know that people often learn best in small steps, which means that you have to be on the lookout for, and reward, behaviors that are done even a little better, or for a little longer, than before.

That brings us to structured exchanges. Last week you learned that certain ways of interacting with your children, and even with yourselves, are productive. That is, some structured exchanges produce beneficial, healthy, or desirable behavior changes. Other exchanges, however, produce harmful and generally undesirable behavior changes. So, let's briefly review the different kinds of structured exchanges. (Encourage parents to list and describe the various productive and counterproductive exchanges and to indicate the kinds of behavior changes that are likely to occur in the short-run and in the long-run.)

Excellent job! You learn fast. This brings us to the program plans that you instituted last week. What did you do? You began to prepare the way for change. You pinpointed both productive exchanges and counterproductive exchanges. You increased your use of productive exchanges and you replaced some counterproductive exchanges with productive ones. And you did many things that will help you to be successful in conducting your program to institute productive exchanges, as well as the many teaching programs you will be conducting a few weeks from now. For example, you were learning to wait and plan, instead of react to problems; to reinforce yourselves and each other; to cooperate even more than before; to take scheduled breaks; to get help from others in this group; and to get others involved in your program. In addition, you learned, or at least saw that it is possible to believe, that you are not totally responsible for changing your child's behavior, but only responsible for your own behavior—for helping to discover the conditions of learning that are right for your child, and seeing that those conditions are in place—conditions such as productive exchanges!

Were you completely successful last week? Well, we know that you got a good start! You started to change your own behaviors and you started to produce change in your children's behaviors. If you had problems in successfully performing all the tasks on the Weekly Contract, and if the plan for instituting productive exchanges was not perfect, and if your children did not make remarkable improvement in one week—all of it was to be expected!! You see, as we said many times, the goal of our work together is not just to help your children to change their behaviors in a beneficial way, but our goal is also to help you to learn how to pinpoint and solve problems. So, if your own observations and notes showed you that there were some difficulties, that is the first step toward achieving your goal of learning how to solve problems. In other words, it is good to make some mistakes at first! That way, you learn how to prevent or correct them.

This leads us to the business of our work together for this week, which is: (1) to review, evaluate, update, or revise your programs for instituting productive exchanges; (2) to learn about rewards and how to use them, both now and in the future; and (3) to firm up your own skills at instituting productive exchanges and in doing all the things we have talked about which were on your Weekly Contract for last week, and which will help you to be successful at conducting and maintaining a good home program.

The above introduction and review should last about 15 minutes, with parents, as always, having the chance to ask questions and discuss what is said.

III. MAIN BUSINESS

During this portion of the meeting, you can address the items of business in the order in which they were listed above. Note that from this unit on, parents are helped to apply and generalize concepts, principles, and methods. Thus, when asking for examples and suggestions, encourage brainstorming and creativity, as described in the Introduction of Chapter 5.

Reviewing and Evaluating Parents' Programs to Institute Productive Exchanges

First, have parents take out their copy of their last Weekly Contract, all logs or notes written during the week, their copy of *Educating Children with Learning and Behavior Problems,* and fresh paper for taking notes. A good way to review the parents' efforts to institute productive exchanges is as follows:

1. Focus on the families' programs one at a time.

2. When a family is "on stage":

a. The parents describe their plan for instituting productive exchanges. In doing so, they may refer to the section on Teaching Program Plan on their Weekly Contract.

b. The parents then describe what they actually did when instituting productive exchanges. For instance, they might describe the changes they made in the physical environment, how they handled tantrums, gave their child occasions to perform simple tasks, reinforced their child many, many times for making spontaneous eye contact, cooperating, playing, or talking. In addition, the parents can describe any behavior changes in their child, both beneficial and undesirable.

c. If parents have given permission, portions of videotapes made during the last home visit can be shown, illustrating what the parents have just described. portion might be shown several times. The first time, the parents can narrate while the tape is running. At the same time, you and the other parents praise the parents for their efforts and skills, ask questions, and make constructive comments. It is important that the tapes show progress and praiseworthy behaviors of the parents and children, as well as behaviors that need improving. The emphasis, however, is on the praiseworthy. For example:

Mr. Wince: What did she do when you ignored her yelling?

Mrs. Lawrence: Well, she kept on hollering, louder and louder. I thought she was going to bust a gut, she was yelling so hard! But we just left the room.

Mrs. Wince: How could you stand all that noise?

Mrs. Lawrence: Who could stand it?! But Marty said that it would probably work, as long as we kept rewarding her whenever she was quiet. So we decided to try it and do just as our plan said. And Bill and I coached ourselves to relax and let her yell. When she finally stopped, we smiled at each other and started rewarding her for being quiet.

Mr. Wince: You did a great job! But I don't know if I could have done it.

Mr. Lawrence: Done what?

Mr. Wince: Stood all that yelling! Ignored it!

Mr. Lawrence: Well, what choice did we have? We either do something to replace her yelling now, or we listen to it on and off for the rest of our lives. Listen, if your Irving had been yelling for as many years as our Sally, you could do what we have been doing.

Mr. Wince: Yeah, I guess you're right. But I've still got to give you a lot of credit.

Consultant: That's right. You folks did a great job! I really liked the way you talked about replacing yelling, and the way you talked about the difference between the short run and the long run—doing something now, even though it may be hard, to replace a problem behavior in order to live a more peaceful life later.

Or,

Mrs. Daring: It looked like it was hard to reward her all of the time when she was not yelling and when she was speaking more softly.

Mrs. Lawrence: Yeah. You are right. Lots of times she would stop for a little while and we didn't notice. . . . .

Mrs. Daring: Don't get me wrong! I thought you did a terrific job. I was just thinking about myself, too. It's hard to be on your toes all the time.

Mrs. Lawrence: Well, we will all get better at it.

Consultant: Yes, you will! Slowly but surely, you will all fine-tune your skills until they are second nature. I think your comments (addressed to Mrs. Daring) were good ones. And you made them in a helpful way. You were praising the Lawrences at the same time that you were raising a general issue—the issue of being on the lookout for good behaviors to reward.

After the first showing, the same portions can be shown again, to allow everyone to more carefully observe and evaluate what was going on. This time, though, rerun portions of the tape several times, so that the signals, behaviors, and consequences in important exchanges can be pinpointed, described, and analyzed. Again, encourage parents who are "on stage" to describe what is happening in each exchange. For example,

(1) They can pinpoint signals, behaviors, and consequences:

> See, here we're not even looking at her while she is yelling. We are looking away. But look at her! She is watching us out of the corner of her eye.

(2) They can indicate the principles of learning that are operating and the type of exchange that is taking place:

> Here we are replacing the escape exchange with the riding-it-out exchange. We are ignoring the hollering and reinforcing her whenever she is quiet for a minute or so or whenever she talks softly.

(3) They can pinpoint those of their performances that are skillful and those that they feel need to be improved. For example:

> We got real good at ignoring the yelling, but we have to be more careful about rewarding her when she is quiet or speaking properly.

(4) They can pinpoint aspects of their plan that seem to be appropriate (and should be continued) and aspects of their plan that might not be right for their child (and which might need to be revised).

When necessary, the discussion leader can: **(1)** Reiterate or clarify what the parents are saying:

Mr. Lawrence: So, whenever she would stop yelling for a minute or so, we would reward her with praise and things like that.

Consultant:	What might she be doing when you rewarded her?
Mr. Lawrence:	Oh, watching TV, speaking more softly, walking around, sitting and looking at a book.
Consultant:	So, you were rewarding a number of other specific behaviors, target behaviors, to replace the yelling.

(2) Point out things that the parents might not have noticed or described (especially "small" or fleeting movements).

Consultant:	Oops, let's watch that one again (rewinds tape) . . . . What do you see?
Mrs. Lawrence:	Oh, damn! I was talking to her while she was flapping her hands. I just rewarded her. What a dope!
Consultant:	What do you mean, "dope?" You just spotted that boo-boo on your own. And you probably won't do it as often now. You are doing just fine. A bit better each week—that's what you are after.
Consultant:	(After watching another portion) Ah, that was great! Let's see that again. This time, watch what Sally is doing right before you give her the signal to close the door. . . . Did you see it?
Mr. Lawrence:	Nope, I didn't see anything special. Let's watch it again. . . . I see. She had her hands down at her side and was looking me right in the eye.
Consultant:	Right! So, you paid attention to her when her hands were down and she was making eye contact. You rewarded two important behaviors. Do you all see that? That is an important method. You give signals when your child is quiet, still, paying attention. Otherwise, your child is not likely to follow the signal and you are likely to reward your child for some problem behavior. Remember, it is more important to conduct a few exchanges just right than lots of them that have some shortcomings.

and **(3)** Pinpoint and enthusiastically reinforce the parents for their efforts, improvements since the baseline and over the past weeks, skillful performances, and successfully or almost successfully performing other tasks on the Weekly Contract. For example:

Consultant:	There! Did you see that? That was great the way you turned and walked away just at the instant when she started to get that yell out. Remember what you used to do when she looked like she was working up to a good yell?
Mrs. Lawrence:	Oh, boy! I would do just about anything to keep her from yelling.
Consultant:	The placation exchange?
Mrs. Lawrence:	Yup!
Consultant:	Well, you have sure come a long way in a short time. Great work!

Or,

Consultant: I like the way the two of you are cooperating in these exchanges. You are coaching and rewarding one another a lot. Good teamwork!

Note that other parents should be encouraged to comment and ask questions, just as you are doing.

In sum, when examining the videotapes, all participants should use, or be reminded to use, the proper terms and principles to describe and analyze what they are seeing; reinforce the parents who are on stage for their efforts, improvements, and skills; and, in as positive a manner as possible, should make helpful suggestions. For example:

> Try to use a little more ''oomph'' in your praise, okay? You want to light up her face!
>
> You might reward her in different ways from time to time. Praise, then a pat on the head, then a big hug. You know, mix it up!

d. After showing and analyzing the videotape for a family, the parents can summarize their program and their efforts for the week, pinpointing both progress and shortcomings and making suggestions of what to do during the coming week; for instance, portions of the plan to revise and portions to continue. If necessary, other parents, and then you, can also make suggestions.

In summarizing and evaluating their work, it might be helpful for parents to read or at least refer to logs or notes written during the week. For instance, they might point out that they had a hard time remembering to take scheduled breaks, and that perhaps they should post more signs.

If videotape equipment is not available, parents can still describe their programs as completely as possible and role-play illustrative exchanges.

e. During all of the above, you and the parents take notes on teaching methods that seem to be working, problems which can occur, and methods for correcting problems. In fact, important points can be written on a blackboard. For example, ''Switch the ways you reward your children''; ''When you ignore a behavior, you do not even see it.''

f. Regarding problems or shortcomings, you can demonstrate and role-play proper methods. For example, if parents give multiple signals, you might first demonstrate the difference between multiple signals and single signals. Then, you and the parent who used multiple signals can role-play multiple versus single signals, changing between the role of ''parent'' and ''child'' several times.

g. All indications of shortcomings and all suggestions for changes are made in a positive way. For example, it is unwise to say "Don't do that"; "I think that is the wrong way to present signals"; or, addressing the group, "What do you think of what you just saw?" Instead, comments and questions are framed in such a way as to give the parents themselves a chance to pinpoint and solve potential or actual problems or shortcomings, and constitute reinforcement for or recognition of improvement, effort, and skill. For example:

Consultant: Okay, let's focus on signals. What is happening here? (Shows a portion of tape.)

Parent: I asked him four times to close the door, didn't I?

Consultant: Sure looks like it. But that's okay. You pinpointed it by yourself. And that will help you to replace multiple signals with single signals. Besides, you have improved a lot already. Just think of the way you gave signals during the baseline. . . . Now, the next time you give him a signal and he does not cooperate, what do you do?

(4) After the families have made their presentations, you can further strengthen esprit de corps in the group by:

1. Again describing the common career experiences and interests of the families (especially if this was not done last week).
2. Stressing the important changes that the parents can make in their families and in the services available to children and families, by working together during and after the Program.
3. Pinpointing the areas in which the parents and children have so far made progress, enthusiastically praising them for hard work and success.

Rewards

In general, this portion of the meeting follows Chapter 3 of *Educating Children*, using brief presentations backed up by demonstrations, role-playing, portions of videotape, and discussions. When possible, the ideas from Chapter 3 are applied to the parents' programs to institute productive exchanges and to future teaching programs for various target behaviors, such as eye contact, cooperating, playing, chores and self-help routines, and speech. While reviewing Chapter 3, parents should have their copy of *Educating Children* handy, so that they can reread and ask questions concerning certain passages, and answer questions in the review sections. They are encouraged to take notes on ideas that arise in the meeting. Finally, important points can be written on a blackboard. When possible, transcripts from our Programs are presented below.

What is a Reward? First, make sure that the parents understand what is meant by "reward" and "positive reinforcer." The main idea to convey is that there may be a difference between the technical meaning and the everyday meaning of ''reward'' and ''reinforcer.''

Defining ''Reward''

We have often used the words ''reward'' and ''reinforcer.'' We have talked about ways that behaviors are rewarded or reinforced. But just what is meant by these words? Well, these words mean several things at once. First, rewards and reinforcers are events. They can usually be observed in some way. For instance, a good meal, a pat on the back, a smile, a pay check, or the opportunity to go bowling, are all events that happen.

Second, rewards and reinforcers are consequences of our behaviors. They are events that follow or come after some behavior. Notice that this does not mean that a smile always follows the behaviors that it should! We might smile at our child when our child is throwing a tantrum, or right after our child has hit himself in the face. The point is that a certain event in the environment has followed a certain behavior, no matter what the behavior is and no matter whether it is beneficial for the person that his behavior was followed by that consequence—that reward or reinforcer.

Third, the consequent events that we are calling rewards and positive reinforcers, usually amount to some sort of change in the world around us. Now sometimes the change is a big deal or is an obvious kind of change. And sometimes the change is subtle or hard to notice. For instance, if someone smiles at us after we say ''Hello,'' isn't that smile a change in their facial expression? And if we go bowling after we have done the dishes, isn't the event of going bowling a change in what we were doing? And if we swing an axe in such a way that the swing of the axe is followed by the log splitting in half—isn't that splitting of the log a change in the log? Of course, the answer is ''yes.'' All of those events that followed—were consequences of—our behaviors were changes in the world—the environment—around us.

And finally, those changes in our environment that are the consequences of our behaviors, often represent the effects of our behaviors on the world. In other words, we have usually acted or behaved in such a way as to produce those changes. Of course, sometimes the environment seems to accidentally change. I might not have planned or expected that a certain behavior of mine was going to be followed by a certain change in my world. But the change—the event—happened anyway. For instance, I might be looking for a job and might happen to call a friend of mine to say hello. Well, my friend might tell me that she knows of someone who is looking for a guy like me for a certain job. Well, hearing that there is a job available to me, would be a change in my world, wouldn't it? And, you know as well as I do that if I ever need a job again, I am going to call that friend of mine, or at least I am going to call on my other friends, call on other people, or at least use the phone to find a job. Why? Because even though my first phone-call behavior accidentally resulted in a change that was a reward for me, it was rewarding nevertheless. And that rewarding change will strengthen the behavior (using the phone) that led to the rewarding change. (You might want to elaborate on the above and discuss superstitious behavior.)

Sometimes the relationship between behaviors and consequences is not accidental or does not seem accidental. For example, our economic system is set up so that working behavior is somehow followed by pay checks—though not necessarily large enough pay checks. The same thing goes for everyday life with people. When we greet people, when we compliment them, when we help them out, or when we invite them to our homes—all of these behaviors of ours are usually followed by some change in their behaviors. They smile at us, say nice things to us, or invite us back to their homes.

In other words, our behaviors and the consequences of our behaviors in social life are often arranged in structured exchanges. Certain behaviors are followed by certain consequences. Some of the consequences are rewards. Others are punishers.

So, rewards and reinforcers are events; they are consequent events—consequences of our behaviors. They amount to changes in our environment—either in the physical environment—like logs that split—or in the social environment, in the behavior of other people—our bosses, our neighbors, the clerk at the drug store, and the passerby. And in many cases, rewards or reinforcers represent the effects of our behaviors or actions. Sometimes the changes seem to accidentally follow our behaviors. But most of the time, it seems that the world is structured so that certain behaviors are followed by certain kinds of consequences. If you swing the axe a certain way, the logs are bound to split. That is the way logs are made. In social life, however, it is a different story. People don't have to smile when you tell them that they look nice. They smile out of convention, custom, or etiquette. Sometimes, certain behaviors receive certain kinds of consequences because of the law. Well, even though in social life the arrangements between certain behaviors and certain consequences don't have to be that way, those arrangements or structured exchanges are that way consistently enough that we can count on them. We assume that if we work we will get paid; if we are nice to certain people, they will be nice in return.

Obvious Versus Subtle Rewards

Now, let's turn to another idea. Some consequences most people consider to be rewards—like money, smiles, pats on the back, bowling, and other activities. These events are obvious kinds of changes in our lives; everybody knows about them and can see them. When talking about money, smiles, compliments, and certain activities, people use words like "want," "need," "desire," "like," "turns me on," "pleasure," and "enjoy." In other words, people say that they expect or want certain events to be consequences of their behaviors. They want their behaviors to be followed by or to produce certain consequences. They say that they want to go bowling, that they enjoy dressing up and being complimented, that they look forward to going on vacation, or that they need the next pay check. Well, these events are the kinds of events that are usually called "rewards."

Now, what does Chapter 3 say that rewards are? (Give parents a chance to answer.) Yes, rewards are consequent events that increase the behaviors that they follow. The behaviors happen more often or for a longer time, are done with more skill or more effort. Okay, do the events that people usually call rewards, and say that they want, need, enjoy, or hope to get—do those events generally increase the behaviors that they follow? Do they increase the behaviors that result in our getting those things? (Give parents the chance to respond.) Sure! For example, if we want to go to some nice place for a vacation, and if we have to take on an extra job for awhile to earn the money for that vacation, we are likely to do more extra work in the future in order to go on other vacations.

But the rewarding or reinforcing events that increase our behaviors are not always so obvious; people don't necessarily use words like "want," "enjoy," or "need" when talking about some events. There are many events that people think have nothing to do with increasing our behaviors, even though they are actually rewards or positive reinforcers. In fact, some of the events I will tell you about are the kinds of events that people might call "punishers," but they are actually rewards, because they increase behaviors.

For example, events, changes, or consequences like looking at another person, like taking away a puzzle piece from a child when the child is fiddling around with it, like turning away from a child when he is doing some strange behavior, like fighting with a person, or even spanking a child—all of these can increase the behaviors they follow!

Strange, huh? Who would think that looking at a child could be a reward for that child? Who would think that spanking a child could be a reward? Now, I do not mean that the child says that he wants, needs, likes, enjoys, or desires a spanking. And I don't mean that the child, or anyone, really craves, desires, or gets great pleasure out of being looked at! The point is simply that under some conditions, these events, strange as it seems, and unobvious as it usually is, will increase the behaviors they follow. Sometimes, if a child is making a mess in the kitchen and you look at him, and he sees you looking at him, looking at him is a change in your behavior that will increase the chances of the child's making messes. And sometimes spanking a child when the child is throwing a tantrum will increase the chances that the child will throw tantrums in the future.

What is the message of all this? The message is that just because most people do not think of looking at a child as being a reward, this does not mean that it is not a reward! It may be. And just because people usually think that a spanking is punishment, a spanking may nevertheless do what a reward is supposed to do—namely, increase the behaviors it follows. So, it's not the word that is important, and it's not what people think an event ought to be that is important. What is important is what the event does to the behavior!! If the behavior increases after it has been followed a bunch of times by a certain event, that event is a reward, pure and simple. And if a certain behavior is followed a number of times by a certain event, and the behavior decreases, that event is probably just not a reward for that person at that time, even if it is the kind of event that people often think of as a reward.

How Unobvious Events can be Rewards

But how could looking at a child be a reward? How could taking a puzzle piece away from a child or fighting with a child be a reward? And how in Heaven's name could a spanking actually reward the behavior that resulted in the spanking? (Give parents a chance to answer.) Well, let's look carefully at these events. Sure, a spank usually produces pain. But what else is the child getting? What else is changing when someone spanks him? And when you take a puzzle piece away from the child, sure, the child is losing the piece, but what else is happening in that whole event? (Give parents a chance to answer.)

In all of these events, the child is getting contact with or attention from another person. And that attention may be a reward for him. In fact, he may do all sorts of strange things with the puzzle piece—spinning or flipping it over and over—because it results in your reaching out to him, touching him, and tugging at his hand. As far as you are concerned, you simply took away a puzzle piece. In fact, maybe you thought that it was punishment! But the child was turned on to the attention or contact with you. Taking away the puzzle piece may have been a reward. Now, can you tell me how a slap could actually be a reward for the behavior that resulted in the slap? (Give parents a chance to answer that the slap constitutes attention. And, in a situation in which few behaviors produce attention, even a slap may be worth the pain.)

At this point, you can turn to the different rewards or positive reinforcers.

Kinds of Rewards. First, ask the parents to list the major categories of rewards: primary and learned (social, general, and activity). Write each category on the blackboard and then ask parents to give examples of specific events that are rewards for them and for their children in each category (for instance, from Table 3-1 of *Educating Children*, which they were to fill out). Help the parents to be as specific as possible. For instance, if a parent says that food is a reward for his child, ask him which foods, since it is not likely that all foods are rewards for his child. Similarly, if a parent says that praise is a reward for herself or her child, ask her to specify statements that are the most "rewarding."

Moreover, since you have already shown parents that even subtle and fleeting contact with another person (such as eye contact) can be a reward—a social reward—have them give examples of subtle forms of attention in their lives that may be rewards for them and their children. For example, a subtle, though powerful, social reward for the wife or husband may be a gentle touch on the shoulder, the word "Honey," a wink, or statements that communicate regard for the other's hard work. And similar social rewards (forms of attention or social contact) for their children might be eye contact, holding the child's hand, yelling at the child, telling the child to stop an activity, or a kiss, but not necessarily words like "Good boy."

To make sure that the parents are listing events that actually satisfy the earlier functional definition of reward or positive reinforcer, ask them to explain why they have listed the events that they have. The criteria for events being categorized as rewards include the following:

1. The events follow, are consequences of, behaviors.
2. The person makes efforts to acquire such events.
3. The person repeats the behaviors that have been followed by, or have enabled the person to get, those events.
4. The presentation of such events may make the person feel good, as indicated by statements to that effect, by smiles, giggles, and other culturally-accepted expressions or communications of pleasure.

However, make sure to remind parents that item 3 above is the only relatively certain criterion than an event is a reward. The others are only tentative. Number three is the test. Also point out that in some conditions an event that usually results in an increase in a behavior does not produce an increase in that behavior, namely, when the person has been satiated, has been presented with (or consumed) that event too often or in too great an amount.

How Rewards are Learned. Next, you can point out the difference between primary and learned rewards. For example:

> As you know, some events are generally always rewards for most people, and other events have to become rewards. Well, events that are generally always rewards for most people most of the time are called "primary" rewards. Events that are not always rewards for us are called "learned rewards." And, as you know, there are several types—social rewards (kinds of contact with others); general rewards (some kind of medium of exchange that we use to buy other rewards); and activity rewards (simply activities that we are likely to do if we have the choice). And, behind all of the rewarding events produced by our behaviors is control. That is, it may be rewarding simply to be able to produce changes in our physical and social world in a predictable way.
>
> Now, why is it that some events have always been rewards for our behavior? What is it about primary rewards that makes them so special? Basically, they are events that affect our bodies in an important way. After all, we have bodies that are programmed to be sensitive to certain events. Some events and things are needed if we are to stay alive, like food and water. Others can injure us, like strong light in our eyes, extreme heat or cold. Our bodies are simply programmed to be affected by such events and things. And without much if any learning or experience, those events and things can change our behaviors. Almost any behavior that brings food to a hungry person will be rewarded by the food, and will increase. And almost any behavior that results in our becoming warm—such as putting on a coat—when we are cold, will be rewarded by the consequent event of becoming warm, and we will do that behavior more often when we are cold.
>
> Notice that these primary rewards are strong under certain conditions and weak in others. When are primary rewards strong? When are they most likely to increase the behaviors that follow them? (At this point, you can discuss satiation.)

Having discussed primary rewards, you can begin discussing learned rewards.

> As you know from Chapter 3, primary rewards are important. You may need to use them to increase certain of your children's behaviors at the beginning of their educational programs. But primary rewards have some shortcomings. What are they? (Give parents the chance to answer and discuss the issues of satiation; that most behaviors in social life are maintained by various learned rewards; and that "normality" means both that a behavior is performed like "most people" perform it and that the behavior is maintained by the kinds of rewards that maintain most people's behaviors.)

> So, even though food may be an important kind of reward (at least for some children at the start of their educational program), we need to know how to teach children to be rewarded by the other, more common, kinds of rewards. So. here is the question: how do things like praise, hugs, or physical contact, general rewards like tokens and money, and various activities, become rewards? How do these become events that turn us on and that will increase our behaviors?

As usual, give parents the opportunity to answer the above questions. The main points to stress are that events and activities become rewards because: (1) they are consistently paired or associated with events that are already rewards (for instance, praise, smiles, and eye contact are given to an infant at the same time the infant is being fed; we might experience an enjoyable activity in the presence of a particular person, or we might learn to perform a chore while being praised or given food); (2) they may repeatedly be followed by events that are already rewarding (for example, praising a child and then giving the child food; having the child perform a chore and following the chore with an activity that is already a reward for the child—which may make the chore more rewarding in itself). Make sure to discuss Grandma's Law as a way of both using rewarding activities to strengthen weak behaviors and to create new rewarding activities.

Review Questions on the above. At this point you can have the parents read and give answers to the review questions on pages 50 to 51 in Chapter 3 of *Educating Children*. While the parents are answering the questions, encourage them both to give many examples to illustrate the main points and apply the points to their present or future home programs (for example, Question 2 on withholding rewards, Question 3 on satiation, Question 10 on activity rewards, and Questions 11 and 12 on Grandma's Law).

Reward Schedules. The next topic is reward schedules—the kinds of schedules, the effects of certain schedules on behavior, and the kinds of rewards and reward schedules to use at different times in a teaching program. You might set the occasion for this topic with statements like the following.

> We have talked about kinds of rewards and about how events that were not rewards become rewards. Now, it may have sounded like our behaviors are being rewarded every time or all of the time. But that is not so. For instance, I am not praised or given money after every class that I teach. The logs that I am chopping don't split with every swing of the axe. I don't get a strike every time I roll a bowling ball. People don't jump up and down and tell me what a great guy I am every time I help them out. And I don't win every pot in a poker game. Yet, I continue to engage in those behaviors.
>
> Not only is it unnecessary for me to be rewarded for every behavior I perform, but it would be unusual if I did get rewarded every time! Sure, it would be nice if everyone praised and did nice things for others more often. But if we praised each other for

everything we did, it would be a strange world. After a few days, all we would be doing is praising each other for praising each other. "Thank you for thanking me." "You're welcome." "And thank you for thanking me for thanking you. . . ."

Nope, we sure don't get rewarded for every behavior we perform. Now, what would happen if you did reward your child with a bite of food every time that your child made a sound, especially if you used the same reward? (Encourage parents to answer that the child would become satiated, and the behavior of making sounds would quickly decrease.) And even if your child would never become satiated, would it even be possible to reward him every time he made a sound? ("Of course not. Many sounds would not be heard. In addition, as the behavior increased in frequency because of past rewards, it would become even harder to reward every sound.") Finally, even if your child would never become satiated, and even if you could reward every behavior every time, would your child be "normal?" ("No, because 'normal' means both that the behavior is performed 'like most people perform it' and is kept going or maintained with the same kinds of events—rewards—and the same reward schedules that keep most people's behavior going.")

So, in order to run effective teaching programs, and in order to help our children to become more normal, we have to do two things. First, we have to teach them to be rewarded by more common rewards. Food may be needed at first. But after a while, it is not normal or necessary to use it. And second, we have to teach them to keep on learning and doing what they have learned, even though they are not rewarded every time. How often a reward is given for a certain behavior is called a reward schedule. Let's look at the different kinds of reward schedules and how and when to use them.

In discussing reward schedules, the main points to convey are the following:

1. A behavior can be rewarded every time (continuous schedule) or once in a while (intermittent schedule).
2. The reward can be given either because behavior was done a certain number of times (number or "ratio" schedule) or because a certain amount of time went by since the last reward (interval schedule).
3. The number of times the behavior is performed, or the amount of time that goes by since the last reward, can either be the same all the time (fixed) or it can change after each reward (changing or "variable" schedule).
4. Continuous schedules usually increase behaviors quickly, but result in satiation quickly.
5. Intermittent schedules usually make behaviors rather durable. That is, the person continues to perform the behavior many times, even when rewards are no longer given. Thus, if problem behaviors have been rewarded on an intermittent schedule, merely ignoring them will not result in their decreasing quickly.
6. Fixed schedules usually result in a pause or a decrease in the rate of behavior after it has been rewarded. The longer the interval in a fixed interval schedule, or the higher the number of responses required in a fixed number

schedule, the longer the pause. Changing (variable) schedules produce a more even rate of responding. Thus, changing schedules may be better to use.

At this time, you and the parents can role-play a teaching session (or show a videotape) illustrating the different schedules. Good target behaviors to use as illustrations include stacking blocks, working puzzles, reading words, solving simple arithmetic problems, and making eye contact, because these behaviors can be emitted so quickly.

At the start of a child's educational program, and at the start of some teaching programs, the parents may have to use strong rewards (like food) and a continuous schedule to quickly increase target behaviors. As target behaviors increase and begin to level off (as shown on page 60 of Chapter 3 in *Educating Children*), the parents can and should slowly move to more usual rewards (such as praise and activities), and to leaner schedules.

To illustrate the importance of a slow transition to learned rewards and intermittent schedules, you and a parent can again role-play a teaching session (or, again, show a videotape). For example, for a minute or so, you might reward the parent (playing the role of child) with small pieces of candy on a continuous schedule, and then suddenly change to a fixed number schedule, in which the target behavior is rewarded one out of ten times. Then, you might return to a continuous schedule of food rewards for a minute or so, quickly stop using food, and use praise alone.

After each of the abrupt transitions, you might ask the role-playing parent and the other parents how the child might feel when such abrupt changes are made (frustrated? bewildered?). You can make the point that abrupt changes are likely to result in a marked decrease in the target behavior and an increase in noncompliance, inattention, and problem behaviors.

Next, to demonstrate and practice smoother transitions, the parents themselves can role-play the same teaching session, only this time you can coach them to:

1. Gradually stretch the schedule of reinforcement from every response to three out of four, two out of three, one out of two, etc.
2. Slowly reduce the use of food and increase the use of social rewards, such as praise and physical contact.
3. Present social rewards just before the primary rewards are given.

Of course, such transitions might take a number of days in home programs. In addition, demonstrate how behaviors such as eye contact or performing chores can be rewarded in more natural ways, such as letting the child engage in an enjoyable activity after a less enjoyable activity has been performed (that is, Grandma's Law).

After the role-playing exercises on reward schedules, the parents can review answers to questions on pages 65 to 67 in Chapter 3 of *Educating Children*. When the review is finished, take a break.

Finding and Using Rewards. At this point, teach parents to find and use rewards in a systematic, planned way in their programs to institute productive exchanges.

First, have the parents turn to pages 68 and 69 in their book. The parents were to have filled out the Reward List on page 69 for this week. Go from family to family, and have the parents again list some of the rewards in each category. Teach them to carefully specify exactly what the rewarding consequence is. It is particularly important to have them generate a long list of possible activity rewards, adding the suggestions of other parents to their list.

Second, you can show portions of videotapes, either from past Programs or from this Program (for example, baseline tapes or tapes made during the first or second week), to give examples of possible activity rewards that the parents can use, as in Grandma's Law (for example, watching TV, roughhousing, going outside, being pushed on a swing, or taking a bath). Try to present situations in which the parents on the tapes are using Grandma's Law, that is, having the child to do a little of a "good" behavior (such as a short math lesson or cooperating with a simple request) before the child does a behavior that the child usually enjoys). Encourage the parents to give additional examples of how they might use Grandma's Law in their programs. You and the parents can role-play the use of Grandma's Law.

Third, focus on the proper use of rewards. Have the parents turn to pages 70 and 71 in Chapter 3 of *Educating Children* and review the three questions on those pages. Encourage them to give examples of: (1) the ways they might have accidentally rewarded problem behaviors (the escape, placation, and multiple signals exchanges); (2) weak behaviors that have not been rewarded often (such as eye contact, cooperating, and playing). Make sure the parents give examples of rewards they can and will use to strengthen weak behaviors; and (3) behaviors that the child has been performing rather well, but which have not been rewarded often, perhaps because the parents have not noticed those behaviors or have expected them of the child. Have the parents discuss ways to maintain such behaviors.

Fourth, discuss ways to find events that are rewarding to their children. For example: (1) carefully observing the events that "turn on" or "light up" their children, (2) using a reward menu, and (3) carefully observing which events or activities the child "goes after," tries to get, indicates that he "wants," and which the child does more often than other activities.

Summarizing the Main Points and Giving an Extended Example. A good way to conclude this portion of the main business is to restate and illustrate the major points (with videotapes or role-playing). The use of videotape or role-playing to demonstrate the proper use of rewards and reward schedules can also teach the parents how to teach their children certain behaviors for which the children are ready, such as spontaneous eye contact, cooperation with simple spoken requests, large or small motor activities, speech, or self-help skills.

Here are the main points (teaching methods) to illustrate at this time. They are some components of APG Item 18. Note that if you will be demonstrating methods for teaching a target behavior in one of the skill areas covered in *Educating Children*, refer to the relevant chapter.

1. Before conducting a teaching program, parents carefully select target behavior(s) on the basis of the child's evaluation, and the child should have already learned the necessary "basic behaviors." The target behavior(s) are clearly defined and goals established for the teaching program; for example, how much to increase (or decrease) the behavior(s), or how much skill the child is to acquire over a certain number of weeks.

2. If used, teaching sessions are short (at first), and held just before a favorite activity and in a place that is relatively free of disruptions. If used, food rewards and materials are kept handy. Parents can sit facing their child unless it is unnecessary or would be distracting. Note that we are not recommending that parents actually conduct teaching sessions at this early time.

3. The target behavior is broken down into small steps. The parents start working on (signaling, prompting, and rewarding) the easiest step with which the child needs help. That is, the target behavior is shaped.

4. If signals are to be used, they are given only when the child is paying attention; they are simple and clear; single signals, rather than multiple signals, are used.

5. If necessary, the parents prompt the child to correctly perform the movements on the step being worked on. The parents try the minimal prompt needed. Prompts are slowly faded out as the child begins to perform the behavior more on his own.

6. As much as possible, rewards to be used in the teaching program are saved during the rest of the day.

7. At the start of their children's education, and at the start of some teaching programs later, the parents may have to use strong rewards and a high rate of reinforcement—continuous schedules.

8. Nevertheless, the parents must shift from primary rewards to more common or natural rewards (social, general, and activity rewards) and from continuous to more intermittent schedules, particularly changing number ("variable ratio") schedules. But they must make the transition to leaner schedules slowly, and when beginning to use more common (and perhaps weaker) rewards, they use the strong and weak rewards together, gradually fading out the stronger rewards.

9. Behaviors are rewarded immediately, especially weak target behaviors and behaviors that are likely to be followed quickly by a different behavior. Thus, you can role-play the difference between immediate rewarding and delayed rewarding, showing that when rewards are given too slowly, the child is likely to initiate a different behavior, perhaps a problem behavior, which then may be the one that is rewarded and strengthened. Consequently, parents should be on the lookout for target behaviors, should be prepared to reward them, and should have tangible rewards handy.

10. Relatively weak rewards (or events that may not be rewards yet, such as praise) are paired with events that are already rewards (such as food).

11. Parents bridge the time gap between the behavior just performed by the child and the strong reward they are going to use to reward that behavior. For example, if the parents are going to reward spontaneous eye contact with food, but the child makes eye contact with them from across the room, the parents bridge the gap between the eye contact and the food reward by praising the child while they run across the room with the food.

In addition to stating the above points, illustrate them with a videotape or at least an extended demonstration of a teaching program to strengthen a behavior likely to be one of the first worked on by the parents—such as spontaneous eye contact, cooperation, small motor activities, or self-help tasks. As in the past uses of videotape, run some portions several times until all parents can pinpoint and describe the different parts of the exchanges and the teaching methods being used. It is a good idea for the tape(s) to show the teaching programs at different points in time, such as: (1) the beginning (when strong rewards, a continuous schedule, and perhaps much prompting are used); (2) several days or weeks later, when the target behavior has accelerated (and the transition is being made to more usual rewards and schedules, and prompts are being faded out); and (3) still later, when the behavior is being maintained and generalized to other settings (with social and activity rewards—Grandma's Law—and more intermittent schedules being used, and with several target behaviors being chained together). For example, the child might make eye contact and then be given a puzzle piece to put in, or make eye contact and be allowed to enter the kitchen, or cooperate with a request and be allowed to go outside. Naturally, the parents are encouraged to ask questions and generalize to their own programs while the tapes are being shown. It might be useful to have parents role-play some same basic teaching methods.

Note, again, that the above basic teaching methods are listed under APG Item 18. Parents' skills regarding the methods are assessed with and scored on the APG during the coming weeks.

Again, we are not saying that parents begin to conduct teaching programs for target behaviors. The idea is to show them how to use signals, prompts, rewards, and reward schedules to strengthen some of the appropriate behaviors that they are already strengthening in their programs to institute productive exchanges—behaviors that they are likely to begin to start working on in a more systematic way in a few weeks. That is, a major goal is still to strengthen the parents' ability to discriminate their children's appropriate and inappropriate behavior, productive and counterproductive exchanges, and their proper and improper use of general teaching methods, before they conduct teaching sessions.

"What About Punishment?" (1) Some children engage in behaviors that are so disruptive, durable, or harmful to themselves or others that the suggested methods (namely, ignoring or perhaps timing out problem behaviors and rewarding replacement behaviors) may be ineffective and, indeed, harmful. (2) Some parents may have used punishment in the past, perhaps with apparent success, and may be tempted to use it now, though it may not be the method of choice. In either case, this is a good time to openly discuss the time and place for punishment procedures (to the extent that you agree with me, of course), the danger and possible benefits of punishment, and the right and wrong way to use it.

Punishment is discussed on pages 382 and 383 of *Educating Children*, and in Section III of Chapter 9 of this book. Here are some major points to discuss.

1. As much as possible, we should try to affect each other's behaviors through the use of rewards.
2. Sometimes, however, a child engages in long-standing, harmful, and durable problem behaviors.
3. Punishment (in my opinion) should be used only after other, less aversive methods have either been tried and shown to be ineffective or are likely to involve more injury to the child or others.
4. Punishment should never be used in anger or out of desperation, that is, as an escape behavior, but only as part of a carefully prepared teaching plan.
5. To be most effective, the punishing event must be used every time the problem behavior occurs, immediately, and must be painful or noxious enough to quickly disrupt the problem behavior, resulting in a longer and longer time interval between episodes of the behavior. In the interval between episodes of the problem behavior, the parents must be reinforcing appropriate behaviors.
6. The child must not be given reinforcement immediately after the punishment or else the punishment may become a signal for the reinforcement, resulting in an increase in the punished behavior.
7. Alternative behaviors must be rewarded immediately and as often as possible, or else the problem behavior being punished may not decrease, but may actually increase.
8. The problem behavior must be punished wherever and whenever it happens, and by many different people.

After reviewing alternatives to punishment, the decision to use it and the proper method for doing so, you and the parents can discuss questions the parents may have. Moreover, if children in the group engage in serious problem behaviors that are not likely to be replaced quickly by differentially reinforcing appropriate behaviors, you and the parents can discuss the possible use of other methods during the Individual Consultation and/or home visit. In that case, parents might also be assigned Chapter 15 of *Educating Children*.

Pulling it all Together

The last item of main business is to: (1) help the parents to apply what they have learned about rewards (as well as other teaching methods) to their program for instituting productive exchanges and (2) continue to strengthen the APG items that seem important for success in a home educational program. While final plans will be discussed and written on a Weekly Contract form during the Individual Consultation, this is a good time to stress certain points.

Revising the Plan for Instituting Productive Exchanges. The past week's plan can be updated and/or revised by:

1. Adding the basic teaching methods described above to the existing plans.
2. Discussing and solving problems in the past week's teaching plan and home program.
3. If appropriate, planning how to conduct simple teaching sessions on certain target behaviors (such as eye contact, self-help, cooperation, small motor activities, or even academic skills).

First, briefly review the general teaching methods that were discussed and illustrated during the meeting, that is, the methods noted on pages 227–248, regarding planning and setting up teaching sessions, shaping, signaling, prompting, and rewarding. Again, illustrate the methods by referring to examples that parents described from their home programs, or that were role-played or shown on videotapes. For example:

> Now, you remember how important it is to reward target behaviors immediately, especially when a target behavior is weak. And you know that if you reward too slowly, your child may have done some other behavior in the meantime, and that is the behavior you will be rewarding. So, be ready to reward! Have the food handy, or in your hand, if you are using food rewards, and be on the lookout for the behaviors that you are going to reward.
>
> For example, if you are going to strengthen spontaneous eye contact, have the food ready and be on the lookout for spontaneous eye contact. And when your child looks at you, say "Good boy" and shoot the food to him while he is looking at you.

Second, you might give parents another opportunity to briefly describe their progress and problems, using their logs and notes so that they can be specific. Pinpoint and reinforce parents for their effort, use of proper terms, and use of proper teaching methods. When the parents describe problems, on the other hand, such as an increase in disruptive behavior or a lack of increase in ''good'' behaviors, help them try to pinpoint the source of the problems—for example, in the teaching methods that were used.

At this time, you might also introduce the Checklist of Common Problems of Teaching (Table 7-1, page 169) in *Educating Children*, for it lists many sources of problems or apparent problems in applying general teaching methods (Item 18). For instance, as parents describe problems in their home programs, they can be given the chance to look through their copy of the Checklist to determine which Checklist items might account for the problems they were having. You can elaborate on each problem source as needed. For instance:

Parent: Well, one of the behaviors that we were on the lookout to reward was cooperation. And Cindy just didn't get any more cooperative during the week.

Consultant: Does the Checklist give you any hint as to why Cindy's cooperation did not seem to increase?

Parent: I'm not sure.

Consultant: Well, looking at the Checklist, do any of the items apply to your work last week?

Parent: Let's see. . . . Well, not item 1; we were careful to take notes on what was going on. . . .

Consultant: Great. So, you think that your measurement was correct. Mm hmm. . . .

Parent: And not item 2. . . . We used strong rewards—food. And she didn't get any snacks at all during the day. All food, except meals, had to be earned by cooperating and making eye contact. So, not number three either.

Consultant: Great!

Parent: But maybe it is item 4: ''Consequences are not given often enough.'' Yeah, that could be it! See, sometimes she would cooperate and then sort of walk away. And we wouldn't reward her. We figured that she didn't want the food.

Consultant: Any other reason why she might have walked away?

Parent: You mean maybe she didn't know that she was going to be rewarded?

Consultant: Could be? . . . And were there lots of times when she seemed to ignore your request, just walked away or maybe even whined when you gave her a signal?

Parent: Yeah. That's right. . . . Okay, so we'll make sure to be right there! When she cooperates, why, we'll reward her immediately and every time, even if she doesn't look like she knows that she is going to be rewarded.

Consultant: Fine! Try that for a few days and see what happens. But, keep using the Checklist; it will help you to remind yourselves of proper teaching methods.

Parents are asked to use the Checklist both to remind themselves of proper teaching methods and to pinpoint the sources of any problems in their teaching programs. Note that a general problem-solving sequence (which includes the use of the Checklist of Common Problems of Teaching) is presented in detail for Unit Six in Chapter 8.

Some problems, however, may not be the result of parents' lack of skill at using basic teaching methods. For example, the parents might be consistently ignoring tantrums and frequently rewarding their child for many nontantrum behaviors, and yet the child's tantrums continue at a high rate, perhaps because in the past the child's tantrums were intermittently reinforced. Thus, you and the parents must: 1) make sure that none of the common problems of teaching are occurring (for instance, accidentally rewarding tantrums) and 2) then make a choice between either continuing with the plan as it was written and conducted during the past week (because the teaching methods are simply going to require more time) or trying another teaching method. At this time, discuss the above two points with the group and stress the importance of parents' writing accurate logs or notes so that the proper choices can be made. The specific choice between continuing with or revising the teaching plan, however, can be made either during the Individual Consultation or later during the home visit, when you will have another chance to observe the parent-child interaction. For example:

Consultant: Mr. and Mrs. Fernandez. How about some last comments on how your program has been going? What to continue? What might need to be changed?

Parent: Most of the things . . . exchanges . . . were working well. Jose is becoming more cooperative and is starting to do some chores! So, we are satisfied with the plans for those behaviors. But his whining is another thing! We did just what our plan said to do. We completely ignored the whining and waited for him to stop. Then when he was quiet for a little while, we would reward him with all sorts of things, like praise, bites of food.

Consultant: Mm hmm. So, what is the problem?

Parent: Well, he started whining louder and longer than ever. We are not sure if the plan is right. Maybe we should try another method.

Consultant: Okay. First of all, are you sure that the common problems of teaching—on the Checklist—do not apply?

Parent: We're pretty sure. We never talked to him, or even looked at him, when he was whining. We rewarded him many, many times, all day long, when he was doing other than whining. And the rewards were good, strong ones.

Consultant: Well, you may be right that the teaching plan needs to be revised. But it may be that it will just take more time for the present plan to work. You remember how you handled whining before you started in this Program?

Parent: Yeah, we used to pay attention to him—the escape exchange.

Consultant: And remember what you read about reward schedules? Did you used to reward Joe's whining every time?

Parent: No, only once in a while—when we couldn't stand it. . . . Ah, I see! That means that Jose will keep trying to get attention by whining, at least for a while.

Consultant: Right! An intermittent schedule can make the behavior durable. His sudden increase in whining is called an "extinction burst." Like when the can of soda pop does not come down the chute after you have put your money in. What do you do? . . . . You try again and again. Maybe you kick the machine! But when you finally realize that the machine is not going to reward you for putting your money in it, then you stop trying.

Parent: So, Jose is going to keep putting his money in. He's going to keep trying to get our attention back.

Consultant: Right. So, why don't we see what happens if you continue ignoring the whining and rewarding nonwhining for another week?

Parent: Okay. And if the whining doesn't slow down then, we can try something else.

Consultant: Mm hmm. So, for the coming week, keep up the same program. Hang in there; stick to your guns! When I make a home visit we can check it out in more detail.

Continuing to Strengthen Other APG Items. Finally, you can spend some time reminding parents of the importance of, encouraging them to discuss, and helping them to solve problems regarding other APG items. These were listed in the beginning of this chapter.

IV. INTRODUCING THE NEXT WEEK'S WORK

The focus of work during the coming week is APG Item 14: planning a comprehensive, long-term educational program. It is not necessary at this time to describe for parents all that is involved in Item 14. Instead, merely repeat some of what was said during the first meeting, on pages 157–158 in Chapter 5, regarding skill areas, the Behavior Evaluation Scale (BES) and Behavior Evaluation Table (BET), the Skill Sequence Table, and the Table of Basic Behaviors, which are used to answer three questions:

> What are my child's strengths and weaknesses?
>
> Where do I start my child's educational program and how do I find out which skill areas I should work on?
>
> Where do I go next?

The parents' assignment, then, is to read relevant APG items and to read and do the written tasks in Chapter 4 of *Educating Children*. The bulk of their written task consists of filling out the Behavior Evaluation Scale. Emphasize the importance of the parents' working together—observing their child, discussing their observations, and filling out the BES and BET. Of course, depending on the needs of the children, additional assessment instruments could be used.

Before the group divides up for Individual Consultations, briefly discuss and complete any plans for continuing or extending an interfamily network, such as scheduled phone calls, home visits, or backup services. If the group seems ready, you might ask for a volunteer to play the role of rotating leader.

V. INDIVIDUAL CONSULTATION

As in the past week's meeting, there are two tasks to accomplish during the Individual Consultation: 1) reviewing the work done so far and 2) planning the next week's work and writing the plans on a Weekly Contract. In general, the format for this and future Individual Consultations follows the description in Section V of Chapter 6. In particular:

1. Parents are to read and do all written assignments in Chapter 4 of *Educating Children*. Most of this assignment is to be completed before the home visit. Parents might also read APG Item 14 (and possibly Items 12 and 13).

2. You and the parents decide either to continue the last week's plan for instituting productive exchanges or to update/revise it. For instance, new behaviors might be added to the plan or different teaching methods might be tried.

3. Parents discuss and write their plans for cooperating with one another; insuring the proper organization in home life; scheduling and taking breaks; reinforcing themselves and each other; making scheduled phone calls (and possibly making a home visit or providing a backup service) to other families; generalizing teaching methods and their child's gains to other persons and places (slowly involving siblings and frequent visitors more and more); using logs or notes, their APG, Weekly Contract, and book to pinpoint and solve problems; and making a scheduled phone call to you.

4. A day and time for the home visit is arranged.

All plans are written on a Weekly Contract, as in Table 6–3 of Chapter 6. Additional details can be written on the Contract during the home visit or after a phone call.

If a parent has volunteered to be a rotating leader, you can help the parent plan the portion of the meeting to be led, for instance, by reviewing part of the assignment in Chapter 4 of *Educating Children* or reviewing parents' past home programs. Again, the parent might be a coleader, rather than assume full responsibility at this time.

VI. HOME VISIT

This is an important home visit because the parents, by this time, should have become more skilled at instituting productive exchanges and in learning and using many other APG items. Here is what we have done during this week's home visit.

Coaching Parents to Conduct Their Teaching Program

All families are continuing to institute productive exchanges, and some may be focusing on certain target behaviors. It is important to observe and coach parents at work and, if possible, to videotape what they are doing. In preparing for the home visit, refer to the recent APG scoring for the family, especially Item 16 (waiting and planning, rather than reacting), Item 17 (instituting productive exchanges), and Item 18 (general teaching methods). Naturally, be sensitive to cooperation between the spouses (Item 19) and organization in the home life (Item 20).

While the parents are interacting with their child, coach them on all of the above items (using the minimum coaching necessary), show them the videotape so that they can assess their own performance, demonstrate proper methods (for instance, how to use a certain teaching method or how to cooperate with one's spouse), and role-play methods with the parents.

Discussion and Work on Planning an Educational Program

Next, review with parents the methods they used to score their child on the Behavior Evaluation Scale (BES). If necessary, help them to solve any problems they may have had, such as how to score a particular behavior. In addition, you and the parents can discuss the remainder of the assignment in Chapter 4 of *Educating Children,* namely: (1) using a sample Behavior Evaluation Table (BET) to plan part of a child's educational program and especially (2) using the BES which they have filled out for their own child, to pick the first skill area to work on and the first target behavior to work on in that skill area. Moreover, you might discuss the long-term educational program for the child by referring to both the Skill Sequence Table and the goals of the parents, as discussed during the Pre-Program stage. Show parents how the small steps in the child's educational program help them to achieve long-term goals.

Discussion and Work on Other APG Items

Many APG items which the parents have contracted to work on are not so easy to observe: scheduled breaks, reinforcement for oneself and one another, interfamily hotline, objectivity, confidence in learning principles and long-term perspective, honesty, generalization, and personal problems. Thus, it may be necessary to set the occasion for the parents to indicate how they have been faring on such items. For example, you can:

1. Read the parents' logs or notes or ask the parents to read them.
2. Ask general questions, such as, "Well, how do you feel about the Program and about how it is going for you?"
3. Ask specific questions regarding APG items, such as:

> Last week you mentioned that you have a hard time waiting and planning when Sally throws tantrums, because you said you are so tense. Would you tell me more about those feelings of tension?

Here is an example of what we have said during this part of home visits:

Consultant: Okay, now, tell me how you think your home program has been working out. (A general question.)

Mrs. Oaks: Just fine. Really! Everything is working just fine. (Parents may be right. On the other hand, there may be some problems, both in their child's progress or in their work. Therefore, the consultant asks for "specifics" and seeks comparative evidence by referring both to notes made while observing and parents' logs.)

Consultant: Great! Let's get more specific, though. Let's focus on each item on your Weekly Contract. Perhaps you could read from your logs so that you can remember some details. We've already discussed the assignment from Chapter 4 of *Educating Children,* and you have done a terrific job. How about the program for instituting productive exchanges?

As the parents describe the way they have conducted their teaching program, praise them for their efforts and for improved or successful performance. Probe regarding their performance on related items from the APG; for instance, planning rather than reacting, confidence in learning principles, or agreeing to use certain behavioral methods. For example:

Mrs. Oaks: (Parent describes much of what consultant has already seen during this home visit.) So, we have been following the teaching plan just as it is written on the Contract for this week.

Mr. Oaks: Yeah, that's right. I think we have done pretty well.

Consultant: I agree! You are doing a fine job. Your description and your logs match what I have seen. In other words, you folks are objective and honest, and I appreciate it. It makes it easier for all of us to evaluate how well your program is working. . . . Now, you remember a few minutes ago when Chris was biting her hand and you almost went to her to stop her? Well, you didn't go to her. You seemed on the verge of reacting, but you stopped yourself. I thought that was great! But what I want to know is this—do her problem behaviors make you tense? You haven't mentioned it to me or written about it in your logs.

Mrs. Oaks: Well, I guess you're right. It gets me pretty tense when she starts biting herself, but Al coaches me to wait and plan, and I coach myself so that I don't react. I should have written about those feelings, huh?

Consultant: Yes, I think so. Because if those feelings become uncomfortable during the day, or if they interfere with your conducting your teaching program, we want to pinpoint those feelings and perhaps teach you to relax.

Mrs. Oaks: Yeah. I guess I was a little embarrassed to tell you.

Consultant: Got any idea why?

Mrs. Oaks: Well, you know the other parents have kids who bite themselves, and they don't seem to get too tense about it. I guess I didn't want to come out looking like a weakling.

Consultant: Do you think that it would make you a weakling to have those feelings? To be upset when Chris bites herself? (Consultant helps parent to reinterpret her feelings—as a rather "natural" response of a caring, sensitive person and parent. Consultant stresses the importance of parent accurately describing feelings during discussions and in logs; reinforces parent for being so honest during the present discussion.)

Consultant: So, Chris has been making progress. Your notes, your descriptions, and my observations all jibe. Now tell me, do you think her problem behaviors will be replaced by next month? (Consultant probes for information on parents' expectations of success, confidence in learning principles, and long-term time perspective.)

Mr. Oaks: Well, that would be nice, but we don't believe in miracles.

Consultant: You don't? What do you believe in?

Mr. Oaks: Hard work!

Mrs. Oaks: You know! Like you have said. If we do our part, she is likely to change. A little at a time. Rome wasn't built in a day, you know!

Consultant: You've got the right attitude!

Of course, if you suspect that the parents' expectations, confidence, or long-term perspective are weakening, work on those items by:

1. Reminding parents of the progress made by other families.
2. Helping parents to see how much they and their child have changed already.
3. Reminding them of the garden metaphor.
4. Urging them to practice making key statements to themselves ("One week at a time") and to vividly imagine realistic, short-term progress and the pleasant consequences of that progress, such as the parents' good feelings and their child's improved behaviors (see Section II of Chapter 10, on the use of imagery).

In a similar fashion, you might focus on the remaining assignment items on the Weekly Contract. For example:

Consultant: Has anything been hampering your efforts to do your assignments? (Consultant has noticed disruptive behaviors of siblings.)

Mrs. Oaks: No, I don't think so.

Consultant: How about the sounds from the TV and from the other kids? I noticed that little Andy was running around . . .

Mrs. Oaks: Yeah. He's on wheels today. (A description, not an explanation.)

Consultant: Does it seem to you that he might have been fishing for some attention while you were working with Chris.

Mrs. Oaks: Yeah, you're right. He's a pretty active boy. Maybe he felt left out. (The beginning of an explanation.)

Consultant: You may be right. Well, we sure don't want to ignore him. He has his needs—to feel part of the action, to be recognized. What are we going to do? He needs to be given attention, and yet you need to be able to work with Chris without being too interrupted.

Mrs. Oaks: I think that maybe we'll give him lots of attention before we have our sessions with Chris, and tell him that after the sessions we will also do something with him. What do you think?

Consultant: Sounds like a good idea. Good thinking!

Mr. Oaks: Or, when the wife works with Chris, I can spend time with Andy, and vice versa.

Mrs. Oaks: That's a good idea, too.

Consultant: Fine! Let's put it on the Weekly Contract, in the section on "Generalization."

Consultant: (Reading copy of Weekly Contract.) Now, it says here that you are going to work together to institute some productive exchanges, and that you are going to coach and praise each other, that Al is going to do the wash one day a week, and that Mrs. Oaks is going to make Mr. Oaks a chocolate cake on Sunday. This ties in with Item 19 of your APG.

Mrs. Oaks: Well, I've already bought the ingredients for the cake. He's been so good. It was cute to see him do the wash.

Mr. Oaks: Don't rub it in, dear (said with a grin). Yeah, I did the wash last night. She deserved it. She works hard.

Consultant: (However, consultant noticed that Mr. Oaks spent most of the time in another room when Mrs. Oaks was working with Chris. Raising this issue is tricky because it partly contradicts what the parents have said.) That's great to hear that you are working together like that. How about when Mrs. Oaks is working with Chris? (Sets occasion for raising the issue.)

Mrs. Oaks: Well, we work together pretty much. (Vague.)

Consultant: Can you give me more details? How else are you working together?

Mrs. Oaks: Well, Al rewards Chris a lot, and I mean a lot! When she cooperates, makes eye contact, and sits and eats properly at the table. (Mr. Oaks smiles and so consultant turns to him.)

Consultant: Very good, Al! And Chris is cooperating more and more, huh?

Mr. Oaks: She sure is. Makes me feel real good.

Consultant: I did notice, though, that when Chris starts some of her disruptive behaviors, you (Mrs. Oaks) seem to deal with them mostly. (Raises the issue.)

Mr. Oaks: Well, I guess that's my habit. She's (Mrs. Oaks) always been the one to handle Chris when Chris starts up.

Consultant: Any ideas why?

Mr. Oaks: I don't know. She seems better at it.

Consultant: Mm hmm. (Waits for elaboration.)

Mr. Oaks: I guess it's sort of how we've worked things out over the years. It upsets me when Chris bites herself and makes noises. I don't know why.

Consultant: You say that it bothers you. (Repeats parent's message.)

Mr. Oaks: I guess I just have a hard time taking it. I don't know what to do to stop her.

Consultant: So, you sort of back off?

Mr. Oaks: Yeah. I guess it's the easy way out. (Seems somewhat upset.)

Consultant: So, you're not happy with your way of dealing with her disruptive behaviors. (Sets occasion for an effort to change.)

Mr. Oaks: No, I guess not. It sort of eats at me that I don't do something—that I let the wife do it.

Consultant: Well, do you think that there is any reason for not trying to handle a few of Chris' disruptive behaviors now? What about the methods that you have learned? (Suggests the beginning of a solution.)

Mr. Oaks: Yeah, well, I guess I do know what to do. We have talked about it, and the methods are on our plan.

Consultant: Mm hmm. (Sets occasion for Mr. Oaks to continue—to find his own solution.)

Mr. Oaks: I guess I could try. I could jump in and try some of the methods.

Consultant: Right! Like what? (Sets occasion for more details.)

Mr. Oaks: Well, like timing her out when she screams. Aren't Mr. and Mrs. Lawrence doing that?

Consultant: They sure are. Getting good results, too, I hear!

Mr. Oaks: Okay. Hell! I'll give it a whirl.

Consultant: Yeah?

Mr. Oaks: Yeah.

Consultant: Okay. That's great. Now can we think of some ways to insure your success at this. (Consultant encourages parents to suggest, for example, self-reinforcement, reinforcement from wife, or relaxation procedures.)

At this point, you might provide the parent with a set of simple instructions (e.g., relaxation, self-reinforcement, covert rehearsal) to prepare himself for working on the behaviors which are so aversive and which make him feel that he has been a failure (see Chapter 10). Moreover, you might conduct a practice session on using the methods.

In sum, by the end of the home visit, you and the parents should have pinpointed and discussed the progress of parents and children; pinpointed and discussed problems (both in the child's progress, in the parents' satisfactory completion of their assigned tasks, and regarding various items on the APG); developed partial solutions to some problems; and written all program revisions and new plans on the Weekly Contract. In addition, the parents might be asked to phone you regarding their efforts to strengthen any weak points, and are reminded to bring their materials to the next meeting (the APG, *Educating Children,* and a completed Behavior Evaluation Scale). Finally, if a parent will be acting as rotating leader at the next meeting, you might discuss and even role-play with the parent.

VII. PLANNING THE ACTIVITIES FOR THE FOURTH UNIT

As in the past weeks use your notes to update your copy of the parents' APG, pinpoint problems to work on during the week, and plan the details of the agenda for the next meeting(s).

8 UNITS FOUR (PLANNING AN EDUCATIONAL PROGRAM AND MEASURING BEHAVIOR), FIVE (PLANNING AND CONDUCTING THE FIRST TEACHING PROGRAM), AND SIX (EVALUATING THE FIRST TEACHING PROGRAM)

I. INTRODUCTION

This chapter describes three units of work, the activities of which are closely connected. Specifically, in Unit Four the parents complete the evaluation of their child and the planning of a comprehensive educational program, learn how to count and chart behaviors, and conduct a Baseline on the first target behavior to increase in a teaching program. In Unit Five, they plan and conduct a teaching program for the first target behavior. And in Unit Six, they learn how to evaluate the first teaching program and update or revise it using a general problem-solving sequence. Although it is possible to complete each unit in one week, you can spread the activities over several weeks, depending on the progress of the children and parents or the type of Program you are conducting (i.e., intensive or extended).

COMMON ASSESSMENT AND PROGRAMMING GUIDE (APG) ITEMS TO WORK ON IN THE THREE UNITS

The following items and components are important in all three units:

Item 11: Productive participation: Continue the contract-credit system (checking performance and providing backup consequences as quickly as possible). During meetings, continue to measure verbal behaviors, reinforce productive verbal behaviors, and teach parents to do the same. During Individual Consultations and home visits, discuss participation; help parents to pinpoint and analyze strengths, progress, and weaknesses; plan and conduct special programs if needed. Continue to gradually help parents to assume the roles of rotating leader and temporary expert. For example, as rotating leader, a parent can conduct the review of reading and written assignments or the review of parents' home programs. On the other hand, a parent might be temporary expert on handling certain problem behaviors, teaching certain appropriate behaviors, or using a particular teaching method (e.g., Grandma's Law, shaping, relaxation).

Item 12: Objectivity: This is important in all three units, but most of the instruction is in Units Four and Five.

Item 13: Confidence in general learning principles and a long-term perspective: Continue to help parents to see that their task is to do the best they can to find and institute the conditions their child needs in order to learn, so that more general, deterministic processes can operate through their own behaviors. Continue to help parents to examine and plan both long- and short-term goals. Work on this item in all three units.

Item 14: Planning an educational program: Focus on this item in Units Four and Five.

Item 15: Agreeing to try certain behavioral methods: Address this item when the parents are planning and conducting their first teaching program (i.e., Units Five and Six).

Item 16: Planning rather than reacting: Continue to emphasize the importance of not reacting to problems, whether they are specific behaviors of the child, behaviors or feelings of the parents, problems in teaching programs, or other problems in the family. The emphasis is on teaching parents not to be so reinforced by short-run or immediate efforts to escape or avoid problems that, in the long run, the problems remain unsolved or worsen. Instead, help parents to wait and plan what to do, using a problem-solving strategy (see Items 16 and 27 on the APG).

Item 17: Instituting productive exchanges: Continue to strengthen and/or revise patterns of productive interaction or exchange between parents and children. That is, even though the parents may be conducting teaching programs on specific behaviors, they should maintain and accentuate productive exchanges at other times and places. Thus, help parents to continue to institute the program on productive exchanges which they wrote during the second unit of work (see Chapters 6 and 7).

Item 18: General teaching methods: Continue to strengthen parents' understanding and use of general teaching methods. For instance, in discussing the home programs, showing videotapes, role-playing and demonstrating methods, and in home visits, help parents to pinpoint certain teaching methods that are being used or could be used, as well as strengths and weaknesses in performance; help them to properly use the methods and see the ways that methods can be generalized and modified for teaching behaviors in many skill areas. Focus on all components of this item in the three units.

Item 19: Cooperation of spouses or partners: Continue teaching parents to work together in all aspects of their home program.

Item 20: Organized home life: Continue to stress the importance of this item. Work on it as needed.

Item 21: Personal problems: Work on anticipating, describing, analyzing, and solving personal problems. Problems that are common to parents in a group, or methods that might be used by many parents, can be focused on in group meetings (e.g., relaxation or covert rehearsal).

Item 22: Honesty: Continue to work on this item by comparing parents' logs, notes, and descriptions with your observations.

Item 23: Scheduled breaks: Stress the importance of scheduling and taking breaks. Have parents discuss their taking of breaks. Teach methods for maintaining children's gains when the parents are on break. Emphasize this item when parents are about to start their first teaching program (Units Five and Six).

Item 24: Reinforcement for each other: Continue to strengthen this item.

Item 25: Linkage with networks: If successful so far, help parents to extend a telephone and home visit network; for instance, helping one another to conduct their first teaching program and/or providing baby-sitting services. At this time, you might also invite specialists to meetings, as temporary experts in teaching certain skills.

Item 26: Generalization: Especially prior to starting their first teaching program, help the parents plan how to generalize their own and their children's behaviors (e.g., the role of siblings in the teaching program, what to do in public, how grandparents and neighbors can help).

Item 27: Pinpointing and solving problems: Especially during Unit Six, teach parents how to use various materials to pinpoint, describe, analyze, and solve problems, particularly in their first teaching program (e.g., using Chapter 7 (Handling Common Problems of Teaching) and chapters on relevant skill areas in *Educating Children*, their copy of the APG, and other materials).

Remember, if problems arise regarding any item above, see Chapter 10 for special methods that might be used.

II. UNIT FOUR: PLANNING AN EDUCATIONAL PROGRAM, LEARNING HOW TO COUNT AND CHART BEHAVIORS, AND CONDUCTING A BASELINE

Starting the Meeting

After the performance check, briefly review what has been done to date in the Program, showing parents that their work has been leading up to the topic for this and future weeks. For example, so far they have: (1) learned a new way of viewing their child's needs and the family situation (the behavioral-educational approach) and some general principles and methods of behavior change; (2) begun to institute a program for changing patterns of interaction or exchange with their children so as to start their child's educational program and give them more confidence in themselves; and (3) learned about an important condition that helps people to learn, namely, rewards.

Reviewing Rewards

Either you or a parent serving as rotating leader can review the following points from Chapter 3 of *Educating Children:*

1. Types of rewards (primary, social, general, activity).

2. How rewards are learned (through being paired with or followed by events that are already rewards).

3. Types of reward schedules and how they affect the speed with which behaviors are acquired and how durably they will be maintained.

4. Which kinds of rewards and reward schedules it might be best to use at the start of a child's educational program and at the start of some teaching programs.

5. Why it is important to move to more common rewards and reward schedules and how to make the transition.

6. How to find rewarding events.

Reviewing Parents' Programs to Institute Productive Exchanges. Next, either you or a parent reviews the parents' work during the past week on instituting productive exchanges. The review can proceed in the manner described in Section III of Chapter 7. In particular, the leader addresses the following: (1) rewards (which parents are using, could be using, and have found; how the parents are using rewards, e.g., rewarding immediately, requiring their child to earn them; how the parents can use more common rewards, such as activities—Grandma's Law); (2) other general teaching skills (such as signaling, prompting, rearranging the physical environment, and replacing problem behaviors); and (3) additional important APG items which increase the chances of success, such as planning rather than reacting, cooperation between the spouses, and methods for pinpointing and working to solve problems (especially using Chapter 7 of *Educating Children*).

If parents are having similar problems on any item above, the problems can be described and analyzed in more detail; parents can suggest methods to employ; and consultants can demonstrate those which might be useful. For example, you (or an outside specialist) might make a presentation on progressive relaxation training, indicating how it can be used to help replace reacting rather than planning or tension, and demonstrating specific procedures. When possible, parents then practice the methods during the meeting (e.g., through role-playing), discuss when and how they might use the methods at home, and are provided with materials describing the steps to follow (see Chapter 10).

Later, during Individual Consultations and home visits, help parents to plan and institute special methods, writing the details of the plan on the Weekly Contract. As with their teaching programs, progress can be discussed in future meetings.

Main Business

The main business for this unit of work is APG Item 14: planning a comprehensive, long-term educational program for their child. Prior to the meeting, parents should have read and completed the assignment in Chapter 4 of *Educating Children*. During this portion of the meeting review and discuss the main points in that chapter and the parents' written assignment. Here is what we have done.

First, remind parents to work in a businesslike way. That is, they should:

1. Know which behaviors of their child are strengths to be accentuated and which behaviors need to be improved.
2. Teach behaviors for which thier child is ready.
3. Conduct their child's educational program in a sequence of carefully planned steps.
4. Always work to replace problem behaviors with appropriate behaviors.

Second, review Table 4-3 (Steps to Follow in Planning an Educational Program) on page 91 of *Educating Children*, to provide parents with a framework within which they can view their assignment for this week and future activities. Emphasize that use of Table 4-3 helps achieve long-term goals by moving in a series of carefully planned steps, and that they use Table 4-3 from now on to become more independent in planning and conducting their child's home program.

Third, review the main points in Chapter 4 of *Educating Children*. For example:

1. Point out that an educational program consists of a series of teaching programs.

2. Define "skill area" and briefly describe the skill areas on the BES. If appropriate to the children's needs, describe other skill areas as well (e.g., reading, math).

3. Point out that by filling out the BES and BET (and/or other behavioral assessments), the parents can answer the first questions which must be answered in planning an educational program, namely:

What are my child's strengths and weaknesses?

With which behaviors does my child need help?

In which way(s) does my child need help on the different behaviors?

4. Describe the Skill Sequence Table, pointing out that it helps to answer the question: "In what order do I teach the target behaviors with which my child needs help, as shown by my scoring of the BES?" Also, indicate that, just because the parents might move from one skill area to another, they do not stop working on earlier skill areas. Rather, they continue to give their child practice on earlier behaviors and work on harder behaviors in earlier skill areas.

5. Describe Table 4-2 (Basic Behaviors Child Must Learn Before He Can Work in Each Skill Area) on pages 84–85 of *Educating Children*. Stress the importance of this table in pinpointing behaviors for which their child is ready, so that their child's progress will be smoother.

Fourth, review the assignment at the end of Chapter 4 of *Educating Children*. While this may have been done during the last home visit, a second review helps to strengthen the main ideas and methods and enables parents to share information.

Regarding Part Three of that assignment (filling out the BES and BET), have the parents briefly review how they worked on the task, noting any difficulties they encountered and reactions they had. We have found that parents sometimes experience the following difficulties:

(1) the definitions and scale for some behaviors on the BES may be ambiguous, e.g., the meaning of "sometimes," "often," and "rarely" (in which case we try to clear up such ambiguities); (2) the parents may feel that, since their child needs so little help on a particular behavior, it need not be circled (in which case, we stress the importance of erring on the side of caution); (3) spouses may have disagreed in their ratings (in which case we help them try to resolve disagreements by referring to more general and objective criteria and rules, e.g., both parents observing a behavior at the same time and making a decision to err

on the side of caution); and (4) some parents' confidence may weaken when they see just how much their child needs to learn (in which case we emphasize that the BES also shows them that their child has skills which they might not have seen before and that having pinpointed the behaviors with which their child needs help (even if the list is long), the parents (and others) are now better able to plan and conduct a program that will help the parents to achieve goals).

Regarding Part Four of their assignment (picking the first skill area and target behavior to increase), have the parents briefly describe how they used the Table of Basic Behaviors (4-2) and the rule—start with the easiest behavior on the list with which the child needs help—to complete this part of the assignment. Moreover, to give parents practice for the future, have them suggest: (1) the second target behavior that they might work on in that first skill area and (2) any other skill areas for which their child may be ready.

In bringing the assignment to a close, you can point out that the BES does not list all of the behaviors with which their child might need help or might benefit from learning. Nor is it certain that, even if they carefully plan their child's educational program and conduct teaching programs, their child's progress will be smooth. Prerequisite behaviors may not be included on the Table of Basic Behaviors and/or their child may have additional problems which interfere with learning. Thus, encourage parents to: (1) think of and teach behaviors that are not on the BES, so long as they try to ensure that their child has the basic behaviors which seem to be needed; and (2) consult specialists to determine if their child has other difficulties (e.g., visual, auditory, metabolic, motor) and how to help remedy them. Parents should incorporate the specialists' recommendations in their educational program and teaching program plans.

After taking a break, introduce the next week's work (measuring behavior). However, if there is not enough time, you and the parents can meet in Individual Consultations, with the next week's assignment being to read and do the assignment in Chapter 5 of *Educating Children*. Measuring behavior would then be the main business for the next meeting.

Introducing the Next Week's Work (Measuring Behavior)

Measuring behavior is part of APG Item 12. First, to introduce this topic, point out that it is important to: (1) measure many pinpointed behaviors before planning a teaching program (i.e., take a baseline), so that the parents can see precisely if, in which ways, and how much a behavior needs to be changed; and (2) continue to measure the target behavior(s) and some of their own behaviors during a teaching program, so that they can evaluate progress, pinpoint or avoid problems, and revise their programs if needed.

Second, briefly present some main ideas from Chapter 5 of *Educating Children*. In Particular:

1. How we measure things in daily life (scales, thermometers, calorie counters).
2. How measurements can help in a teaching program (to determine if target behaviors are changing as expected; to help us wait and plan, rather than react; to maintain enthusiasm by showing that progress is being made; to sensitize us to our own behaviors).
3. Which behaviors to pinpoint and measure (target behaviors of child and teaching behaviors of parents, e.g., signals, prompts, consequences).
4. How to define behaviors (in terms of movements).
5. What to measure or count (number of times or how long a behavior occurs, settings in which a behavior occurs, how fast a behavior occurs after a signal has been given).
6. When to count behaviors and how much time to spend counting (during and outside of teaching sessions, the length of time depending on how much the behavior occurs and how many behaviors are to be counted).
7. What to do if the length of the observation time varies (calculate the rate).
8. Why and how to check reliability.
9. How to count behaviors (pencil and paper, counters, calendars, wristwatches, stopwatches, clocks).
10. How to chart what is counted.
11. How to conduct a baseline (planning the baseline—using Table 5-2, page 123 in *Educating Children*—and what to do during the baseline period).

Third, if time remains, give parents practice at pinpointing, defining, counting, and charting behaviors. If there is not enough time, however, the practice session (described below) can be on the agenda for the next meeting.

The following is a list of steps we have used in teaching parents to measure behavior.

1. Parents watch a portion of a teaching session, either on videotape or role-played by consultants and parents. The behavior(s) in the session are those which the parents are likely to be measuring as part of their baseline assignment for the coming week; for example, correct responses on small motor tasks, tantrums or noncompliance, requests made by the parent, prompts, social rewards. As was done earlier in this and in past meetings, parents are encouraged to pinpoint the important behaviors, objectively define each one, and write the definitions.

To help parents pinpoint important behaviors, we write the Signal–Child's Behavior–Consequence sequence on a blackboard, and ask them to note behaviors in each category which they see on the tape or in the demonstration. For example:

Consultant: (Portion of videotape has been shown.) Okay, what is going on here? Can we break it down in terms of the Signal–Child's Behavior–Consequence sequence? That's a good way to make sense out of a fast-moving sequence of events.

Mr. Lawrence: Well, the parent was signaling the little girl to put in puzzle pieces.

Mrs. Wince: Yeah, he said, "Here, put this one in," and "Now put in the bear."

Consultant: Good! Can we give a name to that kind of signal?

Mr. Daring: How about calling them "requests"?

Consultant: Group?

Mrs. Lawrence: Sure, "requests" is a good word.

Mrs. Wince: I agree.

Consultant: Good. Great observing and pinpointing! So, we have one kind of signal—requests. (Writes "requests" under the category for "Signals" on the blackboard and writes down the two examples that were given next to the word "requests.") Any other kinds of requests? . . . . (also encourages parents to pinpoint and define other kinds of signals, e.g., models, threats, Grandma's Law.). . . .

Mrs. Fernandez: Well, I think we have covered all of the kinds of signals. I didn't see any more.

Mr. Daring: Yeah, I agree. (Perhaps the portion of tape would be rerun to make sure.)

Mrs. Fernandez: How about the child's behaviors? I saw her put in three puzzle pieces by herself.

Mr. Lawrence: Right!

Consultant: So, you are pinpointing how she worked with puzzle pieces—the way she handled them according to the task, which was to put them in. Terrific! What shall we call that behavior?

Mr. Wince: Well, how about "correct"?

Mr. Daring: Sounds good to me. Good word, Wince!

Mr. Wince: Nothing to it!

Consultant: I'm not sure of just what we mean or what we see when we call it a "correct" response. (Probes for operational definition.)

Mr. Fernandez: When she puts a puzzle in the right spot.

Mrs. Daring: Even if she does it wrong a few times. As long as she finally gets it in the right spot.

Mr. Fernandez: Right. And as long as she got no help—no prompts.

Mr. Daring: Right! I'll buy that.

Consultant: Will somebody summarize the definition? (Note that consultant is letting parents do more and more of the talking.)

Mrs. Lawrence: Okay. It's a correct response if she puts a puzzle piece in the right spot without help, even if she did it over and over until she finally got it in the right one. All of the times when she did not get it in the right spot are just called "incorrect."

Consultant: Can you all live with that?

Mrs. Wince: Heavens. That's pretty complicated!

Consultant: Good point. Notice that there is no rule book in the sky that tells us what a correct response is. It is up to us to define it. So, how exact should we be? I mean, she's never going to put in any two pieces in exactly the same way. . . .

Mr. Lawrence: Shoot for the main ingredients. The right spot and no prompts.

Consultant: Great! And we want a useful definition. Does it help us to check the child's progress on working puzzles by defining correct responses that way?

Mrs. Lawrence: Yeah. We can keep track of errors and we can see if she needs less help as time goes by.

Consultant: Fine. Really fine! Okay. Any other kinds of behaviors of the child that we ought to look at? And remember, we don't have to pinpoint everything—just enough that we can keep track of what's going on. (The discussion can continue in this fashion until other important behaviors of the child, for example, whining, and consequences delivered by the parents—social rewards and primary rewards—have been pinpointed and defined.)

2. When all parents have pinpointed and defined each behavior, they select a few behaviors to count and chart. Make sure that several parents are counting the same behaviors. Then they decide what to count regarding each behavior (number of occurrences, duration) and how to count each (stopwatch, wrist-counter, hashmarks made on paper). In our Programs, we have also provided parents with several wrist-counters to use at home.

Next, parents are provided with a "Behavior Count Table" (recording sheet) and a "Behavior Chart." Examples are on pages 124, 125, and 150 through 153 of *Educating Children*. Of course, for this exercise, parents might divide the chart and table into 1-minute or 30-second intervals, instead of sessions or days.

3. The same portion of tape is run (or the same type of session is role-played) again for several minutes while the parents take data. If you are using tape, the parents can take data a second time, to check intra-observer reliability. The point is to help them to make sure that their definitions are clear and precise enough and that their counts are accurate. All of the above can be repeated with different segments of tape or role-playing for extra practice.

4. When parents feel more comfortable observing and recording, and when they are accurately and reliably counting their assigned behaviors, the tape is run in its entirety or a more lengthy session is role-played. Again, parents take data and record their observations on the Behavior Count Table, perhaps for consecutive 1-minute intervals. When the session has been recorded, the parents compare their data (to check interobserver reliability) and work toward solving problems of definition and observation. Help parents to compute the rate of certain behaviors.

5. Parents then plot their data on Behavior Charts.

6. Finally, you and the parents discuss the observed teaching session in light of the data. For example: Did the person in the role of parent seem to be providing enough reinforcement or prompting, given the number of occurrences of correct responses made by the child? Were appropriate behaviors increasing, decreasing, or remaining steady during the session? Were behaviors of the parent changing during the session?

Note that, if you are working individually with parents, you can still generally follow the above steps. Moreover, practice on measuring behavior can be obtained in a classroom setting.

Fourth, you can deal with reservations some parents may have about measuring behavior. Common reservations are: 1) the time spent measuring behavior is unnecessary, interferes with teaching or is too much of a burden; and 2) it will be impossible to measure behavior (as they have just done) when they are working on several behaviors at once in teaching programs. Give parents a chance to solve such problems by themselves or as a group. For example, you might say something like:

> I think I understand your concerns. I think you are saying that since your major goal involves helping your child by conducting teaching programs in the home, measuring behavior will be difficult and may interfere with your teaching. Okay. First of all, do we agree that measuring behavior is important for good teaching? (Here, parents can be encouraged to list and discuss the ways in which measuring behavior will contribute to good teaching, for example, objectivity, keeping track of progress or problems, sensitivity to parents' own behaviors.)
>
> All right. Since we agree that both measuring behavior and conducting teaching programs are important (and actually go together), can we think of how measuring behavior is likely to become easier, or ways that we can make it easier? (Here, parents can be encouraged to see that: the task of measuring behavior will become easier with practice; spouses and siblings can share tasks so that one teaches while another person takes data; and when several behaviors are being worked on at the same time, time sampling can be used to obtain an estimate of how often behaviors are occurring, by measuring different behaviors at different times of day.)

Fifth, you can briefly discuss the assignment for the coming week, which is to:

1. Read Chapter 5 of *Educating Children*.
2. Plan and conduct a baseline on the first target behavior to increase (which was pinpointed as part of the past week's assignment).

3. Read Chapter 6 of *Educating Children* (parents might tentatively fill out the General Teaching Program Plan on page 146 but should not start the teaching program).
4. Read that portion of a later chapter in *Educating Children* that describes methods for teaching the first target behavior pinpointed.
5. Perhaps read APG Items 12 and 18.

When introducing the assignment for the fifth unit, we have said something like the following:

> Please open your book (*Educating Children*) to page 91. As you can see from Table 4-3, we have completed steps 1 through 4. You have evaluated your children using the BES and BET. You have used Table 4-1 (Skill Sequence Table), Table 4-2 (Basic Behaviors), and the BES and BET which you have filled out to pick a skill area in which to start your children's educational programs. And you have pinpointed the first target behavior to work on, and determined how it needs to be changed.
>
> Well, as you see from Table 4-3, the next several steps involve taking a baseline on the target behavior (so you can see precisely how your child performs the behavior and can have a basis for judging progress when you start a teaching program), reading how to change the target behavior, and writing a teaching program plan.
>
> So, during the coming week, you will be doing those next few steps. Then we will be ready to conduct teaching programs. . . .

In addition, you can discuss phone calls and home visits which parents may be making among themselves and plan future steps in the development of a network of backup support (e.g., baby-sitting, joining organizations, or locating sources of respite care). Finally, you can discuss parents' assuming the roles of rotating leader and temporary expert during the coming week.

Individual Consultation

As usual, discuss the progress of parents, children, and family to date, focusing on and updating specific APG items. (e.g., by reviewing the last Weekly Contract). Plans for solving new or continuing problems can be suggested at this point and finalized over the phone or during a home visit. A Weekly Contract for the coming week should be filled out. Any revisions in the plan for instituting productive exchanges should be written. Moreover, you can help the parents to fill out Table 5-2 (Planning a Baseline) on page 123 in *Educating Children*. A copy of that table can be affixed to the weekly Contract.

In helping parents to plan the baseline, you might remind them of the teaching sessions they conducted when you were assessing the family during the Pre-Program stage. In other words, for some target behaviors, the baseline can be conducted during "teaching sessions" (e.g., eye contact on request, correct responses on small motor tasks, or correct answers to certain questions). For other target behaviors, the baseline might be conducted in more common settings and at various times (e.g., the number of times that the child uses the toilet on his or her own, the amount of time the child spends playing, or the number of times the child cooperates with requests).

It might be easiest if parents complete assignments in the following order. First, parents read APG Item 12 and Chapter 5 in *Educating Children*. Then they begin the baseline, which will take the rest of the week. Toward the middle of the week, they begin to read APG Item 18, Chapter 6, and portions of a later chapter in *Educating Children* which describe how to teach the target behavior they have been measuring. If necessary, at this time, help the parents to choose the right section to read in a later chapter.

If a parent has volunteered to be rotating leader or temporary expert, help the parent to plan what to do. Finally, parents are reminded to bring their copy of *Educating Children,* the APG, handouts they have received, their Weekly Contract, and current logs, notes, and other data to all meetings.

Home Visit

A home visit may not be needed this week. A good policy to follow is to have the parents phone you in the middle of the week to discuss their reading, conducting of the baseline, and efforts to continue their plan to institute productive exchanges. If they are having any problems that cannot be solved over the phone, then a home visit can be made. In any event, parents are reminded to govern and keep track of their own behavior, using their book, the APG, the Weekly Contract, logs, notes, and other data, and any handouts they have received. They might also be reminded of the possibility that another parent can help, either through a phone call or visit.

III. UNIT FIVE: PLANNING AND CONDUCTING THE FIRST TEACHING PROGRAM

Starting the Meeting

After the performance check, introduce the meeting by briefly noting the work to be accomplished, which focuses on a review of parents' baselines (APG Item 12, objectivity), planning the first teaching program (Item 18, general teaching methods), and other APG items. Parents' continuing effort to institute productive exchanges can be discussed later in the meeting so as to integrate it with their first teaching program plan.

Reviewing Parents' Baselines. At this time, review the assignment to read Chapter 5 of *Educating Children* and conduct a baseline on the first target behavior. Here are the steps you might follow:

First, cite the main ideas in Chapter 5.

Second, ask each family to present their baseline briefly. Parents can read their plan and then describe what they did and subsequently learned. For instance:

1. Did the baseline indicate that the target behavior needs to be increased?
2. Precisely in which way(s) and how much does the target behavior need to be changed?
3. What subtle or minute aspects of the child's performance did the parents notice? For example, if they were counting the number of times the behavior occurred, what did they also notice about the child's skill, the way the child moved his hands, what he looked at?
4. In what ways did the baseline sensitize them to other behaviors of the child and to their own behaviors?

Third, if it appears that parents are weak on any component of objectivity (Item 12) at this point, it is important that they learn to pinpoint their needs and work to strengthen their skills. Thus, either in the meetings, in home visits, or during in-class instruction, give the parents extra practice, e.g., by helping them to observe and record behaviors from videotape or live sessions.

Main Business

The main business focuses on APG Item 18: applying general teaching skills. At this time, you can: 1) present, discuss, and illustrate the main ideas and methods in Chapter 6 of *Educating Children* and in sections of later chapters which the parents may have read concerning the first target behavior; 2) help parents to finalize their first teaching program plan; and 3) continue to strengthen additional items from the APG.

Here are the steps we have followed in our Programs:

Stressing and Explaining the Naturalness of Behavioral-Education Methods. Although the parents may tentatively accept the behavioral approach (APG Item 10), they may still have some misconceptions. A common one is that behavioral methods are not "natural," that they are tricks or mere techniques that might be used only when more accepted teaching methods are not working. Consequently, some parents may not be agreeable to trying certain methods (APG Item 15) or may not learn to use the methods creatively. Therefore, stress and explain the naturalness of behavioral methods either before or after the presentation on main ideas and teaching methods. Here is what we have said:

You have read and heard about rewards, reward schedules, shaping, prompting, chaining, and extinction. Well, at this point in our work, it is important that we are seeing these things from the same perspective. Often, because of newspaper articles and TV programs, because of the way materials are written, or even because of the way we have been presenting behavioral methods, you may see the methods as unnatural, as tricks or mere techniques. The result is that you may have a hard time using the methods with good conscience because you think you may be doing your children a disservice in the long run. Or, if you use the methods, you might figure that it is only temporary, that as soon as your children are making progress, you should go back to more natural ways of teaching.

Well, as I said, these hesitations are certainly understandable. I used to have the same hesitations myself. But let's look at behavioral-education methods more carefully. What I want to get across is that there is nothing unnatural about them.

First, we are all working to achieve certain goals. We want our children's behaviors and your own behaviors to change in certain ways. (Ask for examples of such goals.)

Now, in working to achieve goals, we are making certain assumptions about how behavior changes and about why problems occur. Well, what do we assume? Do we assume or believe that behavior change is magical or random? (Give parents a chance to respond.) Of course not! If we believed that, then we would be practicing certain rituals here or we would be sitting around waiting for change to happen. We would not be carefully planning and we would not be working to change our own behaviors.

And when problems occur (and over the years they certainly have occurred), do we assume that the source of the problems is solely in the children or in ourselves? Again, the answer is "No."

Well, then, what do we assume about behavior change and about problems? And what do we do to produce change and solve problems? . . . . Yes, we assume that behaviors change as they do because of the way the learning environment (which consists of people and their behaviors, objects, and places) is organized in a certain way. We assume that when behaviors are not changing in the desired way, it is because the environment is not arranged in a way which suits the needs of the people involved. And we assume that when we find out what arrangements people need, and when we put those arrangements into effect, behaviors eventually change in the desired direction. In other words, we assume that there is a rather tight cause-and-effect relationship between the organization of the learning environment and the behaviors of persons in the environment.

Well, we already know this! What does this have to do with behavioral methods, such as rewarding behaviors, using certain reward schedules, prompting, and so forth?

Here is the way we see it. The learning environment—now consider your homes here—can be described in terms of a number of dimensions or components, and those components are precisely the ones meant by certain behavioral terms. They are also the very things that we arrange when we use the behavioral methods.

For example, all environments have arrangements of objects which are somehow connected to our behaviors. Some objects are like tools—spoons, chairs, ladders. They help us to perform certain behaviors. Other objects are reinforcers; for instance, the TV and radio. And still others may be instructional, such as books, puzzles, flash cards.

As you can see, our behaviors are affected by the arrangement of objects. If the TV is playing loudly when we need to concentrate, our concentration may break down. If instructional materials are too far away, we may not use them. If our tools are too hard to use, they will not help us to perform our tasks.

We have already talked about engineering the environment. Can you see that there is nothing unnatural about it? We are just intentionally arranging the objects for successful learning.

Let's look at some other components. All environments somehow respond to our behaviors. Changes may be produced by our behaviors. Putting on a coat removes us from the cold; opening a door gives us access to things we might want; doing a good job may produce praise. As you know, many types of changes produced by our behaviors affect the way we perform the behaviors in the future. Those changes or events are called rewards or reinforcers. Behaviors that produce reinforcement are likely to be done more often or with more skill. So, just because we intentionally arrange the environment so that rewarding consequences follow appropriate behaviors, it does not mean we are doing anything unnatural. We are just using our knowledge to intentionally encourage change.

We can also describe an environment in terms of how predictably it changes as a result of our behaviors, or how much behavior we have to engage in before a reinforcing change occurs. What behavioral term covers predictability and the amount of behavior needed for a rewarding change to take place? (Reward schedule or schedule of reinforcement.) So, again, intentionally arranging the environment so that a certain reward schedule is in effect, so as to promote behavior change, is not unnatural. Reward schedules are there anyway. But, only by thinking about and arranging them can we be more certain of providing our children and ourselves with the ones we need.

Don't we generally know that not all environments provide rewarding events for all our behaviors? Don't we usually know that some environments or people in them do not reinforce certain behaviors? Of course we do. The behavioral term for this is simply "ignoring" or "extinction." Knowing this, we can consciously arrange it so that problem behaviors do not produce reinforcing events.

Here's another natural component—recognition of improvement, especially in skill. All environments can be described as to the recognition of improvements in skill or level of difficulty. We know some people who are quick to point out that we are doing a job better and better, and we know others who could not care less. What is the behavioral term for recognition or reinforcement of improvements in skill? (Shaping.) So, again we see that the behavioral method called "shaping" merely describes a process that takes place anyway.

We can do the same thing with the natural component that we might call "help" or "performance aid." Some environments provide more aid than others. The behavioral term is "prompts." And we can use prompts to help children and ourselves perform behaviors with more skill.

Here's another. You have heard of "chaining." Can you think of a natural example of chaining in the environment? (The point is that many behaviors consist of smaller behaviors performed in a sequence, such as bed-making or saying sentences.) So, the behavioral method of chaining simply involves intentionally teaching a person to perform a behavior in a sequence of steps which lead to some ending.

And now for a big item. This one is the heart of the matter. It refers to the naturalness of behavioral methods themselves. We make a common everyday distinction between environments that are coercive and dominating and those in which people are relatively free. Interestingly enough, the behavioral approach makes the same distinction. We will be talking about it more in later meetings. But, for now, what do we mean by coercive? We tend to mean that some people have control over the events that are rewards and punishers; that they can force us to perform by severely depriving us of reinforcers or by threatening to punish us; and that they benefit from the behaviors they coerce from us more than we do. Well, in behavioral terms, this is called "arbitrary reinforcement."

Similarly, in a relatively free environment reinforcement tends to naturally flow from our behaviors, where we are not forced to perform through severe deprivation or threats, and where we benefit from what we learn and do. In behavioral terms, this is "natural reinforcement."

The point is this. Behavioral methods are not in themselves unnatural or coercive. In fact, as behavioral educators, we can intentionally arrange the environment so that it encourages and strengthens behaviors in a way that is more natural and free.

Given this way of looking at behavioral methods, when we teach children we are intentionally arranging the naturally occurring components of the environment so as to help the children learn and perform desirable behaviors. And we keep on rearranging the environment until we find the arrangements that the children need so they can learn.

So, behavioral methods are not a bag of tricks, and they are not something we use once in a while. We are using them all the time.

Allow time for discussion of the above points.

Presenting, Discussing, and Illustrating Main Ideas and Teaching Methods. First, show parents that many components of a teaching program (in particular, their teaching behaviors) occur in a sequence that is usually repeated many times as they interact with their child. This should remind them of their past analyses of signals, behaviors, and consequences. It is helpful to draw the following figure on a blackboard, and then discuss it.

In addition, you can illustrate the sequence by role-playing or showing portions of videotapes on teaching sessions for several appropriate target behaviors, making sure that parents pinpoint each step.

Second, and most important, focus on each general teaching method (APG Item 18) and each component of a general teaching program plan (Table 6-2, page 146 of *Educating Children*). In doing so, you can make a brief presentation on each teaching method or component; role-play, demonstrate, or show videotapes illustrating the teaching methods; and discuss and answer questions on each. Parents are encouraged to take notes on how to apply to their own home programs the methods presented. Also, it might be helpful if they read along from Chapter 6 and APG Item 18. Below are some important points to make and

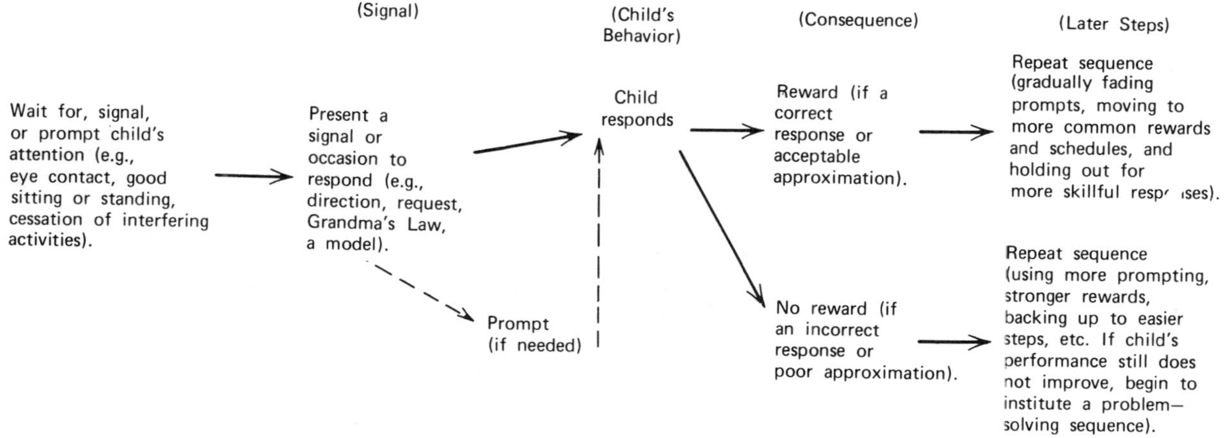

Figure 8-1 General teaching sequence.

methods to illustrate them. Since the APG and *Educating Children* discuss each component, there is no need for us to do that in detail here.

1. Program Planning. As to the first steps in program planning, briefly remind parents of: (a) how to determine the right skill areas and target behaviors to work on in their teaching programs; (b) the importance of defining the target behavior in terms of movements, so that they know just what they are teaching and how much progress is being made; and (c) the importance of specifying just how the target behavior needs to be changed and how they will measure such change. You can also ask the parents to specify the skill area and target behavior for their first teaching program.

2. Arranging the Physical Environment for Success. Point out that some problem behaviors can be reduced by temporarily making certain objects or places inaccessible while the child is taught to be more cooperative, and that many appropriate behaviors can be facilitated by making toys and instructional materials more accessible or by providing the child with materials (e.g., clothes, eating utensils) that are easier to use. Encourage parents to brainstorm a number of ways that they might arrange the home environment as suggested by APG Item 18B. For example, ask them to list some appropriate behaviors to increase and some problem behaviors to decrease. Then, focus on each behavior and ask: "Now, let's have some examples of arrangements in the home which may increase this behavior and those which may decrease it." By having parents examine the way that different arrangements may have opposite effects on a behavior, the parents' ability to pinpoint those arrangements and see how they affect behaviors is likely to be sharpened.

Some parents' hesitations, here, might involve the unusualness of certain arrangements (e.g., a lock on the refrigerator for a child who is constantly gorging himself or herself), the effort required to make the changes, or the fear that certain arrangements will always be needed. You can either defuse such hesitations by anticipating them or respond when parents voice them. In either case, stress that: a) the initial effort is likely to produce long-term benefits and b) most arrangements, even if unusual, are temporary. For example, the parents might also be teaching a child to earn access to the refrigerator and large eating utensils would be replaced by regular ones as the child acquired small motor skills.

3. The "Where and When" of Teaching the First Target Behavior.

a. At first, the parents might do their teaching at a certain time or place (e.g., teaching sessions), especially just before their child's favorite activities.

b. Sessions should be short at first, so that they can end on a good note.

c. If possible, teaching sessions can be constructed around or integrated with the child's favorite activities or interests (e.g., working on face-washing when the child is taking a bath; learning to read, spell, or do arithmetic with materials that deal with sports; increasing hand-eye coordination while working with tools; increasing cooperation by encouraging the child to help the parent while the parent is cooking the child's favorite meal).

d. Events and objects that are known to disrupt the child's performance might be removed (as noted in Item 18B).

e. The parents should provide the child with many occasions to perform, and reinforcement for performing, the target behavior and many other appropriate behaviors outside of teaching sessions.

4. Shaping. Ask the parents to define shaping. Then demonstrate shaping and give parents practice at breaking down target behaviors (i.e., task analysis).

A demonstration we have used is to have one consultant or parent in the group shape another parent to find a dollar bill that is hidden in the room. The "finder" leaves the room while the dollar is hidden. For the first few minutes after the finder returns, no one says anything, allowing the finder to search in trial-and-error fashion. This illustrates the difficulty of learning by trial and error. Or, the "shaper" criticizes and nags the finder. For example: "Hurry up! . . . . No, that's wrong! . . . . No, not there, either. . . . Come on, will you?" In either case, the finder is not likely to find the dollar and is likely to become frustrated. The group then discusses the poor shaping methods that were used (perhaps while viewing a videotape of the exercise) and suggests concrete alternatives (written on the blackboard).

Next, the exercise is repeated, with the shaper reinforcing the finder for closer and closer approximations to finding the dollar (using praise or words such as "warm" and "cold"), perhaps using prompts and even engineering the physical environment for easy finding. This time, the finder is likely to find the dollar quickly.

The group then analyzes and discusses shaping, emphasizing:

a. The fact that the finder enacted a number of steps leading to the dollar.

b. The kinds of movements involved in the search (e.g., turning, looking, walking, reaching), many of which were repeated in the process.

c. The importance of immediate feedback regarding the correctness of each approximation (e.g., if the word "warmer" was given a second too late, the finder may have already turned, reached, walked, or looked in the wrong direction).

d. The importance of reinforcing small enough steps (e.g., if the finder was not reinforced for a movement as small or subtle as turning in the right direction, the finder might have returned to a strategy of trial and error, perhaps leading to a deterioration in shaping).

e. The importance of not reinforcing errors (e.g., looking or walking in the opposite direction) and not reinforcing movements at an earlier step in the shaping sequence (e.g., if the finder went back to the door), unless performance had already deteriorated and the process had to be started again at an earlier step.

f. The importance of providing some kind of prompt (pointing, directions, moving the finder through some of the right motions), if the consequences alone (''warm,'' ''cold'') were not sufficient.

Note that you can also provide practice at shaping by using a Skinner box (e.g., shaping a pigeon to peck a lighted disc), or you could show films or videotapes.

In addition to a demonstration of shaping, give parents practice at breaking down behaviors into both successively closer approximations to the terminal (goal) performance (i.e., levels of skill), as well as the sequence of behavioral steps or movements by which a ''task'' is accomplished or an activity is conducted. The first breakdown refers to the quality or skillfulness of the performance as defined by another person (e.g., poor, fair, and perfect articulation). The second refers to the fact that most behaviors occur in sequences or chains (some short and some long) leading to some state of affairs, as defined by both the actor and others (e.g., getting a drink or making a bed, getting ready for school, doing one's job at work). Although both ways of analyzing behavior are important, usually only the first is emphasized in educational programs. The result is that behaviors are shaped in skill, but the now-skillful performances may be isolated from the larger activity sequences of which they could be a part. The child has thus learned ''splinter skills.''

At this point, then:

a. Have parents suggest several behaviors or tasks to break down (perhaps those relevant to early teaching programs).

b. Ask them to suggest the steps (movements) in the sequence by which the behaviors or tasks are generally performed.

c. Ask them to suggest the approximations of skill by which the behaviors or tasks might be taught.

d. Show videotapes of or role-play the behaviors or tasks. Parents' suggestions could be listed on a blackboard.

In reviewing the parents' ideas, emphasize the following:

a. Any behavior can be broken down into infinitely small movements (as seen when carefully observing a task being performed). If a child is having great difficulty learning or performing a behavior, we may have to break down that behavior into small movements (e.g., movements of the child's thumb when buttoning a shirt, movements of the eyes when working a puzzle).

b. When we break down a task into the sequence of component movements, we must consider both the child's skill in performing the component movements and the child's ability to chain the movements into a smooth sequence (that is, the child's ability to discriminate when to go on to the next step; for instance, when his socks are on well enough that he can reach for the shoes).

c. Even if the child cannot perform a target behavior or sequence of behaviors very well, it may be important to teach the child that there is a sequence involved, that behaviors generally occur before and after certain events. Thus, you can demonstrate forward-chaining and back-chaining, and stress the importance of teaching children to use even "small" behaviors (eye contact, properly placing objects) in larger sequences or activities (such as when socializing and performing chores).

5. Signals:

a. Have parents give examples of signals in the different categories (e.g., requests, questions, Grandma's Law).

b. Point out that some signals are used to start a session or a more lengthy task (e.g., "Okay, let's do these puzzles"), while others are used to start or stop a specific behavior ("What is this called?"; "Please put in this piece"; "Hands on the table"; or "Look at me").

c. Stress again the importance of obtaining the child's attention before giving most signals.

d. Point out the difference between signals that are complicated, overly long, wordy, stated as threats, or irrelevant (e.g., "Damnit, tell me what this is!" or "Can you tell me the name of this thing?") versus more simple and direct signals (e.g., "What is this?").

e. Discuss what to do if the child does not cooperate with signals (e.g., turns or walks away from the parent; puts up a fuss; tries to comply, but makes an incorrect response or poor approximation).

6. Prompting. It is important to:

a. Describe the three main types of prompts (visual, verbal, physical or manual).

b. Encourage parents to think of specific ways of using different prompts for various behaviors, and to list alternative prompts for the same behavior, from the least to the most intrusive (e.g., several ways of prompting eye contact, working at small motor tasks, writing letters of the alphabet, adding numbers, making a bed).

c. Give demonstrations and have parents role-play and discuss their suggestions.

d. Remind parents of how signaling, prompting, and rewarding go together, as noted on Figure 8-1 and in the shaping exercise.

*7. **Rewards,*** simply review the component on rewards in APG Item 18 and some main points made in Chapters 3 and 6 of *Educating Children.*

*8. **Replacing problem behaviors*** may require a more lengthy discussion. First, review the guidelines suggested on the APG (Item 18I). Remind parents that if they do not react to problem behaviors, if they make interaction with their child enjoyable for the child (by working on easy enough tasks and by delivering reinforcement frequently), if they systematically reinforce replacement behaviors, and if they operate in that fashion consistently and for long enough, many problem behaviors will begin to be replaced.

However, if the children engage in some behaviors that are disruptive, dangerous, or interfere with learning, more direct efforts might be required to replace them. Thus, you can discuss methods for weakening and replacing problem behaviors which the parents might use during the next weeks. For example, discuss and demonstrate time out, ignoring, the reinforcement of shorter episodes of a problem behavior, and the immediate reinforcement of alternative behaviors. Parents might also be assigned Chapter 15 in *Educating Children.* Section III of Chapter 9 below discusses methods for replacing problem behaviors in more detail.

At this time in the meeting, you can illustrate the above eight components and teaching methods with videotapes or demonstrations of teaching sessions on target behaviors relevant to the parents' first teaching program; for instance, eye contact (with a severely impaired child), cooperation tasks, motor or play skills, speech and language, chores, or academic subjects. Present small portions of the session several times, until the parents can pinpoint all of the important events. Indicate how the various methods contribute to success. Parents can role-play the methods to use in teaching the target behaviors selected for their first teaching program. Note that parents can also receive practice by first observing another parent or a teacher in a classroom and then working with children in the class.

Other Important APG Items. Next, briefly address additional APG items, particularly:

Item 13, Confidence in learning principles

Now remember, don't expect or hope for immediate change in your children. Just make sure that you conduct your teaching program according to the plan you will write. If the plan is proper for them, they will eventually change.

Item 17, Instituting productive exchanges

Although you will now be concentrating on certain target behaviors, remember the more general and frequent exchanges you have with your children. Continue to institute productive exchanges. Give your children lots of occasions to learn and do appropriate behaviors; reinforce good behaviors frequently; make your signals count.

Item 19, Cooperation; Item 23, Scheduled breaks; and Item 24, Reinforcement for self and spouse

Remember to give yourselves the reinforcement you need and deserve. Pay attention to one another. Coach one another and lend a hand. Praise one another. Schedule reinforcement for yourselves and for each other. And, take breaks.

Item 25, Linkage with networks

At this point, you folks have been getting to know one another better. You know what you have been through over the years and you know that it's a good idea to work together. So, we strongly suggest that you call one another and possibly make a home visit or exchange some services.

Item 26, Generalization

As you know, in many cases, the more chances your children have to learn and perform appropriate behaviors, and the more settings in which they learn and perform them, the faster they will learn and the more their behaviors will generalize. So, discuss your teaching program plan with siblings and others, such as neighbors and grandparents. Get them involved. But make sure to give them lots of reinforcement for their efforts. And make a special effort to pay attention to and express appreciation to your other children.

If parents have been experiencing difficulties with any of the above items (or others), discuss it during the Individual Consultation and write a plan for remedying the problems, either during the Individual Consultation or home visit.

Evaluation. Briefly discuss ways parents can evaluate their teaching program (Item 18J) and solve problems (Items 16 and 27) during the coming week. Since problem-solving is a major topic for the next unit, it is sufficient during this meeting to: (a) stress the importance of parents' keeping track of teaching programs by observing the child's and their own behavior and following a problem-solving sequence when problems are noted; (b) review the steps listed in Item 18J on evaluation and revision; and (c) describe what parents should do to solve problems they note. In particular, during the next week or two, they refer to their written teaching program plan to remind themselves of how to teach. In addition, they take data using Table 6-3 (Behavior Count Table) and Figure 6-2 (Behavior

Chart) in *Educating Children,* as well as write a log of important events and their feelings. Also from *Educating Children* assign pages 143 to 145 in Chapter 6 on how to judge the effectiveness of the teaching program, and Chapter 7 if the target behavior does not seem to be increasing. Finally, each parent asks another person to observe his or her teaching behaviors (in particular, APG Items 16 through 18).

In sum, if the teaching program does not seem to be effective during the first week or so, the parents, as much as possible, continue to conduct the program as planned (unless changes are necessary) and try to increase progress by first improving their teaching behaviors, as indicated by Chapter 7 of *Educating Children.* This helps parents to evaluate their programs and solve problems in a businesslike way. Unless they do so, their problem-solving efforts may become haphazard.

Before the Individual Consultations, you might end this portion of the meeting with a short pep talk.

Individual Consultation

Up to now, the consultations might have been between yourself and one family. While you can continue in that fashion, you can also conduct consultations with small groups of parents whose teaching programs for the next week(s) are similar. As mentioned, small groups of this sort may be necessary if the group is large. In any case, small groups may facilitate different families' learning to work together.

The major task for this week's Individual Consultation is to fill out a general teaching program plan (Table 6-2) on pages 146 to 149 of *Educating Children.* Since the parents have already read about how to change the target behavior, seen a videotape or demonstration on how to teach it, and reviewed all components of a teaching program, it should not be difficult or time-consuming to write the plan. However, you may have to help the parents with details of the plan, for example, just which rewards, signals, and prompts to use; when and where to conduct their teaching; which shaping step to start on; how to measure their own and the child's behavior; what short-term goal to work toward; and how to continue to institute productive exchanges at other times of the day. The parents conduct the program as written, at least until they see or speak with you again. In addition, they should read pages 143 to 145 in Chapter 6 and all of Chapter 7 of *Educating Children,* and other APG items (such as 16, 18, and 27) to help them evaluate their program and solve problems.

Finally, discuss and plan parents' work on other APG items, such as cooperation, self-reinforcement, and scheduled breaks. If the parents were having problems on some items, either start or continue a program for remedying them.

Home Visit

This important home visit is best held within a few days after the parents have started their program, both to reinforce them for progress and to correct difficulties before they worsen. In general, the home visit can be conducted much like those described in Chapters 6 and 7.

1. Discuss with parents the components of their overall program thus far, as specified on their Weekly Contract, asking them to refer to their charts and logs. Reinforce effort and progress; label events and processes which illustrate concepts, principles, key ideas, and past suggestions; and help them to develop their own solutions to problems. For instance:

Mrs. Wince: As for the teaching program, we have been trying to increase Marion's cooperation with simple requests, which is Item A4 on the BES. (Parents describe teaching program plan.)

Consultant: Yes. And what does your evaluation indicate?

Mrs. Wince: Well, she is cooperating more often, but then we are asking her to do more things. (Does not sound enthusiastic.)

Consultant: Giving her more occasions or opportunities. . . .

Mrs. Wince: Mm hmm. But I don't think she is more likely to cooperate than before.

Consultant: And you know this because? (Probes objectivity.)

Mr. Wince: The chart. We have counted the number of our requests and the number of her cooperations. Well, both lines have gone up, but they are still separated, about as much as during the baseline. (Shows consultant the charts.)

Consultant: I see. Excellent charts and good description! Now, do you have any ideas why?

Mrs. Wince: Well, I believe we are following the teaching program plan to the letter.

Consultant: Okay, let's look at her behavior and your behavior—the teaching program—more closely. Which rewards are you using? And when is she most and when is she least likely to cooperate? (As part of problem-solving sequence, consultant works toward a description of problem.)

Mrs. Wince: Using activity rewards at certain times, like TV, bath, records, reading to her, wrestling. Oh, and social rewards. Lots of praise and hugging.

Consultant: Mm hmm. That's a nice variety!

Mr. Wince: Our logs show that she cooperates most often as the activity times get closer—mid-morning, afternoon, after supper when I am home, and before her bedtime.

Consultant: Excellent observation! Any explanation?

Mrs. Wince: I guess she knows that if she cooperates at those times, she will get the activity rewards.

Consultant: Very good!

Mr. Wince: And maybe activity rewards are stronger. Sure!! That must be it.

Consultant: You may be right. Good point. What about the social rewards. Are they useless? Should we start putting all of our money on the activity rewards? Should we revise the teaching program? (Prompts parents to use their observations and analysis to make a decision regarding future.)

Mr. Wince: No, I don't think so. She likes the socials. She really lights up when she gets physical contact and enthusiastic praise!

Consultant: Then?

Mrs. Wince: Maybe we should continue as we have been and just make sure that we use lots of enthusiastic social rewards.

Consultant: I agree. But you can't be screaming out praise and squeezing her all of her life. How can you increase the value of the more usual social rewards? (Prompts parents to think about short-run and long-run.)

Mr. Wince: Okay. I got you. Pair 'em up.

Mrs. Wince: Sure, pair up the socials and the activity rewards so that she starts liking the praise more.

Consultant: (Asks for a description of how parents will pair the reinforcers.) . . . Great. I think you two have worked it out. Let's summarize what you've said. . . . Also, I want you to know that you are making very nice progress in being objective, taking part in meetings, learning the principles and methods. And, to hear you talk, it seems as though you are thinking alike and working together. . . . Now, how about other parts of your program? What about scheduled breaks, reinforcement for yourselves, working with other families? . . . .

2. Ask parents to conduct a teaching session. Videotape it (if permissible) and/or take notes; coach, if necessary; and praise efforts and accomplishments. Afterward, you can review your observations, show the videotape, analyze the session, pinpoint parents' strengths, and make suggestions. If the child has been making satisfactory progress, the parents continue the teaching program as planned, at least until the next meeting. If the child has not been making satisfactory progress and if, in light of the parents' skills, the teaching program plan itself seems unsatisfactory, discuss possible revisions, select one, and write it on the Weekly Contract. The parents conduct the revised teaching program until their next contact with you.

3. In general, when helping parents to evaluate their teaching program and solve problems, refer to APG Items 16 and 27 and to the relevant places in *Educating Children* (pages 143 to 145 in Chapter 6, and Chapter 7).

4. Follow the problem-solving sequence if there are problems with other APG items, such as productive participation, cooperation, or personal problems. Chapter 10 suggests alternative methods for solving many problems.

IV. UNIT SIX: EVALUATING THE FIRST TEACHING PROGRAM AND USING A PROBLEM-SOLVING SEQUENCE

The goal for this unit of work is to teach parents to evaluate their home educational program and solve problems in a systematic way. If there is time, introduce the main ideas from Chapter 8 of *Educating Children* on planning and conducting advanced teaching programs (i.e., when several target behaviors are being worked on), and describe methods for teaching new target behaviors for which the children may be ready. After the credit check, move to the main business of the meeting.

Main Business

The main business has three parts: (1) introductory comments, (2) a presentation on program evaluation and problem-solving, and (3) practice exercises on problem-solving and applications to the past week's and future weeks' home programs. You might introduce the main business with comments, such as:

> Well, for the past several weeks you have been making changes in the home. For instance, you have been instituting a program for changing general patterns of interaction or exchange, so as to get your child's behavior changing in a beneficial direction and to help you to learn some of the basic principles of learning and methods of teaching. In addition, you have been working on such things as cooperation in the home, cooperation with people outside the home, self-reinforcement, and possibly methods for relaxing. Finally, you have evaluated your children's strengths and needs, planned a long-term educational program, conducted a baseline on the first target behavior, planned a teaching program for that target behavior, and conducted your first teaching program for about a week. All of this might be called your home program. As you can see, there are many parts to it.
>
> The question is, how do you keep track of how well your whole program is working? How do you keep track of progress in the parts, like the teaching program for your children or the programs you might be following for changing some of your own behaviors? And, most important, how do you go about correcting problems in the overall home program or its parts? For instance, what do you do if you simply have a feeling that your child is not making progress in a certain teaching program? What do you do if, day after day, you conduct sessions to teach some behavior, and your child keeps making errors or becomes whiney? What do you do if your charts show that a target behavior is not changing much in the right direction? Or, concerning yourselves, what if you begin to make pessimistic statements to yourselves, feel that you have less energy to run your programs, or find that your efforts to learn how to relax do not seem to be working?

Well, one thing is certain. You should not lose hope or become desperate, because you have all made progress in a rather short time. You have become more skillful in many ways, and your children's behaviors have started to change in a beneficial direction. But hope, as you know, is not enough. You have to do something about problems before they get out of hand, before you do lose hope and motivation, before your home programs come to a standstill or deteriorate.

Today we are going to talk about how to keep track of your home programs, or evaluate them, and to solve problems in a businesslike way, that is, by moving in a sequence of small, planned steps. Now, you may be saying to yourselves, "Oh, God! Another bunch of small steps. More to do!!" Well, the task of evaluating your programs and solving problems is not as complex or difficult as you may think. Here is why:

First, you have already done complex tasks. Remember when you used Chapter 4 of *Educating Children* to evaluate your children and plan a long-term educational program? Surely that seemed like a tall order at the time. It had a lot of steps and involved many new ideas. But it wasn't impossible. And, looking back, was it such a big deal? . . . Second, even though you have been learning and doing many, many new things in the home, your lives are no more complicated than before this program. Sure, you may still feel a bit uncomfortable about all the new words and methods, but there are still only 24 hours in the day. The fact is, with practice, the new ideas and methods become second nature or habit. In addition, if we are successful, your lives are likely to be easier in the future because of them. Evaluating your home program and solving problems in a businesslike way is better than insurance. It will help you to make sense out of your whole program and all that you are doing, and will help you to keep the ship tight and on course.

One last point. The steps involved in evaluating and problem-solving can be applied to all parts of your home program. In fact, the steps are so general that you can use them to help other people in other settings. We are going to be using the same steps for keeping track of and solving problems in this Program. But, we have to start somewhere. Since you have been conducting your first teaching program for about a week, and since that is probably on your minds the most right now, let's apply the methods of evaluation and problem-solving to it.

Presenting Program Evaluating and Problem-Solving. Before examining each step, you might: (1) point out that the steps and methods involved in evaluation and problem-solving are found in APG Items 16, 18J, and 27, and Chapters 6 (pages 143–145) and 7 of *Educating Children* and that the steps can be applied to any part of their overall home program; (2) ask parents to read the steps in their APG as you examine each step; and (3) provide parents with a written summary or copy of the following pages and a copy of Figure 8-2.

Here, then, are the steps in the evaluation and problem solving sequence. (See also Goldfried and Davison, 1976; Haley, 1976; and Mahoney, 1977.)

1. As a program is being conducted (e.g., a teaching program), measure progress or change through direct observation, and record observations on logs, behavior count tables, charts, videotape, or audiotape.

2. Evaluate the apparent effectiveness of a program (e.g., as noted on pages 143 to 145 of *Educating Children*).

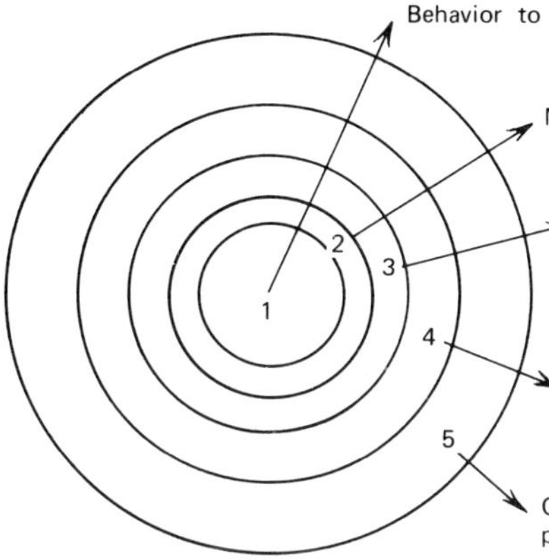

Figure 8-2 Relationships between parts of the overall home program.

a. If data and/or parents' perceptions seem to indicate that a program is going well, parents recheck their measurements and obtain another opinion (reliability). For example, they examine definitions of target behaviors for clarity and observability; check charts for accuracy; compare videotapes or audiotapes with observations and charts. If it is confirmed that the program is going well, they continue it as planned for another week or so to produce more improvement in target behaviors. Then, they institute the next steps in the program (e.g., work on harder steps in shaping; shift to a more intermittent schedule of rewards; fade prompts; use more common rewards) or plan and conduct teaching programs for the next target behaviors or skill areas (as described in Chapter 8 of *Educating Children*).

b. If data and/or parents' perceptions indicate that a program is not going well, parents contain or manage the problem for the time being and begin to institute a problem-solving sequence (using APG Items 14, 16 through 18, and 27, Chapter 7 of *Educating Children*, and perhaps a written summary of this presentation). Parents respond to perceived problems with statements, such as:

> Relax. Now, just what is going on here? How do I correct this? What is the next step in solving problems?

rather than

> Oh, good grief. It's not working. I don't know what to do.

In addition, parents seek help from others (e.g., teachers, language specialists, physicians) to confirm their evaluation; pinpoint, describe, and analyze the problem; and plan and institute a program to solve it.

3. Pinpoint, describe, and analyze the problem situation or events. In general, problems can be defined as the disparity between goals and what is actually occurring. Our major assumption is that beneficial behavior change will eventually occur (i.e., goals will be achieved) if we can arrange the proper learning environment. Therefore, to solve problems, we must determine just what the present learning environment is like (both for children and parents), how it is related to the changes that are or are not occurring satisfactorily, and what can be done to change the environment so as to generate change in relation to goals (i.e, solve the problem).

a. Pinpointing and describing problems within the environment means answering the questions: What? When? Where? How Long? How Often? Who? For example, if the problem is a decrease in the child's cooperation, just what does the child do when the child fails to cooperate and when the child does cooperate? How often do cooperation and noncooperation occur in relation to the number of requests given? Are some types of requests more likely to produce cooperation or noncooperation? Are certain prompts more helpful than others? Are some rewards more effective than others? Is the child more likely to cooperate at certain times, in certain settings, or with some people? How long has cooperation been decreasing? That is, did cooperation increase for a time and then begin to decrease (in which case, the child may have become satiated, overworked, or the parents may have stopped teaching according to their plan)? Did cooperation decrease almost as soon as the teaching program began (in which case, the plan may have been poor, e.g., ineffective rewards, tasks too hard)? Or is the present decrease in cooperation part of a trend that started long ago? (In this case, the teaching program may simply be poor and/or the parents may not be following it).

Note that the same questions would be asked if the problem concerned behaviors of the parents (e.g., lack of progress in their use of a program in progressive relaxation training or in scheduling breaks).

b. On the other hand, analyzing or explaining the problem means showing the probable relationships between parts of the overall home program (the learning environment for parents and children) and the lack of beneficial change in the targeted behavior. One way of depicting and analyzing relationships involves the use of concentric circles representing clusters of items influencing behavior. Each circle consists of APG items and chapters in *Educating Children*.

By examining the overall program, beginning with circle 1 and moving outward, both you and the parents can: (1) see how the parts seem to be interrelated and (2) tentatively decide where in the overall program to intervene so as to solve the problem.

For example, regarding circle 1, it may be that the target behavior is not changing satisfactorily due to interference of certain problem behaviors. If so, the overall program might be left alone at first and efforts might be directed toward replacing the problem behaviors. On the other hand, as indicated by circle 2, measurement may be inaccurate or incomplete. Perhaps the behavior is changing satisfactorily, but progress is not reflected in the data. On the other hand, perhaps a problem has not been noticed at all. In effect, to solve the apparent or actual problem the parents may have to become stronger on APG Items 12 (objectivity) or 22 (honesty). For instance, they might continue their teaching program as planned, but receive extra practice on objectivity, increase the number of times they measure the target behavior, or measure it in a different way.

Regarding circle 3, two questions must be answered. First, is the program being carried out as planned? In particular, are the parents replacing counter-productive with productive exchanges? Are they instituting productive exchanges properly and often enough? Are they using the specified teaching methods with enough skill? To answer these questions, the parents, you, and others examine the parents' teaching behaviors using APG Items 17 and 18, the Checklist on Common Problems of Teaching in Chapter 7 of *Educating Children*, as well as later chapters in *Educating Children* which describe methods for teaching target behaviors.

If it is found that parents are not skilled enough in using the methods specified on the program plan, the plan itself can be left alone while the parents are given more practice in using the methods. Failure to actually carry out the program plan, on the other hand, may be traced to a lack of clarity in the plan or to difficulties with other aspects of their home program, such as marital problems, personal problems, or fatigue. These difficulties are addressed in circle 5.

Second, is the program plan itself adequate? For instance, is the target behavior broken down into small enough steps? Are effective rewards, prompts, and signals being used? Are teaching sessions scheduled often enough and at the best times? Additional problems here are noted on the Checklist of Common Problems of Teaching on page 169 of *Educating Children*. If the teaching program plan does not seem adequate, it should be revised and the parents can try again. In revising the plan, however, it may be best to revise few components of it at first, changing more components later, if necessary. Chapter 7 of *Educating Children* (pp. 167–168) offers guidelines on what to change.

With respect to circle 4, it may be that the child is not yet ready to work on the pinpointed target behavior or in the chosen skill area, or that the child has needs that were not determined earlier. Thus, you and the parents check the parents' evaluation of their child (i.e., their scoring of the Behavior Evaluation Scale) and their selection of the skill area and target behavior. In addition, more evaluation information might be obtained to see if different behaviors or skill areas should be worked on at this time, or if different teaching methods might be used (and specified on a revised program plan). For instance, the child may have an undetected hearing problem. Hence, even if the parents are working on the right behaviors (such as cooperation), the child might be supplied with a hearing aide and/or more use should be made of visual prompts.

Finally, concerning circle 5, the parents' ability to plan or conduct their programs may be hampered by difficulties with other items noted on the APG. Thus, you and the parents should examine those items to see: (1) if, in fact, there are weaknesses or difficulties and (2) how any difficulties may be interfering with the program the parents are running. Remedial programs are then planned and conducted. For example, the teaching program plan may be adequate and the parents may have sufficient skill to conduct it, but may be bothered by extreme tension or by marital difficulties. Indeed, Readiness to Change may have weakened, e.g., expectations of success. In this case, the teaching program plans might be left alone while efforts are made to decrease tension, improve marital interaction, and increase expectations of success. Chapter 10 addresses such problems.

Note that in using Figure 8-2, trace possible interrelationships among the concentric circles. For example, a problem in measurement may have led the parents to underestimate the amount of beneficial change taking place, leading to pessimism and self-blame, a decrease in motivation and energy, a deterioration in teaching skills and performance of the teaching program itself, and a worsening of the behaviors being worked on. An understanding of such relationships may prevent parents from blaming one element of the family system (e.g., themselves or their child) for a lack of progress. The question of where to intervene in solving problems is addressed in the fourth and fifth steps discussed below.

4. Reframe or reconceptualize the problem and goals as needed. In order to solve a problem, you and the parents may have to reframe your conception of the situation and/or goals for the future.

By "reframing" is meant seeing a problem or situation from a different perspective, and perhaps seeing how one's past point of view has led to unproductive solutions or prevented one from seeing any solution. For example, a 6-year-old child may not know how to bathe herself. When put in the bathtub, she yells louder and louder for her parents to come back. Her father may conceptualize the situation as follows:

> Janet is 6 years old. She is old enough to learn how to bathe herself. Yet, she may need someone to teach her how. However, she is yelling. If I go to her and help her to bathe herself, I will be reinforcing yelling, which is counterproductive. If I do not go to her, she will not learn how to bathe herself, which is also not productive. So, I am damned if I do and damned if I don't.

The problem appears unsolvable to her father because of the way he is viewing the situation. He is framing it as a situation in which teaching her to bathe requires actually putting her through the motions while she is in the tub. Thus, his view presents him with only two solutions, which constitute a dilemma: either he helps her bathe or he does not. However, the situation can be viewed in a different way, from which other solutions can be derived. To develop a new point of view or framework, he might ask himself and answer several questions; for instance:

> How am I viewing this situation?
>
> What assumptions am I making about the problem and about solutions?
>
> How is my point of view and set of assumptions preventing me from arriving at a productive solution?
>
> Can I view this situation in another way?

As a result, he might realize the following:

> Of course!! I have been assuming that Janet is yelling for me to bathe her. But she may be yelling for me to be with her as well. Also, I have been assuming that I have to put her through the motions in order to teach her to bathe herself, and that the teaching has to be done while she is in the bathtub. But, there are other ways and places to teach her. And, I have been assuming that it is an either-or situation: either I am with her or I am not. But there are degrees. I can be partially with her; I can be with her for greater or lesser amounts of time and distances.
>
> So, how do I give her attention, teach her without actually putting her through the motions, and teach her not to yell for me? How can I be with her and not be with her? I've got it!!!I can sit with her in the bathroom while she is in the tub. I can give her instructions and praise her while she follows the directions for bathing herself. That will teach her to bathe herself. . . .Uh oh! How do I avoid reinforcing her yelling? . . . . Okay. This time I'll wait until she stops yelling and then go in and try my new program. Next time I will explain the deal to her beforehand—that I will stay with her as long as she is not yelling or whining. Gradually, I will fade myself out of the bathroom. When she is having a good time, I will leave for a few seconds and then return, slowly increasing the amount of time. Or I can teach her to bathe in her bedroom—how to soap the wash cloth and rub herself. Then she can try it in the tub.

In sum, reframing the situation is aided by the following:

a. Discovering and describing past or present conceptions of and efforts to solve the problem.

b. Discovering and describing the results of past or present conceptions of and efforts to solve the problem. Specifically, how has the conception of the problem helped or hindered efforts to solve it? How have efforts to solve the problem affected people's expectations, feelings, relationships? For instance, has ignoring disruptive behaviors worked in the past? How were parents affected when they found that their past efforts did not work? The point is to help people see how their view of and assumptions regarding a problem partly determine the solutions they develop, and that certain of their past problem-solving efforts may have been more successful than others (in which case, they might be considered for use now and in the future).

c. Developing new conceptions or frames by:

1. Trying to consider more of the components of the situation.
2. Trying to discover the "bigger picture" (e.g., that the situation may be more than just a child yelling for help).
3. Using analogies and paradoxes (e.g., "How can I be with someone and not be with someone at the same time? . . . By seeing my presence at any time as part of a process of fading my presence.").
4. Brainstorming as many new frames and solutions as possible.

Excellent discussions of reframing are found in Watzlawick et al. (1974), Prince (1976), and Haley (1976, especially Chapter 3).

It may also be important to reexamine and perhaps revise goals. This issue was discussed at the end of Chapter 4. In particular, parents might be helped to reexamine their reasons for wanting to achieve certain goals, that is, what they think will be the consequences of attaining or failing to attain their goals. For example, the parents may dread what will happen if they are not successful. This may be partly responsible for inaccurate measurement or for tension that interferes with skillfully using certain teaching methods. Or, a belief that there will be little difference in their lives even if they achieve their short-term goals (e.g., their lives will not be more satisfying or their child's opportunities in life will not be increased if they teach their child to communicate) may be responsible for their not carrying out their program as it was planned.

It may be necessary to revise long-term and/or short-term goals. Specifically, in view of additional evaluations and present teaching efforts, are the long-term goals as likely to be achieved as was anticipated during the Pre-Program stage? Are present teaching programs too costly as currently planned and conducted? Should goals be broken down into still-smaller steps? For example, given a child's slow progress in a well-run speech training program, even if the goal of teaching the child to talk still seems feasible (but perhaps more distant), it may be better to put speech as a goal on the "back burner" and work toward goals such as self-help skills, which may be easier to accomplish and in a shorter time, thus increasing the success of parents and children.

After the situation, problem, and goals have been reframed, solutions are sought.

5. Develop alternative plans for solving the problem (achieving short-term goals) in the context of long-term goals, and select the first plan to try. In developing plans, specify just what will be done (i.e., methods) and what resources will be used (e.g., people, places, time, materials, responsibilities of participants). For instance, if the problem is a lack of increase in the child's cooperation, alternative plans might involve:

a. Continuing the current teaching programs for several more days, but measuring the behavior more carefully or in a different way.

b. Giving parents extra practice on using the prescribed teaching methods.

c. Continuing the current teaching program, but also starting a program to decrease problem behaviors.

d. Revising the teaching program in minor ways (e.g., different rewards, more prompts).

e. Working on a different target behavior or skill area.

f. Strengthening other APG items that have a bearing on the parents' conducting their programs.

Alternative plans should be listed in the order for trying them.

The first plan to try might be selected on the basis of the following criteria: (a) The plan may produce the most beneficial change at the least cost (i.e., the most "bang for the buck"). While I am not able to say exactly what produces the most payoff for the least cost, improving parents' skills for conducting their teaching programs is imperative and is likely to increase their ability to decide for themselves. (b) The prerequisites for instituting the plan are available. For example, the parents have (or should be taught) the necessary teaching skills; additional personnel are willing and able to assist; the child has the "basic behaviors" needed. (c) The plan will be inhibited by the fewest factors. For instance, it is consistent with parents' goals (old or revised) and point of view; it will disrupt home life the least.

6. After selecting the first plan, write it (using much the same format as a teaching program plan).

7. Institute the problem-solving plan and measure progress and problems.

8. After conducting the plan for a week or so, evaluate it and decide what to do next. If it is working satisfactorily (e.g., the child's behavior has started to improve), continue the plan as noted in item 2a above. If it does not seem to be working, follow steps 2b through 7 above and try again (e.g., select the second problem-solving plan).

Practice Exercises on Problem-Solving and Applications to the Home Program. One way of strengthening parents' use of the problem-solving sequence is to describe several hypothetical problem situations similar to those they may be encountering. The goal is for the parents to follow the problem-solving sequence and use their book, APG, and data which you provide, to ask appropriate questions and develop solutions. You might describe hypothetical problems with the following data: a sample child's BES and supplementary evaluations; the teaching program plan for a target behavior being worked on (the plan may or may not be suited to the evaluation and may or may not be detailed enough); behavior count tables and charts (which may or may not be accurate and which might show that the target behavior is not changing satisfactorily); portions of the sample parents' logs, indicating their expectations, feelings, cooperation; and videotape showing how the sample parents conduct teaching sessions on the target behavior. Instead of presenting the entire case at once, you might give parents portions of the above information, setting the occasion for them to ask for more on the basis of steps in the problem-solving sequence.

During the exercise, encourage parents to search for the right questions, analyze and reframe the situation, and make recommendations for problem-solving plans. If needed, you might encourage them with statements and questions, such as:

1. Okay, here is a behavior chart. What does it seem to be saying? How can we find out if it is accurate? Is there anything else that we ought to know about the child's behavior, about the rest of the home program, or about the family situation?

2. Compare the teaching program plan with the BES. Are they working in the right skill area and on the right behaviors? Is the teaching program plan adequate in itself?

3. What do the parents' logs tell us? (Marital problems? Personal problems? Decline in Readiness to Change?)

4. Do we know enough about the child's strengths and needs? What other problems of the child might account for the lack of progress? Where might we find this information?

5. What is happening on the videotape? Look at the details of the child's performance. (For example, hand-eye coordination, apparent muscle tension, apparent satisfaction or dissatisfaction.) Are the parents building on the child's strengths? Are they remedying apparent weaknesses? (For example, do they fail to physically prompt a child with obvious motor deficits?) Look at the parents' behaviors. Are they following the teaching program plan? Compare their teaching skills with the list in Item 18. How well do they signal, prompt, and reward? How well are they shaping? How well is the teaching setting designed?

6. How might the lack of progress in the child affect the parents?

7. Okay. You have suggested one thing they might do to solve the problem (e.g., to reward the child more often for approximations or to practice relaxation.) What are all of the possible results that you can think of? How might such a plan affect the teaching program, the parents themselves, and the rest of the family situation?

8. Let's see if we can view this situation in a different way.

9. What else needs to be considered or included in carrying out the plan you suggested?

10. Why do you think that is the best plan to try first?

11. How many ways can you think of to improve the parents' teaching skills?

12. How would you know if the plan you just suggested were working well or not?

13. What other things might you try if the first plan were clearly not working?

After, or instead of, the above exercise, you can help the parents to apply the problem-solving sequence to their own first teaching program. In general, you can follow the same procedures as in the suggested practice exercise. That is, the parents describe their teaching program plan and how they conducted the program; the parents then present their data and evaluate apparent results (with comments from the group); a videotape is shown, and is analyzed by the parents and the group; problems are pinpointed, described, and analyzed; suggestions are made; new and old methods are demonstrated and role-played; and plans for the next week are tentatively established (to be firmed up during the Individual Consultation and home visit).

Activities for the Next Week.

If time remains and progress was satisfactory during the past week, present some of the main ideas in Chapter 8 of *Educating Children* on how to plan and conduct a teaching program for several target behaviors at the same time. Describe teaching methods the parents can use for the next target behaviors. Both of the above topics are discussed in the next chapter.

Before dividing into small groups for the Individual Consultation, give the parents time to voice any fears, changes in expectations or self-confidence, or other problems. In many cases, these can be handled through group discussion and by the leader's stressing that: much progress has been made already; the Program has worked for many others; less than complete success is expected and even desirable; we are moving in small steps (one of which is to determine the conditions of learning and behavior change that are adequate for everyone involved); and that we may travel down several dark alleys and make several false starts before we find the right conditions.

Activities for the next week, then, include continuing to conduct the past week's teaching program, making minor revisions as indicated, and/or conducting a program to solve problems. In addition, in preparation for later meetings, assign Chapter 8 of *Educating Children* and perhaps a later chapter on how to teach the next target behavior.

Individual (or Small Group) Consultation

During the consultation, you and other parents can help each family to plan its overall home program, which is to be written on a Weekly Contract, specifying as much as possible the teaching program plan, any plans to solve problems, phone calls and/or home visits with the consultant and others, the scheduling of breaks, self-reinforcement, and so on.

Home Visit

A home visit from you is important if the parents had problems in their first teaching program. Help them to review their overall program in terms of the problem-solving sequence; discuss and demonstrate methods to use in working with their child or in conducting special programs for themselves (such as relaxation training); finalize their overall program plans; observe and coach them in conducting their programs.

9 ACTIVITIES FOR THE REMAINING UNITS OR MEETINGS

In general, meetings for the remaining units of work can be conducted like earlier ones: credit-check; reviewing and evaluating the past weeks' home programs; giving a presentation on the main business (e.g., how to teach the next skill area, or a special topic, such as generalization, solving personal problems or long-term planning); giving the assignment for the next week (conducting teaching programs based on readings from Chapters 9 through 15 in *Educating Children* and working on other APG items; holding an individual or small group consultation; and, during the week, making phone calls and/or home visits.

The following sections address topics that can be part of the main business of remaining meetings or units. As noted in Chapters 3 and 4, meetings might be weekly, biweekly, or scheduled at longer intervals.

I. ADVANCED TEACHING PROGRAMS

In our programs, this topic is part of the main business for the seventh meeting or unit of work. That is why the assignment given at the end of the sixth meeting or unit was Chapter 8 in *Educating Children*. In addition to discussing advanced teaching programs, you can give a presentation on how to teach more difficult target behaviors in the skill area the parents have been working on or, if the children are ready, the next skill area on the skill sequence. For example, if most parents' first teaching programs were in the Learning Readiness skills area, the seventh unit might focus on Looking, Listening, and Moving skills.

Reviewing the Main Points on Advanced Teaching Programs

The main points in Chapter 8 of *Educating Children* to review and apply to the home programs are as follows:

Selecting the Next Target Behavior or Skill Area. Parents select the next target behavior or skill area using the child's evaluation (e.g., the Behavior Evaluation Scale and Table), the Table of Basic Behaviors, the Skill Sequence

Table, and baseline measurements on the behavior they have tentatively selected. For practice during the meeting, the parents can select the next target behavior or skill area for their own children (as well as hypothetical children) using the above materials, discussing their decision-making process with the other parents.

Maintaining Old Target Behaviors. When working on new target behaviors, old behaviors are increased in strength and maintained by continuing to provide the child both with occasions to respond and reinforcement during teaching sessions and at other times during the day.

Strengthening New Target Behaviors. Remind the parents that when starting new teaching programs, they may have to use stronger and more frequent rewards and provide more extensive prompting. For certain behaviors, they might institute some variety of token system. For instance, to strengthen cooperation with requests, chores and self-help routines, or to strengthen performance during sit-down sessions (attending, working at the tasks), the parents might reinforce the child with tokens, stars, check-marks, or even money. Token and contract systems are described in Chapter 8 of *Educating Children*, and in Homme et al. (1970), Patterson (1971), Miller (1975), Walker and Buckley (1974), and Christopherson et al. (1972). At this time, the parents might brainstorm possible token systems to use in the near future.

Avoiding Satiation and Boredom. Remind parents to switch tasks and rewards during sessions and from day-to-day. Also, give them the opportunity to generate and share a rather long list of possible reinforcers. Although this was done during the third unit of work, the children may now be reinforced by many more events which the parents should be able to pinpoint.

Recognizing and Strengthening Spontaneous Behaviors. The parents also keep their eyes open for seemingly spontaneous appropriate behaviors. For example, there may be improvements in behaviors that the parents are not working on (e.g., increased cooperation or smiling) or the child may begin to emit behaviors without being signaled (e.g., performing chores without being asked). Parents should reinforce such behaviors with much enthusiasm, describe them in their logs, and perhaps begin planning to further strengthen them in a teaching program.

Normalizing Behavior. Parents begin working toward the normalization of behavior. So far, they have been increasing the skill, frequency, and duration of certain appropriate behaviors. But, normalization also involves learning and performing behaviors under more usual or common conditions, as well as performing behaviors in more complex sequences or chains, either independently or with others. The latter two aspects of normalization should be addressed at this time.

First, stress that as a target behavior increases in frequency or skill, the parents should: hold teaching sessions and reinforce the child in a wider variety of settings and times, use more common social and activity rewards, move toward intermittent reward schedules, and have additional persons work with and reinforce the child.

Second, pay special attention to the ways parents might use activity rewards (e.g., in Grandma's Law). For example, they can discuss and list various ways to arrange for enjoyable activities to follow productive teaching sessions and the performance of appropriate behaviors during the day.

Third, address the distinction that Ferster (1967a, 1967b), Ferster and Simons (1966), and Peterson (1976) have made between ''arbitrary'' and ''natural'' reinforcement contingencies or exchanges. Their ideas can be presented, discussed, and applied to the parents' home programs.

In particular, Ferster and Simons state the following about natural reinforcers and contingencies (exchanges):

> Natural reinforcement contingencies persist without the intervention of the parent and therapist, and they do not require collateral aversive stimuli to be effective. (Ferster, 1967a:346.)
>
> Natural reinforcement begins with a performance already in the individual's repertoire reinforced by an event which occurs reliably in the millieu. (Ferster, 1967a:343.)
>
> We speak of reinforcements being natural when the other environments available to the child . . . would also reinforce the same behavior in the same way.'' (Ferster and Simons, 1966:66.)
>
> The individual is reinforced by the immediate and specific behaviors generated by the stimulus.

The above statements apply both to negative reinforcement (aversive control) and positive reinforcement. For instance, putting on sunglasses, squinting, or turning one's head constitute a class of behaviors that are negatively reinforced in a natural way by the escape from or future avoidance of bright light. In this contingency, ''any behavior which reduces the aversive stimulus'' will be reinforced (Ferster, 1967a:342). Similarly, turning a door knob (in any way which results in the door opening) may be positively reinforced because it enables the person to come into contact with positive reinforcers in the next room. These contingencies are natural because: some approximation of the necessary class of behavior is already in the person's repertoire; the class of behavior reinforced is large; no extra aversive stimuli are required to encourage the person to engage in the behaviors; no other persons are necessarily needed to manage the contingency; the contingency operates in many environments; and the individual directly benefits from the behaviors.

In contrast to natural reinforcement, arbitrary reinforcement involves the following (Ferster, 1967a, pp. 343–344):

> . . . the . . . stimulus . . . is applied arbitrarily by one person to control the behavior of another.
>
> . . . the performance that is reinforced is specified narrowly. . . .
>
> Arbitrary reinforcement does not need to take the individual's current repertoire into account nearly as much as is the case with natural reinforcement.
>
> [The relationship between the behavior and the reinforcement is socially rather than physically determined. For example, the] . . . child cannot simply escape from the parent's anger as he could from a hot fire because there is no behavior in his repertoire which has any physical relation to the aversive stimulus. The parents require a particular performance and adjust the application of the aversive stimulus until they get it.
>
> The person may be able to temporarily terminate the aversive stimulus (in an arbitrary aversive contingency), but the controller can reapply it any time he or she wants another performance.
>
> . . . control by an arbitrary reinforcer . . . is designed to preempt the rest of the individual's behavior. . . . The requirement that he emit a particular performance will preempt all other behaviors. . . . The person who applies an arbitrary reinforcer intends to produce a particular form of behavior.
>
> The reinforcement is arbitrary because there is no reinforcer currently maintaining the desired behavior or behavior similar to it in the child's repertoire. With an arbitrary stimulus, the controller can coerce a particular performance, whatever the child's current repertoire.
>
> [The behavior] which is arbitrarily reinforced without reference to the child's repertoire may disappear as soon as the acute intervention ends unless there is planned transition to a natural reinforcer.
>
> The immediate and specific behavior generated by the arbitrary stimulus reinforces the controller.

Like natural reinforcement, arbitrary reinforcement can be either negative or positive. For example, one can arbitrarily reinforce a child negatively by removing threats (aversive stimuli) when the child starts working on or finishes tasks. On the other hand, one can arbitrarily reinforce the child's performance positively with food and tokens. Note that the use of activity rewards, as in Grandma's Law, does not insure that the contingency or exchange is natural. The exchange—"If you put on your coat, you can have a cookie"—is arbitrary because the relationship between putting on a coat and receiving a cookie is socially determined; the behavior that produces the cookie (putting on a coat) is narrowly defined; control of the contingency is in the hands of another person; the behavior is likely to disappear when it no longer produces cookies; and the contingency can be reapplied any time the controller wants the child to put on a coat. A more natural contingency would be. "As soon as you put on your coat, you will be warm" (where the coat will protect the child from the cold).

After presenting some of the above points (which it would be well for the parents to write down), you can give the parents practice at: pinpointing, describing, and analyzing a number of arbitrary and natural contingencies; brainstorming ways of strengthening behaviors with natural contingencies; and applying the ideas to their home programs. Specifically, parents should begin to find ways of shifting from arbitrary exchanges they may be using to more natural ones, and find possible behaviors which they may be able to strengthen with natural exchanges alone.

The following table of arbitrary and corresponding natural exchanges might be useful for parents to have. Most examples are adapted from Ferster and Simons (1966) and Ferster (1967b). Encourage parents to think of and list others as well.

Fourth, discuss ways to build more complex sequences, chains, or units of behavior. This is an extremely important aspect of normalization for, if target behaviors are taught in isolation from one another, and are not integrated into larger units of activity, there may be little qualitative improvement in the children's participation in the social world. In effect, they may acquire a number of "splinter skills" which occur in few settings and are rarely emitted unless signaled by others. The too-common example of this is children who learn to work puzzles or to sort shapes with no end other than the completion of the puzzle or the sorting of the shapes, and who do so only at the table when the parent or teacher is present. Moreover, the subskills or movements involved in these tasks (e.g., hand-eye coordination) may not transfer to the performance of other tasks.

The topic might be introduced with the following comments:

> This question may sound strange, but here it is. You are all working to increase certain target behaviors. Why? (Give parents a chance to respond. They may say that some behaviors are important in and of themselves or that some behaviors must be learned before others.)
>
> You are right that some behaviors seem to be prerequisites for the learning of harder behaviors, and that some behaviors seem important in and of themselves. But what makes any behavior important? . . .
>
> Okay, behaviors are important because they help the child to participate in this world, in this society, and in your family. As you know, there is a world out there—a world of objects, space, time, people, and events—which surrounds us till the day we die. Somehow we learn to fit into it and take part in it. We learn about objects, spaces, and time. We learn what people do and we learn to do things alone and with others. We learn how to move through space and among objects without falling all over and getting bruised. We learn how to come into contact with things with our vision, hearing and touching. We learn how to take hold of and manipulate things by reaching, grasping, picking up, holding, turning, twisting, placing, and fitting. We learn how to fit into social activities with many of the same behaviors. We learn to look for, look at, reach for, go to, touch and hold, listen to and understand other people. And we learn how to do things like others do them, both alone and with others.
>
> So, you teach your child to make eye contact! What for? So that he will get a piece of food?! No, that can't be the reason!! That's an arbitrary exchange. Eye contact,

TABLE 9-1 Arbitrary and Natural Exchanges or Contingencies

Arbitrary Exchanges	*Natural Exchanges*
1. Child would rather roughhouse with parent than work puzzles. So, child is reinforced with candy for working puzzles.	1. Parent interrupts roughhousing, brings child to table and helps child to put in the last puzzle piece; then they return to roughhousing. After a minute or so, they go back to the puzzles. As time goes by, the prompts are faded and child does more and more puzzles in exchange for roughhousing.
2. Child learns to turn doorknob and open door in order to escape or avoid threats or forceful prompting.	2. Child learns to turn doorknob in order to enter room containing enjoyable activities and objects.
3. Child wants to go outside, but has removed shoes and socks. Parent uses food, praise, or tokens to reinforce child for putting them back on, or child puts them back on to escape threatening talk from parent.	3. Parent puts child's socks back on, but child must put shoes on by himself (assuming child can do this) before child can go outside.
4. Parent teaches child to climb using food, praise, or tokens.	4. Parent locates a toy child enjoys and teaches child to climb so as to gain access to the toy. For example, child learns to climb upon a rocking horse in small steps.
5. Parent teaches child to remove jacket using food, praise, tokens.	5. Parent removes jacket from child, except for child's last hand. Child removes hand and goes on to some activity child enjoys, or child is reinforced by escape from uncomfortable heat of jacket. Parent gradually has child remove more of jacket (back-chaining).
6. Child must complete tasks in order to earn token. Child needs one token in order to get snack. No token, no snack.	6. If child's performance of tasks is weak (either lack of skill or noncompliance), parent adjusts performance requirement to match child's repertoire, e.g., at first, child might simply come to parent

(continued)

TABLE 9-1 *(Continued)*

Arbitrary Exchanges	*Natural Exchanges*
	when called in order to get snack; later, child might have to sit at table; still later, child might be required to put in the last piece of puzzle (perhaps with prompting), and still later, child might be required to finish the task.
7. Child throws her plate of food onto the floor. Child is spanked.	7 Child is physically prevented from engaging in any other behaviors except picking up the plate (or some approximation as determined by child's repertoire).
8. Child constantly holds on to her doll. Doll is taken from child's hands. Child cries. Crying is ignored. Crying finally stops. Child is given bites of food (or praise, tokens) for longer and longer intervals of not crying.	8. Parent locates some activity that reinforces noncrying behaviors. For example, parent puts child on rocking horse, while child is holding doll. As child's behavior comes under control of the rocking horse (e.g., child moves in time to the rocking and/or holds on to the handles), doll is removed for a few seconds (short enough that child will not start crying). Doll is returned before crying starts. Intervals of rocking without the doll are gradually increased. Vigor with which parent rocks horse is increased to encourage child to hang on even tighter. Thus, the extinction of crying is a "by-product of the reinforcement of other behaviors" (Ferster, 1967b:147).
9. Child pulls parent's hair. Parent talks to child or struggles to get free. Parent finally decides to ignore hair-pulling or forceably removes child's hands. Child releases grip to escape discomfort resulting from parent's efforts to free hair.	9. Parent holds child's hand close to parent's head so that child cannot pull. Parent releases child's hand as child relaxes grip (negatively reinforces behavior in the right direction).

> working at small motor tasks or talking, just to get food, poker chips, or even praise? No, you might use food, poker chips, and praise to strengthen these behaviors now, but getting food, poker chips, and praise is not what makes these behaviors important. What makes them important is that these and other behaviors are used over and over again in many, many situations and they are somehow strung together into sequences or patterns that enable the child to fit into the patterns of living that are already out there and being performed by others.
>
> Take working puzzles. Who cares!! Is it puzzles that are so important? Can you get a job working puzzles? Can you occupy all of your free time doing that? Of course not! Working at puzzles and other small motor tasks now is important because of the smaller behaviors or movements that are involved. To work a puzzle requires looking at, reaching for, grasping, turning, and fitting. These are the movements that are important. Why? The answer is that these movements are used over and over in many other tasks and in many situations in life.
>
> Also, working puzzles, blocks, or workbooks is a unit of activity—a unit that might be called "working at some kind of task." And isn't that unit important? . . . . Sure, working at something, no matter what it is, occurs over and over in life. We work at chores; we work on a job. It is a unit of activity that has a beginning, middle, and ending. Right now, the children may be learning the small movements involved in working puzzles and other small motor tasks, but they are also learning about the unit of working itself; they are learning about beginnings, middles, and endings of that unit. And if we teach our children properly, they will learn to use that general unit of working in other settings and with other tasks besides puzzles, such as doing chores and lessons.
>
> So, to sum it up, the behaviors you are teaching now are important because they consist of even smaller movements or skills which are used to perform other behaviors. In addition, behaviors are usually performed in larger, socially real units, like making breakfast or getting ready for work in the morning.
>
> Well, what does this mean for us? It means three things. First, we have to see what the units of activity are in the world of everyday life in which we want our children to participate. Second, we have to figure out how to teach our children to use the important small movements and skills in many everyday tasks. For instance. we have to teach them to pay attention, not just when they are working puzzles, but at other times and when working at other tasks. And, third, we have to teach them to participate in the larger units of activity that are going on around them. For instance, a child might be learning to set his place at the table, but it is also important that the child learn about the whole activity called preparing for the evening meal.

Detailed treatments of this topic are found in Pike (1954), Goffman (1971, 1974), and Barker (1963, 1968).

One way to help parents understand and use the above points is to examine the organization of the round of daily life. The goal is to describe the typical sequence of events in daily life as a number of units of activity occurring in time, each of which can be broken down into smaller and smaller units. For instance, a typical day has a number of major segments (such as morning, work-time, and evening). Each segment can be analyzed into smaller units of activity (e.g., in the morning we get out of bed, go to the bathroom, get dressed, eat, and leave the house). Each activity can be broken down into still-smaller tasks or actions (e.g., those involved in dressing). Ultimately, we can break down tasks and actions into microscopic movements. Note, however, that the meaningfulness of almost any unit, no matter how large or small, depends on the larger units of which it is a part. Getting dressed makes little sense in and of itself, unless it occurs within a larger unit, such as getting ready to go out. Similarly, the basic sounds in language (Ah, M, Ee) have no meaning in and of themselves. They create meaning only when uttered in larger units, such as words.

In addition to breaking down the sequence of events in daily life into ever-smaller units, parents learn that the intended end or goal of most units can be accomplished with many combinations of movements and actions. For example, the end of the unit called "getting a drink of water" is water in the mouth (the reinforcer), but many sets of movements result in a mouthful of water. A person can walk to the sink backward, find the faucet with his hands, and turn it on with his nose, if necessary. Similarly, many sequences of vocal movements result in the message-unit "Help me" (screaming "Eeeee" until someone comes or saying "Help"; "Help me, please"; "How about some help?" etc.).

In other words, you want parents to see how they can teach and reinforce their children for accomplishing the same objectives with alternative combinations of behaviors. Not only might this facilitate generalization to new situations, but it may help to teach the children a larger class of behavior called problem-solving.

The following questions, comments, and exercises might help parents learn to: break down the round of daily life into a typical sequence of smaller units; see that the behavioral components of those units occur over and over in daily life; build larger units; and see that the end or goal of various units can be accomplished in a number of ways.

1. Let's look at a typical day in our lives. What are the largest portions or units of a day? The answers, e.g., getting ready for school or work, working, lunch, working in the afternoon, eating supper, evening activities, going to bed, can be written on a blackboard. (See Table 9-2).

2. Notice that the major units or portions in the day are similar for most of you even though the exact activities in each unit may be different. For example, you all get dressed, but you do it in different ways.

3. Now let us take one of the units of the day and break it down into smaller and smaller units of activity. (For example, the parents might break down "getting ready for work" into: responding to the alarm clock, getting out of bed, going to the bathroom, washing, dressing, preparing breakfast, eating breakfast and carrying on breakfast conversation, cleaning up, saying goodbye, and walking out of the door. Again, some of the specific activities or tasks may be different, but the tasks accomplish the same ends—individually and as a

TABLE 9-2 Partial Breakdown of Activity-Units in the Round of Daily Life

Major Portions or Units	Activities or Tasks Involved in Getting Ready for Work	Movements or Actions Involved in Washing
Getting ready for work or school	Responding to the alarm clock	Walking into the bathroom
Morning work	Getting out of bed	Locating the faucet
Lunch	Going to the bathroom	Grasping the faucet
Afternoon work	Washing	Turning on faucet
Eating supper	Dressing	Locating the soap
Evening activities	Preparing breakfast	Reaching for the soap
Going to bed	Eating breakfast and carrying on breakfast conversation	Grasping the soap
	Cleaning up after breakfast	Placing hands and soap under running water
	Saying goodbye	Rubbing hands together
	Walking out the door	Placing soap back on the sink
		Etc.

whole—and the order is similar. This breakdown can also be written on a blackboard.)

4. Now, let us take an even smaller unit. Let's break down one task or activity involved in getting ready for work. (For example, washing might be broken down into walking into the bathroom, locating the faucet, reaching for the faucet, turning it on, locating the soap, reaching for the soap, grasping the soap, placing hands and soap under running water, rubbing hands together, placing soap on the sink, and so on. Of course, the list of movements would be long. Therefore, you might not write down every one. Encourage parents to notice absolutely essential movements, e.g., somehow putting hands in contact with water and soap. Point out that this is the level of organization at which chaining is usually discussed. Parents might then list the steps involved in teaching a simple task through forward- or back-chaining. Also, have parents develop several lists of movement-steps that accomplish the same objective, e.g., alternative ways of washing hands.)

5. Now let's look at the ways many of the small movements involved in certain tasks occur over and over in other tasks. (For example, parents might point out how movements, such as looking at objects, grasping, and fitting occur in tasks as different as opening a can of soup, putting on pants, writing, working puzzles, fixing a carburetor, and sewing.)

6. Now, let us discuss how to build larger and larger sequences. (Here, you and the parents can give examples of: short sequences or units, such as simple exchanges, e.g., reinforcing eye contact with food or using Grandma's Law regarding a simple task; building a larger task through chaining; teaching the child to perform the several tasks involved in a larger activity-unit, such as the evening meal—setting the table, eating, cleaning up, and then going off to play.)

Later in the Program

The points made on advanced teaching programs are reviewed and applied again and again in later meetings; for example, each time the parents begin to work on a new behavior and especially toward the end of the program to prepare them for working more independently.

Assignment

Assign Chapters 9 through 15 in *Educating Children*, depending on the skill area(s) being worked on. The parents will be conducting teaching programs on behaviors in those skill areas, as well as strengthening other APG items, as noted in later sections of this chapter.

II. TEACHING IN THE VARIOUS SKILL AREAS

By the time this chapter is employed, the parents have been working on at least one skill area. In our programs, parents move from one skill area to the next according to the Skill Sequence Table (Table 4-1, page 82) in *Educating Children*. Most children's educational programs begin in the Learning Readiness area, even if they can speak, read, and write, because they still need work on some behaviors in that area, e.g., cooperation with requests. Of course, you may add skill areas to the curriculum as needed.

In general, the same methods can be used to teach parents how to plan and conduct teaching programs in each skill area. Parents first read all or part of the chapter on the skill area; during the next meeting, you can review the major points in the chapter (i.e., the main teaching methods); the methods are demonstrated or shown on videotape or film (the videotapes or demonstrations should illustrate the main methods, as well as subtle but important points, e.g., different types of prompts, methods for shaping the behavior, and errors that can be made); parents then role-play the methods; in the home and/or in a classroom, parents are observed, coached, and perhaps videotaped; progress and problems are assessed and discussed, based on parents' reports, your observation, and review of videotapes of teaching sessions.

To instruct and evaluate, make special videotapes of teaching in various skill areas; show parents short segments of a particular tape; have parents score both correct and incorrect teaching behaviors in each segment and suggest alternative ways of teaching and of correcting the errors (see Section III of Chapter 11).

You and the parents routinely assess the parents' teaching skills, noting both progress and problems, with APG Items 16, 17, and especially 18 and Chapters 9 through 15 of *Educating Children*.

III. PROBLEM BEHAVIORS

When to Teach Parents How to Replace Problem Behaviors

Parents are taught how to plan and conduct programs to replace problem behaviors as necessary. Although the first seven units are designed primarily to teach parents how to strengthen appropriate behaviors, some problem behaviors may be so dangerous, disruptive, or incompatible with the learning of appropriate behaviors that problem behaviors might be part of the main business for one or more of the earlier meetings, whether in a Program for a group or for an individual family.

Instruction in Replacing Problem Behaviors

Instruction in planning, conducting, and evaluating teaching programs for replacing problem behaviors is much the same as that for strengthening appropriate behaviors. Specifically:

1. Parents first read Chapter 15 of *Educating Children* and APG Item 16 (on the problem-solving sequence).
2. Review the main ideas in Chapter 15 of *Educating Children*.
3. Review with parents the steps in the problem-solving sequence (discussed in Section IV, Chapter 8).
4. Give parents practice at using the problem-solving sequence with respect to the problem behaviors they have pinpointed.
5. Discuss alternative methods for replacing the pinpointed problem behaviors.
6. Demonstrate methods the parents might use; show videotapes or films; and, if necessary, provide additional readings (noted below).
7. Allow parents to role-play methods to use.
8. During individual consultations, help parents to write a plan for replacing the targeted problem behavior(s).

9. During home visits, help parents to institute and evaluate their plan.
10. During the next weeks, review with parents their program and, if necessary, revise it.

Factors to Consider

A number of factors are addressed when helping parents to plan programs for replacing problem behaviors.

Aversiveness of Problem Behaviors for Parents. The dangerousness, disruptiveness, social inappropriateness, or resistance to change of certain problem behaviors may have made them highly aversive to some parents. As a result, it may be difficult for the parents to be objective in assessing the seriousness of a problem behavior (e.g., they may overestimate its seriousness), to see the relationship between a problem behavior and other aspects of the family system (e.g., they may see it as a result of their child's willfulness or moodiness or as a medical phenomenon), or to be optimistic about replacing it. In addition, problem behaviors may have been partly responsible for marital difficulties, personal problems, and a pattern of reacting rather than planning.

In view of the above, it is helpful to give parents the chance to discuss the effects of problem behaviors on their feelings and family relationships. At the same time, however, remind them of some key ideas presented in earlier units; for example, that: (1) behaviors tend to change in the desired direction when we arrange the environment so that it suits the child's needs; (2) the same principles that help us to figure out how to strengthen appropriate behaviors help us to plan programs to replace problem behaviors; (3) change may not be as rapid as we wish, but if we carefully plan, conduct, and keep track of our teaching programs to replace problem behaviors, we are likely to see that beneficial change is occurring. Note that, to increase parents' chances of success, it may be necessary to help them deal with personal problems, such as tension or depressed mood, involve siblings and others, and strengthen the marital relationship. (See Chapter 10.)

Another way to reduce the aversiveness of certain problem behaviors is to help parents to see them in relative terms (La Vigna and Walsh, 1976). That is, not all behaviors that are aversive to them are as problematic as they think. Some may be aggravating, but will not greatly hinder the learning of appropriate behaviors. Others may be inappropriate only when emitted in certain situations (e.g., yelling) and hence need not be regarded as problematic in and of themselves. And still others may be aversive primarily because they are considered socially inappropriate and are a source of embarrassment and anger to the parents. The following example may be useful for parents to discuss.

When taken to grocery stores, a child may wander away or remove items from the shelves and play with them on the floor. Not only might the parents be embarrassed by this, as they imagine what others think, but they may become angry with the child. When angry and embarrassed they may yell at or threaten the child, which may produce an escalation (e.g., the child whines or argues back). In sum, the aversiveness of a problem behavior may prevent the parents from responding in a productive way.

At this point, stress how helpful it would be if parents were able to: (1) devalue somewhat the importance they are placing in others' opinions of their child's behavior or their competence; (2) be sensitive to and reinforce improvements in the child's behavior (as when the child stays with them or tries to replace items on the shelves); and (3) plan a program for shaping desirable behavior in public places. Several exercises on assertiveness training and behavior rehearsal may also be useful. (See Chapter 10.) For instance, if greatly bothered by their child's strange hand gestures or vocalizations, partly because they have experienced or imagine others' evaluations, parents might practice (rehearse, role-play): (1) telling others to ignore the child's behaviors or (2) making self-statements, such as:

> Who cares what they think? I've got more important things to do, like carrying out my teaching program.
>
> Okay, so I'm angry with Junior. Why? Because of what others might be thinking? What is more important—trying to look good to others (by jumping on Junior) or teaching Junior the behaviors he needs to learn?

How Long Have Problem Behaviors Been Occurring? Some problem behaviors, such as aggression, tantrums, or bizarre behaviors, may have been occurring for a long time. If they have been intermittently reinforced or intermittently punished, they now may be resistant to ignoring and punishment, even if it is done consistently (Patterson, 1976). In addition, they may now occur in many settings or be started by many signals. Therefore, carefully describe these behaviors, parents' past and present efforts to control them, and the settings in which they occur and do not occur.

On the other hand, some problem behaviors may begin or worsen either when the parents conduct their first home programs or later in their child's education. Examples include oppositional behavior, leaving teaching sessions, throwing tantrums, or more intense whining and bizarre behaviors. Several factors may be involved.

First, there may be common problems in the home educational program (as described in Chapter 7 of *Educating Children*) which make the learning environment less attractive than it was before. For instance, some problem behaviors may constitute the child's efforts to escape or avoid situations experienced as aversive (e.g., boring sessions, tasks requiring too much effort, or tasks on which the child makes many errors). Others may be behaviors that the parents are accidentally reinforcing.

Second, as a result of the parents' reinforcing certain problem behaviors less often or not at all, the child may now be emitting problem behaviors which were formerly of low strength, perhaps in an effort to coerce reinforcement from the parents. Or, third, the classroom and home may differ with respect to tasks worked on and the quality, frequency, and consistency of reinforcement. For example, the tasks worked on at home may be more difficult or the parents may be a bit more likely to reinforce problem behaviors. Such contrast may result in a marked increase in the child's rate of problem behaviors in the home.

In any case, the parents must carefully examine the overall educational program to increase its attractiveness, remove any accidental reinforcement of problem behaviors, systematically reinforce alternative behaviors, and make the home and school programs consistent with one another. This is likely to require that parents and teachers work together. Hence, you might make the coordination of home and school programs part of the main business of one of the earlier meetings, as well as later meetings.

How Often and Where Does a Problem Behavior Occur? As noted in Chapter 15 of *Educating Children*, infrequent problem behaviors may be under the control of a small set of signals (e.g., persons, times, or places). It may be possible to remove those signals, at least temporarily, or teach the child alternative behaviors in their presence. For example, if a child makes messes, generally by getting into kitchen cabinets, the parents might: (1) temporarily put locks on the cabinets; (2) teach the child to cooperate with directions (such as "Do not open these doors. You may play in your own drawer."); and (3) provide the child with his or her own drawer or cabinet of interesting items. Or, if the child engages in many problem behaviors, but usually only in the grocery store, the parents might conduct a program to strengthen appropriate behaviors in stores (e.g., giving the child opportunities to help load and unload the cart, reinforcing improvements, and leaving the store if the child becomes disruptive).

To What Extent is the Problem Behavior Situationally Inappropriate? Although some behaviors may be problematic in and of themselves (e.g., those that are dangerous or that interfere with almost any behavioral improvement), others may be situationally inappropriate. For instance, they may be incompatible with the target behaviors being worked on in a current teaching program or may be inappropriate in a particular setting (masturbating in the living room, nose-picking in public, yelling in the restaurant).

If behaviors are problematic only in certain situations, it may be possible to teach the child to: (1) discriminate those settings in which the behavior is appropriate from those in which it is not; (2) engage in the "problem" behavior only in more acceptable settings (e.g., to masturbate in the bedroom); and (3) engage in alternative behaviors in the settings in which the "problem" behavior had formerly occurred (LaVigna and Walsh, 1976).

How Dangerous is the Behavior? Clearly, dangerous behaviors (self-injury, aggression, running into the street, firesetting) must be dealt with quickly and may initially require aversive methods to weaken them (punishment, over-correction, time out), combined with positive reinforcement for alternative behaviors. However, many aggravating and socially inappropriate behaviors are neither dangerous nor incompatible with behavioral improvement (e.g., muttering, cursing, squinting, seat-squirming). It is helpful to have parents assess the relative unimportance of such behaviors in view of the many others with which their children need help. Thus, while the parents are working to strengthen more important appropriate behaviors, they can reinforce the child for emitting replacements for the minor problem behaviors (e.g., sitting more calmly, expressing feelings without cursing), or, later, when the more important behaviors have been strengthened, the parents might conduct programs to replace the minor problem behaviors.

To What Extent Can the Child Participate in Planning and Conducting a Program to Replace Problem Behaviors? As noted by LaVigna and Walsh (1976), as much as possible the child should participate in programs to replace behaviors. Hence, you and the parents assess the extent to which the child understands the problematic nature of the behaviors in question, shares the same goals as the parents with respect to the behavior (e.g., Does the child feel that the behavior should be replaced? Does the child agree that suggested replacement behaviors are satisfactory?), and is able to participate in conducting the program (e.g., defining the target behaviors, counting in some fashion, practicing relaxation, providing self-reinforcement). As is described later, it may be possible for the child to participate rather fully in the program (e.g., behavioral contracting with the parents).

To What Extent are Alternative Behaviors in the Child's Repertoire? Before selecting replacement behaviors, determine the extent to which replacements (or prerequisites for learning them) are in the child's repertoire at some level of skill or frequency. For example, progressive relaxation may be a good way to replace tantrums the child throws as a result of tension caused by errors. Before selecting progressive relaxation, however, you and the parents should determine the times and places in which the child seems tense versus more relaxed, and how many of the prerequisites of relaxation training the child knows (e.g., eye contact on request, cooperation with simple requests, such as to lie or sit down, allowing himself or herself to be touched).

This information is useful in two ways. First, in general, replacement behaviors that are stronger in the child's repertoire might be the best ones to try first. And, second, the assessment can be used to plan the details of the program itself; for instance, prescribing the level of skill at which to begin teaching the child to relax or the prerequisites of relaxation training to be worked on first.

Aversive Methods. It is important to discuss aversive methods with parents for a number of reasons. Aversive methods may seem necessary when, in fact, they are not. Some parents may have a propensity to use aversive methods because these methods have apparently worked for them in the short run or because the parents have not learned alternative methods. There may be times when, out of desperation, a parent might turn to aversive methods. And, finally, parents should learn to determine when and how to use aversive methods in case they ever do seem to be necessary.

First, enumerate the potential counterproductive effects of using aversive methods.

1. As noted by Ferster (1967a), escape and avoidance behaviors acquired through arbitrary negative reinforcement are likely to constitute a small class of behaviors. In addition, the temporary suppression produced by the use of aversive stimuli may benefit the person delivering the punishment more than the child (i.e., the child may not be learning behaviors that are appropriate in other settings or that constitute alternative, acceptable ways of producing positive reinforcement). Hence, the behavior changes may not occur in other settings. And, finally, the performances coerced through the use of aversive stimuli may not build upon appropriate behaviors already in the child's repertoire. Thus, the child's performance of alternative behaviors may be of short duration, requiring the parents to continue to use the aversive methods.

2. As indicated by Patterson (1976), LaVigna and Walsh (1976), and Hutchinson (1977), aversive stimuli may actually produce an acceleration in the punished behavior, as well as in aggressive-attack behaviors.

> The repetitive, but infrequent delivery of intense aversive stimuli can result in increased responses or facilitation, rather than habituation. . . . Once the process is begun it is possible to terminate all aversive stimulation, yet continue to observe the occurrence of these reactions for hours and even days. [Hutchinson, 1977:422.]

In addition, Hutchinson shows that the effects of aversive stimuli are often unpredictable, but seem to depend in part on the past history of aversive stimulation and on current states of deprivation and schedules of positive reinforcement. Thus, to the extent that the past history of aversive stimulation is not well known, its effects may be just the opposite of what was intended. For example, Hutchinson found that when some subjects were punished for behaviors that had been previously strengthened by escape from or avoidance of aversive stimuli, the punished behaviors actually increased (Hutchinson, 1977:428).

3. If the aversive stimuli are not strong enough to suppress the behavior, the parents may gradually increase the level of aversiveness. However, the child may habituate to the point of tolerating much punishment with little or no weakening in the behaviors. In one sense, this situation may be seen as merely unproductive. In another sense, however, it is tragic. What, for example, are the long-term effects on the child who is learning to tolerate pain? And what will happen to the parents if they stand back and see what they inadvertently have been doing?

To avoid the above situation, Chapter 15 of *Educating Children* suggests that when punishment and time out are used, the aversive consequence should be strong enough to suppress the behavior. For example, if it is used at all, a spanking should be uncomfortable, and the time out at least 10 minutes. As noted however, the spanking may produce counteraggression. My colleagues Barbara Cutler and Dr. Barbara Bruno-Golden have found that short time out intervals may be effective if the child is timed out instantly and every time the problem behavior occurs, and if alternative behaviors are being strengthened concurrently. In any case, there are a number of alternatives to aversive methods, as described below.

4. In the same way that a child can habituate to one type of aversive consequence, the child may habituate to a range of methods that are gradually more aversive. For instance, wishing to be humane, the parents may start with a mildly aversive method, such as time out. If that does not work, they might try physical punishment. However, the child may habituate to aversive consequences in general. Simultaneously, the child may learn to escape or avoid aversive stimuli in more problematic ways than the original problem behavior (e.g., counteraggression or withdrawal from the parents' touch).

5. If aversive methods do temporarily suppress problem behaviors, the parents may use aversive methods more and more and, without thinking about it, use them when other methods would be more effective and humane.

Alternatives to the Use of Aversive Methods. After discussing problems in the use of aversive methods (such as punishment, time out, negative practice, and possibly overcorrection), you and the parents should discuss alternatives. Chapter 15 of *Educating Children* describes methods such as ignoring, satiation, and the reinforcement of alternative appropriate behaviors (a method which should be used in any case). In addition, LaVigna and Walsh (1976) describe the following methods. It might be a good idea to provide the parents with a copy of their paper or at least a summary of the main points.

1. Differential Reinforcement of Low Rates of Responding (DRL). One way to decrease a problem behavior is to systematically reinforce the child for engaging in the behavior at lower and lower rates. For example, the parents can: count the number of times the behavior occurs during several periods; calculate the average rate of the behavior; and reinforce the child at the end of intervals in which the rate was lower. Or, they might reinforce the child if a specified amount of time has elapsed since the last occurrence of the behavior (LaVigna and Walsh, 1976:13). In the first version, the parents reinforce the child for performing the behavior fewer times in an interval; in the second, they reinforce the child for waiting longer and longer between episodes of the behavior.

Either version might involve the use of a timer or watch. If the problem behavior occurs too many times during an interval, or if too little time has occurred since the last episode, the parents either reset the timer and start the interval again or simply let the interval run out and then reset the timer.

Ultimately, the parents reinforce the child for longer and longer intervals in which the problem behavior has not occurred at all.

For example, if the child engages in hand-flapping at a high rate, but stops periodically for short intervals, the parents might determine the average time between episodes of intense flapping and reinforce the child only when the child waits longer between episodes. Using the same principles, but in a different way, if the child is usually late in doing chores or in coming home from playing, the paents can reinforce the child for being less and less late. It is also possible for the child to participate actively in such programs. The child who yells or talks back an average of twenty times a day might take data on his or her talking back. The child would be reinforced at the end of the day if fewer episodes occurred.

2. Stimulus Control. In this method, the child is reinforced only when he or she performs the problem behavior in a particular setting or after a certain signal. The purpose is to teach the child to discriminate when or where to perform the problem behavior. This method might be used for behaviors that are problematic only because they occur in the ''wrong'' situations (e.g., masturbation in nonprivate places). If the parents would be satisfied with the child's masturbating in private (e.g., in the child's room at certain times of day), they can encourage the child to masturbate at the ''right'' time and place, and reinforce the child for doing so. Or, if the child rocks a great deal in many places, the parents might teach the child to rock only on a rocking horse or on a rocking chair. And if the child argues loudly with the parents in public places or at many times of day, the parents might arrange a special time and place for arguing and for resolving difficulties (Martin and Twentyman, 1976).

3. Stimulus Change. Since many problem behaviors occur in the presence of or following certain signals, one way of breaking up habitual connections is to suddenly alter the setting so that the old signals are no longer there. When the problem behaviors temporarily cease, the parents can begin reinforcing alternative behaviors.

Engineering the environment, as described in APG Item 18, is one type of stimulus change. Examples of additional stimulus changes that may temporarily disrupt habitual problem behaviors include: a) markedly changing the time or place of meals, or the arrangements of seats and utensils (for a child who disrupts meals); b) altering the time for going to bed, activities which precede bedtime, and/or the arrangement of things in the bedroom (for a child with bedtime problems); or c) giving directions and making requests in a different way (for a child who rarely cooperates with parents' usual way of presenting tasks).

4. Instructional Control. Instructional control corresponds to "cooperation with simple spoken requests" on the Behavior Evaluation Scale. If the parents first strengthen the child's cooperation with instructions or requests, they might be able to stop a problem behavior once it starts or avert it before it starts. For example, if the child typically works up to tantrums in a sequence of progressively more-disruptive behaviors, the parents might be able to interrupt the chain with instructions, such as "Relax," or "Tell me what you want in a soft voice." Of course, it is important that the parents teach the child how to perform the behaviors they are requesting as substitutes for the problem behavior.

5. Shaping a Problem Behavior in a More Acceptable Direction. The above methods dealt with changing the rate at which or settings in which problem behaviors occur. It is also possible to change both the way a problem behavior is performed, as well as the duration and intensity of episodes, using shaping procedures. For example, parents might be on the lookout for, and systematically reinforce: (a) shorter and shorter episodes of a problem behavior (such as tantrums, self-injury, or bizarre behavior); (b) less and less intense episodes of tantrums and yelling (e.g., softer yelling); and (c) less harmful self-injurious behaviors (e.g., reinforcing the child for hitting his shoulder or a table rather than his head).

This method may also be a way of avoiding escalated conflict. For example, if a child has typically escaped from certain of the parents' requests by throwing wild tantrums, instead of expecting perfect compliance, the parents might reinforce those episodes of cooperation that involve less "protest" than before.

6. Additive Procedures. LaVigna and Walsh (1976) also suggest that a procedure may not be effective by itself. Instead of switching to another procedure (which may be no better than the first), the parents might use several at once or in a planned sequence. For instance, a child might throw dangerous tantrums at a high rate and in many places. Careful observation might show that the child throws some tantrums when he seems to be bored, others when he is not given what he wants, and still others when he makes several errors in a row in his lessons.

At first, the parents might teach the child to occupy his free time in a constructive way. Later, they might teach the child to relax, to observe them as they intentionally make and calmly correct errors, or even to practice calmly making and correcting errors. At the same time, they might teach the child to wait until they can pay him more attention or teach the child to get things on his own.

Yet, some tantrums—even intense ones—may still occur. Thus, the parents might shape less intense and/or shorter tantrums. As tantrums decrease in intensity and duration, the parents might be able to avert future tantrums by requesting the child to perform alternative behaviors.

*7. **Replacement Behaviors.*** No matter what other methods are used to alter the frequency, duration, setting, or topography, the goal is still to replace problem behaviors with appropriate behaviors. In many cases, alternative behaviors are rather obvious and specific. For example, mess-making might be replaced with constructive play (finger painting, water play), yelling for things might be replaced with proper asking. Sometimes, however, the child benefits from learning a more general skill, i.e., one that is beneficial in many settings and may replace a number of problem behaviors.

For example, after careful observation, you, the parents, and teachers may determine that many problem behaviors occur when the child is tense. The child may become so tense during lessons that the child whines, throws tantrums, and engages in self-stimulation or self-injury. Indeed, tension may interfere with the learning of appropriate behaviors. Thus, it might be helpful to teach the child progressive relaxation. This might involve: (a) setting up relaxation sessions (e.g., 5 minutes each hour); (b) having the child label the different parts of the body; and teaching the child to: (c) discriminate tension versus relaxation (by tensing and relaxing on instruction), (d) tense and relax various parts of the body, (e) relax in other settings, (f) relax his body more independently, and (g) pinpoint the settings in which he or she becomes tense and to relax in those settings. Excellent articles and manuals describing relaxation for children include: Bruno (1974), Cautela and Groden (1978), Graziano and Kean (1968), Koeppen (1974), Putre et al. (1977), and Weil and Goldfried (1973).

In addition to tension, some problem behaviors are associated with a child's poor social and problem-solving skills. For example, excessive fantasizing, resistance to change, withdrawal, tantrums, and outbursts of aggression may result from the child's difficulty in telling others to stop bothering him, discriminating accidental from intentional injury, unfamiliarity with certain roles (e.g., patient in a dentist's office), or difficulty in correcting errors. Along with (or besides) the above methods, it may be helpful to teach the child more general problem-solving and role-playing (behavior rehearsal) skills.

For example, the parents might teach the child how to make and correct errors (beginning with tasks that are not too important for the child), play the role of patient, tell others not to bother him, make and take jokes or criticism, or tell the difference between accidental and intentional injury.

Even more generally, a child might benefit from learning self-control; for example, pinpointing behaviors to change, planning a program, using certain change procedures (e.g., relaxation), taking data, and providing reinforcement.

Methods for teaching the above skills can be found in the following sources: (1)*self-control* (Bolstad and Johnson, 1972; Cautela, 1969; Goldiamond, 1965; O'Leary, 1977; Schneider and Robin, 1975; Brown et al., 1976; Aronfreed, 1968; Lazarus and Abramovitz, 1962; Sherman and Plummer, 1973; Thoresen and Mahoney, 1974; Bornstein and Quevillon, 1976; Bandura and Perloff, 1967;

Glynn, 1970; Felixbrod and O'Leary, 1973; Broden et al., 1971; Meichenbaum, 1977; Meichenbaum and Goodman, 1977; Drabman et al., 1973; Kanfer, 1970); (2) *problem-solving* (Goldfried and Davison, 1976; Spivak and Shure, 1974); (3) *rehearsal and role-playing* (Goldfried and Davison, 1976; Shaftel and Shaftel, 1967; Bandura, 1969: Chapter 3).

8. ***Participation of the Child.*** As much as possible, the child should participate in planning and conducting a program to replace problem behaviors. For example, to the extent that the child has the receptive language skills, the parents can discuss with the child each party's perception of the overall situation, seeking at least a compromise. If possible, parents and children can develop a behavioral contract (Homme et al., 1970), with the child taking data on himself or herself. For instance, the child might keep track of the number of episodes of rocking or tantrums during the day by dropping tokens in a can, making hash-marks on a calendar, or by punching holes in a 3 × 5 card.

Applying the Above Ideas to the Parents' Programs

After the above ideas are presented, the parents are given a chance to think of ways to use them. For instance, having pinpointed and described a problem behavior (perhaps one common to families in the group), the group can brainstorm ways of applying each above-mentioned method to replace it. Then, parents can practice adapting and generalizing the methods to other behaviors. For example, "Okay, you've talked about how to use stimulus control to handle making messes in the bathroom. Now, how would you use stimulus control to handle arguing?"

IV. PARENTS AS ROTATING LEADERS AND TEMPORARY EXPERTS

As described in Chapter 5, the role of leader consists primarily of guiding communication in the group, while the role of expert consists of presenting a certain body of knowledge or helping others to apply that knowledge. Parents' learning to play the roles of rotating leader and temporary expert has several benefits. First, it helps to de-mythify conceptions of authority and expertise as statuses and qualities held only by a special few called "professionals." Second, it may increase parents' commitment in the Program since they will be more responsible for outcomes. And, third, the parents will be acquiring skills enabling them to help others (making suggestions, guiding decision-making, coaching, conducting Programs). Moreover, as the parents begin to assume the tasks of running group meetings and possibly home visits, you will have more time, either for helping those with special difficulties or for working with new parents.

Parents can assume the tasks of rotating leader and temporary expert in a sequence of small steps. As rotating leaders, they might: review the main ideas in a reading assignment; review videotapes of other families' home programs, providing reinforcement and corrective feedback; conduct role-playing exercises; guide the group in brainstorming ideas on how to solve a particular problem or how to apply a teaching method to the home programs; handle conflicts or disagreements in the group; schedule meetings; develop lists of persons or organizations from whom the parents might be able to obtain backup support (e.g., evaluations, baby-sitting, respite care); or plan parties for the group.

As temporary experts, on the other hand, parents can: give presentations on how to teach certain target behaviors; give presentations on how to solve certain problems (e.g., how to handle tension, depressed mood, low level of marital cooperation or sibling involvement); play the role of "outside observer" who sits in on a group meeting and evaluates how well the group is doing (e.g., commenting on group participation, interaction between parents and consultants, or presentations).

If necessary, you (or parents who have previously assumed these roles) prepare parents who will be acting as rotating leader or temporary expert by rehearsing with them what they might do, coaching them if needed, and providing them with reinforcement and suggestions after the meeting.

V. GENERALIZATION OF PARENTS' AND CHILDREN'S SKILLS

This topic corresponds to APG Item 26. It can be worked on in small steps. For example, the importance of promoting generalization, and some methods for doing so, can be discussed in early meetings, with parents referring to their own copies of the APG. After the parents have conducted their first teaching program (about the fifth week), generalization can again be part of the main business of a meeting. That is, parents begin to systematically program generalization of the skills they have learned and those they are teaching their children. In later meetings, parents' generalization efforts are reviewed in the group, revised, and upgraded. Good sources of ideas on generalization include Rose (1977) and Conway and Bucher (1976).

Defining Generalization

In essence, generalization involves the parents and children performing their new skills in different situations. For instance:

1. The parents have new people work with their child (siblings, friends, grandparents).

2. The child engages in newly learned behaviors in new settings, such as public places and other people's homes.
3. The parents increase the number of people who come into their home (especially if they have been isolated).
4. The parents learn to adapt to changes in the Program itself (for instance, different consultants, changes in the style of instruction, changes in the place where meetings are held).

Programming Generalization

Generalization can be planned and implemented like other intentional efforts to change behavior. Here are some steps that might be followed:

1. Pinpointing and Describing. The parents pinpoint and describe the behaviors they want to generalize (their own and their children's), the settings in which they want generalization to occur, the behaviors they want others in the settings to engage in with respect to themselves and their children, the problems they anticipate, and the potential solutions for such problems.

For instance, part of the parents' first teaching program might involve strengthening cooperation with simple requests. After several weeks, the child's cooperation may greatly increase and so the parents now wish to teach the child to cooperate in other people's homes and in certain public places, such as the grocery store and restaurant. They describe the kinds of requests with which they want the child to cooperate. They also note that they want several adult friends and the grocery clerk whom they know to also give the child several simple requests, to ignore noncooperation and to reinforce cooperation. They specify just what the others should do and say. However, they anticipate several problems. Perhaps the clerk may not want to cooperate with them or will not carry out the program properly; perhaps their child will not only be uncooperative, but will throw a wild tantrum when another person makes a request. Consequently, they decide to discuss with others their goals and the importance of help. If possible, they arrange for some kind of exchange with those who help them (e.g., a certificate of appreciation from the Program). In addition, before implementing the program, they practice with the other persons what the others are supposed to do.

Parents also pinpoint reinforcement for themselves; for instance, social reinforcement they might give each other, a snack that will be awaiting them at home, or a movie they will see the next night. It might be a good idea if the reinforcement for the parents is something made available by the generalization of the child's behavior. For example, to the extent that the child is cooperative in the grocery store, the parents have the time to buy themselves (and the child) a special treat. Similarly, as the child's behavior at home with new people improves, the parents may be more able to utilize baby-sitters.

2. Finalizing a Plan. In developing plans, it is a good idea for the group to brainstorm certain components (e.g., places to generalize various behaviors, how to encourage others to cooperate, potential problems and solutions). In addition, you might invite parents from former programs to give a presentation at a meeting, describing their efforts at generalization, successes and problems. These "old hands" can then serve as models or even on-site coaches for the present families. Plans might be written on a Weekly Contract.

3. Practicing the Plan. Prior to implementing the plan, parents, yourself, and others who might be involved practice the necessary skills. For instance, the parents can:

a. Rehearse soliciting cooperation, coaching others, ignoring stares and whispers in public places, the actual methods for interacting with the child and handling problems that may arise. Rehearsal can take place through role-playing with you and others, as well as through imagination (covert behavioral rehearsal). For instance, the parents can imagine: explaining to a hesitant grandparent the importance of the grandparent cooperating with them; handling objections; and eventually persuading the grandparent. (See Chapter 10 on behavioral rehearsal.)

b. Practice statements they can make to themselves when implementing a program. For example:

> Rome wasn't built in a day. A little improvement now is better than none at all. Change will add up.
>
> Excellent, I'm doing a good job! Okay, so this person won't help. He's not the only grocer in town!
>
> Okay, a problem. Betsy is starting to whine. Let them look. Handling Betsy the right way is what is important, not what they think. Now what would Mr. Fernandez do (using another parent as model)?

c. Practice assertiveness exercises. The reason for this is that despite a carefully thought-out plan and a number of optimistic self-statements, some parents may be too timid to actually solicit cooperation, handle objections (e.g., from overprotective grandparents), coach others who are making errors when interacting with the child (e.g., giving multiple signals, reinforcing tantrums), or even to take their child to places where they envision problems. Assertiveness training, as described in Chapter 10, may help.

4. Implementing the Plan. The plan can be implemented in small steps. For example, the parents might go to a restaurant with you or another parent (especially one who has conducted a similar program). The "buddy" rehearses the plan with the parent, observes the parent in action, coaches or helps if necessary, and provides reinforcement and suggestions afterward. As progress is made, the buddy can be faded out. Similarly, if parents want to generalize cooperation and proper eating to a restaurant, they might first have snacks or meals at the homes of others. Each time the plan is conducted, the parents take data on what they did and what happened.

5. Review and Evaluation. After the parents have conducted a generalization program for about one week, it is reviewed and evaluated in meetings; other parents and consultants can provide reinforcement and suggestions for the future; and the plan can be revised or upgraded (e.g., new settings, more difficult behaviors).

In the Classroom (and the Homes of Others)

As noted in an earlier chapter, it is helpful to give parents practice working in a classroom. This enables them to generalize their skills to another situation, as well as to children with different problem behaviors and needs. In addition, parents can generalize their skills to other people's homes (e.g., by observing and coaching other parents and even working with their children).

Changing the Group Climate

Another way to help parents generalize their skills is to change the group climate (see Rose, 1977, Chapter 11). For example, new consultants can be brought in, giving the parents practice talking to and learning from a person with a different style; meetings can be held in other places (parents' homes, classrooms); and you can change your own roles or style (for instance, a different consultant can assume responsibility for presenting the main business of meetings).

Bringing the Outside In

In addition to generalizing their own and their children's skills to settings outside the home, the parents can bring the outside world in. This, too, can be done in small steps. First, some families may have become isolated, perhaps for the reasons mentioned in Chapter 2. It may be possible to decrease isolation by having: (1) parents in the Program call one another to chat and, later, to discuss their home program; (2) other parents visit isolated families, either with regard to the teaching program (i.e., to coach) or simply for a social call; and (3) the formerly-isolated parents plan how to open their door to still others (e.g., phoning neighbors and relatives, inviting others in for coffee).

Second, parents can begin to request the cooperation of those who visit or who have other contacts with their child, such as neighbors, relatives, bus and taxi drivers. It may also be helpful to have a meeting for siblings, grandparents, friends, and drivers. These persons might be invited to attend either a regular meeting of the group or a special meeting given on their behalf. During the meetings, you (or, better, parents) stress the importance of such persons' contacts with the children and describe basic ways of interacting with the children in a productive way. The guests are given a chance to voice the difficulties they have interacting with the children (e.g., aggravation caused by problem behavior, pity, or fear of doing something wrong). Simple programs can then be worked out.

Guests might be given certificates of appreciation. Those who show an interest in working with the children or families in a more formal way can be given the chance to do so, and might even attend some future group meetings or be given a short training program of their own (conducted, perhaps, by some of the parents).

Siblings may require special attention. Either you or certain parents might have a short series of meetings for them, backed up with much reinforcement. Siblings can be given a chance to air their feelings about themselves and the child with learning and behavior problems. Those who wish to participate in some way can be taught how (e.g., taking data, instituting productive exchanges, coaching and reinforcing their parents, or participating in teaching programs for certain target behaviors).

VI. PERSISTENCE, MAINTENANCE, AND FOLLOW-UP

This section describes ways to help parents persist at conducting and to maintain a good home educational program. It treats APG Items 22 through 27, except 26 on generalization, which is addressed in Section V above. All of the items important for persistence and maintenance were part of the main business in earlier units of work. For instance, you have already helped parents to schedule and take breaks, reinforce themselves, and start a network of extended support. Toward the end of a Program, however, Items 22 through 27 are focused on again. Some items, such as scheduling breaks and self-reinforcement, can be worked on along with methods for teaching behaviors in certain skill areas. It might be best, however, to work on building a network of extended support and on long-term problem-solving as the sole items of main business in several meetings.

During a later meeting, the topic of maintenance might be introduced as follows:

> We have come a long way together. You have learned how to evaluate your children's strengths and needs, as well as your own. You have learned to see that beneficial changes can be produced when we arrange the family environment in a way that suits people's learning needs and accentuates their strengths. As a result, you have instituted productive exchanges, planned teaching programs for many

target behaviors, conducted teaching programs, and have been getting good results. Well, as you know, our intensive, week-by-week meetings together are coming to a close. Of course, we will continue to meet, but not as regularly; the bulk of the instruction is about over. So, at this time, it is important to think about and plan for the future.

What does it take to persist at conducting and maintaining your good home educational programs? We have to think about and do something to produce persistence and maintenance as much as we did to simply conduct good teaching programs. We can't take beneficial change for granted. Well, what does the APG tell us we need to think about and do? (APG Items 22 through 27 can be referred to.) As you know, we talked about these items from the very beginning. And we have worked in small steps on some components of the items. For example, you have been (making phone calls to one another, making home visits, reinforcing yourselves, taking scheduled breaks). Now we have to deal with these important items in more detail.

Long-Term Planning and Problem-Solving (APG Item 27)

This topic can receive special attention during the last several meetings of the Program stage and can be returned to during Follow-up and Maintenance meetings. The following exercises and discussions may be helpful.

Pinpointing and Planning Programs for Future Target Behaviors. First, parents can use their child's most recent evaluation to pinpoint behaviors to teach in the near and distant future. In particular, given their child's place on the Skill Sequence Table and their child's strengths and needs as indicated by the BES, the parents try to answer the question: "What are the next skill areas, and behaviors in those skill areas, to work on?" In addition, parents can be encouraged to brainstorm possible behaviors or skill areas to teach which are not found in the materials with which they were provided (e.g., which are not on the BES). As when first planning their child's educational program, some ideas can come from the children's teachers.

After individual and group discussion, parents list future behaviors to work on, and a tentative sequence for doing so. They keep one copy of the list with their teaching materials; you file another copy.

Next, you, the parents, and possibly the children's teachers can discuss methods for teaching several of the behaviors pinpointed for the future. As in past units of work, the methods can be demonstrated, shown on videotape or film, and role-played. Tentative teaching programs might then be written for the next several target behaviors.

Evaluating Teaching Skills. Following the first exercise, parents can be given another opportunity to observe and evaluate both their own and others' teaching skills. For instance, they can demonstrate how they would teach behaviors they have not yet worked on (e.g., on the list of future target behaviors they just made), or observe themselves and others on videotape, teaching both new and old behaviors. As in earlier meetings, parents can observe short segments, evaluate and score the teaching according to APG Items 17 and 18, and suggest improvements, as well as alternative teaching methods. With respect to their own teaching skills, parents pinpoint strengths and needs, writing them on the APG or a separate list. Keep a copy of such a list. In later Individual Consultations and home visits, help parents to improve teaching skills prior to phasing out the Program stage.

Scenarios. In a third exercise, parents can use their analytical skills to anticipate, avoid, or solve future problems. You might introduce the exercise with remarks such as:

> Early in the Program you examined your experiences from the time you recognized that something was wrong with your child to the present. Well, what did you find? (Encourage parents to briefly describe the worsening of problems and the connections among problems, as described in Chapter 2. For example, they might recall how their children's problems were a burden at home and produced unkind reactions from outsiders; that various structured exchanges produced a worsening of the children's problem behaviors, and fatigue and tension in the parents; and that continuing problems led to pessimism, hypervigilance, personal problems, and perhaps marital difficulties.)
>
> So far, you have been learning and using a number of ideas and methods for producing beneficial change in the home. Now let us apply them to the future. What kinds of things might happen which can slowly but surely make the change process grind to a halt? How can we avoid or correct initial problems that can lead to a deterioration in your home programs? And what can we do to remedy your programs if they do begin to deteriorate?

After the introduction, encourage parents to pinpoint and write some factors that can engender a deterioration in the change process. Examples include:

1. Too little perceived change in the child's behavior.
2. Parents' realization of how much the child still needs to learn.
3. The sudden appearance or recognition of problem behaviors.
4. Parents' fatigue.
5. A decrease in the value to parents of changes in future target behaviors.
6. Job-related and other family difficulties (e.g., layoffs, firing, job dissatisfaction, pregnancy).
7. Difficulty in obtaining help when problems arise.

Given the list of factors, help parents to develop alternative scenarios of both deterioration and effective problem-solving. For instance:

Consultant: Okay, let's take the first factor we've listed. What might happen after we notice that our child is not learning—say functional speech—as fast as we expect?

Mr. Fernandez: Well, I think that if my child didn't learn much for several weeks, I might begin to feel less enthusiastic about teaching sessions. (The changes described by parents can be diagrammed on a blackboard.)

Mrs. Wince: And I would also be tense before sessions—you know, sort of expecting the worst.

Mrs. Blake: Yes, I can see myself feeling that way too.

Consultant: Okay, so a lack of progress in light of your expectations could result in less optimism and in more tension. Could this affect your teaching?

Mrs. Fernandez: Yes.

Consultant: How?

Mrs. Fernandez: Uh, well, I might push harder.

Mr. Wince: How? What do you mean?

Mrs. Fernandez: Well, I might start to see my child as a brat, that he can do what I'm teaching him, but won't.

Consultant: And?

Mrs. Fernandez: And I might become angry when he makes errors.

Mr. Wince: Yeah, and maybe give less prompts because you figure he can do the behavior.

Mrs. Fernandez: Yeah.

Consultant: Would this type of teaching affect the child?

Mrs. Wince: You'd probably get even less progress. The poor kid would try to get out of sessions or would whine and stop paying attention.

Consultant: So, as your own teaching performance deteriorates, so might your children's behaviors. See the vicious cycle? . . . . Okay, now that your children's behaviors are deteriorating, what else might happen?

Mr. Levine: Well, after a while, I might have sessions less and less. And I might be less consistent. I mean, I might stop some sessions when my daughter makes a few errors, because it aggravates me so much, and I might run some sessions too long, trying to force her to learn.

Consultant: So, your changing mood would affect how often or how long you run sessions. That would be quite a change, wouldn't it folks? For so long, you were conducting sessions on the basis of your children's needs and a written program plan, but then you run sessions on the basis of your feelings, which does not mean that you will be satisfying your children's needs.

Mr. Levine: Yeah, that could happen. Pretty sad, huh?

Mrs. Wince: I can see it happening, though, if you're not prepared. And our children would get even worse. They might throw some whopping tantrums just to keep from having sessions.

Mrs. Levine: And we would become even more upset and pessimistic.

Consultant: And the rest of the day?

Mr. Wince: Ignore the kid. Yeah, the kid would remind me of my failure. So, I would stay away. Give the child fewer chances to learn, fewer rewards and prompts.

Consultant: And?

Mr. Wince: She would get even worse. Probably stop doing chores, stop cooperating, go back to goofy behavior.

Consultant: And at some point?

Mrs. Wince: We'd feel like giving up.

Mr. Fernandez: No hope. Just where we started.

Consultant: But, that's not the way it has to be! And look, just because we've predicted what could happen, that is no reason to make it come true!! You don't have to live up to the prediction. So, let's start over. What can you do to make sure that the prediction of mutual deterioration does not come true? Here's a hint—problem-solving!!!

Mrs. Levine: Well, let me see. I'll just check Item 16 on the APG here . . . . Okay, first, I'd check my measurements.

Consultant: Right!! And if your measurements turned out to be accurate—there really is little progress in the teaching program?

Mrs. Levine: Describe the behavior or problem. Is there no progress at all? What kinds of errors is my child making?

Consultant: And then?

Mr. Wince: Let's see. Maybe only a minor adjustment is needed. You know. Maybe the teaching program plan is okay. Maybe the kid needs a little more prompting to get her over the hump.

Consultant: Excellent! But let's say that more or different prompts still aren't enough. How do you keep yourselves from becoming too upset and desperate?

Mr. Fernandez: Well, just keep looking, following the problem-solving sequence. Uh, check the teaching program plan and my own teaching. Maybe I'm not doing what it says or maybe it isn't good.

Mrs. Fernandez: And we could watch and coach each other.

Consultant: Okay, but let's say you revise the teaching program plan and that your teaching skills are up to par, but still little progress results.

Mr. Blake: Well, I can imagine this pretty well. In the pit of my stomach I would start to feel a bit queasy. But let's say I just tell myself that the answer must be somewhere! Okay, so I ask if the kid is even ready for this skill area.

Consultant: Good! And?

Mr. Blake:	Check the BES and Table of Basic Behaviors.
Consultant:	And?
Mr. Blake:	And back up to an easier skill area and work on a different behavior.
Consultant:	Excellent job! Only I think I might add one more thing. Why try the problem-solving all alone?
Mr. Wince:	I've got it! Outside help. Call in a language specialist; check with my child's teacher.
Consultant:	Great! Okay, now let's try it with a different problem. What if you just plain start feeling real tired? What could that lead to? . . . .

In concluding an exercise on alternative scenarios, stress the importance of parents using their own copies of the APG to remind themselves of how to strengthen the items important for conducting, persisting at, and maintaining a good home educational program (Items 11 through 27) and how to solve problems that may arise. In particular, at this time, address such items as marital cooperation, solving personal problems, scheduling and taking breaks, and providing reinforcement for themselves.

Section I of Chapter 10 describes methods you can use if the parents' productive participation and home programs begin to deteriorate either during or after the Program stage.

Linkage in Networks of Backup Support (APG Item 25)

In earlier meetings, the parents began to establish a support network among themselves; for example, through phone calls and interfamily home visits. They also might have started to exchange services with one another, such as babysitting or weekend respite. Toward the end of and following the Program stage, help parents to extend the support network in the following ways:

1. A larger and perhaps more formal (i.e., agreed upon and written) network can be planned and instituted, consisting of periodic telephone calls, a hotline, periodic and emergency home visits, interfamily service exchanges, and linkages with respite care facilities. Parents from past and present Programs, specialists, administrators, and teachers can be part of the network. Moreover, you can conduct training programs for siblings and students who can then provide babysitting, tutoring, and respite services in exchange for certification credit, course credit, and money.

2. Specialists and administrators in special education and mental health can be invited to meetings, both to discuss their possible participation in the network and to provide information useful to the parents' home educational programs.

3. Either parents in Programs or, better, the whole network can be given a name, to increase esprit de corps, formalize the association, and establish it as a potential source of strength in working to plan services and obtain funds from local, state, and federal agencies. The community network need not be an alternative to existing organizations, such as the Association for Retarded Citizens or the National Society for Autistic Children. Rather, if members of the network join these organizations, the network model might be more easily disseminated through them, thereby helping many more people.

4. Parents and other members of the network can be encouraged to give presentations in other educational or mental health facilities, as well as at conferences.

Follow-up and Maintenance Meetings

When the series of instructional meetings (i.e., the Program stage) has ended, the Follow-up stage begins. In our programs, follow-up meetings are scheduled at progressively longer intervals, e.g., bi-weekly, monthly, bi-monthly. It may be, however, that a more variable schedule would help to maintain a smooth change process in the home. Follow-up or maintenance meetings can be conducted like those in the Program stage. The main business might consist of new behaviors or skill areas to work on, a review and evaluation of the overall home program, anticipating and solving problems, and extensions of the support network.

In addition to meetings, we continue to conduct home visits, both to check the parents' assessments of their programs and to provide help if needed. To the extent that the support network has been established, meetings and home visits can be conducted more and more by parents from past and present programs. This helps to strengthen and generalize their skills.

10 HANDLING POTENTIAL AND ACTUAL PROBLEMS

The parents may experience a variety of problems. Some may be of long standing. Others may develop or worsen during the Program. Most are painful in and of themselves. All interfere with conducting, persisting at, and maintaining a good home educational program. In helping parents to remedy problems, you can follow the steps in the problem-solving sequence which you are teaching parents.

I. DECREASE IN READINESS TO CONTINUE WORKING FOR CHANGE AND IN PRODUCTIVE PARTICIPATION

During the Pre-Program stage you worked to strengthen readiness to change (APG Items 2 through 10). The continued strength of those items cannot be taken for granted, however. A number of factors can weaken them, leading to a decrease in productive participation and a deterioration in the home educational program. Examples of a decline in readiness to continue working for change (i.e., "motivation") and in productive participation are as follows.

1. *Decline in parents' belief that they still need to conduct a home educational program.* For instance, they may say that the school is now doing a good job, that the child no longer needs additional help, or that further changes are not worth the effort or time.

2. *Decline in parents' recognition of a need to maintain the changes they have made in their own behaviors or to learn new teaching methods.* For instance, they may say that they do not have to be as consistent in managing productive exchanges or disagree that there is a need to learn special methods to teach their child to relax.

3. *Decline in expectations of success.* That is, parents may lose some of their self-confidence or optimism regarding the chances of further improvement.

> I don't know. Do you think she'll make it?
>
> I'm not sure I've got the brains to teach Billy arithmetic.

4. *Decline in willingness to continue putting in needed time and effort.* For example, a parent might say that he feels he has his own life to lead and is no longer willing to give up his time after a hard day's work.

5. *Decline in energy* sufficient to participate in meetings or to maintain current programs.

> It's getting pretty hard to keep this up. Always on the lookout for behaviors to reward, thinking about the next teaching session. . . .

6. *Decline in acceptance of the behavioral-education approach.* For instance, having encountered an apparent obstacle in their child's educational program (e.g., in speech), a parent may say that his child has a medical problem or one that simply cannot be remedied with educational methods.

> You know, I'm beginning to wonder if Mary really has an allergy. Perhaps if we could find out what kind of allergy she has, and could treat it, she would talk.

Of course, the search for a cure or a faster remedy is reasonable. The problem is that the search may begin to replace productive interaction in the home.

7. *Decrease in parents' taking their turns,* making optimistic and prescriptive statements, asking for concrete suggestions, or in encouraging and reinforcing the productive participation of others; an increase in joking, off-the-subject talk, or in self-pitying remarks; parents coming late or missing meetings, failing to do written and reading assignments or failing to carry out their home program as specified on the Weekly Contract.

Reasons for Decline in Readiness to Continue Working and Productive Participation.

1. *Decline or leveling-off in the child's progress.* For example, the child's overall progress may be slower than the parents expected; new behaviors may improve slower than earlier ones; or progress with a particular behavior may slow down. This may result in a decrease in the parents' self-confidence, optimism, or perceived energy; self-blame or mutual blaming; a decline in cooperative working relationships; anxiety about the future and a depressed mood.

> Why did she slow down!? We were trying so hard.
>
> What's happening? I feel like its all slipping away.

2. *Decline in support parents might have received for having a child with special needs* or for having borne so many problems. For example, the parents may have gotten sympathy in the past, but now that their child has improved, or now that people see that they are getting help, they may not receive as much support as before.

For many parents, past sympathy was accepted somewhat begrudgingly.

> Who wanted their sympathy? We wanted help! or
>
> We were just doing what we had to do.

For them, a decrease in sympathy is not perceived as deprivation; improvement in the children and in their own competence is sufficient. For others, however, a decrease in support (despite improvement in the child) is perceived as deprivation, which may result in a depressed mood and sympathy-seeking behavior. The long-term result may be a deterioration in productive participation.

> Nobody understands what we've been through. Nobody seems to care.
>
> You have to laugh or else you'll cry.

3. *Decrease in the value of improvements in future behaviors with which their children need help.* For instance, an increase in cooperation and a decrease in tantrums early in the Program may be highly gratifying; later improvements in motor imitation or academic tasks may seem relatively less important. The result may be a decline in a recognition to conduct further home programs, to change their own behavior (e.g., to learn new teaching skills) or a general decline in productive participation in meetings (e.g., indifference or argumentativeness).

> Why should we teach that? That doesn't look too important to me.

4. *Fear of the future.* Parents may fear what they cannot predict or feel they can do little about. For example, as a result of having evaluated their child and conducted several successful teaching programs, they may conclude that they are certainly in a position to produce much change. However, the previously obscure mountain is clearly visible; they see how much their child still needs to learn and worry about whether they can give the child what the child needs or whether the child can learn it all.

Similarly, they may worry that services and settings for their child will not be available, that they may die or become disabled and have no one to continue their work or to care for their child. This, too, may result in a depressed mood and difficulty in becoming ''fired-up'' about conducting future teaching programs.

> What's the use? Okay, so she's learning to talk, play, pay attention, and cooperate. But what about 10 years from now when her schooling is no longer covered by the law?

5. *Decrease in the actual need for parents to work as hard or to put in as much time.* When their children improve enough that the parents need not work as hard or as long, or when meetings and home visits become less frequent, some parents may experience difficulties. They may have a depressed mood (perhaps feeling less needed or that they have lost an important source of social reinforcement) or they may have a hard time just filling the now-available time. Some parents overreact. That is, they begin to work much less than is actually needed, resulting in a deterioration in the child's behavior.

Well, he was doing so good that we stopped having sessions and just sort of worked with him now and then. . . . Oh, yeah, he's still doing pretty good, but I guess he could be doing better. . . . Well, maybe he has slipped back some. . . .

6. *Excessive feelings of personal responsibility for behavior change.* Sometimes, parents whose goals are high, who have a strong sense of responsibility for helping their child, who in the past felt guilty for their child's problems, or who have been strongly reinforced for their teaching efforts, may work so hard and put in so much time, that they burn out from overwork. Similarly, they may "push" the child so hard that the child becomes tense or depressed and/or attempts to escape or avoid the parents' teaching efforts through tantrums, withdrawal, or whining. This of course, can start a vicious cycle in which the parents push the child even harder or inadvertently return to counterproductive exchanges.

Damn it! I know you can read this! . . .

Okay, that's it!! No TV, no playing outside, no nothing until you pay attention!

7. *Personal and marital problems* can hinder productive participation and produce a decline in readiness to continue working for change. For instance, although an unassertive parent might have become more secure and self-confident with you during the Pre-Program stage, the parent may be so tense in a group that the parent learns little or comes to fewer and fewer meetings. Similarly, anxiety, a depressed mood, or a lack of mutual reinforcement and cooperation in the home may make it hard for one or both parents to conduct effective programs.

There are two ways to deal with the above problems: avoid them (that is, maintain motivation and productive participation from the start) and/or re-strengthen motivation and participation should they weaken.

Maintaining Readiness to Change and Productive Participation

In the beginning of the Program, describe the potential problems noted above. Stress that they are natural, that you even expect some of them to happen, but that they are avoidable and solvable. Encourage parents to pinpoint problems before they worsen and to air them in meetings, where they can be shared, further discussed, and solutions can be suggested. In fact, you can periodically hold special "state-of-the-Program" meetings, to set the occasion for discussion and solution of difficulties.

Teach parents how to maintain high motivation by: (1) using logs, progress data, the observations of others, and an updating of their child's evaluation so they can keep track of their child's progress, (2) using Items 17 and 18 of their APG to assess their own teaching skills, and (3) systematically scheduling breaks, cooperative activity, and reinforcement.

Restrengthening Readiness to Change and Productive Participation

When problems are common to a group, you might work on them in the group. If not common to the group, you can work on them in Individual Consultations and home visits. Here are methods you can use.

Expectations are not being met. If parents feel that change is too slow, help them to objectively assess how much change has taken place by showing videotapes of their child at different points in the Program. They might also obtain opinions from other parents and outside specialists. In addition, you can stress some of the key ideas presented in earlier units:

1. We are working in small steps.
2. Small changes add up to important ones.
3. Even if we seem to be unsuccessful in several teaching programs, it does not mean that the methods are useless, the parents are incompetent, or that the child is hopeless, but that we have not yet arranged the learning environment to suit the child's needs and must try again.
4. Since other parents and children have eventually achieved beneficial change, so can the parents and children in the present program.

Of course, it is also necessary to assess and if necessary improve the parents' teaching skills and the teaching program plans they are using.

Here is an example of an interchange between a consultant and a parent who does not feel that his expectations are being met.

Parent:	I feel like a flop. It's just awfully hard living with Betty. She's such a pill. (The child has been making progress in the Program, however.)
Consultant:	Pill?
Parent:	Yeah. The way she messes her room and dawdles at the table.
Consultant:	And it's awfully hard to live with that. (Stated in a neutral tone of voice.)
Parent:	Yeah.
Consultant:	Do you think that she should be acting like a perfect lady now? (States what parent seems to want.)
Parent:	(Laughs) Well, I don't know about that. That's a large order.
Consultant:	It is? Why? (Encourages parent to adjust expectations.)
Parent:	Well, I can't expect her to be a perfect lady in a few months.
Consultant:	But it sounds like that's what you want.
Parent:	Sure I do. Wouldn't you?
Consultant:	Yes, but the question is when? When do you want her to be a perfect lady? (Introduces time perspective.)

Parent: I want it now, but I know that I can't have it now. I know that it takes time. That's what aggravates me! (Parent is not gratified by short-run changes.)

Consultant: Aggravated because the goal—her behaving better—isn't achieved yet. And what else is aggravating?

Parent: Well, the disruptions, the behavior.

Consultant: Okay, the disruptions are aggravating. For sure! They would aggravate me, too. But is Betty as disruptive as before?

Parent: Well, no. She's lots better.

Consultant: Yes, she certainly has improved. But, you seem to have your feelings tied to the long-term goals. And since the goals aren't achieved yet, you feel lousy, even about minor disruptions.

Parent: I guess so.

Consultant: Can you tie your feelings to something else besides the long-term goal? (Encourages parent to find more-immediate reinforcers.)

Parent: Smaller steps? Small improvements?

Consultant: Right! To the small changes that add up to your goals. Let's reframe the situation. You feel bad because she hasn't changed as much as you want—yet. Now, how can you view it so that you feel better?

Parent: By seeing how far she has come?

Consultant: Good! How far has she come?

Parent: (Describes improvements.)

Consultant: And she changed all by herself, right? (Encourages parent to reinforce himself.)

Parent: What!! Are you kidding? We've worked our butts off!

Consultant: You think you've done pretty well, huh?

Parent: Yeah! You know what a mess she was when we started!

Consultant: Well, then, what might you say to yourself to reinforce yourself for your successes? . . .

At this point, the parent might be shown videotapes of himself and the child before and during the Program, so that he can pinpoint improvements and reinforce himself ("Hey! I did real well there, didn't I!")

It is possible, of course, that some of the parents' long- or short-term goals need to be revised. Certain goals may be less feasible than had been thought. If so, help parents to break down goals into smaller and easier-to-achieve steps, and to see that the small improvements are important for them and their child. This issue is discussed in Section VII of Chapter 4.

Parents are overwhelmed by the future. If parents seem overwhelmed by the future needs of their child, still have an exaggerated sense of personal responsibility for changing their child, and/or seem to be burning out from overwork, again stress key ideas. Here is what we have said in our Programs.

> So, you seem to be afraid of the future. You have been rather successful in your first couple of teaching programs, and now you see just how much remains to be done. Maybe you see that your children have a long way to go. Maybe you are worrying about what will happen to your children when you pass away. Or maybe you feel so responsible for your children's futures that you feel anxious a lot or have a hard time keeping the task of teaching off your mind. Well, if that is how you feel, it is pretty common. It is disturbing to you, but I assure you that it is common. In fact, it is a good sign! A good sign of how objective you are becoming and of how well you have been teaching!
>
> But let's stand back from your thoughts and feelings for a moment. These things you are worrying about—is this the first time you have ever worried about them? Probably not. You've had these fears for a long time. And even if you have not been worrying for awhile now, the issues have been there all along, haven't they?
>
> What seems to be happening is that knowledge and success have made you so objective that it is hard to keep from looking at the future. Okay, but that does not mean that you must worry about the future! You should be concerned, perhaps, but not worry yourselves sick!
>
> Haven't we learned how to deal with what needs to be done? Of course! That's what this program is all about. We face a problem, describe it, analyze it, plan what to do, and institute our plans. Can't we do the same thing regarding the things that worry you now? Sure we can!
>
> You worry that your children have so much left to learn. Well, as I said, your children always did have much to learn. And you have been working to decrease the size of the task. So, it still looks mighty large?! Well, who said that the job has to be done next week! Can we really rush it anyway? No, we have to go in small steps. Maybe, the way you see it, speech skills are near the top of the mountain. Well you are no longer at the foothills! You have brought your children part way up. Let's look at the remaining steps in teaching speech. . . .
>
> Maybe you are worried that you don't have the skills to teach the remaining behaviors your children need to learn. Is that reasonable? Really, now! If you've learned so much already, why should the rest be any harder? Actually, the methods are no harder. The basic teaching methods (APG Item 18) are just about the same no matter what you teach.
>
> Do you feel that you have to be "on" all the time or your child will slip back? Do you feel that unless you are teaching or thnking about teaching all the time, you are short-changing your child? Have you learned anything that makes such a fear unreasonable? . . . Of course you have! You know that it is not you as a person, but what you and others do. And you also know that you need reinforcement and breaks. You aren't machines. And even if you were, machines can burn out if you push them. Now don't let that happen to you. Take breaks; rest; gratify yourselves. As long as you maintain your child's gains through reinforcement and opportunities to use the skills he or she has learned, the child will not slip back. As long as you continue to institute productive exchanges, and not go and reinforce problem behaviors, your child will keep making progress. Besides, the child needs a break, too. . . .

At this point, you can discuss with parents the ways they have been cooperating, taking breaks, and reinforcing themselves. If necessary, help them to improve these aspects of their home programs, for example, finding more powerful reinforcers for themselves, taking more frequent scheduled breaks, and sharing more tasks. In addition, it is possible that the long- and short-term goals for some children should be revised. Although some children have been making progress on playing skills, imitation, and speech, it may be more important at this time to teach them self-help skills and skills that clearly lead to vocational opportunities.

Increase in Self-Pitying and Pessimistic Remarks. If the frequency of pessimistic, self-pitying remarks is increasing (or has not decreased after the first several weeks of a Program), perhaps because of a decline in support from others or difficulties in the home educational program, make sure to increase the reinforcement you give parents and parents give one another for: (1) having done so well in the Program; (2) making optimistic, activistic, self-congratulatory statements; and (3) remaining oriented to practical teaching tasks. When pessimistic, self-pitying statements occur, do not let parents commiserate. Instead, point out that such behaviors are ultimately worse than useless; they strengthen inactivity and resignation, allowing precious time to go by. Thus, encourage parents to immediately replace such behaviors by pinpointing their strengths and progress. For example:

> You seem to be upset that people don't understand what you've been going through. Do you really think that anyone can understand? . . . Besides, how much help would sympathy and understanding be! Suppose, God forbid, your children had leukemia or were completely paralyzed. Sympathy and understanding might be nice—might make you feel a little better—but would they help your children? No, sympathy and understanding would do nothing for your children!
>
> Well, your children have problems, alright, but luckily for you and for them, they can be corrected (at least in part). So, the question is, what are you going to do about it to make your life easier and your children's lives richer? . . .
>
> There's another angle to consider, namely you. Let's say that you get all the sympathy and understanding you want. People say things to you like "Oh, it must be very hard to live with Bobby" and "I can imagine what you've been through." Well, what is that going to do to you? Which of your behaviors will be reinforced by that kind of talk from others? . . . Sure! Pretty soon you'll be walking around and moaning, either out loud or to yourself. Do you want to see yourself as a person who needs pity from others? Do you want others to see you as being in need of their pity? Do you want people to reinforce you for being pitiful or for being a victor?
>
> Now, I'm not saying that it isn't hard. I'm saying that you have to ask yourself what is in your best interests. Is short-run sympathy really going to help you and your children in the long run? Or is it better to work hard now to change your children, to give and receive practical teaching suggestions, to give and receive reinforcement for hard word and for success?

If necessary, help parents to conduct a special program. For example, a parent might:

a. Pinpoint, describe, and list his pessimistic, self-pitying statements and thoughts and alternative optimistic, self-congratulatory statements and thoughts.

b. Count the number of each type of statement or thought during the day.

c. Practice immediately stopping each pessimistic, self-pitying statement or thought and providing an acceptable replacement.

d. Immediately reinforce himself for the replacement.

e. Arrange to reinforce himself (and/or have another person reinforce him) for daily or weekly increases in the percent of optimistic, self-congratulatory statements and thoughts (Meichenbaum, 1977).

Examples of counterproductive statements and thoughts and productive alternatives, include the following:

Counterproductive	*Productive*
1. No one understands or cares what we've been through.	1. So what? Understanding from others is better for them than for me. Besides it doesn't get the job donc.
2. But Marvin's got so far to go.	2. Yes, but Marvin's come a long way. What a mess he used to be. . . .
3. I just don't have the brains (patience, strength).	3. Of course I've got the brains (patience, strength)! If I've come this far, I can go the rest of the way. It doesn't get any harder.
4. I just can't stand it when Bobby has tantrums. It makes me so nervous . . . .!	4. Baloney! Its unpleasant as hell, but I can stand it. In fact, I won't even try to stand it; I'll just relax my way through it and think about how the graph shows that the number of tantrums is decreasing.
5. What if I fail?	5. Nonsense! What does "fail" mean? So if I run into a problem, I'll correct it. How? I check the book; I check the APG; I call another parent. Finally, I discover the answer. You never fail; you only give up!
6. What if Sally doesn't get any better?	6. What if, what if, what if! I'll do my best and that's it. If she never talks, we'll try signs; if she can't learn signs, at least she'll learn something that will be an improvement.

Decrease in the Value of Future Changes. If parents seem to feel that future behaviors to work on, or further improvements in their child, are not worth the time and effort, first help them to examine the steps between the present situation and their goals. Then it may be possible to increase motivation by helping parents to: 1) teach in a less-effortful fashion (e.g., using more natural exchanges and fewer teaching sessions, and by sharing or splitting tasks in the home); 2) increase the amount of reinforcement they provide themselves or receive from others in the Program; and 3) see that further changes really are important for them and their child (e.g., that further changes will help them to achieve their long-term goals, make their own lives easier and more enjoyable, and increase their child's chances in life). This topic might be addressed in group discussions. Parents from past Programs who have had similar feelings might be asked to attend the meeting.

Decrease in Cooperation with Consultant, Productive Verbal Behavior, and Doing Assignments. If productive participation has remained weak or has declined (e.g., not speaking up and taking turns, complaining and making self-pitying statements, arriving late or missing meetings, not satisfactorily completing assignments), try to strengthen it in the following ways.

First, resolve any problems in the relationship between parents and yourself. For instance:

1. You might not provide enough feedback on performance or enough social reinforcement.
2. Presentations and discussions may be too abstract or seem irrelevent.
3. Instruction might not be individualized enough.
4. The same consultant or different consultants might give conflicting messages and suggestions.
5. Suggested methods might not be working.
6. Parents might feel that you do not like them or their child
7. You may seem to have lost interest.

One way to overcome the above difficulties is to have parents evaluate the Program periodically, either in group discussions or by indicating on a short checklist which aspects of the Program are satisfactory and which they might want changed or improved. By remaining open to parents' perceptions and by revising the program when necessary, the parent-consultant relationship is more likely to remain honest and businesslike. An example of such a checklist is in Appendix 6.

Second, problems of productive participation which are common to the group can be addressed in the group, with parents brainstorming possible solutions and implementing the plan. For example, if engaging in off-the-subject conversation more often, the group might decide to have one member count the number of minutes of off-the-subject talk and graph it. Or if many persons have been arriving late, the group might decide to increase the number of credits for arriving on time. Or, finally, if many parents are experiencing tension, group instruction on relaxation training might be employed.

It is also possible for the group to seek solutions to the problems of an individual or family. For example, in a Program conducted by Dr. Kenneth Kaufman and his staff, one parent was having many problems which made it hard for her to continue in the Program. Instead of simply allowing the parent to drop out, and instead of subtly driving the parent out, the group decided to give the parent extra emotional support in meetings and over the phone until she was able to fully participate again. In this way, the parents see that even if full participation is impossible at the time, they are still members in good standing and are expected to return.

Third, some individual problems should be handled more in private, especially those that would embarrass the parents or worsen the marital relationship. In particular, if parents are arriving late, not doing their assignments, not verbally participating in a constructive way, or simply continuing to make errors in a teaching program, you and the parents can discuss the terms of the Program Contract or Weekly Contract and the parents' performance. You and the parents might then develop a program for strengthening participation.

For example, many problems in doing assignments can be solved by the manner in which suggestions and directions are given. In general, when making suggestions and assigning tasks, point out how the suggestion or task is relevant to the parents' goals and how it follows from the approach that is being used for program planning and problem-solving. As noted in an earlier chapter, disagreements about a certain aspect of a task can often be resolved by leaving it up to the parents to suggest an alternative, carry out their suggestion, evaluate the results, and, if indicated, revise their plan.

Some problems can be handled through tighter scheduling and additional reinforcement. For instance, the parent who does not finish his reading assignments or who often skips teaching sessions, might write a weekly schedule of tasks and arrange for strong reinforcers to follow completion of the tasks. Often, a parent's difficulty in using a certain teaching method (e.g., ignoring bizarre behaviors) can be remedied with extra rehearsal, on-site coaching, and feedback (e.g., videotape).

Problems of productive participation are not always so easily solved, however. A parent might continually:

1. Argue or disagree with your suggestions or directions ("It won't work" or "We've tried that").

2. Fail to do or complete agreed-upon tasks or assignments (''Things came up''; ''I've got my own life to live'').
3. Make many errors despite extra practice and coaching (''I guess I'm just incompetent''; ''Help me. I can't control myself'').

According to Watzlawick et al. (1974), Haley (1976), and Rabkin (1977), the above difficulties represent a number of things. Some parents (a few in my experience) may be trying to gain or maintain control over the parent-consultant relationship or to maintain situations as they are in the home (e.g., by showing that your suggestions do not work). In Chapter 4 we called such behavior communication games. On the other hand, a parent's behavior might be so habitual and long-standing that the parent seems unable to change it. And finally, often, a parent may be so tense and try so hard to carry out an assignment correctly, that the parent makes the very errors he or she is afraid of making.

The works of the three writers cited above are useful in helping parents who persistently fail to perform agreed-upon tasks or continue to make errors in their teaching programs. Briefly, they suggest the following.

1. When assignments are not done, and there is no good reason, do not provide or accept excuses (such as ''Things just came up'' or ''I forgot''). To do so may weaken the basis of the parent-consultant relationship (honesty, working together). In fact, Haley suggests that you tell the parent that the task was important; that it would have been beneficial had the parent done it, but now the parent may never know; and that any problems the parent is now having may be the result of not having done the assignment (Haley, 1976:64).

2. When working with parents who often have excuses for failing to do assignments, you can, after reviewing the next assignment, ask how they think they will avoid the tasks during the next week. If the parents do not suggest ways that they might avoid doing the tasks, give them suggestions—perhaps ways that have been typical. For example: ''Well, perhaps you will be too tired. What will you do then?'' or ''What if someone forgets?'' According to Haley (1976:59), having the parents anticipate and express their own excuses may block them from avoiding the tasks and more fully commit them to doing the tasks.

3. Encourage parents to talk about their problems, which they may experience as serious or desperate. Instead of reassuring them that the problem is not so bad (which excuses them from doing assignments), agree that the problem is indeed desperate and may worsen. Or, if they indicate that improvements have been made, you can agree. In the former case, stress that the assigned tasks will improve the situation and avert an even worse future; in the latter, stress that the tasks will further the improvements (Haley, 1976:55–56).

4. Discuss the parents' difficulty in following directions or doing assignments and ask them what they would advise if they were you (role-reversal). This may motivate them to follow what is, in effect, their own advice (Haley, 1976:54).

5. Present suggestions and assignments in a way that avoids debate and motivates the reluctant parent to follow the suggestion if for no other reason than to prove you wrong. For example, Haley recommends that suggestions sometimes be stated as follows:

> This will probably not work, but you can. . . .
>
> This is going to sound silly, but I want you to do it anyway. . . .
>
> I have a task that I want you to do. I have my reasons for it, but I don't want to go into them now. I just want you to do the task this week. . . .

6. Giving instructions that are the opposite of what the parents expect sometimes helps them to do the assignment or perform a teaching method with fewer errors. In giving such "paradoxical" instructions, communicate that you care for the parents and children and that the instruction will benefit the family. That is, do not present the instruction in a fashion that could be perceived as sarcastic.

For instance, if a parent continues to reinforce tantrums by talking to the child, despite much past reading, rehearsal, and coaching, you might say,

> During the next week, I want you to stop trying to ignore tantrums. In fact, I want you to reinforce them! Talk to Sally when she is throwing tantrums. Look at her. Go to her. This will help you to be more objective about her behavior and your own behavior.

You might specify how many tantrums to reinforce. Similarly, if a parent continues to placate the child, providing free reinforcers during the day and prompting which is no longer needed, you might say:

> During the coming week, I want you to continue to do things for Mickey. Don't try to get him to do things for himself and don't wait for him to do so. Instead, I want you to pay attention to him when he is wandering around the house. Also, help him to dress himself. And give him snacks when he is watching TV, instead of after he does his chores. This will help you to observe Mickey's behavior and to evaluate how much help he needs.

Or, if parents are beginning to revert to counterproductive exchanges with their child, or say that they no longer need to be as consistent, you can give the following instruction and explanation.

> Okay, I think that we may be moving ahead too fast. So, I want you to go back to dealing with Arlo the way you used to. Specifically, I want you to ask him again and again to follow your directions. I want you to pay attention to him when he is whining. And when he is playing constructively, just ignore it. Now this will be beneficial, because if we change things too fast, it may be upsetting to everyone.

If the parents follow the instruction to reinstitute counterproductive exchanges, congratulate them and move ahead to reinstituting productive exchanges. If they do not follow the instruction (and instead, improve their use of productive exchanges), that is what you wanted anyway.

There are several things you can do if a parent is so tense or anxious (especially about making errors) that he or she either cannot carry out a task properly or avoids doing tasks altogether (see also Section II below). First, you might teach progressive relaxation and instruct the parent to practice relaxation exercises prior to the tasks (e.g., teaching sessions). Second, you might teach the parent behavioral rehearsal. In particular, the parent might repeatedly imagine (or practice) performing the tasks, making errors, correcting errors, and finally being successful.

Third, you might teach the use of *self-instructions* while carrying out difficult tasks. For example, the parent might say to himself or herself:

> Okay, now give those signals nice and slow. . . . That was good. . . . Now she's working on the task. She's paying attention very well. . . . Okay, she's almost done. . . . Uh oh! She's having trouble with this problem!! She usually gets upset. What can I do? . . . Easy, relax. Let's see. Okay, try a little prompt. Show her that you understand her difficulty. Point to the answer. . . . Good, real good!

Fourth, you can deal directly with beliefs about incompetence and the supposedly awful consequences of making errors. Cognitive relabeling helps the parent to see that making certain errors does not mean that the parent is a failure, will continue to make errors, or that making errors is so terrible.

Finally, you can give the parent the paradoxical instruction to intentionally make some inexpensive errors each day (Watzlawick et al., 1974:127). For example:

> Now, here is what I want you to do. Every so often, I want you to pay attention to Pat when she hollers at you. And every so often, I want you to leave a snack on the table so that Pat can snitch it. And once in awhile, I want you to have meals too early or too late. Now, you think of several simple errors that you can make. . . . This may sound silly, but it will help you to be less concerned about making errors.

II. PERSONAL AND MARITAL PROBLEMS

Like anyone else, parents of children with learning and behavior problems may experience personal and marital difficulties. For example, they may have a difficult time voicing opinions, taking turns in meetings, requesting help from and instructing others who interact with their children. There may be much role-segregation between the spouses or partners, too little recognition of the other's efforts by one or both spouses, too little emotional support and expressions of affection, and perhaps blaming and criticizing. In addition, parents may experience anxiety and panic; a depressed mood, low level of interest or energy, and sleep disturbances; sensations such as tension, nausea, headaches, heart palpitations, weakness in muscles, and a feeling of unreality. And finally, perhaps accompanying many of the above, parents may make a number of counterproductive self-statements such as "I am a failure"; "Things are hopeless"; or "I am going crazy."

This section does not provide complete clinical solutions to marital and personal problems. Rather it suggests how certain methods might be incorporated in programs for families. More detailed descriptions of clinical procedures can be found in the works cited below. I am not encouraging persons without clinical training and certification to attempt to treat serious problems. If, for example, a Program is being conducted by a teacher, and the parents have problems that are not likely to be remedied by relatively simple suggestions, the teacher should certainly refer the parents to clinically competent persons.

Some Current Ideas

For the past 20 years or so, the behavioral literature has reported the application of numerous therapeutic procedures to equally numerous personal and interpersonal problems. Recently, three ideas have been growing in acceptance.

First, many problems are now seen to be multi-dimensional. For example, a person who has been experiencing the sensations called "anxiety" for a considerable period of time, may also make a number of self-statements, exist in marital or occupational relationships, and utilize methods of coping that all contribute to or worsen the anxiety and engender additional problems.

Second, procedures that seem to be simple are actually complex and affect the client in many ways. In fact, it is often not clear just why a procedure is producing improvement (Goldfried and Davison, 1976; Wachtel, 1977). For instance, simply helping a person to describe fears and self-statements, assuring the person that he or she is not going crazy, may help to reduce unpleasant sensations, replace counterproductive self-statements, and increase the boldness with which the client confronts feared situations.

Third, in view of the above, strategies for helping people to overcome problems are likely to be more effective in the long run if a variety of procedures are utilized, for instance, relaxation to reduce tension; disputation and persuasion to replace counterproductive self-statements and beliefs; problem-solving and "stress inoculation" training to teach a new framework for coping; modeling, behavioral rehearsal, and assertiveness training to teach new skills; and reinforcement contingencies to motivate and strengthen the performance of new skills (Lazarus, 1977; Wolpe, 1973; Goldfried and Davison, 1976; Weekes, 1969, 1972).

Strategies for remedying personal and marital problems generally consist of combinations of the following methods.

Relaxation Training

Relaxation training has been used in many ways: (1) as part of systematic or symbolic desensitization (e.g., in the treatment of phobias and anxiety states); (2) to help persons confront anxiety-provoking situations (i.e., as a coping skill); (3) to facilitate behavior rehearsal; (4) to facilitate work on cognitive relabeling and the client's participation in therapeutic conversation; (5) to remedy headaches, insomnia, and mild depression; and (6) to reduce general tenseness and fear of anxiety (Goldfried and Davison, 1976; Bernstein and Borkovec, 1973; Rimm and Masters, 1974). The training itself has been provided by clinicians, audiotapes, and manuals (such as those of Cautela and Groden, 1978; Jacobson, 1964, 1976; Walker, 1975; and Benson, 1975), both in individual consultant-client relationships and in groups (Wolpe, 1973; Rose, 1977).

In general, relaxation training involves the development of three skills. First, the person is taught to relax all parts of the body. Second, the person might be taught to use "differential relaxation." This is based on the observation that a person's muscles may be more tense than is required to successfully perform an activity, the result being "residual tension which contributes nothing to the behavior and which needlessly increases psychological stress" (Bernstein and Borkovek, 1973:39). When using differential relaxation,

> Deep relaxation is induced and maintained in the muscles not required for the ongoing activity. For muscles involved in the activity, excess tension is eliminated; only the amount of tension necessary for behavioral performance remains. The result is that the client can perform most daily activities with a minimum of tension and a maximum of relaxed comfort. [Bernstein and Borkovec, 1973:39]

Third, the person might be taught conditioned relaxation. As noted by Bernstein and Borkovec, the goal is to enable the person to achieve a relaxed state in response to self-produced cues, such as "calm," "relax." Conditioned relaxation is taught by associating the state of muscle relaxation with the self-produced cues. The result is that the person may be able to reduce tension when it occurs or avoid tension in formerly-stressful situations through the use of the cues.

Replacing Erroneous and "Irrational" (Counterproductive) Self-Statements

Many researchers and clinicians argue that feelings and actions are mediated by the cognitive structures, schemas, and belief systems that develop on the basis of experience, and which may be represented by the statements people habitually make to themselves. To the extent that self-statements made in response to past, present, and anticipated events are erroneous, overgeneralized, arbitrary, or overly magnified, they may elicit, maintain, or worsen painful feelings and set in motion vicious cycles of counterproductive action. The literature documenting the above points is large, but has been partially summarized in Ellis and Grieger (1977).

Common examples of erroneus or irrational self-statements include:

I am inferior.

They will think (or what if they think) I'm stupid (sick, weak).

I will never feel better. (or What if I don't feel better?)

I should always be successful.

I am going crazy.

I always fail (make a fool of myself).

I can't stop feeling this way.

I don't deserve this. (This shouldn't happen to me.)

I can't help (change) myself.

I deserve this because I'm stupid (weak, evil).

I should always feel good.

I can't stand to feel bad (fail).

I must be loved (given recognition) by everyone (at all times).

I must continuc to think about my problems and try to understand them, until they are solved.

I desperately need others to depend or rely on.

My personal miseries come from external events. (Therefore, either nothing can be done and I must remain miserable or I must rely on others to help me.)

It is easy to see how the above self-statement can produce or worsen problems. For example, a parent might:

1. Judge several teaching programs to be unsuccessful and overgeneralize to all future programs (''What if the next program is a failure?''; ''I am worthless''; ''Billy is hopeless'').
2. Experience sadness or anxiety, and then magnify, overreact to, or ''catastrophize'' it (Ellis, 1962) so much that the feelings worsen, giving the parent even more to worry about (''Oh, God! I can't stand it! I'm coming unglued'').
3. Blame the other for marital difficulties or personal problems (''If he weren't so cold I would feel all right. It's all his fault'').
4. Burn out from overwork (''If I stop I'll fail my child'' or ''It's now or never'').

5. Continually fail to perform assigned tasks, justifying nonperformance ("Well, I'm just a jerk [so I'm not responsible]" or "What does it matter? I'll probably fail, anyway").

6. Continue to make errors or be tense before and during teaching sessions ("What if I do it wrong"; "I've made so many mistakes that I'm bound to make more mistakes"; or "What will they think when they find out?").

The method for helping to replace counterproductive self-statements has several labels (rational-emotive therapy, cognitive therapy, cognitive restructuring, and cognitive relabeling) and is found in the works of Ellis and Grieger (1977), Ellis and Harper (1961, 1973, 1975), Ellis (1975), Beck (1972, 1976), Meichenbaum (1977), Goldfried and Davison (1976), Mahoney (1974), Wolpe (1973, Chapter 4); and Weekes (1969, 1972). The following steps are used.

First, the consultant provides the client with a rationale (i.e., how emotions and actions are affected by our beliefs, interpretations, and self-statements). In addition, the consultant might encourage the client to analyze irrational or erroneous beliefs by reversing roles with the client (Goldfried and Davison, 1976). For example, the client might be asked to assess the reasonableness of the consultant's beliefs that the consultant should be successful or happy at all times, be approved of by everyone, or be terrified and made helpless by sadness, tension, or anxiety.

Second, the consultant helps the client to analyze his or her problems in terms of cognitive-behavioral theory. In particular, the client learns to describe the relationships between problematic situations or events (e.g., perceived failure, marital difficulties, depressed mood), irrational self-statements made in response to such events (e.g., "This is terrible"; "Its her fault"; or "I can't stand it"), the worsening of the painful feelings (e.g., increased depression or anxiety), and counterproductive efforts to cope (e.g., withdrawal, counteraggression).

Third, the consultant helps the client to actively replace counterproductive beliefs and self-statements by:

1. Pinpointing and describing unpleasant feelings when they occur.

2. Stopping and pinpointing irrational self-statements ("Now, what am I telling myself? What 'shoulds,' 'oughts,' 'what-ifs,' and 'Oh, my's' am I saying to myself?"), thereby breaking up habitual connections among events, counterproductive self-statements, and feelings.

3. Immediately replacing any irrational beliefs and self-statements with more reasonable ones:

> Okay, here comes that familiar sinking feeling. Just let it come. It won't kill me, drive me mad, or interfere with my work.

Time for another teaching session. Afraid of failing? So what? If you make errors, write them down and practice correcting them. It won't be the end of the world. Relax.

4. Practicing the above steps by imagining real-life situations:

Okay, now imagine that you are in a meeting and it is almost your turn to describe your home program. . . . How do you feel? . . . What are you telling yourself? . . . Is it reasonable to believe that? . . . What can you tell yourself that is more reasonable? . . .

5. Applying the above steps in real-life situations. Here, the client is prepared for less-than-complete success at first, perhaps uses self-relaxation in difficult situations, and imagines the consultant as a model (e.g., "What would she say to herself if she were getting tense?").

Modeling and Behavior Rehearsal

Modeling and behavior rehearsal are used to (1) teach new skills; (2) facilitate the performance of behaviors already in the person's repertoire, but which may be inhibited by anxiety and counterproductive thoughts; or (3) inhibit the performance of inappropriate behaviors. In general, behavior rehearsal involves practicing new performances and then applying them to real-life situations. Modeling involves observing another (the model) engage in a performance. From this, the person learns what to do and/or what not to do and applies what he or she has learned to real-life situations.

The actual training in behavior rehearsal and modeling can be conducted in individual sessions and groups, either in live (in vivo) situations (e.g., in the office, in the home, in meetings) or symbolically (i.e., in imagination). Both methods have been studied and used a great deal (Bandura, 1969; Bandura and Walters, 1963; McFall and Lillesand, 1971; Kelly, 1955; Cautela et al., 1974; Mahoney, 1974; Rose, 1977; Goldfried and Davison, 1976; Kazdin, 1974a, 1974b; Suinn, 1972).

As described by Goldfried and Davison (1976), training in behavior rehearsal and modeling has four steps. First, the consultant prepares the client by explaining how rehearsal or modeling can be beneficial and that, while the methods may seem artificial, the training can generalize to real-life situations. Second, the consultant and client select target situations or behaviors to focus upon. These may be listed in a hierarchy, beginning with the easiest.

The third and fourth steps consist of rehearsal or modeling and then application. The amount of time between the last two steps seems to depend on the difficulty of the performance to be learned, the specific training method used, and the progress of the client. Alternative methods are as follows.

1. In Vivo (Live) Rehearsal. This is about the same as role-playing described in earlier chapters. The client practices the new performances in small steps. The consultant provides coaching, immediate and follow-up feedback (e.g., verbally or with video and audiotape), and reinforcement. When the appropriate performances have been learned in practice sessions, the client begins to apply them in real-life situations, perhaps with initial coaching from the consultant or another. The client now prompts and reinforces himself (with self-statements) before, during, and after the performances. For example:

> Its okay if I make some errors. I've had lots of practice. I can do it. . . . Hey! I'm doing real well. Keep it up. . . . That's it. . . . Well, that wasn't so hard. Think I'll have a beer.

In addition, the client might use self-relaxation before and during the performance. Goldfried and Davison (1976) also suggest that the client keep records of his or her behavior, noting strong points to continue, weak points to correct, and the consequences of the new performances, such as reactions of others and feelings of self-satisfaction.

2. Covert or Symbolic Rehearsal. The person imagines performing the appropriate behaviors, making and correcting errors, and producing successful outcomes (Cautela, 1970; McFall and Lillesand, 1971). Covert rehearsal might be used both when it is difficult to obtain practice in real-life situations and as preparation for novel or troublesome activities. For example, a parent who has been experiencing difficulties speaking up in meetings, or who has become anxious about doing well in teaching sessions, might engage in covert rehearsal prior to meetings and teaching sessions. For instance:

> Well, now. Let's imagine this afternoon's session. I see myself getting a little nervous. So, I breathe out slowly and say "calm, calm." Yeah, I can even feel it now! A little more relaxed. . . . Well, now I'll call Nan to the table. She says, "Aw, Mom, I want to watch TV." And I say, "I know you do. It's 15 minutes 'till the Peartree Family comes on. As soon as we do your lesson, you can watch it." She fusses a little, but I ignore it. Then. . . .

3. In Vivo Modeling. The client observes the consultant or another person perform the appropriate behaviors and then is given the opportunity to perform the same behaviors (as in behavioral rehearsal). The sequence of observation and practice are repeated until the proper level of skill is achieved. When modeling is used, the model must have certain characteristics, such as warmth, credibility, and attractiveness to the observer-learner. In addition, the observer-learner should see the model receive reinforcement for the appropriate performance. For example, if the model is demonstrating teaching methods, the methods should be successful or if the model is demonstrating methods for being assertive, the model's behaviors should produce satisfactory outcomes. Similarly, when practicing behaviors he or she has observed, the learner should be reinforced.

There are several variations of modeling. In *reverse modeling,* the client plays the role of model for others acting as observers who are to learn from the client-model. This may be a useful way of practicing new skills before actually applying them. In *negative modeling,* on the other hand, the client observes a model engage in inappropriate or incorrect performances. For example, the model can demonstrate incorrect teaching procedures, marital conflicts, and counterproductive exchanges between parents and children. This may facilitate the discrimination of productive and unproductive behaviors.

4. Covert Modeling. The client imagines how a model would perform appropriate behaviors (Cautela et al., 1974; Kazdin, 1973, 1974a, 1974b; Mahoney, 1974). Again, the characteristics of the imagined model and the reinforcement received by the imagined model are important. According to Mahoney, of the covert procedures, covert modeling "stands alone as the most consistently effective procedure" (Mahoney, 1974:118). There are several ways it could be used in programs for parents. For example, prior to instituting a new teaching program, a parent might imagine how the consultant would conduct the first session. Or, if a child began to engage in problem behaviors for which the parent was not prepared, the parent might imagine how a parent who has been quite successful in similar situations would handle the behavior.

Reinforcement Contingencies. In general, some type of reinforcement contingency is useful to motivate and strengthen performance of behaviors designed to remedy problems. Naturally, the consultant should reinforce the parents for learning and applying their skills. In addition, parents should reinforce themselves and each other. In some cases (e.g., programs for remedying marital difficulties) contingency contracts can be written, which specify the expected behaviors of each party and the reinforcing consequences for appropriate performance.

Applications

There are several ways in which the above methods might be used to help parents with personal and marital problems. Information indicating the existence of such problems may have been acquired from the Assessment Interview, your own observations during the Program, or parents' self-reports. As noted in Chapter 2, parents may have had problems for many years, possibly engendered or worsened by the difficulties encountered during their career. On the other hand, problems may have begin, or worsened, during the Program itself, because of the personal and interpersonal changes required by participation, perceived slow progress or failure, or factors largely outside the scope of the Program (e.g., job layoff).

Tension and Anxiety

Classic anxiety consists of a syndrome of feelings and physical sensations (restlessness, palpitations, muscle tension, fatigue, rapid pulse, pains, choking feeling in the throat, nausea, giddiness), thoughts or self-statements (''I can't stand this''; ''I'm going crazy''; ''What if this doesn't go away''; ''I'm afraid of that'') and behaviors (e.g., avoidance of situations in which the above reactions occur). Strategies for remedying tension and anxiety involve combinations of the methods described earlier, generally applied in three stages.

First, the consultant explains the condition to the client. This might involve replacing erroneous, anxiety-producing misconceptions, such as that the condition is chronic, will worsen, lead to insanity, or produce physical breakdown. Of course, the explanation and reconceptualization depend on the consultant's theoretical orientation, for example, respondent conditioning (Wolpe, 1973, Salter, 1961), autonomic oversensitivity (Weekes, 1969, 1972), or cognitive-behavioral interactions (Goldfried and Davison, 1976; Ellis and Harper, 1961; Lazarus, 1977).

Second, the consultant and client assess the condition by pinpointing and describing:

1. The external situations in which tension and anxiety occur.
2. The internal events (self-statements, images, and sensations) that elicit, prolong, or worsen the tension and anxiety.
3. The client's efforts to cope with the feared situations and sensations.
4. Possibly the relationships between the client and others (e.g., reinforcement for avoidance behavior, lack of reinforcement for efforts to cope, marital conflict, occupational vulnerability).

Assessment may consist of structured self-report, for example, the Willoughby Neuroticism Schedule (Willoughby, 1934), the Bernreuter Scale, the Fear Survey Schedule (Wolpe and Lang, 1969), or the Assertion Inventory (Gambrill and Richey, 1975); observation of the client in the natural environment (e.g., observing the parent in meetings, in the home, and in public places); and self-recording by the client (e.g., the parent might describe the times and places when tension and anxiety occur, self-statements, and responses to the sensations and thoughts).

Third, methods are used for teaching the client to reduce and control tension and anxiety.

In systematic (symbolic) desensitization, developed by Wolpe (1973), the consultant and client develop a hierarchy consisting of the sensations, thoughts, and situations to which the client has been responding with tension and anxiety. The client is taught how to vividly imagine various scenes and how to progressively relax his or her muscles. Then, the consultant teaches the client to relax while vividly imagining scenes from the hierarchy, starting with those associated with the least tension and anxiety. Gradually, the client learns to remain relaxed while imagining more and more fearful scenes.

The following are examples of partial hierarchies that may be used by parents with Program-related fears.

Tension and Anxiety Associated with Describing Home Program in Meetings
I am:

1. Watching the sun set.
2. Watching TV and remember that there is a meeting in five days.
3. Reading the assigned chapter to be discussed at the next meeting, which is in three days.
4. Conducting a teaching program which will be videotaped the next day and shown at the meeting.
5. Waking up and remember that the meeting is tonight.
6. Getting dressed for the meeting.
7. Driving to the meeting.
8. Walking up the stairs to the meeting room.
9. In the room and see other parents.
10. Talking to parents and consultants before the meeting starts.
11. Sitting in the group while the consultant reviews ideas presented at the last meeting.
12. Listening to another parent describe her home program.
13. Listening to the parent who finishes talking and it is my turn.
14. Describing my home program, reading from my notes.
15. Describing my home program, not reading from my notes.
16. Describing my home program while a videotape of my teaching session is running.
17. Asked by another parent how well the teaching program worked.
18. Told by another parent that I made several errors.

Tension and Anxiety Associated with Conducting a Teaching Program
I am:

1. Watching my favorite TV program.

2. Reading how to teach the new target behavior.

3. Sitting in a chair counting the target behavior during the baseline.

4. Sitting at the table, writing the teaching program plan.

5. Arranging the room and materials before the teaching session.

6. Starting the teaching session. The child sits, pays attention to me, cooperates with my directions, and makes three correct responses in a row.

7. Starting the teaching session and giving the child a direction even though the child is not paying attention.

I am teaching and:

8. Forget to reinforce a correct response.

9. The child makes several errors in a row.

10. The child begins to whine.

11. The child throws a tantrum.

Naturally, the parents may have other fears, both related and unrelated to the Program (their child's future, taking the child to public places, illness and death, being in closed spaces, being in open spaces, being anxious). Both Goldfried and Davison (1976) and Wolpe (1973) describe methods for developing hierarchies for fears such as these.

A number of other methods may be used, either in addition to or instead of symbolic desensitization.

1. Teach the parent to use relaxation prior to and during otherwise-stressful situations (i.e., as a coping response). For example, a parent who is tense and anxious about participating in meetings, might practice relaxation before the meeting (perhaps imagining scenes in a hierarchy) and use conditioned relaxation during the meeting.

2. Teach the parent to pinpoint and replace counterproductive self-statements when in new situations or situations which formerly produced anxiety. For example, the parent might learn to tell himself or herself:

> (In public with the child) Their opinions aren't important.
>
> (Before a teaching session) It's not bad to make mistakes. It teaches me to correct them.
>
> (After several weeks of slow progress) Billy won't regress just because we've had two slow weeks.

(During a "spell" of anxiety) I'm not going crazy. This is just uncomfortable. It'll pass.

(During a teaching session) I'm not a failure. I merely made a few errors, I'll correct them next time.

(Before falling asleep) Okay, so I don't know exactly what the future holds in store. Well, I don't have to know what will be in order to work effectively now. Anyway, there's only so much a human can do.

3. Help the parent to use in vivo desensitization (gradual exposure to real-life situations). As preparation for exposure, the parent might practice correct responses (through in vivo or covert behavior rehearsal) or observe others engage in appropriate behaviors (through in vivo or covert modeling). For example, prior to conducting teaching sessions, the parent might, in reality or in imagination, practice conducting sessions, making errors, becoming tense, relaxing, replacing counterproductive thoughts, correcting errors, and eventually succeeding. Or, the parent might, in reality or in imagination, observe others conducting teaching sessions.

The above preparatory methods have been systematized in an approach called "stress inoculation training" (Meichenbaum, 1977; Meichenbaum and Turk, 1976; Gambrill, 1977). Briefly, the client is taught to:

a. Prepare for a stressful situation (planning what to do, not making irrational self-statements).

b. Confront and handle a stressful situation (going one step at a time, focusing on the task and not the fear, using tension and fear as a cue to cope via relaxation).

c. Cope with feelings of being overwhelmed (label fear, plan how to cope with it, keep it manageable, make optimistic self-statements).

d. Provide reinforcing self-statements for having successfully coped.

Having prepared to successfully cope with stressful or anxiety-producing situations, the person is gradually exposed to real-life situations. As in the preparatory period, the person:

a. is coached as needed:

Okay, now if anxiety starts to build, you know what to do.

Stand back from it. Look at it. Let it happen. Relax through it. . . . You're doing fine.

b. employs relaxation if tension and anxiety occur:

Here it comes. . . . Good! A chance to show myself what I can do. . . . Relax. . . . Breath slowly. . . . That's it. . . .

c. replaces irrational self-statements if they occur:

Nothing to worry about. A few errors won't hurt.

d. guides performance with self-instructions:

Now, what is happening here?. . . . Maybe the task is too hard. . . . Let's see. Good prompting, clear signals, good rewards. . . . Yep. The task is too hard for her. Okay, let's back up to easier problems. . . .

e. perhaps uses covert modeling to generate solutions to ongoing difficulties or as a source of reinforcement:

Now how would Mr. Fernandez handle this? He always seems so cool. . . . Yeah, I can just see him relaxing and telling himself to try, try again. . . . Good job. I can hear him saying that I did it right.

f. and provides self-reinforcement for successful action:

Well, that was just fine. You're doing real well. Keep it up champ!

4. Finally, when planning and instituting a program to remedy tension and anxiety, determine the ways that others in the parents' environment might be involved. For example, other parents might serve as models and coaches or the spouse might help the anxious partner to practice relaxation exercises, remind the partner to replace counterproductive thoughts, and reinforce the partner for successfully coping with stressful situations.

Again, while not suggested as an alternative to necessary clinical intervention, the following books may be helpful for parents: *Relaxation* (Cautela and Groden, 1978), *Anxiety and Tension Control* (Jacobson, 1964), *You Must Relax* (Jacobson, 1976), *A Guide to Rational Living* (Ellis and Harper, 1961), *A New Guide to Rational Living* (Ellis and Harper, 1975), and the extraordinarily sensitive and clear *Hope and Help for Your Nerves* (Weekes, 1969) and *Peace From Nervous Suffering* (Weekes, 1972).

Note that the above methods and books can be used in individual consultant-parent relationships and in groups (Rose, 1977; Lazarus, 1961; Paul and Shannon, 1966).

Unassertiveness

This refers to a variety of interpersonal difficulties, such as:

1. Not speaking up for or asserting personal and perhaps legal rights (e.g., failing to return shoddy merchandise or allowing oneself to be belittled by others).

2. Not speaking up or taking one's turn in conversations and group discussions (e.g., allowing others to hog a conversation or remaining silent in meetings).
3. Not initiating beneficial interactions (e.g., failing to ask for help).
4. Not preventing oneself from being drawn into (or not terminating) unpleasant situations (e.g., going to a boring meeting as a result of pressure from peers or spouse or allowing arguments to continue).

As noted by Gambrill (1977), the short- and long-term results of unassertiveness include the loss of opportunities; unpleasant physiological responses ("stress"); rumination and counterproductive self-statements ("I'm such a jerk"); accumulated resentment and anger; and perhaps unproductive ways of responding to the problems generated by unassertiveness (e.g., "blowing up," drinking, or social isolation). On a larger scale, unassertiveness helps to maintain an unequitable distribution of resources and inadequate service delivery systems.

According to Goldfried and Davison (1976), unassertiveness may involve at least five factors. A person may:

1. Not know what to do or say in various situations.
2. Not know how to respond.
3. Experience anxiety before and during social encounters, which interferes with productive action (Wolpe, 1973; Salter, 1961: Chapters 11 to 13; Gambrill, 1977).
4. Have "vague and perhaps unrealistic concerns" about the consequences of self-assertion (Goldfried and Davison, 1976:238) for example, that it results in punishment.
5. Have values and beliefs that make the person feel incapable of self-assertion or that self-assertion is improper (Lange, 1977; Wolpe, 1973).

Consequently, strategies for remedying unassertiveness incorporate a number of methods as described in the literature on individual consultant-client relationships (Salter, 1961; Wolpe, 1973; Goldfried and Davison, 1976) and on programs for groups (Cotler and Guerra, 1976; Shoemaker and Paulson, 1976; Lange, 1977; Lange and Jakubowski, 1976; Rathus, 1972; Rose, 1977).

Assertiveness training involves the following general steps and methods.

First, the consultant helps the client to see the need for and likely benefits of becoming more assertive. As Wolpe writes:

> Simple direct coaxing and goading is often all that is necessary. This consists in part of emphasizing the disadvantages of non-assertion—its inevitable winlessness, its frequently unpleasant emotional consequences, the unfavorable image it gives to others—and in part of promising increasing ease of execution of assertive acts as anxiety diminishes. [Wolpe, 1973:83.]

Second, the nature and extent of assertiveness and unassertiveness are assessed. Information may be obtained through: self-monitoring (e.g., the client can observe and record his or her behavior in various situations); questionnaires such as the "Assertion Questionnaire" (Wolpe and Lazarus, 1966), "Conflict Resolution Inventory" (Gambrill and Richey, 1975), "Rathus Assertiveness Schedule" (Rathus, 1973), "Behavioral Assertiveness Test" (Eisler et al., 1973) and the "Assertiveness Inventory" (Alberti and Emmons, 1974); observations made by the consultant or another person (e.g., what the client does in meetings or public places); and through various exercises with the consultant (such as the client's demonstrating or answering questions about what the client does in certain situations). On the basis of the assessment, a hierarchy of problematic situations can be developed.

Third, the consultant and client develop plans for properly assertive behavior in pinpointed situations. This involves defining: (1) what the client's rights seem to be; (2) the difference between unassertive, properly-assertive, and aggressive action; (3) what the client might actually do or say; and (4) the likely consequences of proper assertiveness.

Fourth, the client learns how to be properly assertive in the pinpointed situations through: (1) modeling and behavior rehearsal (perhaps reading from a script at first and role-playing); (2) symbolic desensitization to reduce anxiety; and (3) cognitive relabeling via disputation and persuasion to help the client pinpoint and replace counterproductive beliefs and self-statements about his or her capabilities, the likely outcomes, and the alleged impropriety of self-assertion.

Finally, during practice sessions and actual applications, the client might use self-instructions, self-relaxation, rational self-statements, and covert modeling to facilitate proper action, and receive coaching, feedback, and reinforcement from the consultant or others.

Assertiveness training has several uses in a Program for parents. First, some parents may have particular problems related to unassertiveness, for example, not speaking up or taking turns in meetings, having self-confidence shaken by more assertive parents, or making negative self-statements based on perception of past failure. In this case, you can work with parents during Individual Consultations and home visits, using the methods described in the above writings. In addition, parents might read books such as *Your Perfect Right* (Alberti and Emmons, 1974), *When I Say No, I Feel Guilty* (Smith, 1975), *A Guide to Rational Living* (Ellis and Harper, 1961) or *A New Guide to Rational Living* (Ellis and Harper, 1975).

On the other hand, parents may have common interests or face difficulties for which group assertiveness training is relevant. For example, in preparing to generalize their own and their children's skills, parents can list the situations to which they wish to generalize behaviors; describe the actions they might take in those situations; and write scripts and role-play properly-assertive actions to enlist cooperation or help, respond to unkind remarks, and handle interference from others.

Special attention should be paid to the parents' role in the implementation of Public Law 94-142 (the Education for All Handicapped Children Act). As noted in Chapter 1, the situation in many communities contains elements that can foster conflictual-adversary relationships between parents, administrators in education and mental health, specialists, teachers and aides, for instance:

1. Past lack of services.
2. Parents' rising expectations and legal rights.
3. The complexity of relationships (regarding authority and communication) in community service delivery systems.
4. The difficulty administrators have in obtaining needed resources.
5. The need for teacher and teacher-aide training.
6. The lack of a shared framework for evaluating children, planning their programs, guiding their movement through the system, coordinating and evaluating services.
7. The complex motives and sentiments of persons in the system (hostility, distrust, caring, frustration, vulnerability).

In my opinion, there are occasions when social change may require conflictual-adversary relationships (as when persons have absolutely irreconcilable interests). More often, however, such relationships are both unnecessary and have consequences that are the opposite of what was wanted—for example, increased suffering, deep hostility, the development of motives unrelated to the original issue (such as securing one's job or beating the opponent rather than serving the children), and perhaps the creation of a system that is no better than the old (e.g., a proliferation of services that are neither coordinated nor appropriate to children's needs).

In view of the above, group assertiveness training may be one way of helping parents to determine when an adversary relationship seems necessary, how to work with teachers, and how to de-escalate adversary relationships. Specifically:

1. Parents can read and discuss materials concerning Public Law 94-142, their rights, and due process, such as *Making School Work* (Brown and Spofford, 1973); *Primer on Due Process* (Abeson et al.); articles in *The Exceptional Parent;* "Your Rights Under the Education for All Handicapped Children Act" (Children's Defense Fund, 1520 New Hampshire Ave., N.W., Washington, D.C. 20036); past and future reports from *Closer Look* (National Information Center for the Handicapped, 1201 16th St., N.W., Washington, D.C. 20036); and materials from various organizations, such as National Association for Retarded Citizens (2709 Avenue E, East Arlington, Texas 76011); United Cerebral

Palsy Associations (66 East 34th St., New York, N.Y. 10016); National Association of the Physically Handicapped (6423 Grandville Ave., Detroit, Mich. 48228); International Association for Parents of the Deaf (814 Thayer Ave., Silver Spring, Md. 20910); Association for Children with Learning Disabilities (5225 Grace St., Pittsburgh, Pa. 15236); American Council of the Blind (1211 Connecticut Ave., N.W., Suite 506, Washington, D.C. 20036); American Coalition of Citizens with Disabilities (1346 Connecticut Ave., N.W., Rm. 817, Washington, D.C. 20036), National Society for Autistic Children (169 Tampa Ave., Albany, N.Y. 12208), and National Center for Law and the Handicapped (1235 North Eddy St., South Bend, Ind. 46617).

2. Parents can pinpoint the circumstances in which they might interact with teachers, specialists, and administrators (e.g., during their child's evaluation; to find out what methods the teachers are using; to ask for suggestions or to suggest changes in the educational program; or to request additional services). Then parents can plan and practice how to initiate interaction with and/or respond by phone, letter, or in person, for example, when:

a teacher is open to the parent's queries and suggestions.

a teacher is uneasy, reluctant to describe methods being used or child's progress, blames parent for problems child is having.

an administrator is happy to speak with the parent, accepts parent's suggestion that the educational system needs to be improved, works to provide services that are requested.

an administrator is hard to reach, argues that child is receiving adequate services, seems to stall.

members of child's evaluation committee ignore parents' presence, speak in jargon, imply that parents do not have the expertise to contribute to evaluation or planning decisions, imply that parents are to blame for child's problems or are themselves intellectually or emotionally impaired.

specialists describe what is being done or will be done, adequately answer parents' questions, translate findings into procedures parents can use at home.

specialists do not adequately describe procedures or answer parents' questions, do not translate findings into methods parents can use at home, imply that parents are not qualified to judge services provided, tell parents to see the business office if they are not satisfied with the bill.

3. To reduce or avoid a conflictual-adversary relationship, administrators, teachers, specialists, and aides can be invited to participate in the Program. In this way, it may be possible to slowly develop a larger framework within which cooperative problem-solving can take place.

Depression

The syndrome of depression, which has several levels of severity, consists of many symptoms, including sadness, loss of gratification and interest, apathy and boredom; a decrease in social participation, sexual activity, rate of speech, communication with others, and ability to perform usual behaviors; complaints about guilt, memory, loneliness, and material losses (e.g., money, job); excessive crying, weeping, and indecisiveness; sleep disturbances, fatigue, headaches, dizziness, generalized pain, gastrointestinal problems; and negative self-statements, for example, self-blame, pessimism, helplessness, inadequacy, and powerlessness (Lewinsohn et al., 1976). There are many models of depression, each trying to describe relationships among the symptoms and between the symptoms and other aspects of the person's life. On the one hand, some working within the biogenic approach see depression as the result of imbalances in the chemistry of the brain, possibly based on a genetic predisposition and precipitated or worsened by acute or chronic life stress (Rosenthal, 1970).

Within the behavioral approach, on the other hand, McLean (1976a) has summarized six models. The "behavioral reinforcement" model focuses on the reduction in reinforcement, the rate of reinforceable behaviors, and reinforcer effectiveness, and on the reinforcement of depressive behavior. The "cognitive distortion" model, best represented by the work of Beck (1972, 1976), Beck and Shaw (1977) and Shaw and Beck (1977) is based on the proposition that "the idiosyncratic, distorted conceptions of depressed patients are central in the development and maintenance of depressive symptomatology" (Beck and Shaw, 1977:119). Specifically, Beck and Shaw argue that the depressed person's view of the world is a "cognitive triad" consisting of a negative view of the self, the world, and the future. Moreover, the depressed person tends to distort experiences, for example, by misinterpreting irrelevant events in terms of personal failure, rejection, or deprivation; exaggerating and overgeneralizing events that bear a semblance of negative information regarding the self; and preseverating in making "indiscriminate, negative predictions of the future" (Beck and Shaw, 1977:121).

The "life stress events" model points to the experience of acute or chronic stressors impinging on the person, which elicit or worsen depression (e.g., marital conflicts, separation, divorce, illness, death, and job difficulties). The "interpersonal disturbance" model focuses on the person's failure to successfully control the interpersonal environment, either because of a skill deficiency or because of the greater power of others in the environment (e.g., in a coercive marital relationship). Similarly, the "learned helplessness" model sees depression as resulting from the continual frustration of goal-attainment, which results both in the belief that responding is useless and in general feelings of helplessness (Wolpe, 1973; Seligman, 1975).

Finally, the "variable cause" model is based on the assumption that depression is caused by a number of factors. For instance. Weekes (1969, 1972) argues that depression sometimes results from chronic sensitization, fatigue, anxiety, and apparently-unsolvable conflicts, coupled with the person's misunderstanding, exaggeration, and fear of the symptoms themselves.

Many current treatment strategies explicitly utilize a number of methods in a sequence of steps.

1. In view of the many factors that may be involved in depression, the actual suffering, and the potential consequences of inadequate help (namely suicide), proper assessment is essential. As described by Lewinsohn et al. (1976), depression can be measured via: a) interview rating scales (Hamilton, 1960; Grinker et al., 1961); b) self-report (Beck, 1967; Zung, 1965; Lubin, 1965, 1967); and c) behavioral observation (Williams et al., 1972; Lewinsohn et al., 1971), which might involve home observations by the consultant.

2. When the initial assessment is completed, the consultant summarizes the collected information, goals are established, and treatment procedures are described. Other family members may be present, so as to establish a mutual understanding of the client's difficulties, the goals, and procedures.

3. In some cases, medication and/or electrical stimulation are used to produce a relatively quick relief from certain symptoms.

4. Other family members may be involved in the treatment. First, the spouse may be asked to act as a "resource person" to help the client to perform some of the later tasks (e.g., increased social activity). According to McLean, regarding spouses of patients, a wife is generally more cooperative in this regard, but a husband's participation can be facilitated by speaking with him, describing the benefits of his participation, and insuring him that he is not to blame for his wife's condition (McLean, 1976a:86).

Second, a program may be employed to replace aversive marital exchanges which tend to both punish the weaker (i.e., depressed) member and reduce the amount of verbal communication. Specifically, the spouses may be taught to:

a. Pinpoint positive and negative verbal behaviors.

b. Arrange a time for talking each day (e.g., about one another's daily experiences).

c. Monitor interaction to ensure that they speak to one another in a positive way and to self-correct negative verbalizations (e.g., sarcasm).

d. Terminate the talk sessions with positive feedback that will benefit each person (McLean, 1976a).

Third, if necessary, the spouses might be taught to work together to increase social encounters with familiar sources (e.g., neighbors, relatives), beginning with relatively simple task demands.

5. A most important phase of treatment consists of increasing the performance of everyday tasks, social interactions, and gratifying activities (McLean, 1976a; Lewinsohn et al., 1976; Burgess, 1969). In helping the client to increase the performance of usual tasks, McLean (1976a) employs the following steps: (a) establishing the client's goals (i.e., activities or changes that the client feels would make him or her feel better); (b) teaching the client to recognize realistic and unrealistic performance standards; (c) transforming goals into actual performance by grading tasks into small units that guarantee success, making the graded steps explicit (e.g., in writing), focusing on the degree of accomplishment rather than on how much remains to be done, providing reinforcement contingent upon performance, and enlisting the help of others (such as the spouse), perhaps through behavioral contracts specifying reciprocal commitments.

It is also important to increase social interaction, for, as McLean notes (1976a:81): "Social interaction can moderate the experience of depression by acting as a reinforcer and as an incompatible response with depressive withdrawal." The following steps are used to increase social interaction:

a. Surveying the client's social interests.

b. Determining available social resources (e.g., friends, relatives, community activities).

c. Using a number of graduated performance assignments regarding social engagements.

d. Perhaps establishing social interaction commitments among the spouses so as to prevent procrastination.

e. Later helping the client to choose and initiate social interactions.

If needed, several auxiliary procedures might be employed:

a. Systematic desensitization to reduce tension and anxiety associated with social interaction (Lewinsohn et al., 1976; Wolpe, 1973).

b. Assertiveness training, rehearsal, and modeling to improve social skills.

Efforts to increase the client's involvement in pleasurable activities involve:

a. Assessing the rate at which the client engages in pleasant activities and the amount of pleasure obtained in each.

b. The client's keeping a record of pleasurable activities he or she engages in.

c. Helping the client to increase the overall level of pleasant activity, especially activities most closely related to mood (Lewinsohn et al., 1976).

6. Many strategies also address the client's interpretations, cognitive structures, and self-statements. For instance, after increasing activity through graded task assignments, Shaw and Beck (1977) help the client to:

a. Collect, examine, and test the cognitive assumptions that seem to lead to depression.

b. Search for alternative solutions to and interpretations of apparent problems.

c. Identify, evaluate, and change the more chronic beliefs and assumptions by which the patient constructs and organizes his world, such as I must be successful at all times (Shaw and Beck, 1977).

Moreover, to reduce obsessional thinking and negative self-statements, the client might be taught thought stopping (Wolpe, 1973); to carry a number of cards containing positive self-statements which the client can read in order to replace negative ones (Mahoney, 1971); or to systematically make positive self-statements and to reinforce himself or herself (Lewinsohn et al., 1976).

7. In addition to methods for reducing the symptoms of depression, the client might be taught more general problem-solving techniques as a way of avoiding or remedying current or future difficulties (e.g., marital or occupational).

8. In several strategies also the client takes data, for example, on counter-productive self-statements (Shaw and Beck, 1977) or on the scheduling and performance of activities (McLean, 1976a). The purpose, in part, is to teach the client to divert attention from mood to behavioral improvement, facilitate performance, and perhaps help the client to see himself or herself as capable of self-control.

9. Finally, reinforcement contingencies might be used to motivate and strengthen performance of the various treatment programs. Reinforcement might be self-administered or delivered by the spouse or by the consultant. Lewinsohn et al. (1976) also suggest that future appointments and the return of portions of a money deposit can be made contingent upon the completion of assigned tasks.

In view of past research, it is reasonable to assume that the life circumstances of families of special-needs children can promote or worsen depression, which then makes effective parenting difficult (McLean, 1976b). Although several APG Items correspond closely with some of the above mentioned methods for reducing depression (Item 19 on marital cooperation, 23 on scheduled breaks, 24 on reinforcement, and 27 on problem-solving), I am not suggesting that strengthening those items alone prevents or remedies depression; the seriousness of depression deserves special attention. Some parents may benefit by reading the works of Claire Weekes (1969, 1972).

Marital Problems

The literature on family interaction suggests that conflict and unhappiness, harmony and satisfaction are determined by a similar process. In adapting to or coping with the external environment and each other, family members develop typical patterns of exchange in which rewards and punishments are delivered. Members also explain, justify, and guide their interpersonal exchanges with a number of beliefs and self-statements. The exchanges and self-statements then become self-perpetuating. For example, to the extent that reciprocal positive reinforcement is predominant, each person is likely to become more valuable to the others, and will be more likely to maintain the reinforcing interaction. To the extent that persons frequently threaten, deprive, or physically punish one another, however, patterns of coercion (in which the others give in, thereby reinforcing coercive behavior), mutual punishment (in which the aversive exchanges escalate), or withdrawal may develop, perpetuated by sentiments of fear or dislike and beliefs that change is impossible.

There are several reasons why it is important to be sensitive to marital interaction in a Program for families of children with learning and behavior problems. First, marital problems are simply painful for one or both spouses, may harm the children, are likely to interfere with participation in the Program and with the parents' efforts to conduct a good home educational program, and may worsen personal problems, such as depression. Second, the great strains to which many families have been subjected over the years, may predispose them to internal problems (as noted in Chapter 2). And third, the Program itself may precipitate or worsen marital problems. For example:

> Now that we're in this program, you'd better start helping out around here!
>
> See, I told you that you were spoiling her!
>
> So what if Mr. Fernandez is such a great teacher!
>
> Don't talk that way about my mother. She's only trying to help.
>
> Okay, so Gina is changing. But what about my needs? You expect me to do this for the rest of my life?

You can help parents to remedy marital problems either individually or in groups (Liberman, 1975; McClellan and Stieper, 1977; Rose, 1977). The rest of this section describes the methods that can be used and a general sequence for doing so.

1. According to Minuchin (1974), maintain a leadership stance and avoid being "sucked into" conflicts (e.g., inadvertently siding with one spouse against the other). While you must adapt to the family organization so as to enter it, maintain enough freedom to intervene in ways that challenge the organization, encouraging members to change in the direction of treatment goals.

2. Assessment can be obtained through videotape or direct observation in the home; self-observation (Knox, 1971), and through various interview scales and questionnaires, such as the "Locke Wallace Marital Adjustment Scale" (Burgess et al., 1971), the "Family Pre-counseling Inventory" (Stuart and Stuart, 1975), the "Area of Change Scale" (Weiss et al., 1973), and the "Marital Happiness Scale" (Azrin et al., 1973). Additional instruments are described by Gambrill (1977).

Somewhat broader in scope than most behavioral assessments, Minuchin's (1974) concentrates on six areas:

a. Family structure, transactional patterns (exchanges), and available alternatives.

b. Flexibility and the capacity for restructuring and elaborating relationships.

c. Sensitivity of members to each other's actions.

d. Context of family life (e.g., sources of support and stress).

e. Family's developmental stages and the performance of tasks appropriate to that stage. This, clearly, is a problem for many families of special-needs children, since parents and siblings may move through stages of the life cycle faster than the special-needs child.

f. Ways one member's problems may be used to maintain the family's current interaction patterns.

3. Many workers begin marital counseling by discussing the ways marital problems develop and are maintained. Some important points are:

a. Certain irrational or erroneous beliefs may produce or maintain marital conflict and deprivation, for example, that one can demand love, approval, and affection and that things be done one's own way; that people don't have the power to control their emotions; that external events (e.g., the behaviors of others) rather than one's own expectations and interpretations, lead to unpleasant feelings (McClellan and Stieper, 1977).

b. Thoughts and feelings are the antecedents of actions which lead to the reactions of others, which then lead to changes in thoughts and feelings (Stuart, 1976).

c. Spouses can best initiate change by increasing their rate of exchanging positive behaviors (Stuart, 1976).

d. The treatment program focuses on the present, since accounts of the past are often distorted and negative, and the past cannot be changed anyway (Stuart, 1976).

e. The spouses should address themselves to observable changes that can be monitored and "fully appreciated by one another" (Stuart, 1976).

f. Even desired attitude changes should be translated into specific behavior change objectives (Stuart, 1976).

g. To change the interaction, each person must assume the initiative in changing his or her own behavior before expecting change in the other, which may help to reverse the belief that it is the other's fault and responsibility (Stuart, 1969).

At this point, goals may be established. In Milton Erickson's work, even goals that might otherwise be considered long-term are transformed into immediate goals, for the long-term goal ''cannot be achieved as long as the living situation is inappropriate; the problem is to bring about a more normal context of living'' (Haley, 1973:188).

4. An early step in several strategies is to enhance communication and replace counterproductive with productive (that is, mutually rewarding) exchanges. In the work of McClellan and Stieper (1977), spouses are first taught to pinpoint and change unreasonable expectations. They are then given practice in accurate listening. That is, they learn to listen to and paraphrase (to the other's satisfaction) what the other has said. Similarly, Stuart (1976) teaches spouses to communicate honest, timely and constructive messages; to censor messages that are distortions; and to avoid communicating messages that are too far in advance of or too late after a troublesome situation.

A second way of enhancing communication is to have the spouses list specific behaviors that they want from each other and which can be delivered at least every few days, such as expressions of affection, asking for opinions, or performing simple tasks. Each person is to act independently of the other, that is, not wait for the other to initiate. Success, it is assumed, facilitates working on larger problems (Stuart, 1976).

Third, the couple might be instructed to establish a time each day to talk about daily events, when accurate listening is to be practiced and the spouses are to communicate with each other in a positive way (McLean, 1976a).

Fourth, the spouses begin to work on increasing exchanges of desirable behaviors. At first, each spouse might list three specific behaviors he or she desires from the other and post the list. These should be behaviors to accelerate, not decelerate, since requesting that the other stop performing a certain behavior is part of the same old pattern (Watzlawick et al., 1974). Each then records the daily frequency with which the other performs the desired behaviors (Stuart, 1969). As productive exchanges increase, the spouses might begin to change some of their more global interaction problems, for example, in the areas of role responsibility, the management of conflict, and trust (i.e., allowing each other more freedom). This might be done via behavioral contracts specifying the performance of certain desired behaviors in return for certain privileges. Stuart (1976) cautions that the exchange should not be on the basis of ''I'll do this for

you if you do that for me,'' since one or both parties may never initiate the behaviors desired by the other. Instead, for instance, the husband might agree to conduct teaching sessions with the child for about 30 minutes, three times per week; assume responsibility for planning and initiating one evening out per week for the couple; and handle any bills that arrive each week. In exchange, he can choose among several privileges, such as his wife cooking his favorite meal one day per week; his wife keeping a list of chores she wants done, rather than nagging; or the opportunity to go bowling one evening or afternoon per week. Additional examples of marital contracts are found in Knox (1971), Stuart (1971), Blechman and Olson (1976), and Weiss et al. (1973).

Fifth, when the spouses have learned to successfully manage their behavioral contracts, they might begin to work on a strategy for managing future issues, such as role responsibilities. In particular, they might be taught to use a problem-solving strategy, for example, formulating their goals, planning the steps to achieve their goals, instituting a program, and evaluating the outcomes (Stuart, 1976).

Finally, an effort is made to help the spouses to maintain beneficial change. In Stuart's work (1976), the spouses are provided with ''relationship rules'' summarizing their agreed upon arrangements; they are taught to expect that perhaps they will begin to test (back-slide on) their new life style; and they periodically assess themselves.

While many of the above steps can be accomplished through discussion with you, role-playing, modeling, and homework assignments can also be used. For example, when teaching spouses to pinpoint erroneous beliefs, accurately listen, and replace counterproductive exchanges, have them demonstrate how they have interacted regarding certain problem situations, have each spouse observe while you role-play counterproductive and productive interaction, and have them observe and imitate the productive interaction of others. Moreover, the couple might benefit from reading such books as *A Couple's Guide to Communication* (Gottman et al., 1976); *Families* (Patterson, 1971); *Keeping Happiness in Your Marriage* (Knox, 1972).

Of course, the above methods are of no value if parents do not use them. Therefore, your behavior when interacting with parents is important. Minuchin (1974) describes seven methods for encouraging families to ''restructure'' their relationships. They are as follows.

1. Encourage family members to ''actualize'' or perform family exchanges by instructing them to enact the patterns (''Show me how you tell him to do his chores''); by directing members to talk to one another rather than just to you; and by manipulating the seating so as to facilitate or block certain interactions (e.g., sitting next to the husband so that he is more likely to talk to his wife).

2. Helping members to mark and define ''boundaries'' by directing them to talk to rather than about one another; asking members to let each person speak for himself or herself; and instructing parents to enact their authority in the home, for example, to maintain their private spaces, set clear limits, and explicitly make decisions (Haley, 1973:212–221).

3. Escalate stress so as to enable the family to experiment with change. This can be done by blocking old exchanges (e.g., stopping one member from speaking for another, thereby enabling the other to speak); emphasizing problems that have been glossed over (e.g., asking for more details, disagreeing with members' accounts); joining and shifting alliances with different members, e.g., temporarily siding with the wife so as to provoke the husband to respond (Haley, 1973:Chapter 7).

4. Assign tasks within sessions and as homework, both to pinpoint and explore areas (e.g., to discuss a problem, to ignore another's interruptions).

5. Use symptoms or problems themselves to remedy difficulties. For instance, by focusing on one person's problems, helping relationships may be established, perhaps altering other patterns as well. By instructing a person to enact and exaggerate a symptom (e.g., "depressive complaining") the person may find that he can control it or may become bored with it, thus helping the person to begin working to change other behaviors. (See Frankl, 1960; Watzlawick et al., 1967, 1974; and Rabkin, 1977 on the use of therapeutic paradox.) You can relabel a problem so as to encourage a different response to it (e.g., seeing a husband's poor performance of chores as the result of lack of reinforcement, rather than noncompliance).

6. Manipulate your mood so as to facilitate change (e.g., speaking more aggressively with an aggressive family, so as to force members to alter their style; sympathizing with a parent who seems overly concerned with some matter, so that he will be more likely to listen to you).

7. Provide support, education, and guidance (e.g., teaching family members how they might interact and solve problems).

11 PROGRAM EVALUATION

I. INTRODUCTION

The purpose of program evaluation is twofold. First, it enables both you and the parents to judge the extent and nature of change in behaviors and relationships within the family and between the family and other persons, families, and organizations. Second, it enables you to make decisions regarding the operation of ongoing and future Programs conducted by yourself and others. For instance, you might decide that additional written materials are needed, videotape should perhaps be used more often, fewer home visits are needed, future Programs are likely to be just as effective when more families are in a group, or that Programs might be more effective if the ages and/or needs of the children are more similar.

A Program is an extremely complex interaction system. The description of family career experiences, the number of items on the Assessment and Programming Guide (APG), and the amount of detail provided in earlier chapters all testify to the complexities and represent my effort to somehow make sense of them. Nevertheless, in the absence of studies of many families divided into comparison groups differing on selected variables and exposed to a variety of Programs, most judgments concerning the relationship between a certain component of a Program and a certain change (or lack of change) in a family are tentative. While the ideas and instruments provided by this book should make your judgments and decisions better than those produced through trial and error, it is important that you take accurate data on as many aspects of a Program as you can and are sensitive to the unexpected.

One way of reducing the complexity is to focus on four clusters of factors in a Program.

1. *Factors that describe the operation of the Program itself* (e.g., the number of consultants and specialists involved; written materials used; the number, spacing, and duration of meetings; instructional methods employed, such as videotape, demonstrations, role-playing exercises, discussions, and lectures; the type of contract-credit system; the number, spacing, and duration of home visits; the number of families involved; and the nature and similarity of children's problems). Note that with the exception of the last two variables, all of the above represent inputs provided to the parents and are, simultaneously, the costs of the Program.

2. *Behaviors of the parents* (e.g., nature and extent of productive participation; readiness to change; planning, teaching and problem-solving skills actually used when needed; marital relationships; personal problems engendered or remedied; integration in networks of extended support).

3. *Changes in the children* (e.g., reduction in problem behaviors; acquisition and maintenance of appropriate behaviors in different skill areas; changes in educational placement; generalization of behavior change across settings and persons).

4. *Events that may be somewhat outside the scope of the Program* but that nevertheless may affect the family system (e.g., actions of relatives, friends, neighbors, and persons in community settings; sickness; pregnancy; financial and occupational considerations; and availability of backup support resources).

In view of the above, program evaluation involves an examination of each cluster of factors, as well as possible relationships between the clusters. For example, you might ask the following questions:

How many hours per week did consultants spend planning meetings, preparing materials, conducting meetings, and making home visits?

How much money was spent on books, videotapes, other supplies?

What was the average length of meetings and home visits?

How much change and what kinds of changes took place in parents' verbal participation?

How often were parents on time? How many meetings did they attend?

What changes took place in readiness to change, for example, from the time of the first contact to the present?

What changes took place (and did not take place) in structured exchanges in the home between parents and children?

What changes took place (and did not take place) in parents' teaching skills between the Pre-Program, Program, and Follow-up periods?

What changes took place in personal problems, marital cooperation, scheduling of breaks, generalization of parents' skills outside the home, linkage in networks of extended support, organization in home life, and in other APG items?

What changes took place (and did not take place) in children's behaviors between Pre-Program, Program, and Follow-up periods? How much change took place in target behaviors worked on in each teaching program (i.e., week-by-week)? To what new persons and settings did behavior changes generalize? Which behaviors changed, though they were not directly worked on (i.e., response generalization)?

In what ways and to what extent have parents maintained readiness to change and good teaching programs?

To what extent and in what ways were the materials and methods effective in teaching the parents certain skills?

To what extent and in what ways were the methods effective in teaching the children certain behaviors?

Did the number of families in a group, or the composition of the group, facilitate or hinder productive participation?

Did variability in children's needs or ages seem to facilitate or hinder sharing of ideas and overall pacing of the Program?

In what ways might the operation of the Program be changed—either an ongoing Program or future Programs—so that it may be more effective and/or efficient?

II. DESCRIBING THE OPERATION OF THE PROGRAM

Keeping accurate records on the operation of the Program enables you to determine the costs, effectiveness, and efficiency of the Program in producing change. Examples of information to obtain on Program operation are provided in Section I above. Much of the information can be recorded in a ledger, e.g., the number of meetings, duration of each meeting, the number and duration of home visits, the amount of money spent on materials, and the amount of time spent preparing for meetings. Notes are kept on methods of instruction used during meetings and home visits, and on phone calls. In our programs, we often record meetings on videotape or audiotape. This enables us to evaluate instructional methods and interaction processes. Moreover, transcripts of the best presentations and exercises are used in conducting future programs (and were used in writing this book).

While not usually taken into consideration, it is important for consultants to describe changes in themselves during the course of a Program. For example, you might find increases or decreases in your: 1) expectations of success for a family; 2) sentiments of liking for a family or child; 3) perceived energy; 4) willingness to fulfill your part of the Program Contract; 5) understanding of family systems and processes of behavior change; and 6) teaching and consulting skills. Such information is useful in present and future Programs. For instance, it may be important for consultants to reinforce themselves, coach, and share the work more often.

III. BEHAVIORS OF PARENTS

The effectiveness of a Program cannot be assessed simply by describing behavior change in the children. It is possible that some children will change a great deal, although their parents have not learned (or used) many teaching skills; and some children may change little, although their parents have become skillful teachers. Consequently, behavior change in parents must be assessed independently of change in their children.

At least seven categories of parents' behaviors can be evaluated. In all cases, you can summarize evaluative information by scoring relevant items on the parents' APG. Thus, one overall evaluation consists of a comparison of APG scorings before, during, and after the Program stage.

Readiness to Change

The APG can be used to keep track of parents' readiness to change from the time of the Initial Interview through the Follow-up period. Information relevant to APG Items 2 through 10 can be obtained through the Initial and Assessment Interviews, verbal behavior of parents during meetings, home visits and phone calls, and parents' logs or notes.

Information on readiness to change is important in several ways. First, if readiness to change declines during a Program, work to restrengthen it. Second, note apparent relationships between readiness to change and other aspects of parents' behaviors. For example, you might find that certain components of readiness to change typically decrease after parents have had difficulties in teaching their child for several weeks, or that readiness to change can be increased through group discussions. This information is useful in conducting future Programs.

Item 11: Productive Participation

Parents' performance can be summarized periodically on the APG (e.g., at the beginning, toward the middle, and toward the end of the Program stage), and when marked changes are noted. Information relevant to the components of productive participation can be obtained from: (1) parents' written assignments (e.g., have they satisfactorily completed the assignment on time?); (2) data taken on verbal participation during meetings and home visits (see Chapter 5); and (3) Credits-Earned sheets (or notes made each meeting or home visit), indicating if parents attended the meeting, were on time, were available for a scheduled home visit, and completed other assignments listed on their Weekly Contracts.

Item 12: Objectivity

It is hard to evaluate objectivity by itself. However, information on objectivity can be obtained from parents': 1) pinpointing, describing, and analyzing behaviors and exchanges during Initial and Assessment Interviews, videotape and role-playing exercises, and group discussions; answering questions in Chapter 2 of *Educating Children* and describing their home programs in meetings, home visits, and in logs; 2) counting, charting, and evaluating behavior change during practice exercises in meetings, in home teaching programs, and when doing the assignments in Chapters 4 and 5 of *Educating Children*.

Evaluation, Planning, and Teaching Skills

An important category of parents' behavior is described by APG Items 14, 17, and 18.

1. Parents' initial knowledge of general principles of learning, teaching, and exchange can be gleaned from the Assessment Interview. In addition, during the first meeting parents can analyze written or videotaped vignettes. Their responses can then be compared with the assignment on vignettes at the end of Chapter 2 of *Educating Children* and with discussions later in the Program. The questions in Chapter 3 of *Educating Children* also provide some information on parents' understanding of rewards.

To obtain a more standardized method for evaluating parents' knowledge of structured exchanges and teaching methods, have them score videotapes at certain points in the Program. For instance, make a tape on general patterns of exchanges and several tapes showing the teaching of target behaviors in various skill areas. Each tape can be divided into short segments. After each segment is shown, the tape is stopped and the parents respond to what they have seen, using a scoring sheet divided into the same number of segments as the tape. For example, while watching a tape on structured exchanges, they might: a) write the name of the exchange shown and b) suggest possible changes. Or, after each segment of a tape on teaching target behaviors in a certain skill area, they might: a) describe the teaching methods shown (e.g., type of signal used, type of prompting, pairing social and primary rewards) and b) make suggestions (e.g., "Should reward faster"; "Should use physical prompt"; "Kid looks bored. Should switch tasks"; "Parent rewarded whining. Better ignore it.")

Tapes on structured exchanges and teaching methods could be made during several Programs by editing portions of tapes made of interaction in the home or in classroom settings. Naturally, the tapes should show productive and counterproductive exchanges, proper and improper teaching methods.

Such tapes can be used in a number of ways. They can be shown at several points during and after a Program to assess changes in parents' objectivity and knowledge of teaching skills. You can use them for instructional purposes, e.g., to show parents how to teach certain target behaviors and how to avoid making certain errors.

2. Parents' actually instituting productive exchanges and properly using the general teaching methods can be assessed through direct observations (and/or by scoring videotapes) made during home or in-class sessions throughout the Pre-Program, Program, and Follow-up stages. APG Items 17 and 18 help you to pinpoint behaviors to score.

For example, during Baseline Observations, list the kinds, frequencies, or percentages of structured exchanges that actually occur. The same information can be obtained during the Program and Follow-up stages. Comparisons across the three stages indicate changes that have taken place. Data might be organized as follows:

	Reinforcement of Problem Behaviors (Percentage of Episodes Reinforced)	Reinforcement of Cooperation (Percentage of Episodes Reinforced)	Occasions to Respond (Number Given Per Hour)
Baseline (Average)	75	20	3
Program Week Four	20	80	10
Program Week Six	5	85	20
Program Week Eight	0	100	20
Follow-up Visit One	0	90	18

Similarly, using APG Item 18 as a guide, you can score parents' use of general teaching methods. For instance, to what extent do they present signals when the child is attending, use clear and simple signals, deliver reinforcement quickly, prompt when necessary, and keep the noise level down? Improvements and difficulties can be judged by comparing your observations (summarized on the parents' APG) at different points, e.g., baseline and mid-Program; when parents institute new teaching programs during the Program stage; at the end of the Program stage; and during the Maintenance and Follow-up stage.

3. Parents' skill at evaluating their children and planning an educational program can be assessed by the assignment at the end of Chapter 4 of *Educating Children*. The durability of these skills can be evaluated toward the end of a Program by providing parents with a completed Behavior Evaluation Scale for a sample child and having them plan an educational program. Notes made during meetings and home visits provide additional information on this item.

Changes in Other APG Items

The APG lists other items that should be assessed. For example, following a problem-solving sequence (16); cooperation among spouses or partners (19); organization in home life (20); existence of, skillful efforts to remedy, and changes in personal problems (21); honesty (22); scheduling and taking of breaks (23); self-reinforcement (24); linkages with extended support networks (25);

generalization of teaching skills to other persons and places (26); and long-term planning and problem-solving (27). Information on improvements or problems regarding these items can be obtained throughout the Program from interviews, observations in meetings and home visits, and parents' logs. Transfer such information to the parents' APG. Special instruments and methods for evaluating marital relationships and personal problems are cited in Chapter 10.

Parents' Perception of Changes

Program evaluation also includes parents' perceptions of the Program and its apparent effects. Information indicating parents' perceptions can be obtained from their: (1) scoring of the APG at different points in time; (2) logs and notes; (3) comments during phone calls, meetings, and home visits; and (4) responses to a Program evaluation form with which they can be provided at various times. The evaluation form might ask them to rate their satisfaction with various aspects of the Program (written materials; lecture; videotape, role-playing, and demonstration methods of instruction; home visits; the contract-credit system; and inputs from other parents). The form might also ask them to suggest possible changes. An example is in Appendix 6.

Sensitivity to the Unexpected

Program evaluation includes observations made on unexpected events and changes. For instance, you might find that a short segment of one videotape, a particular vignette discussed, or a certain practice exercise was extremely effective in conveying information. Or, you might find that one side effect of an improvement in skills and confidence is that some parents become extremely assertive in their dealings with school administrators (in which case, you might help the parents to work with administrators in a businesslike way, so that the parents' efforts will be productive). You might also decide to work on parent advocacy in a more systematic way in future programs.

IV. BEHAVIORS OF THE CHILDREN

There are at least four sources of information on progress made by the children.

Scoring of Scales and Tests

First, you can compare scorings on the Behavior Evaluation Scale (BES) before, during, and after the Program. Other useful instruments include the Detroit Test of Learning Aptitude (Barker and Leland, 1958, 1967); the Weschler Preschool and Primary Scale of Intelligence (Weschler, 1967); the Peabody Picture Vocabulary Test (Dunn, 1965); the Wide Range Achievement Test (Jastek and Jastek, 1965); the Illinois Test of Psycholinguistic Abilities (McCarthy and Kirk, 1961); the Frostig Test of Visual Perception (Frostig and Horne, 1964); the McCarthy Scales of Children's Abilities (McCarthy, 1972); the Northwestern Syntax Screening Test (Lee, 1969); and the Vineland Social Maturity Scale (Doll, 1965).

Parents' Data

Parents also take data useful for evaluating change in the children. For example, they score their children on the BES, graph certain behaviors during teaching sessions and at other times of day, and take notes on other behavior changes they observe. Parents' data, then, can serve as both a reliability check on your evaluations of the children (and vice versa) and an independent source of data on behaviors that you were not able to observe.

Direct Observation and Scoring of Videotapes on the Teaching-Learning Process

Much more detailed information on children's progress is obtained through direct observation of the children and/or through the later scoring of videotapes. A method for recording children's behavior is described in Chapter 4, in the section entitled "Pencil and Paper Data." The method involves recording the teaching behaviors of parents (inputs) and the behaviors of children (outputs) during observation periods (e.g., teaching sessions). In our Programs, we have recorded the following:

Inputs or Teaching Behaviors of Parents. These include *the number of*:

a. Minutes in each observation period.

b. New tasks worked on in a session (e.g., the number of different small motor tasks, motor imitation models, math problems, or objects to name).

c. Occasions to respond provided to the child for each task (e.g., the number of signals of various types).

d. Prompts (visual, verbal, physical) provided when working on each task.

e. Reinforcements (primary, social, activity, token) given when working on each task.

Outputs or Behaviors of the Child. These include *the number of*:

a. Correct, approximately correct, and incorrect responses to each task worked on (e.g., responses to a particular puzzle or to a certain math problem).

b. New tasks learned (the criterion for calling a task "learned" might be five consecutive correct unprompted responses, but may vary depending on the type of task).

c. And duration of episodes of various types of problem behaviors (e.g., non-cooperation with signals, whining, leaving the session).

d. Minutes or the percentage of observation time attending to or working at tasks.

Clearly, it is impossible to keep an accurate record of all the above variables at once. Thus, when making live recordings you might count the number of new tasks worked on (giving the name of each, e.g., working the "Big Bear" puzzle; imitating "clapping hands," "patting table," and "sticking out tongue"; multiplying 3×15, 5×15, etc.), correct responses, minutes in session, time attending and working, prompts, reinforcements, tasks learned, and number and duration of problem behaviors. If you have recorded sessions on videotape, however, you can record all the variables, though it may be time-consuming.

Analysis of Data. While all the measured behaviors of the children can show the extent and rate of progress, perhaps the most useful measures are of the number of new tasks learned in each skill area, the amount of time attending and working, and the number and duration of episodes of problem behaviors. In our Programs, we evaluate the overall effectiveness of the children's educational programs by accumulating each of the above measures of the children's behaviors and graphing them as a function of accumulated teaching sessions, minutes, days or weeks. The effectiveness of a teaching program in a certain skill area or on a particular target behavior, on the other hand, is gauged by graphing the cumulative number of correct responses (e.g., models imitated, math problems solved, objects correctly labeled) or tasks learned as a function of accumulated sessions, minutes, days, or weeks.

In addition to assessing program effectiveness, you can assess efficiency. In general, efficiency is represented by the ratio of change in outputs to change in inputs (i.e., accumulated increases in appropriate behaviors of the child relative to accumulated increases in parents' teaching behaviors and session time). For example, if a child is learning five new tasks each session, the teaching program may be effective, but if the child continues to require (or is simply given) increasingly larger numbers of occasions to respond, prompts, and reinforcement, then the teaching program is not efficient.

To assess efficiency, we simply graph the cumulative number of new tasks learned (or correct responses) as a function of each of the cumulative inputs provided by the parents. For instance, we might graph the cumulative number of new tasks learned in one skill area (and later in all skill areas) as a function of cumulative session time, cumulative occasions to respond, cumulative prompts, or cumulative reinforcement. Each relationship would be graphed separately. The details of the method include the following:

1. *All measures are cumulative.* This is done because we assume that learning actually is cumulative; what is learned in one session does affect what is learned in the next.

2. *Each session or observation period is one data point.* Each data point, then, represents the current number of new tasks (or correct responses) accumulated (learned) by that time and the corresponding amount of the accumulated input (provided). For example:

Session	1	2	3	4	5	6
New Tasks Learned						
Absolute Number	0	2	4	5	6	8
Cumulative Number	0	2	6	11	17	25
Positive Reinforcements						
Absolute Number	20	25	25	22	23	25
Cumulative Number	20	45	70	92	115	140

3. *The data points are plotted on either arithmetic or log × log coordinates,* with outputs (child's behavior) on the vertical axis. Best-fitting lines are then drawn.

4. *Visual inspection of the lines gives a rough estimate of efficiency in the input-output relationship.* On arithmetic coordinates, upward-curving lines indicate that the child's behavior is accumulating (changing) faster than the parents' teaching inputs are accumulating. That is, the relative cost of each unit of behavior change in the child is decreasing; the relationship is effective and efficient. A downward-curving line, on the other hand, indicates that, while the child's behavior may be accumulating, the parents are providing inputs at a relatively higher rate. Thus, the learning process is inefficient.

On log × log coordinates, which tend to straighten curves, efficiency is indicated by the slope or angle of the line. Lines with a slope of 45 degrees represent a linear function; that is, the ratio of change in the child's behavior to change in the parents' teaching behaviors is approximately constant. There is no change in efficiency. Lines greater than 45 degrees indicate efficiency. And lines less than 45 degrees indicate inefficiency. Of course, the exact equation for each functional (input-output) relationship can be obtained with pencil, paper, and a programmable calculator or with a computer.

5. *Information obtained from such graphs is useful in several ways.* First, you can acquire additional knowledge of the learning process. It may be, for example, that the input-output relationships are different for various target behaviors and skill areas or that the input-output relationships themselves become more efficient as the learning process continues. Second, you can use the information to spot and correct potential deteriorations in the learning process. If a graph shows that increasingly greater amounts of certain inputs (such as prompts or reinforcements) are being used, you might hypothesize that the current rate of inputs is unnecessary (for example, the parents are providing too much reinforcement), the tasks are too hard, or the parents are making some errors in teaching (e.g., not reinforcing approximations or not prompting satisfactorily).

And, third, use the kinds of data described above to keep track of program effectiveness and efficiency across the different stages. For instance, compare graphs of cumulative new tasks learned as a function of session time or reinforcement during the Baseline, Program, and Follow-up stages. In this way, you can see if the child's rate of learning is high, and if selected input-output relationships are as efficient, between the baseline and Program stages and between the Program and Follow-up stages (Kozloff, 1976).

Assessments by Others

Teachers and other specialists can provide evaluations of children's behaviors. For example, like parents, teachers can be measuring the children's progress using tests, behavior scales, and/or direct measurement (as described above), both to help determine the extent to which certain behavior changes are generalizing between the classroom and the home, and to solve problems that may result from differences in the home and classroom environment. Moreover, teachers can provide information on behaviors not being worked on by the parents (some of which parents might then begin to work on at home). Indeed, one measure of the efficacy and efficiency of programs for parents is the difference in the type and rate of change in children whose parents are in programs versus those who are not (Kaufman, 1977).

V. POSSIBLE EFFECTS OF OTHER FACTORS

In addition to the apparent effects (or lack of effects) of various components of a Program on the behaviors of parents and children, and on other aspects of the family system, be sensitive to possible effects of factors outside your control. For example, parents' Readiness to Change and productive participation may decline following illness in the family, a job layoff, a change to another job, or pregnancy and childbirth. Similarly, a child's progress may slow down as an indirect result of the above factors or as a direct result of certain events in the child's neighborhood or school (e.g., the introduction of new or difficult tasks, a new teacher, fights with other children, or differences in teaching methods between home and school). Naturally, discuss with parents the possible effects of such factors and attempt to mitigate them.

Appendix 1 ASSESSMENT AND PROGRAMMING GUIDE (APG)

I. INTRODUCTION

How is the Assessment and Programming Guide Organized?

Your work with families has three stages: Pre-Program, Program, and Maintenance/Follow-up. The Assessment and Programming Guide indicates which skills, attitudes, and interaction patterns seem to be needed for families to be successful and what problems may arise in each stage. The skills, attitudes, and interaction patterns are presented as "items." Most items are complex; therefore, each is broken down into components, which are listed either from easier to harder or in the general order in which they might best be taught. When possible, examples of each component are provided.

At the end of the list of components for each item, the APG notes a number of problems that might interfere with the parents' learning or applying an item to the task of changing themselves and their children. The problems are set off by brackets.

Of What Use is the Assessment and Programming Guide?

The APG can be used in several ways. First, by observing a family during Initial Interviews, Assessment Interviews, and Baseline Observations, and by scoring the family according to each APG item, you can assess the strengths and needs of the family and plan a suitable program. Second, by continually observing a family during the Program, you can update your scoring of the APG, keep track of progress and problems, and revise a Program in light of the ongoing evaluation. And third, by comparing scorings of the APG on families before and after the Program, or by comparing the progress of families exposed to different Program formats, you can evaluate the overall Program.

How is the APG Filled Out?

Although the APG is long, it is easy to fill out and use. Here are the steps.

1. Make a blank copy of the APG for use with each family. You might supply each family with its own copy, so that the parents can see what they need to learn and how they are doing. However, it is advisable to revise the APG for self-administration (e.g., by removing irrelevant and potentially threatening statements). Leave space for notes.

2. When assessing a family during the Pre-Program stage (through Initial Interviews, Assessment Interviews, Baseline Observations) and during the Program (in meetings and home visits), you are gathering data on the parents' behaviors, attitudes, and relationships. Your task is to transfer that information to the relevant items of the APG.

3. The ways to transfer information to the APG include: a) underlining words, phrases, or sentences in the components of an item on the APG that describe how the parents stack up on that item; b) underlining words, phrases, or sentences within the brackets under an item (that is, problems) that describe the parents' behavior; c) writing notes on the APG itself.

4. Indicate on each item differences between parents of the same family. For example, the mother might "pass" one component and the father another component.

5. Indicate the items, components, and problems with which the parents need help (e.g., with notations in the margin). These notations should be dated. It may be helpful for parents to mark their copy of the APG in the same way.

6. Update the APG during the Program by continuing to underline the relevant components or problems or by making notes in the spaces provided. When an item, or certain of its components, is passed, check-mark and date it. Parents can update their copy in the same way.

II. PRE-PROGRAM STAGE

Awareness of you (or the Program) and of what the Program has to offer

In order to begin the change process, the parents have to be aware of you or the Program and of what the Program offers. The following item can be assessed through discussions with teachers, therapists, school and mental health administrators, and members of organizations for parents and professionals.

1. Parents are in Contact with Sources of Information (Persons, Organizations, Media) from Which They can Learn of You and the Program.

Note that this item is related to Item 25.

Problems. [parents are isolated from sources of information. For example, they do not receive bulletins, brochures, and newsletters, do not belong to groups or organizations for parents and professionals, do not have the opportunity to attend, or do not attend, parent-teacher conferences, or their child is out of school.]

Readiness to Change

To be successful in a Program, the parents must have certain attitudes (values, beliefs, motives) regarding themselves, their child, and their potential relationship with you. The words "readiness to change" summarize the necessary attitudes.

Items that describe readiness to change are assessed primarily in the Pre-Program stage, during Initial Contacts, Initial Interview(s), Assessment Interview(s), and, to a lessor extent, Baseline Observations. However, during and after the Program, remain sensitive to and take note of any changes in the parents with respect to the items.

The items are generally listed in the order in which the evidence for them is likely to appear (for instance, during an Initial Interview) and in which it might be best to work on strengthening them.

2. Trust in You (the Consultant)

The parents expect that the consultant will respect their abilities, needs, and intentions; will hold in confidence certain personal information; and will share their interests in meeting the educational needs of the children. For example, parents:

a. Smile and nod frequently at the consultant.

b. Are at ease with consultant (seem physically relaxed, joke, make eye contact, address consultant by name).

c. Discuss emotional topics or share information about themselves that might make them vulnerable (for example, information about personal problems, marital problems, times when they "lost control").

d. Indicate trust in consultant by stating, for example:

> You certainly are different from the others we have seen for help.
>
> You are so relaxed and easy to talk to.
>
> I feel that I can really trust you.

Problems. [parents question the goals of consultant, have concerns with confidentiality issues, are concerned about being observed or videotaped. For example, parents:

a. Rarely smile or nod at consultant.

b. Do not seem at ease (sit erect, have a serious or deadpan expression, address consultant by title only).

c. Avoid emotional topics and present little or no information of a nature that might threaten their public or private image.

d. Make explicit or veiled statements indicating lack of trust, for example:

> You know, some people are more interested in money than in helping parents and children.
>
> How can we be sure that you won't let just anybody see the videotapes that you want to make of us?]

3. Confidence in Consultant and in What Consultant has to offer

Parents expect that the consultant can and will help them to analyze problems and find effective ways to solve them. For example, parents:

a. Explicitly state confidence. For example:

> I'm sure that this will work.
>
> I feel that you can help us.
>
> This is what we've been looking for.
>
> Where have you been all these years?
>
> At last, someone understands.

b. Nod and/or verbally agree with consultant's analysis of child's and parents' behaviors in structured exchanges, or agree with consultant's suggestions of methods that they might try.

Problems. [parents have little confidence in consultant's competence, in the adequacy of consultant's framework for understanding their problems or situation, or in the methods the consultant says that the Program will be teaching them to use. For example, parents:

a. Make explicit or veiled statements indicating a lack of confidence in consultant, such as:

> Yes, but Dr. Evans said. . . .
>
> How much experience have you had with children like our Tommy?
>
> You know, we've been through this sort of program (seen people like you) before.
>
> Don't think that will work at all!

b. Remain expressionless or have a look of disagreement, turn away or do not make eye contact with consultant when consultant is providing an analysis of child's or parents' behaviors, or when consultant is suggesting methods to try.]

4. Recognize the Need to Conduct a Home Educational Program

Parents want to accelerate their child's educational gains, promote generalization of change, teach behaviors that are more "natural" to home life or that are more easily taught in the home, increase their child's chances in life, or to make their own lives and the life of their child more rewarding. For example, parents:

a. Give emphatic nods or agree explicitly with consultant when consultant outlines reasons for conducting a home educational program. For instance:

Yeah, I can see that.

Well, it always has been up to us, anyway.

I always did think that we should have been doing in the home what the teachers were doing in school.

b. Volunteer their reasons for conducting a home educational program, for instance:

We need to learn how to teach Harold to be more independent.

How do we get Joe to stop whining for everything?

We just plain need help in the home.

Problems. [parents may simply be unaware of the need to conduct a home educational program. However, parents may also:

a. Play the communication game of "It's no longer (or It's not) our job."

b. Indicate that they do not see a need for them to conduct a home educational program. For example:

Billy's school is doing a fine job.

We are satisfied with the progress Stan has already made.

Sharon does just fine at home.]

5. Parents Recognize that Their Behavior Affects the Behavior of Their Child, and Vice Versa

More specifically, parents recognize that they and their child, through structured exchanges, teach each other, with the implication that the parents are still in a position to change their child's behavior. For example, parents:

a. Indicate agreement with consultant's descriptions and explanations of structured exchanges in families by nodding, giving "knowing" smiles, laughing (as though expressing a sudden flash of recognition of what has been going on), and through statements such as:

Yeah, that's the way it is.

He sure got us that time.

You mean we've been rewarding (reinforcing) his tantrums all this time?!

b. Volunteer examples of structured exchanges in which their behaviors are affecting their child's behaviors, and vice versa. For example:

We stopped working so hard because Jose just ignored us.

Yes, the more we gave in to Wayland, the more he would whine later on.

When we finally made Conway ask for what he wanted, he started talking more and more.

c. Are somewhat critical of or disagree with those approaches that locate the causes of behavior in factors and processes that are presumably outside of the parents' control (e.g., in the child's body chemistry, nervous system, or mind). For example:

They said that Susie does not talk because she has brain damage. But maybe it is partly because we have not been requiring her to try to ask for what she wants.

They said that maybe we did not really want Nick to change. But the reason we have stopped working with him is that all of our work has gotten us nowhere.

They wanted to use drugs to stop Arlo's tantrums. But drugs are not going to teach Arlo the right way to act. You have to teach him, right?

Problems. [parents do not recognize that their behavior has been affecting, and still is affecting, their child's behavior, and vice versa. For instance, they believe that their child's special disabilities are solely responsible for the fact that past efforts to change the child have been ineffective; they don't believe that their child can affect their behavior; or they do not see themselves as being in a position to change their child's behavior. For example, parents:

a. Have blank facial expressions, express disapproval or disagreement, and do not make eye contact when consultant describes and explains structured exchanges in the home.

Or,

b. Make statements such as:

Yes, but what you just described hardly ever happens in our home.

We are not rewarding Becky by talking to her when she slaps herself on the ear. Besides, that's the way she communicates with us.

I guess it's all been God's will.

This is just our cross to bear.

Bruno is not ready to talk.

Billy is insecure. That is why he stays in his room.

I guess I'm a terrible parent for not working with Tanya very much.

What good would it do to require Ashley to ask for what he wants? After all, he has brain damage.

There is nothing wrong in picking Sonya up when she is pulling out her hair! She is showing that she wants my love.

You can't expect us to teach Gary to walk better. He has cerebral palsy.]

6. Parents Recognize the Need to Alter or Change Their own Behavior so as to Change Their Child's Behavior

For example, parents:

a. Agree with consultant's suggestion that they change certain of their behaviors or agree to use certain methods to change their child's behavior. For example:

I can see that Bob (husband) and I will have to learn to work together if we are going to help Ellen.

I don't think that I even notice the times that Jason is sitting quietly. I'm going to have to pay more attention to his good behaviors.

Problems. [parents may not recognize, or may not admit of, a need to change some of their own behaviors. For example, they may disagree, pay only lip service, or appear expressionless when consultant suggests that certain of their behaviors need to be changed or suggests a few methods they could use with their child. For example, parents might not recognize or admit of a need to change their own behaviors because they:

a. Do not see how their behavior affects the behavior of their child (see Item 5 above).

b. Deny that there is anything special or important about their behavior that might need to be changed, for example:

We ignore Elaine's head-banging most of the time, anyway.

c. Believe that factors other than their own behaviors are more important in changing their child's behaviors, for instance:

If Dr. Pheno settles Mark down with the right drugs, Mark will learn to pay attention.

All Ruth needs is more time.]

7. Expect Success in Changing Their own Behavior, the Behavior of Their Child, and the Behavior of Others

For example, parents:

a. Are enthusiastic about the successes of others as described by consultant:

> Wow! That's terrific. Their boy looks like a different child.

b. Generalize from the successful experiences of others as described by consultant:

> If they can do it, so can we!
>
> So, by reinforcing their child for making eye contact they taught her to pay attention better. Well, we can do that!

c. Believe that, despite any notions they have of their ''inadequacies,'' their ''styles,'' or personalities, they can still alter those behaviors needed to help their child. For example, parents may state:

> I thought that I was basically a weak person, and that I would have to become strong before I could help my child. But now I see that, weak or strong, I can still teach my child. In fact, I may become stronger by doing so.
>
> I'm a shy person, but I can still reward Billy for the right behaviors. In fact, maybe I can teach myself to be more assertive.

d. Make explicit their high expectations. For example:

> That idea of yours, that we put Stu in his room every time he throws a tantrum, sounds like it will work. We're going to try it.
>
> Well, I've never given up and I'm not going to start now!
>
> If those parents could do it, so can we.
>
> I'll make sure that our next door neighbor ignores Lois' whining.

Problems. [parents have low expectations of success at changing their own behaviors, the behavior of their child, or the behavior of others; or they do not feel that the changes they might be able to produce in their child are important (in effect, not worth the effort). For example, the parents:

a. Find and state reasons why the successes of other parents do not apply to their family. For example:

> But their children were not as bad as our Alex.
>
> But those parents (or teachers) were so young.
>
> Yes, but they had other children to help them.
>
> They had a college education.
>
> My mother-in-law is too stubborn to ever cooperate with me.

b. Indicate that they are not impressed with the successes of others. For example:

> Yes, they taught their child some speech, but did they teach their child to read?
>
> What they taught their child to do was great. But Alan can already do those things!
>
> Yes, but the effects of those methods are not long lasting (or they only work on certain behaviors).

c. Seem to feel that they have inadequacies, styles, or personalities that make it difficult or impossible for them to change themselves, their child, or others. For instance, parents make statements such as:

> I'm a weak person. That's why I don't get good results.
>
> I don't think I could do that for long. It would really grate on my nerves. It just isn't my style.

Note that if such statements appear to be aimed at getting sympathy, or at excusing the parents for not trying, they may constitute communication games, such as "Help me, I'm. . . ."

d. Make explicit their pessimism or low expectations. For example:

> I can't believe it will work, we've tried so hard.
>
> Harry is too old.
>
> But Sarah is so handicapped.
>
> We've tried that before and it didn't work.
>
> That sounds great. But it also looks like it would take a lot of work, and after all these years I'm just plain worn out.]

8. Willing and Able to Give up Some Time and Outside Interests, at Least for the Time Being, so as to Attend Meetings and Conduct a Home Educational Program

For example, parents say:

> If anything comes up, why we'll handle it.
>
> Only sickness will keep us from coming.
>
> Sure, I like to bowl. But right now nothing is as important as giving Tommy his chance.
>
> I've got time to fish later.
>
> I'll try like hell to get off early from work on Wednesdays.
>
> We can run teaching sessions right before supper.

Problems. [parents indicate that they do not think that they are willing or able to give the time necessary to attend meetings and conduct a home educational program because of the difficulty of predicting available time, the feeling of being overcommitted, or the presence of outside interests. For example, parents say:

> Sometimes things just come up, you know? That's the way things are in our house.
>
> I don't know if we can make it every Wednesday night. Sitters are pretty hard to find.
>
> Sessions every afternoon?! I don't know. Time is pretty short around our house.
>
> But what about Bill's (husband's) bowling night?
>
> I know this is important. But don't my needs count? I've got my own life to live!]

9. Parents Have (or Believe They Have) Sufficient Energy to Change the Behaviors of Themselves and Their Child

For example, either on their own or in response to the consultant's description of the tasks involved in the Program, parents may say:

> I won't try to kid you. I'm worn out after all of these years of trying. But I'll give it my best shot. You can depend on that!
>
> Sure I've got the energy. And if I don't, I know where to get it.
>
> I'm tired all right, but working to change Eddie now will make me feel lots better in the long run.

Problems. [consultant's observations may indicate that parents are fatigued or drained, worn out through hypervigilance and tension, or lethargic and depressed. Or, parents may not believe that they have enough energy left. For example, parents say:

> I'm not sure if I can do that. It looks awfully hard to me.
>
> You mean we have to do all that!
>
> You know, I'm just not as strong as I used to be.]

10. Accept the Behavioral-Education Approach Tentatively

Parents accept learning theory and the educational methods based on it—"prescriptive teaching," "applied behavior analysis," or "behavior modification." For example, parents:

a. Agree with consultant's description and explanation of certain behaviors of parents and children and various structured exchanges in the home (see examples from Item 5a above).

b. Agree that despite the various professional opinions, theories, and treatments, the important task now is to change their child's behavior. For instance, parents state:

> Well, they said that Franklin may have brain damage, but that doesn't mean that he can't learn.
>
> Maybe Shelley does have an emotional problem, but it seems to me that she can learn to handle her problems and enjoy being with others.

c. Apply or generalize from consultant's descriptions of structured exchanges and various behavioral processes in families, to other situations in the family. For example:

> Oh, then I guess I've been rewarding Ben for crawling around, too. (See Item 5b for more examples.)

d. May have questions requiring clarification, but do not become upset about the prospect of using various behavioral methods, such as requiring child to earn certain reinforcers or ignoring disruptive behaviors. For instance:

> Well, if that's what it will take, by Heaven, that's what we will do.
>
> Sure, it would upset me to see Andy hitting himself. But trying to stop him by cuddling him only seems to make it worse.

Problems. [parents may state a number of philosophical/cultural/ideological objections to the behavioral approach. For example:

> Reinforcement (rewarding my child) amounts to bribery.
>
> People should not be rewarded for what they ought to be doing anyway.
>
> Bad behaviors ought to be punished.
>
> How can you expect me to deprive my (poor) child?
>
> It isn't fair to withhold things these children enjoy.
>
> All children should be treated alike.
>
> My child's problems won't be corrected by something as simple as rewarding appropriate behaviors.
>
> My behaviors have little to do with my child's behaviors.
>
> Nothing much can be done, anyway.
>
> What you are suggesting sounds so mechanical (cruel, simplistic).]

Methods for assessing and strengthening readiness to change are described in detail in Section IV of Chapter 4 and Section I of Chapter 10.

III. PROGRAM STAGE

The Program stage constitutes the bulk of your work with families. The major goals in the Program stage are teaching parents 1) to *conduct* a good home educational program and 2) to *persist* in it and to *maintain* their home educational programs once the working relationship with you has been faded out. In this section, the important behaviors (or skills), attitudes, and interaction patterns, as well as the problems that may interfere with them, are grouped in terms of the two goals.

Assessment information for the following items is extremely important in planning the Program for and with the parents. Some information can be obtained during Initial Interviews. More detailed information can be gathered during Assessment Interviews and Baseline Observations. However, assessment does not stop once the Program begins. Use this Assessment and Programming Guide throughout the Program, noting beneficial change in parents' learning and performance of the items as well as problems that may be occurring. In this way, you can revise the overall Program, introduce special programs if needed (e.g., progressive relaxation), or continue the Program as initially planned.

CONDUCTING A GOOD HOME EDUCATIONAL PROGRAM

11. Productive Participation

Parents participate in the Program in a productive way. Some information on this item can be obtained when discussing the requirements of the Program with the parents, especially when formalizing the working relationship. Most of the information, however, is obtained during the Program itself. For example, parents:

a. Attend all meetings and arrive on time. If one parent or partner is unable to attend, a substitute is sent (e.g., an older sibling, close friend, or relative).

b. Satisfactorily complete weekly assignments (e.g., reading, writing, data-taking, teaching programs).

c. Actively participate in meetings in a productive way. For example, parents:

1. speak in an optimistic and prescriptive fashion.

(To consultant) I can also use the method you just demonstrated to teach Jack to brush his teeth, can't I?

(To another parent) When your daughter leaves the supper table, just remove her plate. Make her wait 'till the next meal.

(In response to a method demonstrated by another parent) Why don't we do what Mr. Sanchez did? It sure worked for him.

(To consultant or group) Sure, it's tough! No one said that it would be easy. But nobody else is gonna do the job for us!

Juanita is pretty hard to live with sometimes, but she is changing for the better.

How can we teach Ambrose to play with toys, instead of spinning things all the time?

2. use proper behavioral terms and principles in describing, analyzing, or explaining behavior and in creatively prescribing methods for solving a variety of problems. (See Item 12 below.)

3. speak up and take their turns, to ask questions, offer suggestions, and describe their work (i.e., share their expertise).

4. encourage and reinforce the productive participation of others (i.e., share leadership role) by:

- **a.** Asking others for suggestions.
- **b.** Asking others what they are doing in their home program.
- **c.** Redirecting others or reminding them of the "ground rules" to be optimistic, prescriptive, and behavioral.
- **d.** Congratulating others for their efforts, successes, and appropriate verbal behavior.

Problems Regarding Productive Participation. Parents may:

- **a.** Miss meetings, send no substitutes, arrive late.
- **b.** Not complete assignments satisfactorily; offer various reasons which, if frequent, may indicate that they are not being taught properly or are having problems, such as fatigue, lack of household order, personal problems, lack of marital cooperation. Examples of "excuses" are:

I just didn't have the time this week.

I just can't be trusted.

Help me, I'm stupid.

- **c.** Make negative or pessimistic statements; ask questions that seek sympathy or answers to "ultimate" questions, rather than prescriptions for behavior change. For example:

That method won't work with Sally.

But I can't remove her plate when she leaves the table! That would be cruel.

It's easy for Mr. Sanchez to do that. But he doesn't know our Andy.

> You have to laugh at our problems or else you'll cry.
>
> It's always a battle. Suzy is a pill.
>
> I know that we are talking about how to teach our kids. But why does Mark spin things? I mean, is something wrong with his brain?

If frequent, such statements may be communication games designed to help the parent save face, to excuse the failure either to fulfill obligations or to make the effort that the others are making, or to gain attention.

d. Use nonbehavioral terms and principles, for example, invoking inferred internal states in order to explain child's actions (''Aldo cries so much because he is insecure''), using the behavior itself as its explanation (''Rita whines so much because she is basically a pill''), or using the wrong behavioral terms or principles (''I extinguished Billy's tantrums by spanking him'').

e. Rarely speak, seem timid or threatened, bored, possibly hostile.

f. Remain isolated from one another in meetings; do not ask teaching-related questions of others; do not make prescriptive suggestions to others or congratulate others; reinforce others' pessimistic/negative verbal behavior by oversympathizing or by attempting to answer unproductive questions; gang-up on or act hostile toward another parent for poor performance or because of other's personal characteristics (e.g., making side comments or jokes about another parent who seems pretentious or ''incompetent'').]

Make sure to start working on productive participation from the first week of the Program. Chapter 5 discusses methods for doing so. If problems arise, however, see Chapter 10.

12. Objectivity in Observing, Describing, Explaining or Analyzing, Predicting, and Evaluating Behavior

Components of objectivity are listed from simpler to more complex. Parents can:

a. Describe or define a target behavior (of self or child) in terms of observable movements.

b. Pinpoint (point out, label, discriminate) a recurring target behavior (that is, the same behavior) in a stream of behavior or series of exchanges. For example, while observing behavior, parents can say: There it is! (Some time goes by) There it is again. (More time goes by) There it is again!

Examples of target behaviors are: repeated ''bizarre hand gestures'' of child, episodes of ''tense'' or ''anxious'' feelings of parent during the day, ''noncompliance'' of child when interacting with parent, people ''looking at'' child when interacting with child.

c. Use basic principles of learning to analyze or explain the strength of a target behavior and to predict its future strength (e.g., the weakening of a behavior during extinction).

d. Write logs or take notes describing daily events.

e. Record frequencies and durations of target behavior(s), for example, by making hash-marks after each occurrence or writing the duration of each episode.

f. Chart or graph recorded measurements.

g. Describe an ongoing stream of behavior or a series of exchanges in terms of observable movements (like a sportscaster). For example:

> Terry turns his head toward his mother; looks at her face; she is looking at his face; he flaps his hands rapidly; she frowns and says, ''Terry, that's silly.''

h. Pinpoint, measure, and chart a recurring behavior of both the child and another person in ongoing exchanges (e.g., correct reading responses of child and social reinforcement from parent).

i. Describe and explain or analyze major aspects of family's career in terms of observable events, using behavioral terms and principles (e.g., parents' fatigue or pessimism, the strength of certain of the child's behaviors, the long-term decrease in parents' efforts to teach child, stronger patterns of cooperation between the parents).

j. Pinpoint small, fleeting, or subtle movements (their own and child's). For example: how the child moves his fingers when trying to button his shirt; how the parent glances at (attends to) child when child is throwing a tantrum.

k. Rate performance of a behavior using a checklist, with alternative rankings of performance (for example, the Behavior Evaluation Scale (BES) in *Educating Children with Learning and Behavior Problems*).

1. evaluate progress using logs or notes, a performance checklist, or a graph of the frequency, rate, or duration of a behavior.

[Problems in Learning to be Objective and to Act in an Objective Way Include the Following. Parents:

a. Are affected by too much noise and activity in the home.

b. Do not focus on observable movements and environmental events, but on child's internal states (''Billy is nervous today'').

c. Focus on (or are so caught up in) the ongoing stream of events that they do not pinpoint the beginning and ending of a target behavior or exchange. That is, they have difficulty cutting up the stream of events into discrete behaviors or exchanges.

d. Focus so much on (are so distracted by) their own internal states (e.g., tension, rumination) that observing and recording are hindered.

e. Focus so much on child's behavior that they fail to notice or accurately describe their own behaviors (e.g., in exchanges with child).

f. Do not generalize the same learning principles from one behavior (or setting) to another.

g. Have trouble describing, analyzing, and understanding problems in the family (especially long-standing ones, e.g., those resulting from the career) because they are fatalistic ("I guess it just had to be this way"); believe that they are somehow to blame for their problems ("If I had only continued trying to teach Harriet she would now be fine"); focus on one aspect of, or problem in, their situation and do not see interrelationships:

It's all because my husband and I don't get along.

It's all because of those doctors.

It's all because we live so far from our relatives.

h. Have trouble recording and charting behaviors because they do not see it as important; delay recording and charting, and then forget to do it or fail to do it correctly; are recording too many behaviors at once; their attention wavers.]

Objectivity, as well as several items described below, is worked on from the second week to about the fifth week. See Chapter 6 for details.

13. Confidence in Learning Principles and Have Long-Term Perspective

This complex item means that the parents believe that regularities in behavior can be described by certain laws or principles; they believe that behavior change is neither impossible to understand, magical, nor chance; they do not believe that behavior change depends on their being "perfect" persons or persons of a certain "type." Moreover, they are satisfied with small changes in the direction of their goals. For example, parents recognize that:

a. Principles of learning apply to all of us.

b. Principles of learning are descriptions of environmental conditions within which behavior change is likely to take place.

c. Both their behaviors and the behaviors of their child eventually change in the desired direction if the proper conditions for a teaching-learning environment are determined and established. That is, parents understand that more general principles operate through their behavior. They are not waiting for the "big breakthrough,'' but believe that by successfully achieving their short-term goals they will eventually achieve long-term, major goals. For example, they say:

If I work properly now, behavior change will take care of itself.

We can wait. If the teaching programs are right for Johnny, he'll change.

Rome wasn't built in a day.

Sam has to walk before he can run.

Small changes add up to big ones.

Jane has a long way to go. But look at where she was before!

[Problems Regarding a Long-term Perspective and Confidence in More General Principles, Include the Following. Parents:

a. Do not believe that principles of learning apply to human behavior in an important way.

b. Are so overinvolved with their child that they feel personally responsible for what their child does and becomes, as though their every movement were important to their child's future. Parents may be depressed, pessimistic, fatigued. For example, they say:

Every time I make a mistake, I feel like I'm hurting Mary's chances.

How can I take a break? Every minute that I'm not working with Jose I feel guilty.

How can I help Sarah? I'm no miracle worker!]

Work on this item begins with the first meeting and continues through the third week. See Chapters 5 and 6 for methods of helping parents to develop a long-term perspective and confidence in general principles of learning. The message is reiterated when parents begin to conduct teaching programs for pinpointed target behaviors (about the fifth week).

14. Planning an Educational Program

Parents can plan a comprehensive, long-term educational program for their child. The steps listed below are part of a longer list in Chapter 4 of *Educating Children*. For example, parents can:

a. Rate (score) their child's performance of various behaviors by filling out the Behavior Evaluation Scale (BES) and Behavior Evaluation Table (BET) (or other assessment instruments). If possible, they obtain or have access to other evaluations.

b. Pinpoint those behaviors with which their child needs some form of help and determine the kind(s) of help the child needs with each behavior.

c. Determine the skill area(s) in which to start their child's educational program, based on their child's readiness (as indicated by a comparison of their scoring of the BES with the Table of Basic Behaviors).

d. Determine the first several target behaviors to work on in each skill area of their child's educational program.

e. Determine a tentative skill sequence to follow in their child's educational program, as indicated by the Skill Sequence Table.

f. In general, adapt methods, activities, and materials (curriculum) to match the needs of the child as indicated by the evaluation.

g. Think of or pinpoint new behaviors to work on, which were not suggested by consultant or materials used in the Program.

Problems. [Parents may:

a. Fail to cooperate with one another when planning their child's educational program.

b. Put off the task of scoring the BES and, when they finally do it, may rush through it so fast that their assessment is invalid.

c. Have trouble obtaining past evaluations.

d. Fail to be objective in assessing their child's performance.]

During the first week of the Program (Chapter 5), the methods for planning a comprehensive educational program can be described briefly. The major work on this item, however, is done during the fourth week (Chapter 8).

The next four items constitute a foundation of good teaching procedures, preparing the parents to conduct their home educational program.

15. Willing to Try Certain Behavioral Methods

For example, so long as the methods and their use have been explained and shown to be beneficial (see Item 10), parents are willing to:

a. Save certain reinforcers (rewards) and provide them contingent upon appropriate behaviors, that is, require child to earn reinforcers by engaging in appropriate behaviors (no "freebies").

b. Let their child experience certain "usual" consequences of noncompliant or disruptive behaviors. For example, if the teaching program calls for the parents to require the child to clean up any messes he makes before he goes outside to play, the parents agree to "stick to their guns" and not let the child go outside until the child cleans up. Parents make statements such as:

> Well, I hate to do it, but nothing else has worked and he's got to learn to be responsible for his actions.

c. When necessary, set aside certain periods of time during the day for intensive, individualized teaching sessions.

d. Emphasize errorless learning (in contrast to trial and error), that is, to help or prompt their child to perform behaviors that the child is having difficulty doing on his own.

e. Systematically use certain methods (ignoring, stimulus controls, etc.) to replace problem behaviors with appropriate behaviors.

Problems. [Parents may:

a. Resist saving reinforcers for use in teaching sessions or to allow child to experience the usual consequences of noncompliant or disruptive behaviors. For example, parents pity child, cannot do enough for child, feel that "depriving" their child would make them "bad" parents.

b. Have difficulty setting aside time for teaching sessions because they feel that they can do just as well on a "catch-as-catch-can" basis or do not seem to have the time.

c. Resist prompting the child because they believe child should learn or perform behaviors on his own (i.e., they rely on trial and error).

d. Resist ignoring certain behaviors because they fear that the child will injure himself. Resist timing out or punishing child as they feel that such methods are inhumane or ineffective. Or, may want to punish child instead of trying to replace problem behaviors.]

Instruction on this item is coordinated with Items 16 (planning, rather than reacting), 17 (instituting productive exchanges), and 18 (using general teaching methods), and is started at the beginning of the Program and continued for about four more weeks, using written materials, videotapes or films, demonstrations, discussions, and especially coaching. (See Chapter 6.)

16. Waiting and Planning, Rather Than Reacting

Parents have a response pattern that involves waiting and planning, rather than reacting to problems immediately and unproductively. When faced with a disruptive behavior of their child or a lack of progress, when experiencing an episode of emotional distress (e.g., anxiety), or when confronted with a new problem or situation (that does not require immediate action), the parents use a problem-solving sequence as follows. Parents:

a. Instead of reacting immediately in an unproductive way, tell themselves, "Stop"; "Relax"; "Think"; or "What is the best thing to do now?" If the situation demands an immediate response, they do what they can to contain the problem and recognize that a more carefully planned program is necessary.

b. Pinpoint, describe, and analyze the problem situation or event.

c. Reframe or reconceptualize the problem situation and goals, as needed.

d. Develop alternative plans for solving the problem, weigh each alternative, and select the first plan to try.

e. Write the problem-solving plan.

f. Institute the problem-solving plan and measure progress and any problems.

g. Evaluate the effectiveness of the first problem-solving plan and decide what to do next (e.g., continue the plan or try another).

The above steps are described in detail in Section IV of Chapter 8.

[Problems With the Parents Learning to Plan Rather Than React, and to Follow a Problem-solving Sequence. For example, parents:

a. Are hypervigilant, ''walking on eggs,'' tense, anxious, or on the lookout for events that are aversive to them, such as disruptive behaviors of their child, painful feelings within themselves, or pain-producing behaviors from each other. Consequently, parents react quickly and seemingly without thinking when aversive events occur. Parents try to stop such events by yelling, punishing, nagging, giving in, ruminating, or leaving the situation.

b. May not react immediately, but the waiting period does not involve planning. Instead, parents are ''desperately ignoring'' the aversive behavior or problem, doing the ''slow burn,'' or making unproductive statements to themselves or others, such as:

> Nothing can be done.
>
> I can't stand it.
>
> Won't you make her stop?

c. Do not cooperate with one another; do not know alternative methods for solving problems.

d. Simply avoid situations in which problems arise, rather than work to establish appropriate behavior in those situations.]

Work on this item is generally begun during the second and third weeks of the program, as the parents are taught to institute productive exchanges. See Chapters 6, 7, and especially 8 for details.

17. Instituting Productive Exchanges in the Home

Specifically, using basic principles of teaching-learning, the parents objectively pinpoint, describe, and analyze the major and most frequent patterns of interaction with their child. They decide which ones are productive and hence should be continued and strengthened, as well as those which are counterproductive and should be replaced with exchanges that teach their child to pay attention, follow directions, perform chores or play. (See Section VI of Chapter 2). For example, the parents:

a. Replace the "escape" exchange (reinforcement of problem behaviors) using a variety of methods (systematic positive reinforcement for appropriate behaviors, ignoring, stimulus control, shaping, time out, differential reinforcement of low rates, or if necessary, punishment).

b. Replace the "placation" or avoidance exchange (giving away rewards so as to avoid more severe disruptions) with an exchange that requires the child to earn rewards.

c. Replace "multiple signals" (repeating signals over and over when the child does not comply) with exchanges involving a presentation of a single, clear signal (e.g., a request) followed, if necessary, by prompts which insure that the child performs the indicated behavior.

d. Increase the number of "occasions" (opportunities, places) that the child has to learn and do appropriate behaviors.

e. Increase the reinforcement of both appropriate behaviors and approximations by reinforcing more often, faster, with higher quality reinforcers, and with a wider variety of reinforcers.

f. Use "natural" reinforcers (e.g., activities) as often as possible, in exchanges arranged, for example, in terms of "Grandma's Law":

> As soon as you do your math, you can go outside.

g. Avoid ineffective or unnecessary punishment or replace it with less aversive methods. If punishment is chosen, it is used in a humane and effective way.

h. Increase the use of productive exchanges that are already in operation, such as rewarding appropriate behaviors, systematically ignoring attention-getting problem behaviors.

[**Problems in Pinpointing and Instituting Productive Exchanges.** For example, parents:

a. Do not see the need to alter certain exchanges.

b. Do not objectively describe and analyze exchanges that need to be changed.

c. Have a pattern of reacting rather than waiting and planning.

d. Do not correctly use basic teaching methods, especially those involving rewards, signals, and ignoring problem behaviors.

e. Do not cooperate with one another. For instance, they do not agree on which behaviors or exchanges need to be changed; may blame one another for the child's behavior problems; may not help one another in instituting (carrying out) new exchanges through emotional support, coaching, or helping one another apply various methods.

f. Indicate there is too much noise and extraneous activity in the home, which interferes with instituting new exchanges in a consistent way.

g. Are too anxious, depressed, or fatigued to consistently institute new exchanges.

h. May locate the problem in the child or others, rather than seeing it as a consequence, in part, of their own fatigue, inadequate skills, or difficulty in defining the problem. They may play communication games such as:

I didn't have the time to do all that!

It just won't work.

We've tried that before.

Help me, I can't cope.

So do me something! I'm not trustworthy.]

Work on this item begins in the second and third weeks of the Program. See Chapters 6 and 7 for details.

18. General Teaching Skills

Parents are skilled at applying general (basic) teaching methods, that is, methods that are used in all productive exchanges and in teaching target behaviors in any skill area. The following list is divided into the major types of teaching methods. You can use the list to assess parents' skills during Baseline Observations, to plan their Program as well as agendas for specific meetings, and to assess their progress during the program. Make sure to teach parents to assess themselves as well. Assess parents' skills regarding the teaching of behaviors in all skill areas of their child's educational program. The following component skills are described in detail (in Chapters 3 through 7) and are then applied to the teaching of behaviors in various skill areas (in Chapters 9 through 15) in *Educating Children*.

A. Planning Teaching Programs for Specific Behaviors. Parents use the following steps:

a. Pinpoint target behaviors on the basis of behavioral assessment (e.g., the Behavior Evaluation Scale, the Table of Basic Behaviors, and the Skill Sequence Table), insuring that the child is educationally and developmentally "ready" to work in the selected skill area.

b. Pinpoint target behaviors for a teaching program, selecting those that are easier for the child and earlier in the skill area.

c. Clearly define target behaviors in terms of movements. Specify the way(s) in which each target behavior needs to be changed.

d. Establish goals with specific criteria for the target behaviors. For instance, to: increase, maintain, or decrease the frequency or duration of the target behavior; to improve the skill with which the child performs the target behavior; to increase the number of settings in which the child performs the target behavior.

e. Write all components of the teaching program plan, e.g., the skill area, definition of target behavior, shaping steps, time and place where teaching will be done, signals, prompts, rewards and reward schedules to be used, other target behaviors to be maintained, and methods for taking data. (See "General Teaching Program Plan," Table 6–2, in *Educating Children*.) Parents can plan teaching programs for behaviors in all skill areas.

B. Arranging the Physical Environment (Engineering for Success). Here, we are referring to some alterations in the physical environment which enable the parents to either avoid problems or make their child's learning of appropriate behaviors easier. Most alterations should be temporary. For example, parents: remove nick-nacks which the child persistently handles, tosses around, or threatens to break; remove newspapers, phone books, and magazines which the child persistently shreds; put locks on cabinets or on the refrigerator if the child habitually steals food or simply makes messes; place the TV in a higher location if the child frequently plays with it or damages it; use various items that facilitate the child's self-help skills, such as cotton socks, pants with elastic waist-bands, loafers, large eating utensils and combs; set aside a special place and container for the child's toys. (See Item 20.)

The physical environment:

a. Is arranged to avoid certain problems and facilitate learning.

b. Can be easily rearranged for different activities during the day and throughout the year.

C. Setting up (the Where and When of) Teaching Sessions. Here are some ground-rules. Parents:

a. Set aside regular times for particular teaching sessions. Keep sessions relatively short at first (e.g., 20 minutes). When possible, construct sessions around or integrated with the child's favorite activities.

b. Are flexible so that the duration of sessions can be changed as the occasion requires; increase session time as the child's work habits improve.

c. Keep sessions relatively free of things that prevent the child from learning.

d. Position themselves so as to signal, prompt, and reward the child properly.

e. Ensure that the effective reinforcers are delivered only at the appropriate times (e.g., if necessary, food is kept out of the child's reach).

D. Shaping. The major steps in shaping are as follows. Parents:

a. Break down the target behavior into small steps by which it is taught, that is, movements that are successively closer approximations to the desired performance (goal). (This step constitutes a task analysis.) Strengthen each shaping step by signals, prompts, and rewards.

b. Write the list of shaping steps on the teaching program plan.

c. Begin the actual teaching program with the first step with which the child needs help. Give the child occasions to respond via signals (to perform the movements), prompt child to correctly perform the movements, and reward the child for correct responses and acceptable approximations.

d. Reward the child if he happens to perform a movement that is on a more advanced step.

e. As the child learns to do the movements on a step without help, gradually fade out prompts, no longer reward less skillful performances, and reward skillful performances intermittently.

f. As child becomes skillful on one step, move to the next step. If child is having trouble on a harder step, back-up to an easier step and try again. If child still has trouble, evaluate, and if necessary improve, their own teaching skills and the teaching program plan.

E. Signals. Parents:

a. Make signals simple and straightforward by using few words and stressing the important ones. For example: Pick up your socks, please. [Not: Can you (will you) pick up your socks?]

b. Make sure the child is paying attention when they give signals (e.g., instructions, models, requests, questions).

c. Give a new signal only once. If the child does not respond within a few seconds, present the signal again and prompt the child to respond.

d. Use Grandma's Law to signal (start) teaching sessions and other activities that can be followed by activity rewards. State it positively (i.e., what the child will get if he or she cooperates, not what the child will lose if he or she does not). And back it up by the stated consequences.

F. Prompting. Parents:

a. Know when to use which type of prompt(s) to help child perform each target behavior: visual (e.g., pointing, demonstrating); verbal (e.g., instruction); and physical (e.g., helping child through the motions).

b. Begin with the least prompting that is necessary in teaching a target behavior. If a minimum prompt is not sufficient, then try a slightly more extensive prompt.

c. Slowly fade prompts as the child begins to perform the target behavior on his own. For example, parents say less of an instruction or say it in a softer voice, wait longer before pointing, or move the child through only a portion of the movements.

d. Enthusiastically reward child when child performs target behavior with less prompting.

G. Rewards. Parents:

a. Find rewards by observing the child, asking the child and others, and using reward menus.

b. Use the most effective available rewards.

c. Save rewards to be used to strengthen target behaviors until the child performs target behaviors. That is, rewards are not "given away."

d. Reward correct responses and acceptable approximations (prompted or unprompted) immediately and every time at the beginning of a teaching program.

e. As the target behavior changes in the desired direction (e.g., more often, longer duration, greater skill), give rewards more and more intermittently (especially on a Changing Number Schedule). Give rewards more and more for correct responses and less and less for approximations and prompted responses.

f. Back up to a schedule of more frequent reinforcement, if the child's performance of a target behavior or child's cooperation begins to deteriorate when less reinforcement is being given. When the child's behavior has improved again, slowly move to a more intermittent schedule.

g. Pair primary, activity, and general rewards with social rewards. For example, hug, praise, talk to, and smile at child just before and while rewarding child with food or the opportunity to engage in a favorite activity. Give social reinforcement with enthusiasm. Give social reinforcement in varied ways.

h. Tell or make clear to child which behavior they are rewarding.

i. Reward target behavior(s) and other desirable behaviors (e.g., those being maintained and those that seem to appear spontaneously).

j. Use activity rewards after child performs demanding tasks.

k. To avoid satiation, recognize that some reinforcers become useless, and so, give food in small bites; switch or rotate reinforcers periodically; give child a choice of reinforcers when possible; and stop enjoyable activities before child is bored or tired.

H. Chaining. Parents:

a. Teach child to perform simpler target behaviors in usual sequences. For example, to get task materials, bring them to table, sit down, work at task, complete task, and put away materials.

b. Know how to use both ''forward-chaining'' (e.g., teaching child to perform the first movement in a chain and, when child has mastered it, to perform the first movement followed by the second and so on) and ''back-chaining'' (e.g., teaching child to perform the last movement in the chain and, when the child has mastered it, to perform the second-to-last followed by the last and so on).

Parents use chaining methods effectively for teaching behaviors in all skill areas, when relevant.

I. Replacing Problem Behaviors. Parents:

a. Wait and plan rather than react to problem behaviors.

b. Ignore extraneous behaviors (e.g., nail-biting, squinting) that do not interfere with the child's learning appropriate behaviors. However, may target extraneous behaviors for future replacement.

c. Know when and how to use a variety of methods for replacing problem behaviors (e.g., systematically reinforcing alternative behaviors, ignoring, time out, overcorrection, punishment, differential reinforcement of low rates, stimulus control, stimulus change, satiation, negative practice, self-recording and contingency management, relaxation).

d. Know that any program for decreasing problem behaviors involves simultaneously a program for strengthening appropriate replacement behaviors.

J. Program Evaluation and Revision. Parents:

a. Routinely measure and chart target behaviors being worked on, for example, during or after sessions.

b. Evaluate progress in terms of goals they have established.

c. If target behaviors are changing satisfactorily, continue the teaching program until the goal is almost reached. Then update the child's behavioral assessment and pinpoint the next target behavior(s) to work on (e.g., with the Behavior Evaluation Scale, Table of Basic Behaviors, and Skill Sequence Table). Write a new teaching program plan.

d. If target behaviors are not changing satisfactorily, examine their own behaviors to make sure they are following the teaching program plan and evaluate the teaching program, for example, according to Chapter 7, "Handling Common Problems of Teaching," in *Educating Children.* Revise teaching program plan, if necessary.

e. If having trouble conducting the overall educational program or specific teaching programs in it, evaluate their own behavior (e.g., using the APG and other materials); pinpoint behaviors of theirs that might need to be changed; discuss possible solutions among themselves and carry out the plan. (See Items 16 and 27 regarding a general problem-solving strategy.)

K. Generalization and Creativity. Parents use the above methods when teaching a) all skill areas of their child's educational program and b) skill areas and behaviors for which they have not received instruction.

Problems. [The list of possible problems that can interfere with the parents' learning and effectively using basic teaching methods is long. Indeed, all of the problems listed in earlier items, and all of those to be listed below, are relevant.]

While the parents receive some exposure to basic teaching methods during the first and second weeks, most of this item is worked on in the third through fifth weeks. As the Program progresses, parents learn to apply the general methods to target behaviors in all skill areas of the educational program for their children.

19. Cooperation of Spouses or Partners

Spouses or partners cooperate with one another in planning and conducting the home educational program and in solving problems. For example, parents:

a. Work toward an agreement on: (1) the behaviors of their child and themselves (as individuals and as a couple) that need to be changed; (2) other family issues that need to be addressed (such as how to involve the siblings, how to train others who come in contact with the child, setting priorities on family routines, e.g., that it is more important to conduct teaching sessions than to have fancy meals every night); and (3) methods to use in producing behavior change and in solving problems.

b. Work together in conducting teaching programs. For instance: (1) one parent might work with the child while the other parent coaches, takes data, sets up the session, cleans up after the session, or watches the other children; (2) when the parent who is working with the child becomes fatigued or seems to be having trouble, the other parent lends a hand.

c. Work together and support one another in solving personal problems, such as tension, anxiety, or depressed mood.

d. Reinforce each other for efforts and successes. For instance, they: (1) give each other unconditional praise, communicate regard, understanding, closeness, and appreciation; (2) give each other praise and "special" reinforcement (such as a favorite meal, flowers, a favor) for specific behaviors (such as remaining calm during a demanding teaching session or making an effort to change one's own behaviors); and (3) gratify themselves as a couple by scheduling reinforcing activities, such as nights out.

e. Share household tasks, such as child-rearing and housekeeping.

[Problems Regarding Cooperation Between the Parents Include the Following. Parents:

a. Disagree on behaviors that need to be changed, problems that need to be solved, and methods to use. Instead of working toward an agreement, parents may become isolated from one another, work against one another, blame one another, or argue.

b. Do not work together. That is, one parent carries the job of working with the child.

c. Do not work together or support one another in solving personal problems. Instead, one parent may ignore the other's problems, blame the other, expect the other to solve problems alone or get help somewhere else. Or, one parent may simply be uncomfortable or not know how to help the other.

d. Do not reinforce or gratify one another. Instead, they: (1) ignore one another's efforts, successes, and contributions to the family or (2) blame, belittle, and criticize one another.

e. Do not share household tasks; are uncomfortable working as a team. There may be much "role-segregation." For example, the father may consider it his wife's job to do all of the work within the house or he may consider it unmanly to work with his children.]

The importance of cooperation is stressed during the first week. Methods for working as a team to plan an educational program, institute productive exchanges, conduct teaching programs, and solve problems are presented throughout the Program. When problems arise, see Chapter 10.

20. Organized Home Life

Aspects of daily life that have a bearing on the child's education are conducted in an organized and coordinated fashion. This does not mean that home life is rigid, but rather a certain order allows parents the time and energy to effectively conduct a home educational program and to participate in the Program in a productive way. For example, parents:

a. Have a regular schedule for everyday events, such as meals, teaching assignments, bedtimes, and certain chores.

b. Do everyday events efficiently enough that there is sufficient time and energy to conduct teaching programs, to participate in the Program in a productive way (e.g., to do reading assignments), and to interact in a gratifying way with spouse and other children.

c. Keep the noise and activity level (from the TV, radio, or other children) low enough that teaching sessions are not disrupted and people's nerves are not kept on edge.

d. Arrange objects and materials in the home (such as toys and teaching materials) for easy access. (See Item 18B.)

e. With family members, discuss and agree upon priorities for certain events and routines.

f. Allow enough flexibility within the overall household organization to meet needs and take advantage of opportunities. For example, family members understand that the mother sometimes may be too tired to cook the usual hot meal, and so there may be nights when everyone will be eating peanut butter and jelly sandwiches. Similarly, the wife understands that, while the husband has agreed to mow the lawn every Saturday, there may be Saturdays when it is more important for him to spend time with the child, siblings, or by himself, putting off the lawn until the next day. (See Item 19.)

[**Problems** of household organization that are likely to interfere with conducting a good home educational program or with productively participating in the Program, include the following.

a. Everyday events occur at irregular times. For instance: (1) meals may be early or late (meaning that the child is full one night and starving the other); (2) bedtimes are either late or at different times (meaning that the child probably wakes up crabby or at least has bedtime problems); (3) chores pile up and must be done all at once, meaning that teaching programs and gratifying activities must be put aside; and (4) breaks are unscheduled (meaning that the educational program begins to deteriorate). In sum, the environment becomes less consistent and predictable.

b. Everyday events are done inefficiently, so that there is little time or energy to conduct teaching programs, participate in the Program (e.g., doing assignments), or interact with the spouse or other children.

c. The noise or activity level is so high (or the parents seem unable to reduce it for long) that the sessions are disrupted and people's "nerves" are on edge.

d. Objects in the house are in disarray, the result being that: (1) the physical environment is inconstant and unpredictable for the child; (2) teaching materials and toys get lost; and (3) tension is produced because of the mess or lost objects.

e. Parents expect themselves or each other to rigidly maintain certain routines or schedules. For example, family members expect or demand a hot meal every night, spotlessly clean floors, or a continually-emptied trash can.]

21. Pinpointing and Solving Personal Problems

Parents pinpoint and work toward the solution of personal problems, such as tension, anxiety, stress, depressed mood, and counterproductive or self-defeating thoughts. Parents handle personal problems by following a ''Problem-solving sequence'' (as described in Item 16). Parents:

a. Pinpoint and describe a personal problem in terms of specific feelings, thoughts (self-statements), and actions.

b. Analyze a personal problem by taking note of when, where, and how the problem occurs. For instance, parents note: (1) the frequency, duration, intensity, and components of problem episodes (e.g., anxiety); (2) antecedent events that seem to ''set-off'' episodes (e.g., fatigue, disruptive behaviors of the child, physical sensations, fearful thoughts of the future, arguing with the spouse); (3) consequent events (such as running to the refrigerator, thinking pessimistic thoughts, having a drink, going to bed, giving in to child or spouse, support or lack of support from spouse, or putting off teaching sessions); (4) the ways the problem interferes with both conducting a good home educational program as well as with other aspects of family life, such as marital relationships, relationships with the child's siblings, or with household organization.

c. Jointly plan, conduct, and evaluate a program for solving the personal problem, for example, progressive relaxation to handle tension, assertiveness training to help the parent deal with shyness and the unkind reactions of outsiders, or cognitive relabeling to help the parent replace counterproductive thoughts.

Problems. [The major obstacles in the way of solving personal problems are:

a. Lack of objectivity in pinpointing, describing, and analyzing the problem.

b. A lack of confidence in general principles of learning (e.g., the parent gives up without trying because parent sees himself as essentially weak or sick or does not believe the methods will work).

c. A lack of cooperation between the spouses.

d. Lack of household organization. For example, there may be so much noise and confusion that the parent cannot conduct relaxation exercises.]

Methods for helping parents to avoid and overcome personal problems are described in Chapter 10.

PERSISTING IN CONDUCTING A GOOD HOME EDUCATIONAL PROGRAM AND MAINTAINING IT AFTER THE WORKING RELATIONSHIP WITH THE CONSULTANT HAS BEEN FADED OUT

22. Honesty

Parents are honest with themselves (as individuals and as partners), with their consultant, and with others who may be in a position to provide advice or support. For example, parents:

a. Accurately describe their own behaviors and behaviors of child (e.g., how they feel, how they run sessions, events that take place during the day).

b. Accurately describe change in child and themselves, both beneficial and problematic.

c. Accurately describe problems in the overall educational program (e.g., difficulty taking breaks, lack of help from relatives).

d. Accurately describe feelings, thoughts, and expectations regarding child, self, each other, family, school, consultant, and future (especially frustration, pessimism, a declining interest in working with consultant, guilt regarding child or failure to carry out agreed-upon tasks, anger or hostility).

e. Keep objective and valid data (for example, recording sheets and graphs).

Problems. [parents do not volunteer descriptions or withhold information on what is going on in their lives. Or they give an inaccurate picture. For instance, they overemphasize problems:

> Nothing is working right.

or progress

> Oh, everything is just fine. Sure, I'm just as motivated as before. We generally follow the teaching program plans. We work with Marty about an hour a day. I'm feeling great.]

The subject of honesty is discussed in the first meeting. If problems occur, conduct special programs using methods described in Chapter 10.

23. Scheduled Breaks

Parents schedule and take ''breaks'' in their home educational program. That is, they put their educational program on the ''back burner'' while they take a needed rest. Specifically, parents:

a. Set aside strenuous teaching sessions and reinforce themselves (and child) for their efforts and progress by: (1) leaving the situation (e.g., taking a walk, reading in another room); (2) engaging in less structured or demanding activities (e.g., following a teaching session on verbal imitation with a task or activity which the parent and child enjoy); and (3) engaging in more spontaneous interaction with the child (e.g., play). Breaks are taken for some time each day, week, and month. As much as possible, breaks are scheduled in advance, so that they are less likely to become escape/avoidance behaviors.

b. Maintain the major features of the educational program when they are on breaks by: (1) giving child occasions to respond at usual times during the day (for example, when it is time for child to do a chore or when child indicates that she wants something); (2) prompting when child needs help; (3) reinforcing the child for correct responses or for good tries; and (4) going ''on break'' in such a way that one parent is still working with child according to the current teaching program plan while the other parent is on break. The parent who is on break provides special reinforcement for the parent who is still working (e.g., a favorite meal or a favor).

[**Problems** in scheduling and taking breaks are as follows. Parents:

a. Expect, and try, to conduct strenuous teaching programs all of the time (thereby ''burning out'' in a few months).

b. Feel guilty, anxious, or on edge when they are not either working with the child or thinking about it.

c. Take scheduled breaks, but fail to at least maintain the major features of their child's educational program. For example, they return to counterproductive patterns of exchange.

d. Take breaks that are longer and longer, more frequent, and less scheduled.]

Discuss the need for scheduled breaks during the first meeting. During the second and third weeks, help parents to schedule and take breaks. Methods for handling problems are discussed in Chapter 10.

24. Self- and Mutual Reinforcement

Parents reinforce (gratify) themselves and one another often enough and in a way that will maintain motivation and performance. For example, each parent:

a. Reinforces himself or herself by scheduling personally-satisfying activities shortly after teaching sessions. That is, parents use "Grandma's Law" with themselves. For instance, the mother might schedule time for reading after a 20-minute teaching session or a more enjoyable teaching session after a harder one.

b. Provides himself or herself with "special" reinforcers contingent upon making progress toward or reaching certain goals (either a change in parent's behavior, such as learning how to relax, or change in child's behavior, such as teaching child to imitate five small motor models). For instance, the father might treat himself to a weekend football game when he finally teaches his child to work a new puzzle.

c. Reinforces (gratifies) the other parent when the other makes progress toward or attains his or her goals and, as often as possible, after teaching sessions. In addition, each parent provides the other with emotional support, understanding, assistance, and unexpected displays of affection.

d. With spouse (or partner) schedules reinforcing activities for themselves as a couple or family, both as a change of pace, after a period of hard work (e.g., during a schedule break), and especially when certain goals are reached.

Problems. [The major sources of difficulty in parents' reinforcing themselves and one another include the following.

a. Parents may have marital problems (antagonisms, competitiveness) which hinder their reinforcing one another. For example, one parent may not want to gratify the other. Moreover, a parent may not be gratified or reinforced by what the other parent has to offer ("You can keep your roses! I needed them years ago.") Or, the parents may be relatively isolated from one another (for example, the husband may bury himself in the newspaper every night); they may frequently engage in blaming and "cutting" one another ("Well, if it weren't for you . . ."); or they may simply feel that it is too late to try to salvage their relationship.

b. The houshold may not be organized enough for the parents to find the time or energy to reinforce themselves.

c. The family may be so isolated from relatives, neighbors, or from potential support networks, that they cannot get out.

d. The parents may be so tired, tense, or unhappy at times that they do not have the energy to reinforce one another, the interest in doing so, or the receptivity to be pleased. For instance, the wife may be so fatigued that she does not have the energy to reinforce her husband. Or the husband may be so unhappy that he would not enjoy going out.]

The importance of parents' reinforcing themselves and each other is stressed during the first and second meeting. Thereafter, parents are taught to specify in writing how they will reinforce themselves and one another. In addition, efforts are made to establish networks between families and to ingegrate families in networks of extended support. The kinds of problems that can hinder parents' reinforcing themselves, and methods to help them overcome such problems, are dealt with in Chapter 10.

25. Linkage with Networks and Organizations

Parents are closely linked with or integrated within networks and organizations offering resources of various kinds, such as (1) information on how to obtain services and on how to work with their child; (2) emotional support; (3) objective feedback on how they and their children are progressing; (4) backup support such as baby-sitting, specialists, respite care, or extra tutoring for their child; and (5) opportunities to work for change in the community service system.

Note that the examples in this item are aimed at solving the problem of isolation that may have developed over the years of the family's career as described in Section V, Chapter 2. For example, parents:

a. Are part of a community-based information network with parents, teachers, and specialists (e.g., telephone hotline or newsletter).

b. Belong to and participate in organizations for parents and professionals (such as the National Society for Autistic Children, the Association for Children with Learning Disabilities, the Association for Retarded Citizens, Council for Exceptional Children, The American Association for the Education of the Severely/Profoundly Handicapped).

c. Belong to parents' groups or parent-teacher groups at the facility attended by their child, and participate in meetings and other activities.

d. Have close working relationships with others (parents, teachers) for the exchange of information, emotional and backup support, direct coaching, and advice.

e. Read articles, journals, books, and newsletters relevant to the education of their children.

Problems. [Parents may be unable to or unwilling to become part of networks and organizations offering help of various kinds. Here are some of the many reasons. The parents may:

a. Have few people upon whose help they can count.

b. Feel uncomfortable in groups. For instance, they feel that they do not have enough intelligence, education, money, power, "class," or experience; would be unwanted or discriminated against because of their sex, race, religion, ethnic background, or social class; or may be so independent that they do not want to get involved.

c. Not see the potential benefits of becoming a part of such networks or organizations.

d. Not feel that they have the energy or time.

e. Make statements such as:

> With all that we have to do, we don't have the time.
>
> We can do it on our own.
>
> What good will those things do for us?
>
> It's what goes on inside the home that counts.
>
> Those organizations are for rich (white, educated) folks or for people who just want to have a good time (complain).

f. Not have a strong commitment to the community; or problems in the family may prevent their extending themselves.]

Parents are helped to become integrated in networks and organizations in small steps during the Program. Methods are discussed in chapters on various weeks, starting with Chapter 6.

26. Generalization

Parents insure that their child's behavioral changes (and their own skills) generalize to other persons and places. For example, parents:

a. Develop plans for teaching child to use specific skills across different settings, times, and activities.

b. Facilitate generalization by: (1) inviting people to their home; (2) accepting invitations to others' homes; and (3) taking their child to various community settings (such as the grocery store, restaurants, variety stores, barber shop) where their child can learn to perform the relevant behaviors.

c. Ask for (or, if necessary, require) cooperation from, instruct and coach others (such as siblings, relatives, neighbors, friends, salespersons) to interact with child in an educational way.

d. Ask for cooperation from, instruct, and coach others (such as siblings, grandparents, physicians, friends) to help them conduct current teaching programs. For instance, the parents might ask (and coach) the child's dentist to ask the child to say his (the child's) name, to say the dentist's name, and to point to the parts of his (the child's) face. Or, the parents might ask and coach the grandparents to have the child perform certain chores and self-help routines when the grandparents are baby sitting.

e. Use a wider range of materials and teaching methods, more spontaneous occasions for learning, and a wider variety of educational goals as child acquires specific skills.

[**Problems** in the parents' insuring the generalization of behavior change are as follows. Parents:

a. Feel uncomfortable about asking for cooperation or instructing others (perhaps because they do not know the teaching methods well enough).

b. Have few persons whose help they can enlist.

c. Receive, or feel that they receive, advice that is confusing or conflicting.

d. Are self-conscious about their child's behavior and want to avoid the embarrassment and difficulty of taking the child out in public.

Others:

a. (e.g., siblings) Feel pressured into working with the child, may feel neglected, may be embarrassed by child or overwhelmed with all of the problems that have accompanied the family's career.]

Methods for teaching parents to generalize their child's gains are discussed early, beginning with the second week, when parents are starting to institute productive exchanges (see Chapters 6 and 9).

27. Pinpointing and Solving Problems

Parents are skilled at anticipating, avoiding, and solving problems in conducting and maintaining their home educational program. (Also see Items 16 and 21.) Problems include all of those described in the preceding items. In avoiding and/or solving problems, the parents follow a "problem-solving sequence." For example, the parents:

a. Use materials (e.g., the APG and the "Behavior Evaluation Scale") both to remind themselves of what they should be doing in their educational program and to periodically assess themselves and their child's progress. For instance, they check to see if they are using correct teaching methods (Item 18) or if they are properly scheduling breaks in their home educational program (Item 23).

b. When problems are noted, do not ignore them or expect them to go away by themselves, but use methods and written materials (e.g., Chapter 7 of *Educating Children*) to pinpoint, describe, and analyze the problem, and to plan and conduct a program to solve it, using a problem-solving sequence.

c. Get help from others (parents, teachers, specialists) when problems seem to be over their heads.

[**Problems** in the parents' using materials, information received in meetings, and *Educating Children* to remind themselves of what they should be doing or to pinpoint and work to solve potential or actual problems, include the following. Parents:

a. Have low interest, motivation, or energy.

b. Are so involved in teaching programs that they do not take the time to observe and plan their behavior.

c. Are fatigued, or have marital problems or various personal problems that interfere with objectively observing the family system and working to correct problems.

d. Feel so personally responsible for changing the child's behavior and for doing well that they feel anxious, guilty, or incompetent when problems arise.]

Throughout the Program you are teaching the parents to use a problem-solving sequence regarding problems in their home educational program. Much work is done toward the middle and again near the end of the Program. Methods for handling special problems are described in Chapter 10.

Appendix 2 PARENTS AS BEHAVIORAL EDUCATORS

A PROGRAM TO TEACH PARENTS TO TEACH THEIR CHILDREN*

The Silent Minority

Within every community is a group of children who seem to be unreachable, unteachable, and unmanageable. They may not be able to communicate effectively, to play, to participate in social activities, and take care of themselves. These children have been called exceptional, autistic, retarded, and oppositional. Until recently, many persons, with the exception of their parents, had just about given up on educating them.

Reaching the Unreachable.

The picture is different now! Within the past decade big advances have been made in the field of education for "exceptional" children. Children who could not speak, play, cooperate, and learn from others are learning to communicate, to take part in family and classroom activities, to read, to occupy their time in constructive and enjoyable ways, and to find pleasure in being with and learning from others.

Who will Educate Your Children?

Unfortunately, it seems to take a long time to put into action new ideas and methods to convince people that new schools are needed, and to train teachers. If your child is not in a school, you no longer have to be content to wait until more schools are available and your child is accepted into one. You can give him a headstart now! And if your child is in a school, you can add to his education and teach him new skills in the home. For, not only have we developed new methods for educating children, but we have developed simple and effective programs for parents, to teach them how to help their children learn the behaviors and skills

*brochure sent to individual families and parents' organizations.

important for their children's development and education. We are offering such a program to you.

Who is this Program for?

This educational program is designed for parents of "exceptional" children, children with emotional and behavioral problems such as infantile autism, speech problems, childhood psychosis, retardation, and oppositional behavior. The program is for parents who feel that:

1. There is more that can and must be done for their child.
2. They need and desire to become more skillful in guiding their child's behavioral and emotional development.
3. Their child should be educated in school and in the home.

Why a Program for Parents?

1. It is usually agreed that the most important persons in a child's life are the parents. Because of the closeness and the amount of time that is spent together, the parents know much about their children and can help to educate them.

2. A child's progress in the classroom or special education program can be increased if the parents work effectively with their children in the home.

3. The parents can increase their child's chances of being accepted into and remaining in a school by giving the child a head start in certain important skill areas, such as language, cooperation, and motor skills, and by reducing the amount of those undesirable or disruptive behaviors that might otherwise hinder the child's chances.

4. By learning to be behavioral educators the parents can help their child learn skills that are so important to the child's homelife and future, such as playing with brothers and sisters; performing chores; washing, dressing, and toileting; asking for things, conversing, and describing experiences; giving and receiving affection.

What is Meant by "Behavioral Educator?"

By "behavioral educator" we mean a person who has an understanding of the ways various skills or behaviors are learned, maintained over time, and can be changed. He or she knows how to teach a child desirable behaviors (such as talking, reading, doing chores) and teach a child to replace undesirable behaviors (such as tantrums, not paying attention, or whining). He or she, finally, can plan and encourage a child's progress and yet allow the child to learn at his or her own pace; can teach the child in such a way that the child enjoys learning; and can evaluate the results of his teaching efforts.

How does the Program Work and What are the Goals?

The program consists of a series of instructional classroom meetings in which all parents participating in the program meet as a group. The classroom meetings include presentations by members of the staff, films, discussion of readings, group discussions, and demonstrations and practical applications of educational programs. In addition, members of the staff meet with parents after each group meeting and in the home to help the parents design and conduct an effective educational program with their child.

The objective of the program is to teach parents how to be behavioral educators. Specifically, parents will learn how:

1. Behaviors or skills are learned, are maintained over time, and can be changed.
2. To determine the educational needs of their child, that is, the child's strengths and weaknesses in important skill areas.
3. To pinpoint specific behaviors or skills to teach the child (desirable behaviors) and specific behaviors to help the child replace (undesirable behaviors).
4. To design a program for teaching their child in each pinpointed area.
5. To conduct a smooth and successful educational program with their child, so that the child learns personally satisfying and useful behavior and the parents become expert and confident in their abilities to help their child learn.
6. To take a knowledgeable and effective stand on the issues affecting their child's education now and in the future.

The Program also provides parents the opportunity to discuss and seek solutions for common problems and receive feedback on the success of their efforts with their children.

How is this Program Different from Other Programs for Parents?

This program differs from other programs because it is more comprehensive. The program is designed not only to provide parents with an understanding of educational principles and techniques, but experience in their use. We are not teaching parents to use just one idea or method, but instead provide parents with a wide range of skills to deal with any or all of their children's behavioral problems. This is an attempt to deal with the whole child. In addition, staff of the program will be available for help and counseling as long as seems necessary.

How much will it Cost?

In terms of money, the cost is nothing or nearly nothing. There is no participation fee. The only monetary costs are for transportation to and from meetings and for study aides. The "cost," in the most important sense, is a commitment to give the necessary time and effort to insure that the parents and their children benefit from the program.

How do I get More Information?

If this program seems as though it may, in some way, serve yourself and your child and you are interested in more information, at your earliest convenience write or call:

Dr. Martin A. Kozloff
Department of Sociology
Boston University
Boston, Mass. 02215

Appendix 3 PROGRAM CONTRACT

During the next several months we are all going to be working hard. So, before we start it is important that we understand exactly what we can expect from one another. First, we are not offering medical or psychiatric services. The purpose of the Program is to teach you to produce desirable behavior changes in yourselves and your children. The Program consists of a series of ____________ meetings, plus home visits for observation and assistance. However, either you or the Program staff may terminate participation in the Program at any time. Here are the terms of participation.

We, the parents, agree to:

1. Attend all meetings and be on time.
2. Allow staff to make home visits at agreed upon times.
3. Be ready for home visits at the agreed upon times.
4. Complete all agreed upon assignments (reading, teaching, data-taking) on time.
5. Actively participate in meetings (for example, asking and trying to answer questions, describing events in the home).
6. Allow consultants to observe and collect data (including videotapes, slides, audiotape, film) at agreed upon times, with the condition that data will not be presented at meetings without our permission and that any use of videotapes, films, slides, audiotapes or written descriptions that might identify us or our child requires our review and written permission.
7. (Additional agreements might be specified, e.g., to write three certified checks for certain amounts, for use in one of the contract-credit contingencies; to give staff permission to observe and/or record the child's behavior in a classroom; to allow the staff access to past evaluations of the child.)

We, the staff (or I), agree to:

1. Attend all meetings and be on time.

2. Try to teach you how to evaluate your child's needs, plan an educational program, teach your child skills which we will agree upon, measure progress, and solve problems that can arise in an educational program.
3. Make home visits at agreed upon times, and arrive on time.
4. Be available to give you help by telephone hotline during scheduled hours.
5. Explain the purpose, nature, and possible effects of all methods we will suggest that you use to teach your child or to change your own behavior. If at any time in the Program you have any questions about these methods or about any aspect of the Program, we will answer you as honestly and completely as we can.
6. Protect your, your child's, and the family's identity by not revealing your name, address, or any other identifying information to any but Program staff, without your written permission.
7. (Parents may want additional agreements specified, e.g., that any slides, films, videotapes, or audiotapes be kept in the child's school.)

Contract-credit option selected by parents ____________________ and consultant ____________________.

Signed and Dated ____________________ Signed and Dated ____________________

(Parents) (Consultant)

Appendix 4 CREDITS EARNED

NAME OF PARTICIPANT: ____________________

WEEK OF: ____________________

Each Parent	Points	Consultant	Points
Coming to meeting	2	Coming to meeting	2
Being on time	1	Being on time	1
Satisfactory completion of reading, written, or data-taking assignment	1	Satisfactory completion of task assignment by the parents	2
Following plan for home educational program	2	Attendance at home visit	2
Attendance at home visit	2	Having materials prepared for meeting	1
Participation in meeting	1		

Any of the following contract-credit systems could be selected by individual parents, families, consultants or by the group, either before the Program starts or during the first meeting(s).

Option 1: Positive Reinforcement

Available backup reinforcers	Prices in credits
Baby-sitting	4 per hour
Extra tutoring for child	8 per hour
Passes to movies, restaurants, bowling, etc.	18
Respite care	36 per day
College credit	to be arranged
Special items	to be arranged

Option 2: Deposit

Each family makes an initial deposit. At each meeting a certain percentage is returned contingent upon attendance or upon the number of credits earned (e.g., $0.25 per credit).

Option 3: Negative Reinforcement

	For Family	For Consultant
Maximum credits possible:	18	8
Minimum credits needed to avoid a check being sent:	16	7

Appendix 5 WEEKLY CONTRACT

CONTRACT FOR WEEK OF: / / **to** / /

Mr. and Mrs. ______________________________ agree to complete all parts of the following assignment for the coming week.

1. READ AND DO ANY WRITTEN ASSIGNMENTS in Chapter ______________
2. TEACHING PROGRAM PLAN FOR: (*skill area, target behavior(s), exchanges*). Table 6-2 in *Educating Children With Learning and Behavior Problems* provides a form that can be filled out and affixed to the weekly contract.
3. COOPERATION (sharing of tasks, etc.)
4. ORGANIZATION (schedules, physical arrangements in the home)
5. SCHEDULED BREAKS (times, who does what)
6. REINFORCEMENT (when and how)
7. LINKAGES (phone calls and home visits to and from other families, etc.)
8. GENERALIZATION (behaviors, situation, helpers)
9. PROBLEM-SOLVING (personal, marital, etc., and plans)
10. OBJECTIVITY AND HONESTY (logs, frequency counts, charts) Behavior Count Tables and Charts are found in Chapter 6 of *Educating Children.*
11. HOME VISIT (date and time)
12. SPECIAL TASK FOR CONSULTANT

Mr. ______________________________ Date __________

Mrs. ______________________________ Date __________

Consultant ______________________________ Date __________

Appendix 6 CHECKLIST FOR PROGRAM EVALUATION

Rate the following teaching materials, aids, and procedures on how much they help you understand and use the subject matter being taught. Rate each from 1 to 5; 1 being those that are MOST helpful and 5, the LEAST helpful.

____________ Readings (e.g., chapters in *Educating Children With Learning and Behavior Problems*)

____________ Questions at the end of readings

____________ Class presentation by consultant (oral)

____________ Open discussion in class with consultant and other parents

____________ Use of the blackboard

____________ Individual Consultations after the classroom meetings

____________ Use of films

____________ Use of videotapes on families

____________ Practicing methods and principles in class

____________ Home visits to coach and answer questions

____________ Carrying out the program with your child in the home

____________ Weekly Contract

____________ Contract-credit system

____________ Telephone calls or home visits with other parents

Comments? (Changes you would like? Things that might be better? Things you like?)

Appendix 7 WORKING WITH THE SINGLE-PARENT FAMILY

Barbara Cutler, M.Ed.
Project Coordinator, APT Project (Assisting Parents and Teachers), Community-based Training Programs,
Funded by the National Institute of Mental Health
Department of Sociology, Boston University

At first glance, single-parent families may appear to present more difficulties than "intact" families. In fact, much of the literature, current and past, is oriented toward finding pathological effects of single-parent families* and little has been done to identify the unique strengths of these families. Generally, single parents do bear greater physical, emotional, financial, and social burdens than do parents in "intact" families. If two-parent families with deviant children are devalued by society, then the single-parent family is subject to even more social stigma. There is greater potential for social rejection which can lead to increased isolation, thus reducing even further the single parent's already limited access to needed community services. Resources are not always delivered according to needs, and families with the greatest needs may find themselves with less than their fair share of services.

If the deviant child is severely handicapped, the single parent may more and more limit activities both within and without the home: siblings may be deprived of normal childhood experiences (e.g., having friends in, special outings with the parent, family events) and may begin to develop problems of their own; the deviant child's world may become increasingly more restricted, and the single parent who seldom has another adult to turn to for relief when the going gets tough must somehow manage alone.

In view of the obvious burdens, isolation, and lack of resources, the professional, embarking on a program with parents, may be understandably reluctant to

*For an extensive review of the literature on single-parent families, see Blechman and Manning (1976). Although this section was prepared prior to the reading of the Blechman and Manning article, many of the writer's observations, experiences, and views are consistent with those presented in the article.

take on a family which, in his or her eyes, presents so little likelihood of success and may prefer to work with a two-parent family whose basic structure appears to hold greater promise.

However, this awareness of the special needs and difficulties should certainly not prevent the consultant from interviewing the single parent. During the interview, there may emerge some personal strengths of the parent and actually some clearcut and unique advantages of the single-parent family situation.

Faced with the single parent looking for help, the consultant should suspend judgment (as with all parents) at least until the Assessment and Programming Guide (APG) is used to measure the presence and strength of those characteristics of parents that are the likely predictors of success.

We can perhaps best test this notion of the ability of the single parent to successfully participate in behavioral education programs by running through the APG, discussing the strengths and weaknesses of the single parent, noting in which items the consultant may need to offer the parent additional but minimal help, and in which items the consultant may discover some unique strengths developed through the single-parent experience.

READINESS TO CHANGE

The single parent is necessarily weaker than the two-parent family in two items: the amount of time that can be committed and the amount of energy. Since these are physical dimensions, the consultant must accept as a given that one parent, however deeply committed, cannot sustain the level of active programming that two committed parents can. Thus, during the Program stage, the consultant must continually be aware of the demands he or she places on the single parent or the demands self-imposed by the parent, so that parent and consultant can plan a realistic Program.

Another item that may present problems is single parents' expectations of success. Given their limited ability to commit time and energy, single parents may need your guidance in shaping realistic expectations of gains achieved through the Program. You should not, of course, attempt to limit long-term goals, but you may need to play a more active role in helping the parent to set manageable and attainable short-term goals in a reasonable time perspective. If you allow parents to work too long without achieving some short-term goals, you run the risk that they may burn out and/or leave the Program.

As for the other readiness to change items, it is possible and perhaps even likely that you as consultant can more easily assess and/or develop these components in the single parent because dealing with one person's attitudes, questions, anxieties, and past experiences is usually simpler than dealing with two. For example, with the single parent you can more easily assess confidence in your competence. Such confidence is either sufficiently strong or generally can be strengthened. In a two-parent family, one's spouse's skepticism or distrust may undermine the confidence of the other and a potential commitment to the Program may be lost. (Two accepting and motivated parents are of course the ideal.)

If the single parent lacks a number of readiness components, it may be easy for you to decide to postpone, or not provide a Program. On the other hand, unless both parents from an intact family score equally well on the readiness items, you may find making decisions about Program options is difficult because the parents differ in attitudes and commitment. Particularly if you are limited in the number of families you can work with, making such decisions can be troublesome. However, if you are impressed by the readiness to change of a single parent, by all means include that parent in your Program. You may be pleased and surprised by the results.

PROGRAM STAGE

When teaching parents how to conduct a good home educational program, continue to keep in mind the physical constraints (time and energy) of single parents. As single parents develop home programs, they may need more guidance in setting reasonable goals and developing manageable programs. During this stage, single parents may benefit from extra contact with you—home visits, phone calls, or both—whereby you can provide reassurance and correct the Program (if needed) so they can maintain efforts without undue fatigue and draining. In the two-parent family, one can reasonably expect each parent to provide support and relief for the other. In the absence of a second parent, however, you as consultant may have to provide some modest additional support in the early days of the Program and may wish to monitor the single-parent family more closely at the start, especially if the parent has recently become single. In particular, you may need to assist the parent in regaining self-esteem, in establishing priorities, and in realistically assessing the merits and deficits of the single-parent family situation.*

For example, the single parent usually has no adult in the household to take over in times of fatigue and stress and is, therefore, always "on." However, even this serious drawback has potential advantages: greater consistency in implementing a home educational program and a better organized and arranged household. In implementing training, there is apt to be less variation in teaching sessions run by one person rather than two. Basic teaching skills may be used more rigorously (i.e., signals, prompts, rewards) and may be more consistent

*See Blechman and Manning (1976) for a discussion of the idealized "superior" two-parent families and the actual benefits of single-parent family status in certain cases.

and clearer to the child, thus increasing the possibility of Program effectiveness in achieving goals.

In organizing the environment, on the other hand, it is possible for one person to establish a streamlined household routine more easily when there is no need to accommodate the schedule or expectations of another adult. For example, meals can be simplified (frozen dinners, paper plates, etc.) and served at regular times so that sufficient and regular time is made available for teaching sessions without either pressure or fatigue for the parent. Dust can be allowed to accumulate for longer periods so long as a schedule of activities is maintained, and materials for living and learning can be easily located and accessible (perhaps for a time the dining room is used solely for teaching sessions and everyone takes meals in the kitchen). A parent who alone bears the responsibility for managing both household and teaching sessions can quickly learn to streamline routines and sort out essential tasks as part of the educational program, thus becoming an effective teacher in spite of the physical limits of time and energy. If there are other children in the family, they will usually adapt to a new routine as long as it is well-organized (i.e., consistent, predictable, and fair).

A problem faced by all parents during the Program stage, but even more so by the single parent, is making sure a portion of their time and attention is reserved for their nondeviant children. Otherwise, siblings may begin to feel that the deviant child is favored at their expense and, in time, may come to feel unwanted and neglected. This situation would obviously create additional problems for the family.

From the beginning of the Program, the needs of the other children must be taken into account. Explanations about the purpose of the Program (i.e., to help the deviant child learn the skills he or she needs to become a happier and contributing member of the family) should be given at the child's level of understanding. Assurances should also be given that, although the Program's focus is on the deviant child, the parent loves equally well, and specially, each of the children.

The parent should answer any questions and, where children express interest and willingness, involve the other children as participants in teaching programs when effective programs have been established. No child should be pushed into working with a deviant sibling unless ready and willing. And parents must remember that assurances of love are cheap unless backed up by actions that demonstrate their caring (e.g., reserving special time for the nondeviant children, kind words of appreciation, spontaneous displays of affection).

If the single parent has children who are interested in assisting in the Program stage, a well-engineered environment with well-defined tasks and times can maximize the children's contributions (table setting, entertaining the deviant child while supper is prepared, and even running teaching programs). To maintain these contributions, the parents can regularly reinforce children's helping activities. Any assistance giving the single parent moments to plan or take a break is a big bonus. The children's contribution must be viewed as special, and parents must not allow themselves to slip into thinking patterns that expect children to assume adult responsibilities.

Although parents and children help each other in certain ways, the parent/child relationship is not one of equal partners. Since the single parent by definition does not have a partner, the development of cooperation skills in the home program becomes a complex item.

The single head of a household, of necessity, makes unilateral decisions within the family. Advice outside of the family may be sought, but experienced single parents are likely to rely on their own judgments, and to act more and more independently over time. This quality of independence is an essential component in the successful functioning of the single-parent family. However, high independence in some parents may interfere with their ability to cooperate with others in reaching decisions affecting their children. Although there is no second parent with whom to practice cooperation, still the parent must cooperate with other adults to realize the goals desired for the child.

First, you, the consultant, have the opportunity to test and develop the parent's ability to cooperate through your partnership in setting goals and planning programs.

Second, there are those persons legally and/or professionally responsible for the child's welfare (i.e., teachers, therapists, and administrators), with whom the parents can practice cooperation. Professionals can be a hard training ground for parents since, in the past, relationships with professionals may have seemed a one-way street ("expert" to "client") or may even have been demeaning (the "expert" seeing parents as the source of problems and implying or articulating this perception to the parent).

You now have the opportunity to alter that experience by being one professional with whom the parent can cooperate as an equal. Your work with the parent, in which you actively recognize the parents' knowledge of their children and the parents' own skills, and accept their difficulties, can help the parents to improve their skills in assertiveness and communication with other professionals. With practice, they can become adept in more clearly stating their expectations for their child and of the professional, and their willingness to collaborate with the professionals in achieving mutually determined goals for the child. If, during the Program, parents return to you with reports of experiences in which they have found themselves to be unsuccessful in dealings with other professionals, those experiences are appropriate subjects for problem-solving skills. Solutions can lead either to improvement of parents' styles and skills, or to the development of other strategies with people who have recognized difficulties in working with parents as equals.

Since the parent must eventually function without your support, by the end of the Program stage you will have faded out your extra supports to the parents as they acquire the skills to manage independently and successfully. If the Program has gone well, entering the Maintenance phase requires that no more contact time be spent with single parents than with couples. However, some aspects of Maintenance items require your special consideration.

MAINTENANCE

Single parents who successfully complete the Program stage are most likely to maintain and persist in good programs if they take very seriously the scheduling of breaks for themselves. Whereas in the intact family parents can trade off times to take breaks, the "always-on" single parent may find that critical times make taking a scheduled break impossible. The crisis is a reality that cannot be ignored and the breaks must occasionally be postponed. You as consultant can help the single parent to understand the importance of breaks and the need for breaks to be the highest priority after a crisis is resolved. It is easy for an active parent to postpone a needed rest, but many such postponements can lead to fatigue, draining, and ultimately to program failure.

Of necessity, single parents must provide their own support and reward system. Self-rewards for performance must be taken as seriously as scheduled breaks, since there is little likelihood that anyone else will provide them. You as consultant may want to help the parents plan a schedule of self-rewards for their program efforts, and to point out that these rewards should be taken not only for visible successes they help their children to achieve, but also (and perhaps even more important) for just plain hard work when success seems slow in coming. Where other children in the family participate, either through direct involvement in teaching programs with the deviant child or through household chores, the single parent especially should regularly recognize and reward the children's activities and efforts, both for the merit of their efforts and for their needs for love and recognition.

The third item requiring special consideration is related to the first two items discussed in this section, and that is linking parents with existing resources. The single-parent family usually has a greater need for respite care, baby-sitting (an opportunity to be with other adults and without children), special services for the handicapped child (to relieve some of the solitary burden), and services for the nonhandicapped siblings who can benefit from the attention of other caring adults who recognize their special qualities and needs. The single parent who is not successfully integrated into a system of services, support, advocacy, and so forth, may, when the Program is ended, return to their former isolation. Isolation increases the burden of the single parent and undermines the success of the Program. If, in your parent group, you have been successful in developing espirit de corps, you will have already established a parent-to-parent network where parents, both single and married, can serve as resources and support to one another.

These three items require special consideration but, in fact, may require little extra time on your part. Efforts you expend in this direction help to maintain the skills you have taught.

The single parent does have a greater burden to carry than parents in "intact" families. That parent is more isolated and devalued, has more emotional and physical responsibilities and problems, and is likely to have fewer supports and resources. When single parents come to you looking for advice, help, or training and are willing to commit themselves to the extra work involved, the fact that they have not only borne these burdens alone but are willing to do more to improve their lives and the lives of the children is in itself a measure of strength and motivation. As single people, they are physically limited in the amounts of time and energy they have available. As single people, they have demonstrated some level of ability to make decisions and manage. As single-parent participants or clients, they present a promise of consistency of good organization, and of a substantial commitment. To be successful participants in the Program, they require from you some special consideration of their situation, some additional guidance and support, and the opportunity to become more skilled and effective parents.

Every family with a handicapped child has its own special difficulties. Single parents do have unique problems, but two-parent families also present problems. In fact, if one disregards social stigma and financial constraints of the single parent, some two-parent families function as single-parent families, that is, one parent carries full physical and emotional responsibility for all child-rearing tasks and for total household management. If, in your work with single-parent families, you can break through the idealized image of the two-parent family, you may have done both single and married parents a service.

A good basic and humanistic assumption for you, the consultant, is that any parent, single or married, who seeks you out for help and is willing to make a commitment to get that help, can probably use and benefit from the Program you provide.

REFERENCES

Abeson, A., N. Bolick and J. Hass (1975). *Primer on Due Process.* Reston, Va. 22091: Council for Exceptional Children.

Alberti, R. E. and M. L. Emmons (1974). *Your Perfect Right: A Guide to Assertive Behavior,* 2nd ed. San Luis Obispo, Calif.: Impact.

Allen, K. E. and F. R. Harris (1966). Elimination of a child's excessive scratching by training the mother in reinforcement procedures. *Behavior Research and Therapy* 4:79–84.

Arnstein, H. S. (1965). An approach to the severely disturbed child. In P. T. B. Weston (Ed.), *Some Approaches to Teaching Autistic Children.* Oxford, England: Pergamon Press, pp. 1–7.

Aronfreed, J. (1968). *Conduct and Conscience.* New York: Academic Press.

Azrin, N. H., B. J. Naster and R. Jones (1973). Reciprocity counseling: A rapid learning-based procedure for marital counseling. *Behavior Research and Therapy* 11:365–382.

Bandura, A. (1969). *Principles of Behavior Modification.* New York: Holt, Rinehart & Winston.

Bandura, A. and B. Perloff (1967). Relative efficacy of self-monitored and externally imposed reinforcement systems. *Journal of Personality and Social Psychology* 7:111–116.

Bandura, A. and R. H. Walters (1963). *Social Learning and Personality Development.* New York: Holt, Rinehart & Winston.

Barker, H. J. and B. Leland (1958). *Detroit Test of Learning Aptitude.* Cincinnati: Public School Publishing.

Barker, H. J. and B. Leland (1967). *Detroit Test of Learning Aptitude Examiner's Handbook.* Indianapolis: Bobbs-Merrill.

Barker, R. G. (Ed.) (1963). *The Stream of Behavior.* New York, Appleton-Century-Crofts.

Barker, R. G. (1968). *Ecological Psychology.* Stanford, Calif.: Stanford University Press.

Beck, A. T. (1967). *Depression: Clinical, Experimental and Theoretical Aspects.* New York: Harper & Row.

Beck, A. T. (1972). *Depression: Causes and Treatment.* Philadelphia: University of Pennsylvania Press.

Beck, A. T. (1976). *Cognitive Therapy and the Emotional Disorders.* New York: International Universities Press.

Beck, A. T. and B. F. Shaw (1977). Cognitive approaches to depression. In A. Ellis and R. Grieger (Eds.), *Handbook of Rational-Emotive Therapy.* New York: Springer, pp. 119–134.

Becker, H. S. (1963). *Outsiders: Studies in the Sociology of Deviance*. New York: Free Press.

Becker, W. C. (1971). *Parents are Teachers*. Champaign, Ill.: Research Press.

Benson, H. (1975). *The Relaxation Response*. New York: William Morrow.

Bernal, M. E., L. F. Delfini, J. A. North, and S. L. Kreutzer (1976). Comparison of boys' behaviors in homes and classrooms. In E. J. Mash, L. A. Hamerlynck, and L. C. Handy (Eds.), *Behavior Modification and Families*. New York: Brunner/Mazel, pp. 204–227.

Bernal, M. E., J. S. Duryee, H. L. Pruett and B. J. Burns (1968). Behavior modification and the brat syndrome. *Journal of Consulting and Clinical Psychology* 32:447–455.

Berne, E. (1964). *Games People Play*. New York: Grove Press.

Bernstein, D. A., and T. D. Borkovec (1973). *Progressive Relaxation Training*. Champaign, Ill.: Research Press.

Birenbaum, A. (1971). The mentally retarded child in the home and the family cycle. *Journal of Health and Social Behavior* 12:55–65.

Blau, P. M. (1964). *Exchange and Power in Social Life*. New York: John Wiley & Sons.

Blauner, R. (1964). *Alienation and Freedom*. Chicago: University of Chicago Press.

Blechman, E. A. and M. Manning (1976). A reward-cost analysis of the single-parent family. In E. J. Mash, L. A. Hamerlynck, and L. C. Handy (Eds.), *Behavior Modification and families*. New York, Brunner/Mazel, pp. 61–90.

Blechman, E. A. and D. H. L. Olson (1976). The family contract game: Description and effectiveness. In D. H. L. Olson (Ed.), *Treating Relationships*. Lake Mills, Iowa: Graphic Publishing, pp. 133–149.

Boguslaw, R. (1965). *The New Utopians*. Englewood Cliffs, N.J.: Prentice-Hall.

Bolstad, O. D. and S. M. Johnson (1972). Self-regulation in the modification of disruptive classroom behavior. *Journal of Applied Behavior Analysis* 5:443–454.

Bornstein, P. and R. Quevillon (1976). The effects of a self-instruction package on overactive preschool boys. *Journal of Applied Behavior Analysis* 9:179–188.

Bott, E. (1971). *Family and Social Network,* 2nd ed. New York: Free Press.

Broden, M., R. V. Hall and B. Mitts (1971). The effect of self-recording on the classroom behavior of two eighth-grade students. *Journal of Applied Behavior Analysis* 4:191–200.

Brown, J. H., A. M. Gamboa Jr., J. Birkimer and R. Brown (1976). Some possible effects of parent self-control training on parent-child interaction. In E. J. Mash, L. C. Handy, and L. A. Hamerlynck (Eds.), *Behavior Modification Approaches to Parenting*. New York: Brunner/Mazel, pp. 180–192.

Brown, L. and T. Spofford (1973). *Making School Work: An Education Handbook for Students, Parents and Professionals*. Boston, Mass.: Massachusetts Advocacy Center and Massachusetts Law Reform Institute.

Bruno, B. (Fall 1974; Summer/Fall 1975). Progressive relaxation training for children: A guide for parents and children (Parts I and II). *Special Education*. A.A.S.E., Box 168, Fryeburg, Maine.

Brutten, M., S. Richardson and C. Mangel (1973). *Something's Wrong with My Child*. New York: Harcourt Brace Jovanovich.

Buckley, W. (1967). *Sociology and Modern Systems Theory*. Englewood Cliffs, N.J.: Prentice-Hall.

Burgess, E. P. (1969). The modification of depressive behavior. In R. O. Rubin and C.

M. Franks (Eds.), *Advances in Behavior Therapy*. New York: Academic Press, pp. 193–199.

Burgess, E. W., J. J. Locke, and M. M. Thomas (1971). *The Family*. New York: Van Nostrand Reinhold.

Carver, J. and Carver, N. (1974). *The Family of the Retarded Child*. Syracuse, N.Y., Syracuse University Division of Special Education and Rehabilitation and the Center on Human Policy.

Cautela, J. (1969). Behavior therapy and self-control: Techniques and implications, in C. Franks (Ed.), *Behavior Therapy: Appraisal and Status*, New York: McGraw-Hill, pp. 323–340.

Cautela, J. (1970). Covert reinforcement. *Behavior Therapy* 1:33–50.

Cautela, J. and J. Groden (1978). *Relaxation*. Champaign, Ill.: Research Press.

Cautela, J. R., R. B. Flannery Jr., and S. Hanley (1974). Covert modeling: an experimental test. *Behavior Therapy* 5:494–502.

Christopherson, E. R., C. M. Arnold, D. H. Hall, and H. R. Quilitch (1972). The home point system: Token reinforcement procedures for application by parents of children with behavior problems. *Journal of Applied Behavior Analysis* 5:485–497.

Closer Look. National Information Center for the Handicapped, 1201 16th St., N.W., Washington, D.C. 10036.

Conway, J. B. and B. D. Bucher (1976). Transfer and maintenance of behavior change in children: A review and suggestions. In E. J. Mash, L. A. Hamerlynck, and L. C. Handy (Eds.), *Behavior Modification and Families*. New York: Brunner/Mazel, pp. 119–159.

Cotler, S. B. and J. J. Guerra (1976). *Assertion Training: A Humanistic-Behavioral Guide to Self-dignity*. Champaign, Ill.: Research Press.

Crain, A. J., M. B. Sussman, and W. B. Weil Jr. (1966). Effects of a diabetic child on marital integration and related measures of family functioning. *Journal of Health and Human Behavior* 7:122–127.

Creer, T. L. and W. P. Christian (1976). *Chronically Ill and Handicapped children*. Champaign, Ill.: Research Press.

Crickmay, M. C. (1966). *Speech Therapy and the Bobath Approach to Cerebral Palsy*. Springfield, Ill.: Charles C. Thomas.

Davis, F. (1963). *Passage Through Crisis: Polio Victims and Their Families*. Indianapolis: Bobbs-Merrill.

Davison, G. C. (1964). A social learning therapy program with an autistic child. *Behavior Research and Therapy* 2:149.

Doll, E. (1965). *Vineland Social Maturity Scale*. Circle Pines, Minn.: American Guidance Service.

Downey, K. J. (1965). Parents' reasons for institutionalizing severely retarded children. *Journal of Health and Human Behavior* 6:147–155.

Drabman, R. S., R. Spitalnik, and K. D. O'Leary (1973). Teaching self-control to disruptive children. *Journal of Abnormal Psychology* 82:10–16.

Dunn, L. M. (1965). *Peabody Picture Vocabulary Test*. Circle Pines, Minn.: American Guidance Service.

Eisler, R. M., P. M. Miller, and M. Hersen (1973). Components of assertive behavior. *Journal of Clinical Psychology* 3:295–299.

Ellis, A. (1962) *Reason and Emotion in Psychotherapy*. New York: Lyle Stuart.

Ellis, A. (1975). *How to Live with a Neurotic,* revised ed. New York: Crown Publishers.

Ellis, A. and R. Grieger (Eds.) (1977). *Handbook of Rational-Emotive Therapy*. New York: Springer.

Ellis, A. and R. A. Harper (1961). *A Guide to Rational Living*. Englewood Cliffs, N. J.: Prentice-Hall.

Ellis, A. and R. A. Harper (1973). *A Guide to Successful Marriage*. Hollywood: Wilshire Books.

Ellis, A. and R. A. Harper (1975). *A New Guide to Rational Living*. Englewood Cliffs, N. J.: Prentice-Hall.

Ellul, J. (1964). *The Technological Society*. New York: Random House.

Engeln, R., R. Knutson, L. Laughy and W. Garlington (1968). Behavior modification techniques applied to a family unit—A case study. *Journal of Child Psychology and Psychiatry* 9:245–252.

Farber, B. (1959). *Effects of a Severely Mentally Retarded Child on Family Interaction*. Monographs of the Society for Research on Child Development. Serial No. 71, 24 (2). Lafayette, Ind.: Child Development Publications, Purdue University.

Farber, B. (1960). Perception of crisis and related variables in the impact of the mentally retarded child on the mother. *Journal of Health and Human Behavior* 1:108–116.

Farber, B., W. Jenne, and R. Toigo (1960). *Family Crisis: The Decision to Institutionalize the Retarded Child*. CEC Research Monograph Series A, No. 1.

Felixbrod, J. J. and K. D. O'Leary (1973). Effects of reinforcement on children's academic behavior as a function of self-determined and externally-imposed contingencies. *Journal of Applied Behavior Analysis* 6:241–250.

Ferster, C. B. (1967a). Arbitrary and natural reinforcement. *Psychological Record* 17:341–347.

Ferster, C. B. (1967b). Perspectives in psychology: XXV, transition from animal laboratory to clinic. *Psychological Record* 17:145–150.

Ferster, C. B. and J. Simons (1966). Behavior therapy with children. *Psychological Record* 16:65–71.

Finnie, N. (1970). *Handling the Young Cerebral Palsied Child at Home*. New York: Dutton.

Frankl, V. (1960). Paradoxical intention: A logotherapeutic technique. *American Journal of Psychotherapy* 14:520–535.

Fredericks, H. B. (1976). *The Teaching Research Curriculum for the Moderately and Severely Handicapped*. Springfield, Ill.: Charles C. Thomas.

Freidson, E. (1965). Disability as social deviance. In M. B. Sussman (Ed.), *Sociology and Rehabilitation*. Washington, D.C.: American Sociological Association, pp. 71–99.

Frostig, M. and D. Horne (1964). *Teacher's Guide: The Frostig Program for the Development of Visual Perception*. Chicago: Follet.

Gambrill, E. (1963). Posthospitalized disabled children. *Journal of Health and Human Behavior* 4:206–210.

Gambrill, E. D. (1977). *Behavior Modification: Handbook of Assessment, Intervention, and Evaluation*. San Francisco: Jossey-Bass.

Gambrill, E. D. and C. A. Richey (1975). An assertion inventory for use in assessment and research. *Behavior Therapy* 6:547–549.

Garfinkel, H. (1956). Conditions of successful degradation ceremonies. *American Journal of Sociology* LXI:420–424.

Glynn, E. L. (1970). Classroom applications of self-determined reinforcement. *Journal of Applied Behavior Analysis* 3:123–132.

Goffman, E. (1963). *Stigma: Notes on the Management of Spoiled Identity*. Englewood Cliffs, N.J.: Spectrum Books.

Goffman, E. (1971). *Relations in Public,* New York: Harper & Row.

Goffman, E. (1974). *Frame Analysis*. New York: Harper & Row.

Goldfried, M. R. and G. C. Davison (1976). *Clinical Behavior Therapy*. New York: Holt, Rinehart & Winston.

Goldiamond, I. (1965). Self-control procedures in personal behavior problems. *Psychological Reports* 17:851–868.

Goldstein, A. P. (1971). *Therapist-Patient Expectancies in Psychotherapy*. New York: Pergamon Press.

Goode, W. J. (1963). *World Revolution and Family Patterns*. New York: Free Press.

Gordon, N. B. and B. Kutner (1965). Long term and fatal illness in the family. *Journal of Health and Human Behavior* 4:190–196.

Gottman, J., C. Notarius, J. Gonso, and H. Markman (1976). *A Couple's Guide to Communication*. Champaign, Ill.: Research Press.

Gray, B. B. and B. Ryan (1973). *A Language Program for the Non-language Child*. Champaign, Ill.: Research Press.

Graziano, A. M. and J. E. Kean (1968). Programmed relaxation and reciprocal inhibition with psychotic children. *Behavior Research and Therapy,* 6:433–437.

Greenfield, J. (1972). *A Child Called Noah*. New York: Holt, Rinehart & Winston.

Grinker, R. R., J. Miller, M. Sabshin et al., (1961). *The Phenomenon of Depression*. New York: Harper & Row.

Guerney, B. G., Jr. (Ed.) (1969). *Psychotherapeutic Agents: New Roles for Nonprofessionals, Parents, and Teachers*. New York: Holt, Rinehart & Winston.

Haley, J. (1973). *Uncommon Therapy*. New York: W. W. Norton.

Haley, J. (1976). *Problem-solving Therapy*. San Francisco: Jossey-Bass.

Hamblin, R. L., D. Buckholdt, D. Ferritor, M. Kozloff, and L. Blackwell (1971). *The Humanization Processes*. New York: John Wiley & Sons.

Hamilton, M. (1960). A rating scale for depression. *Journal of Neurology, Neurosurgery, and Psychiatry* 23:56–61.

Handel, G. (Ed.) (1967). *The Psychosocial Interior of the Family*. Chicago: Aldine.

Hannan, C. (1974). *Parents and Mentally Retarded Children*. Baltimore: Penguin Books.

Hawkins, R. P., R. F. Peterson, E. Schweid, and S. W. Bijou (1966). Behavior therapy in the home: Amelioration of problem parent-child relations with the parent in a therapeutic role. *Journal of Experimental Child Psychology* 4:99–107.

Henry, J. (1966). "Personality and aging—with special reference to hospitals for the aged poor." In J. C. McKinney and F. T. DeVyver (Eds.), *Aging and Social Policy,* New York: Meredith.

Henry, J. (1971). *Pathways to Madness,* New York: Random House.

Holroyd, J. and D. McArthur (1976). Mental retardation and stress on the parents: A contrast between Down's Syndrome and childhood autism. *American Journal of Mental Deficiency* 80:431–436.

Homans, G. C. (1961). Social Behavior: Its Elementary Forms. New York: Harcourt, Brace and World.

Homme, L., A. P. Csanyi, M. A. Gonzales, and J. R. Rechs (1970). *How to Use Contingency Contracting in the Classroom*. Champaign, Ill.: Research Press.

Hutchinson, R. R. (1977). By-products of aversive control. In W. K. Honig and J. E. R. Staddon (Eds.), *Handbook of Operant Behavior*. Englewood Cliffs, N. J.: Prentice-Hall, pp. 415–431.

Jacobson, E. (1964). *Anxiety and Tension Control*. Philadelphia: J. B. Lippincott.

Jacobson, E. (1974). *Progressive Relaxation*. Chicago, University of Chicago Press.

Jacobson, E. (1976). *You Must Relax,* 5th ed., New York: McGraw-Hill.

Jacoby, R. (1975). *Social Amnesia: A Critique of Conformist Psychology from Adler to Laing*. Boston, Mass.: Beacon Press.

Jakubowski-Spector, P., J. Pearlman, and K. Coburn (1973). *Assertion Training for Women: Stimulus Films*. Washington, D.C.: American Personnel and Guidance Association.

Jastek, J. F. and S. R. Jastek (1965). *Wrat Manual*. Wilmington, Del.: Guidance Association.

Johnson, S. M., O. D. Bolstad, and G. K. Lobitz (1976). Generalization and contrast phenomena in behavior modification with children. In E. J. Mash, L. A. Hamerlynck, and L. C. Handy (Eds.), *Behavior Modification and Families*. New York: Brunner/Mazel, pp. 160–188.

Johnson, S. M. and R. A. Brown (1969). Producing behavior change in parents of disturbed children. *Journal of Child Psychology and Psychiatry* 10:107–121.

Kanfer, F. H. (1970). Self-regulation: Research issues and speculation. In C. Neuringer and J. L. Michael (Eds.), *Behavior Modification in Clinical Psychology*. New York: Appleton-Century-Crofts, pp. 178–220.

Kantor, D. and W. Lehr (1976). *Inside the Family*. San Francisco: Jossey-Bass.

Kaufman, K. F. (1976). Teaching parents to teach their children: The behavior modification approach. In B. Feingold and C. Bank (Eds.), *Developmental Disabilities of Early Childhood*. Springfield, Ill.: Charles C. Thomas, pp. 96–120.

Kaufman, K. F. (1977). New directions in comprehensive programming for parents of autistic children. *Proceedings of the Annual Meeting and Conference of the National Society for Autistic Children*. Albany, N.Y.: National Society for Autistic Children.

Kazdin, A. E. (1973). Covert modeling and the reduction of avoidance behavior. *Journal of Abnormal Psychology* 81:87–95.

Kazdin, A. E. (1974a). Effects of covert modeling and model reinforcement on assertive behavior. *Journal of Abnormal Psychology* 83:240–252.

Kazdin, A. E. (1974b). Covert modeling, modeling similarity and reduction of avoidance behavior. *Behavior Therapy* 5:325–340.

Kelly, G. A. (1955). *The Psychology of Personal Constructs*. New York: W. W. Norton.

Kent, L. R. (1974). *Language Acquisition Program for the Severely Retarded*. Champaign, Ill.: Research Press.

Kitsuse, J. I. (1962). Societal reaction to deviant behavior: Problems of theory and method. *Social Problems* 9:247–257.

Knox, D. (1971). *Marriage Happiness*. Champaign, Ill.: Research Press.

Knox, D. (1972). *Keeping Happiness in Your Marriage*. Champaign, Ill.: Research Press.

Koeppen, A. (1974). Relaxation training for children. *Elementary School Guidance and Counseling,* Oct. 14–20.

Korkes, L. (1955). *The Impact of Mentally Ill Children Upon Their Families.* Trenton, N.J.: State Department of Institutions and Agencies.

Kovitz, K. E. (1976). Comparing group and individual methods for training parents in child management techniques. In E. J. Mash, L. C. Handy, and L. A. Hamerlynck (Eds.), *Behavior Modification Approaches to Parenting.* New York: Brunner/Mazel, pp. 124–138.

Kozloff, M. A. (1973). *Reaching the Autistic Child.* Champaign, Ill.: Research Press.

Kozloff, M. A. (1974). *Educating Children with Learning and Behavior Problems.* New York: Wiley-Interscience.

Kozloff, M.A. (1976). Systems of structured exchange: Changing families of severely deviant children. *Sociological Practice* 1:86–104.

Kozloff, M. A. (1977). A comprehensive training program for parents of autistic children. In D. Upper (Ed.), *Perspectives in Behavior Therapy.* Kalamazoo, Mich.: Behaviordelia, pp. 237–269.

Kvaraceus, W. C. and E. N. Hayes (1969). *If Your Child is Handicapped.* Boston: Porter Sargent.

Lange, A. J. (1977). Cognitive-behavioral assertion training. In A. Ellis and R. Grieger (Eds.), *Handbook of Rational-Emotive Therapy.* New York: Springer, pp. 292–308.

Lange, A. and Jakubowski, P. (1976). *Responsible Assertive Behavior: Cognitive-Behavioral Procedures for Trainers.* Champaign, Ill: Research Press.

Lapin, H. and C. Lapin (1976). The plight of parents in obtaining help for the autistic child and the role of the National Society for Autistic Children. In E. R. Ritvo (Ed.), *Autism: Diagnosis, Current Research and Management.* New York: Spectrum Publications, pp. 287–290.

Larson, L. A. and W. A. Bricker (1968). *A Manual for Parents and Teachers of Severely and Moderately Retarded.* Nashville, Tenn.: Peabody College.

LaVigna, G. W. and A. D. Walsh (1976). Alternatives to the use of punishment in the control of undesired behavior. Paper presented at the Tenth Annual Meeting of the Association for the Advancement of Behavior Therapy, New York, N.Y.

Lazarus, A. (1961). Group therapy of phobic disorders by systematic desensitization. *Journal of Abnormal and Social Psychology* 63:504–510.

Lazarus, A. (1977). *Multimodal Behavior Therapy.* New York: Springer.

Lazarus, A. A. and A. Abramovitz (1962). The use of "emotive imagery" in the treatment of children's phobias. *Journal of Mental Science* 108:191–195.

Lee, L. (1969). *Northwestern Syntax Screening Test.* Evanston, Ill.: Northwestern University Press.

Lemert, E. M. (1951). *Social Pathology.* New York: McGraw-Hill.

Lewinsohn, P. M. et al. (1971). *Manual of Instruction for the Behavior Ratings Used for the Observation of Interpersonal Behavior.* Unpublished manuscript, University of Oregon, 1968. Revised.

Lewinsohn, P. M., A. Biglan, and A. M. Zeiss (1976). Behavioral treatment of depression. In P. O. Davidson (Ed.), *The Behavioral Management of Anxiety, Depression and Pain.* New York: Brunner/Mazel, pp. 91–146.

Liberman, R. P. (1975). *Behavioral Marital Therapy: Group Leaders Guide.* Oxnard,

Calif.: Behavior Analysis and Modification Project.

Lindsley, O. R. (1966). An experiment with parents handling behavior at home. *Johnstone Bulletin*, 27–36.

Lovaas, O. I., R. Koegel, J. Q. Simmons, and J. S. Long (1973). Some generalization and follow-up measures on autistic children in behavior therapy. *Journal of Applied Behavior Analysis* 6:131–166.

Lubin, B. (1965). Adjective checklists for the measurement of depression. *Archives of General Psychiatry* 12:57–62.

Lubin, B. (1967). *Manual for the Depression Adjective Check Lists*. San Diego, Calif.: Education and Industrial Testing Service.

Mahoney, M. J. (1971). The self-management of covert behavior. *Behavior Therapy* 2:575–578.

Mahoney, M. J. (1974). *Cognition and Behavior Modification*. Cambridge, Mass.: Ballinger.

Mahoney, M. J. (1977). Personal science: A cognitive learning therapy. In E. Ellis and R. Grieger (Eds.), *Handbook of Rational-Emotive Therapy*. New York: Springer, pp. 352–366.

Marcuse, H. (1964). *One-dimensional Man*. Boston: Beacon Press.

Marcuse, H. (1966). *Eros and Civilization*. Boston: Beacon Press.

Marks, N. C. (1974). *Cerebral Palsied and Learning Disabled Children*. Springfield, Ill.: Charles C. Thomas.

Martin, B. and C. Twentyman (1976). Teaching conflict resolution skills to parents and children. In E. J. Mash, L. C. Handy and L. A. Hamerlynck (Eds.), *Behavior Modification Approaches to Parenting*. New York: Brunner/Mazel, pp. 141–151.

McCarthy, D. (1972). *Manual for the McCarthy Scales of Children's Abilities*. New York: Psychological Corporation.

McCarthy, J. and S. Kirk (1961). *Examiner's Manual: Test of Psycholinguistic Abilities* (experimental edition). Urbana: University of Illinois.

McClellan, T. A. and D. R. Stieper (1977). A structured approach to group marriage counseling. In A. Ellis and R. Grieger (Eds.). *Handbook of Rational-Emotive Therapy*. New York: Springer, pp. 281–297.

McFall, R. M. and D. B. Lillesand (1971). Behavioral rehearsal with modeling and coaching in assertion training. *Journal of Abnormal Psychology* 77:313–323.

McLean, P. (1976a). Therapeutic decision-making in the treatment of depression. In P. O. Davidson (Ed.), *The Behavioral Management of Anxiety, Depression and Pain*. New York: Brunner/Mazel, pp. 54–89.

McLean, P. D. (1976b). Parental depression: Incompatible with effective parenting. In E. J. Mash, L. C. Handy and L. A. Hamerlynck (Eds.), *Behavior Modification Approaches to Parenting*. New York: Brunner/Mazel, pp. 209–220.

Meichenbaum, D. and D. Turk (1976). The cognitive-behavioral management of anxiety, anger, and pain. In P. O. Davidson (Ed.), *The Behavioral Management of Anxiety, Depression and Pain*. New York: Brunner/Mazel. pp. 1–34.

Meichenbaum, D. (1977). *Cognitive-Behavior Modification*. New York: Plenum Press.

Meichenbaum, D. H. and J. Goodman (1977). Training impulsive children to talk to themselves: A means of developing self-control. In A. Ellis and R. Grieger (Eds.), *Handbook of Rational-Emotive Therapy*. New York: Springer Pub. Co., 379–397.

Mercer, J. R. (1973). *Labeling the Mentally Retarded*. Berkeley and Los Angeles, Calif.:

University of California Press.

Miller, W. H. (1975). *Systematic Parent Training*. Champaign, Ill.: Research Press.

Mills, C. W. (1951). *White Collar*. New York: Oxford University Press.

Minuchin, S. (1974). *Families and Family Therapy*. Cambridge, Mass.: Harvard University Press.

Mira, M. (1970). Results of a behavior modification training program for parents and teachers. *Behaviour Research and Therapy* 8:309–311.

Mosher, L. R., D. Feinsilver, M. M. Katz, and L. A. Wienckowski (1970). Special report on schizophrenia. Washington, D.C.: U.S. Department of Health, Education and Welfare, April.

Mumford, L. (1970). *The Myth of the Machine*. New York: Harcourt Brace Jovanovich.

Mussen, P. H. (1969) Early sex-role development. In D. Goslin (Ed.), *Handbook of Socialization Theory and Research*. Chicago: Rand McNally & Co., pp. 707–741.

Noland. R. L. (Ed.) (1975). *Counseling Parents of the Mentally Retarded*. Springfield, Ill.: Charles C Thomas.

Noland, R. L. (Ed.). (1971). *Counseling Parents of the Ill and Handicapped*. Springfield, Ill.: Charles C Thomas.

Noland, R. L. (Ed.) (1973). *Counseling Parents of the Emotionally Disturbed Child*. Springfield, Ill.: Charles C Thomas.

Oakley, A. (1975) *The Sociology of Housework*. New York: Pantheon Books.

O'dell, S. (1974). Training parents in behavior modification. *Psychological Bulletin* 81:418–433.

O'Leary, K. D. (1977). Teaching self-management skills to children. In D. Upper (Ed.), *Perspectives in Behavior Therapy*. Kalamazoo, Mich.: Behaviordelia, pp. 189–210.

Owens, M. and B. Harper (1971). *Sign Language: A Teaching Manual for Cottage Parents of Non-verbal Retardates*. Pineville, La.: Department of Speech and Hearing, Pinecrest State School.

Park, C. C. (1972). *The Seige*. Boston: Little, Brown & Co.

Patterson, G. R. (1966). A learning theory approach to the treatment of the school phobic child. In L. P. Ullmann and L. Krasner (Eds.), *Case Studies in Behavior Modification*. New York: Holt, Rinehart & Winston.

Patterson, G. R. (1971). *Families: Applications of Social Learning to Family Life*. Champaign, Ill.: Research Press.

Patterson, G. R. (1976). The aggressive child: Victim and architect of a coercive system. In E. J. Mash, L. A. Hamerlynck and L. C. Handy (Eds.), *Behavior Modification and Families*. New York: Brunner/Mazel, pp. 267–316.

Patterson. G. R. and C. Brodsky (1966). A behaviour therapy programme for a child with multiple problem behaviors. *Journal of Child Psychology and Psychiatry* 7:277–295.

Patterson, G. R. and J. B. Reid (1970). Reciprocity and coercion: Two facets of social systems. In J. Michaels and C. Neuringer (Eds.) *Behavior Modification in Clinical Psychology*. New York: Appleton-Century-Crofts, pp. 133–177.

Patterson, G. R., D.A. Shaw and M. J. Ebner (1969). Teachers, peers, and parents as agents of change in classrooms. In F. A. M. Benson (Ed.), *Modifying Deviant Social Behaviors in Various Classroom Settings*. Eugene, Ore: Department of Special Education.

Patterson, G. R., J. B. Reid, R. R. Jones, R. E. Conger (1975). *A Social Learning*

Approach to Family Intervention, Volume 1, Families with Aggressive Children. Eugene, Ore.: Castalia Publishing Co.

Paul, G. L. and D. T. Shannon (1966). Treatment of anxiety through systematic desensitization in therapy groups. *Journal of Abnormal Psychology* 71:124–135.

Peine, H. (1971). Training parents using lecture-demonstration procedures and a contingency-managed program. Unpublished doctoral dissertation, University of Utah.

Peterson, R. F. (1976). Power, programming, and punishment: Could we be overcontrolling our children. In E. J. Mash, L. A. Hamerlynck and L. C. Handy (Eds.), *Behavior Modification and Families.* New York: Brunner/Mazel, pp. 338–352.

Pike, K. L. (1954). *Language in Relation to a Unified Theory of the Structure of Human Behavior.* Glendale, Calif.: Summer Institute of Linguistics.

Prince, G. M. (1976). *The Practice of Creativity,* 3rd ed. New York: Collier Books.

Putre, W., K. Loffio, S. Chorost et al. (1977). An effectiveness study of a relaxation training tape with hyperactive children. *Behavior Therapy* 8:355–359.

Rabkin, R. (1977). *Strategic Psychotherapy: Brief and Symptomatic Treatment.* New York: Basic Books.

Rathus, S. A. (1972). An experimental investigation of assertive training in a group setting. *Journal of Behavior Therapy and Experimental Psychiatry* 3:81–86.

Rathus, S. A. (1973). A 30-item schedule for assessing assertive behavior. *Behavior Therapy* 4:398–406.

Reid, J. R., N. Hawkins, C, Keutzer et al. (1967). A marathon behaviour modification of a selectively mute child. *Journal of Child Psychology and Psychiatry* 8:27–30.

Rimm, D. C. and J. C. Masters (1974). *Behavior Therapy: Techniques and Empirical Findings.* New York: Academic Press.

Risley, T. R. and M. M. Wolf (1966). Experimental manipulation of autistic behavior and generalization into the home. In R. Ulrich, T. Stachnik, and J. Mabry (Eds.) *Control of Human Behavior.* Glenview, Ill.: Scott, Foresman & Co.

Rose, S. D. (1977). *Group Therapy: A Behavioral Approach.* Englewood Cliffs, N. J.: Prentice-Hall.

Rosenthal, D. (1970). *Genetic Theory and Abnormal Behavior.* New York: McGraw-Hill.

Rosner, J. (1975). *Helping Children Overcome Learning Disabilities.* New York: Walker and Co.,

Rubington, E. and M. Weinberg (1968). *Deviance: The Interactionist Perspective.* New York: Macmillan.

Russo, S. (1964). Adaptations of behavioral therapy with children. *Behaviour Research and Therapy* 2:43–47.

Salter, A. (1961). *Conditioned Reflex Therapy,* 2nd ed. New York: Capricorn Books.

Scheff, T. J. (1964). The societal reaction to deviance: Ascriptive elements in the psychiatric screening of mental patients in a Midwestern state. *Social Problems* 11:401–413.

Scheff, T. J. (Ed.) (1975). *Labeling Madness.* Englewood Cliffs, N.J.: Prentice-Hall.

Schell, R. E. and W. P. Adams (1968). Training parents of a young child with profound behavior deficits to be teacher-therapists. *Journal of Special Education* 2:439–454.

Schneider, M. and A. Robin (1975). *Turtle Manual.* Stony Brook, N.Y.: Psychology Department, State University of New York at Stony Brook.

Seeman, M. (1972). The signals of '68: Alienation in pre-crisis France. *American Sociological Review* 37:385–402.

Seligman, M. E. P. (1975). *Helplessness: On Depression, Development, and Death*. San Francisco: W. H. Freeman.

Shaftel, F. R. and G. Shaftel (1967). *Role-playing for Social Values: Decision-making in the Social Sciences*. Englewood Cliffs, N.J.: Prentice-Hall.

Shaw, B. F. and A. T. Beck (1977). The treatment of depression with cognitive therapy. In A. Ellis and R. Grieger (Eds.) *Handbook of Rational-Emotive Therapy*. New York: Springer, pp. 309–326.

Sherman, A. and I. Plummer (1973). Training in relaxation as a behavioral self-management skill. An exploratory investigation. *Behavior Therapy* 4:543–550.

Shoemaker, M. E. and T. L. Paulson (1976). Group assertion training for mothers: A family intervention strategy. In E. J. Mash, L. C. Handy, and L. A. Hamerlynck (Eds.), *Behavior Modification Approaches to Parenting*. New York: Brunner/Mazel, pp. 167–179.

Shostak, A. and W. Gomberg (Eds.) (1964). *Blue-collar World*. Englewood Cliffs, N.J.: Prentice-Hall.

Skinner, B. F. (1957). *Verbal Behavior*. New York: Appleton-Century-Crofts.

Smith, M. J. (1975). *When I Say No, I Feel Guilty*. New York: Bantam Books.

Spivak, G. and M. B. Shure (1974). *Social Adjustment of Young Children*. San Francisco: Jossey-Bass.

Stuart, R. B. (1969). Operant-interpersonal treatment for marital discord. *Journal of Consulting and Clinical Psychology* 33:675–682.

Stuart, R. B. (1971). Behavioral contracting with families of delinquents. *Journal of Behavior Therapy and Experimental Psychiatry* 2:1–11.

Stuart, R. B. (1976). An operant interpersonal program for couples. In D. H. L. Olson (Ed.), *Treating Relationships*. Lake Mills, Iowa: Graphic Publishing Co., pp. 119–132.

Stuart, R. B. and F. Stuart (1975). *Family Pre-Counseling Inventory*. Champaign, Ill.: Research Press.

Suinn, R. M. (1972). Behavior rehearsal training for ski racers. *Behavior Therapy* 3:519–520

Szasz, T. S. (1970). *The Manufacture of Madness*. New York: Dell Publishing Co.

Tams, V. and S. Eyberg (1976). A group treatment program for parents. In E. J. Mash, L. C. Handy, and L. A. Hamerlynck (Eds.), *Behavior Modification Approaches to Parenting*. New York: Brunner/Mazel, pp. 101–124.

Tharp, R. G. and R. J. Wetzel (1969). *Behavior Modification in the Natural Environment*. New York: Academic Press.

Thibaut, J. W. and H. H. Kelley (1959). *The Social Psychology of Groups*. New York: John Wiley & Sons.

Thoresen, C. E. and M. J. Mahoney (1974). *Behavioral Self Control*. New York: Holt, Rinehart & Winston.

Truax, C. B. and R. R. Carkhuff (1967). *Toward Effective Counseling and Psychotherapy: Training and Practice*. Chicago: Aldine.

Truax, C. B. and K. M. Mitchell (1971). Research on certain therapist interpersonal skills in relation to process and outcome. In A. E. Bergin and S. L. Garfield (Eds.),

Handbook of Psychotherapy and Behavior Change. New York: John Wiley & Sons, pp. 299–344.

Voysey, M. (1972). Impression management by parents with disabled children. *Journal of Health and Social Behavior* 13:80–89.

Wachtel, P. L. (1977). *Psychoanalysis and Behavior Therapy*. New York: Basic Books.

Wahler, R. G. (1969). Setting generality: Some specific and general effects of child behavior therapy. *Journal of Applied Behavior Analysis* 2:239–246.

Wahler, R. G., G. H. Winkel, R. F. Peterson and D. C. Morrison (1965). Mothers as behavior therapists for their own children. *Behaviour Research and Therapy* 3:113–124.

Walder, L. (1968). *Teaching Parents and Others Principles of Behavioral Control for Modifying the Behavior of Children*. Final Report. Silver Springs, Md.: Institute for Behavioral Research, Inc.

Walker, C. E. (1975). *Learn to Relax*. Englewood Cliffs, N.J.: Prentice-Hall.

Walker, H. M. and N. K. Buckley (1974). *Token Reinforcement Techniques*. Eugene, Ore.: E-B Press.

Watzlawick, P., J. Beavin and D. Jackson (1967). *Pragmatics of Human Communication*. New York: W. W. Norton.

Watzlawick, P., J. Weakland and R. Fisch (1974). *Change: Principles of Problem Formation and Problem Resolution*. New York: W. W. Norton.

Weekes, C. (1969). *Hope and Help for Your Nerves*. New York: Hawthorne Books.

Weekes, C. (1972). *Peace From Nervous Suffering*. New York: Hawthorne Books.

Weil, G. and M. R. Goldfried (1973). Treatment of insomnia of an eleven-year-old child through self-relaxation. *Behavior Therapy* 4:282–284.

Weiss, R. L., H. Hops and G. R. Patterson (1973). A framework for conceptualizing marital conflict, a technology for altering it, some data for evaluating it. In L. A. Hamerlynck, L. C. Handy, and E. J. Mash (Eds.), *Behavior Change: Methodology, Concepts and Practice*. Champaign, Ill.: Research Press, pp. 309–342.

Weschler, D. (1967). *WPPSI Manual*. New York: Psychological Corporation.

Westlake, H. and D. Rutherford (1961). *Speech Therapy for the Cerebral Palsied*. Chicago: National Society for Crippled Children and Adults.

Williams, C. D. (1966). The elimination of tantrum behavior by extinction procedures. In L. P. Ullmann and L. Krasner (Eds.), *Case Studies in Behavior Modification*. New York: Holt, Rinehart and Winston. pp. 295–296.

Williams, J. G.,D. H. Barlow and W. S. Agras (1972). Behavioral measurement of severe depression. *Archives of General Psychiatry* 72:330–337.

Willoughby, R. R. (1934). Norms for the Clark-Thurstone Inventory. *Journal of Social Psychology* 5:91.

Wilson, L. (1968). *This Stranger My Son*. New York: Signet Books.

Winch, R. F., S. Greer and R. L. Blumberg (1967). Ethnicity and extended familism in an upper-middle-class suburb. *American Sociological Review* 32:265–272.

Wolf, M. M., T. R. Risley and H. Mees (1966). Application of operant conditioning procedures to the behavior problems of an autistic child. In R. Ulrich, T. Stachnik, and J. Mabry (Eds.), *Control of Human Behavior*. Glenview, Ill.: Scott, Foresman & Co.

Wolpe, J. and P. J. Lang (1969). *Fear Survey Schedule*. San Diego: Educational and Industrial Testing Service.

Wolpe, J. and A. A. Lazarus (1966). *Behavior Therapy Techniques: A Guide to the Treatment of Neurosis*. New York: Pergamon Press.

Wolpe, J. (1973). *The Practice of Behavior Therapy*. New York: Pergamon Press.

Your rights under the educational for all handicapped children act. 1520 New Hampshire Ave., N.W., Washington, D.C.: Children's Defense Fund.

Zaretsky, E. (1976). *Capitalism, the Family, and Personal Life*. New York: Harper & Row.

Zung, W. W. K. (1965). A self-rating depression scale. *Archives of General Psychiatry* 12:63–70.

INDEX